IOLO MORGANWG AND THE ROMANTIC TRADITION IN WALES

General Editor: Geraint H. Jenkins

Edward Williams (Iolo Morganwg): an etching by Robert Cruikshank

Bardic Circles: National, Regional and Personal Identity in the Bardic Vision of Iolo Morganwg

CATHRYN A. CHARNELL-WHITE

UNIVERSITY OF WALES PRESS
CARDIFF
2007

www.wales.ac.uk/press

British Library Cataloguing-in-Publication Data
A catalogue record for this book is available from the British Library

ISBN 978-0-7083-2067-9

Printed in Wales by Gwasg Dinefwr, Llandybïe

I NANNA,
ELIZABETH VOYLE,
AM EDRYCH AR YR OCHR OLAU

IOLO MORGANWG AND THE ROMANTIC TRADITION IN WALES

Other volumes already published in the series:

A Rattleskull Genius: The Many Faces of Iolo Morganwg, edited by Geraint H. Jenkins (University of Wales Press, 2005)

The Truth Against the World: Iolo Morganwg and Romantic Forgery, by Mary-Ann Constantine (University of Wales Press, 2007)

Contents

Figures

Preface

Iolo Morganwg registered on my cultural radar at a young age. This was unavoidable since I am, like him, a native of the county of Glamorgan. I benefited from a Welsh-medium education which promoted an understanding of how figures who inspired regional pride – Ifor ap Cadifor (Ifor Bach), William Edwards, Iolo Morganwg, David Williams and Evan Davies (Myfyr Morganwg) – were also significant pieces in the broader cultural and linguistic jigsaw that constitutes Wales. Competing in eisteddfodau (another Ioloic connection) involved regular visits to other parts of Wales and served to reinforce the notion of the interdependency of region and nation. Witnessing the supposedly arcane ceremonies of the Gorsedd on the eisteddfod stage also impressed upon me how Iolo had provided Welsh national consciousness with a focus which transcended regional pride. My curiosity kindled (and regional pride primed), I was glad to join a research project which had set itself the aim of reassessing one of the most famous – indeed notorious – figures in the history of Glamorgan and Wales. It was fitting that my role in the project should be that of uncovering the layers of national and regional identity in Iolo's representation of our cultural past. However, as soon as I began my research, I realized that a layer of self-identity was also prominently woven into the fabric of bardism. On the inside cover of the very first Iolo manuscript that I opened (NLW 13087E) I was confronted by the self-aggrandizing epithet 'Iolo Fawr' (Great Iolo)! This book, therefore, offers an interpretation of the dynamic interaction of national, regional and personal identities within the construct which Iolo called 'bardism'. Since the remit of the project includes bringing selections of Iolo's manuscripts into the public domain, I have also included a substantial group of his unpublished writings in the 'Documents' section at the end of the book.

The project 'Iolo Morganwg and the Romantic Tradition in Wales' could not have been established without the generous financial support of the Arts and Humanities Research Council, the British Academy, the Leverhulme Trust and the University of Wales. Nor could it have come to fruition without the collaboration of all the staff at the University of Wales Centre for Advanced Welsh and Celtic Studies, and I am indebted to everyone for their help and support. Geraint H. Jenkins, the Director of the Centre and the editor of this series, and Mary-Ann Constantine, the project leader, have ensured that it has been a thoroughly edifying (and entertaining) experience and I am grateful to members (past and present) of this project for their intellectual generosity and comradeship: Andrew Davies, David Ceri Jones, Eluned Jones, Ffion Mair Jones, Marion Löffler and Hywel Gethin Rhys. I am indebted to Barry J. Lewis for his assistance with translations of the quotations of early Welsh poetry in the Documents section of this book: unless otherwise stated, the quotations were translated by him. The additional expertise provided by the project's Advisory Panel greatly facilitated my work, as did the gracious assistance I received from the Centre's support staff, Vera Bowen, Nia Davies, Glenys Howells and Marian Beech Hughes. The bulk of Iolo's manuscripts and correspondence are housed at the National Library of Wales, Aberystwyth, and I would like to thank its staff for efficiently and patiently assisting me in my researches. Geraint Phillips and Huw Walters, in particular, were characteristically generous with their time and knowledge. Others to whom I owe thanks both for scholarly and moral support include Jane Aaron, Glenda Carr, Moira Dearnley, Martin Fitzpatrick, Paul Frazer, Marged Haycock, E. Wyn James, Branwen Jarvis, Bethan Jenkins, Dafydd Glyn Jones, Mari Elin Jones, John T. Koch, Ceri W. Lewis, Iolo Lewis, Lesa Ní Mhunghaile, Prys Morgan, Ann Parry Owen and Simon Rodway. I am grateful to the staff of the University of Wales Press for their thoroughness at all stages of the publishing process. Finally, for their unstinting support, I would like to thank my friends and family, especially my sister, Nerys.

February 2007 Cathryn A. Charnell-White

Acknowledgements

The National Library of Wales: Frontispiece, Figs. 1, 2, 3, 4, 6, 7, 8

The National Museum Cardiff: Fig. 5

Abbreviations

BL	British Library Manuscripts
BL Add.	British Library Additional Manuscripts
Cardiff	Cardiff Central Library
CD	John Morris-Jones, *Cerdd Dafod: sef Celfyddyd Barddoniaeth Gymraeg* (facsimile edn., Caerdydd, 1980)
CRhIM	P. J. Donovan (ed.), *Cerddi Rhydd Iolo Morganwg* (Caerdydd, 1980)
EHR	*English Historical Review*
GCH III	T. B. Pugh (ed.), *Glamorgan County History, Volume III: The Middle Ages* (Cardiff, 1971)
GCH IV	Glanmor Williams (ed.), *Glamorgan County History, Volume IV: Early Modern Glamorgan from the Act of Union to the Industrial Revolution* (Cardiff, 1974)
GPC	*Geiriadur Prifysgol Cymru* (4 vols., Caerdydd, 1950–2002)
HGB	Geraint and Zonia Bowen, *Hanes Gorsedd y Beirdd* (Abertawe, 1991)
IMChY	G. J. Williams, *Iolo Morganwg a Chywyddau'r Ychwanegiad* (Llundain, 1926)
JHSCW	*Journal of the Historical Society of the Church in Wales*
Lewis: *IM*	Ceri W. Lewis, *Iolo Morganwg* (Caernarfon, 1995)
LlC	*Llên Cymru*
MAW	Owen Jones, Iolo Morganwg and William Owen Pughe, *The Myvyrian Archaiology of Wales* (3 vols., London, 1801–7)
Morgan: *IM*	Prys Morgan, *Iolo Morganwg* (Cardiff, 1975)
NLW	National Library of Wales
NLWJ	*National Library of Wales Journal*
RAEW	Elijah Waring, *Recollections and Anecdotes of Edward Williams* (London, 1850)
Rattleskull Genius	Geraint H. Jenkins (ed.), *A Rattleskull Genius: The Many Faces of Iolo Morganwg* (Cardiff, 2005)
THSC	*Transactions of the Honourable Society of Cymmrodorion*

TLlM	G. J. Williams, *Traddodiad Llenyddol Morgannwg* (Caerdydd, 1948)
WHR	*Welsh History Review*
Williams: *IM*	G. J. Williams, *Iolo Morganwg – Y Gyfrol Gyntaf* (Caerdydd, 1956)
Williams: *PLP*	Edward Williams, *Poems, Lyric and Pastoral* (2 vols., London, 1794)
WOP	Glenda Carr, *William Owen Pughe* (Caerdydd, 1983)

1

Introduction: The Bard and his Vision

The frontispiece to this volume reproduces an etching of Iolo Morganwg (1747–1826) by Robert Cruikshank which appeared in Elijah Waring's influential biography of Iolo, *Recollections and Anecdotes of Edward Williams* (1850). Although its tendency towards caricature reinforces Iolo's misplaced reputation as an eccentric, it remains the best-known portrait of him in his role as Bard. Dressed in his favourite blue jacket with gilt buttons, and a buff-coloured waistcoat, he is portrayed seated in an armchair. His hair is long and unkempt, and his face betrays the ravages of his long-term addiction to laudanum. Yet, he is an animated figure, wagging his index figure as he explains the arcane mysteries of Welsh bardism to his unseen interlocutor. The venerable Bard is surrounded by symbols of his bardic status: the bardic insignia /|\ and the much-vaunted bardic qualification 'B.B.D.' (Bardd Braint a Defod/Bard by Rite and Privilege). Waring explains the significance of Iolo's self-styled title, but also contextualizes a defining moment in the history of Iolo's Gorsedd, namely the eisteddfod held at Carmarthen in 1819, in which the Gorsedd was incorporated into the proceedings of the eisteddfod for the first time, thereby marking its coming of age as a burgeoning national institution. It was also an event which fully endorsed Iolo's bardic reputation:

> The B.B.D. affixed to the name of IOLO MORGANWG, is an initial contraction of the style and title of his order: *Bardd wrth fraint a Defod Beirdd ynys Prydain*; in English, 'Bard, according to the rights and institutes of the Bards of the Island of Britain.' The grounds of this style and title are stated in the Institutional Triades (*Trïoedd Braint a Defod*) to be, because Bardism originated in Britain, was never well understood in any other country, and can only be preserved in its purity by means of the *Voice conventional* of the British Bards. The best authorities agree that Bardism is not an arbitrary system, or a device of recent date: its institutions are unquestionably of very remote antiquity; and not only Iolo Morganwg, but many other learned Welsh antiquaries, assert that the constitutional principles, and ritual of the order, have been preserved unimpaired. It may be doubted whether any man of the age had more diligently studied these institutes, than our Glamorganshire Bard; and when he attended the Eisteddfod at Carmarthen in 1820 [*sic*], he deeply interested the learned Bishop of St David's (Dr Burgess) by his eloquent expositions of them. The ceremonial used in admitting several candidates for Bardic degrees, on that occasion, was described by an eye-witness as very impressive; and the BARDD BRAINT [Iolo Morganwg] maintained the dignity of

> his Order with absolute authority, standing in the midst of a circle of stones on the *Maen Gorsedd*, or Stone of Covenant, from whence he commanded the several aspirants to put off their shoes, before entering the circle; after which they approached him, one by one, and received the symbols of the institution at his hands. The good Bishop was present, and wished the Bard to dispense with some of the initiatory forms; but he would not permit the slightest departure from ancient usage, for within that circle he was, and would be, *Pontifex Maximus*, and beyond his authority there was no appeal.[1]

Waring's explanation also signposts the running themes of this book: the role of bardism and the Gorsedd in bolstering national pride, regional affiliation and Iolo's dynamic presence within the bardic circle.

Bardic Circles provides a textual study and a close reading of Iolo's writings on bardism. It focuses specifically on the way in which bardism allowed him to construct an innovative Welsh national identity based on primitivist principles. The early sixteenth-century Acts of Union between England and Wales had imposed a heavily Anglocentric 'British' identity on Wales and, as the Welsh lost an awareness of their own history, the sense of their own identity was, by the seventeenth century, 'dribbling away . . . into a stagnant and often despicable, provincial obscurity'.[2] Following the Union of Scotland with England and Wales in 1707, it became even more fractured under the emerging British state. Iolo's reconstruction of Welsh identity was thus timely, and was made all the more immediate by contemporary wrangling over the meaning of the terms 'Britain', 'British' and 'Briton', and qualifying terms such as 'Cambro-Britain'. But bardism also expressed Iolo's highly subjective sense of regional identity and even provided the means for him to fashion his own self-identity. This should come as no surprise. Iolo Morganwg was a proud Glamorgan man who lived in London during the political instability of the early 1790s, during which he become acquainted with polite society and a variety of radical circles. He was thus deeply conscious of the contingent nature of identity and self-identity. His voluminous correspondence and assorted writings reveal a social chameleon moving in diverse circles during a period in which identities of a national, regional, political, religious, social and literary nature were constantly being reconfigured.

The ideological matrix for bardism, and indeed for this book, is the response of patriotic antiquarianism to the ambivalent attitudes towards the Celts which characterized the Celtic revival of the Romantic period and the increasingly contested idea of Britishness witnessed during the closing decades of the

1 *RAEW*, pp. 52–3.

2 Gwyn A. Williams, 'Romanticism in Wales' in Roy Porter and Mikuláš Teich (eds.), *Romanticism in National Context* (Cambridge, 1988), p. 11. See also Prys Morgan, 'From a Death to a View: The Hunt for the Welsh Past in the Romantic Period' in Eric Hobsbawm and Terence Ranger (eds.), *The Invention of Tradition* (Cambridge, 1983), pp. 44–5.

eighteenth century. Building on the work of previous generations of Welsh antiquaries and littérateurs – Edward Lhuyd, Lewis Morris and Evan Evans in particular – Iolo's antiquarian interests brought him into the orbit of the Celtic revival whose interest in, and literary appropriation of, the history and mythology of the Celts had provided a brief Romantic respite from the deeply entrenched image of the barbarous and backward Welsh.[3] Even though 'the Bard' became a potent image in contemporary fiction, poetry and art, old prejudices against the nations of the so-called Celtic fringe and their cultural achievements still prevailed, and these were deepened in literary and antiquarian circles by the furious and long-lasting debate caused by the publication of the bardic poetry of Ossian. Much of the debate was conducted against a backdrop of perceived Anglo-Saxon cultural superiority, to which the vision of Wales which Iolo presented in his pseudo-antiquarian vision of Welsh history was a defensive and passionate riposte. Bardism also constituted a reaction to the cultural appropriation which was one of the outcomes of the revival of interest in the history and mythology of the Celtic nations. Crucially, Iolo manipulated the very myths and motifs that had become popular in the Romantic imagination to rehabilitate Wales's image, thereby reclaiming the Bard and 'Ancient British' status for Wales and the Welsh. The aim of this book, therefore, is to acquaint a new readership with Iolo's Welsh background and to reveal new insights into his novel projection of Welsh identity. He was not the *sui generis* architect of Welsh nationhood of common perception. He was rather, insofar as he gave the Welsh language and its ancient bardic tradition enhanced prominence, the heir to a line of scholars and antiquaries in early modern Wales who were instilled with humanist learning: Siôn Dafydd Rhys, Edward Lhuyd and Lewis Morris. But what set Iolo Morganwg apart was his awareness of, and engagement with, broader Celtic and European contexts.

The 'bardic circles' of the title resonate in multiple ways in the following narrative about bardism. In the first place, it alludes to the 'bardic circles' involved in the genesis and development of bardism. The native antiquaries and poets of Glamorgan and London provided its antiquarian and poetic basis and also stimulated its characteristic regional bias. A composite construct, bardism typifies the work of an autodidact and a *bricoleur*: the indigenous Welsh poetic tradition constitutes the 'single text' which accommodates a variety of eclectic and seemingly disparate discourses.[4] These include received notions of druidism, Jacobinism, Unitarian theology, orientalism,

3 Prys Morgan, 'Wild Wales: Civilizing the Welsh from the Sixteenth to the Nineteenth Centuries' in Peter Burke, Brian Harrison and Paul Slack (eds.), *Civil Histories: Essays Presented to Sir Keith Thomas* (Oxford, 2001), p. 266.

4 Jon Mee, *Dangerous Enthusiasm: William Blake and the Culture of Radicalism in the 1790s* (Oxford, 1992), p. 5.

speculative Freemasonry and Arthuriana. It was Iolo's wide and varied circle of correspondents and his position on the periphery of English Romantic and Jacobin circles which gave bardism its eclectic content, primitivist contours and radical colour. After Iolo's days, during the early part of the nineteenth century bardism's dissemination and evolution into an emblem of Welsh national consciousness was overseen by the circles of poets and literary parsons of the Cambrian Societies, some of whom, like Walter Davies and W. J. Rees, had corresponded with the Glamorgan bard.

Secondly, the title conjures up images of the pseudo-druidic circles of stones which adorn the public spaces of many Welsh towns and cities. These stone circles are the vestiges, not of ancient Druids and their rites, as some still believe, but of nineteenth- and twentieth-century eisteddfodau and their attendant Gorsedd ceremonies. Iolo's original Gorsedd ceremonies in the 1790s were simple, minimalist affairs, in which bards, sporting modest arm-bands, assembled around a circle made of small stones:

> The *Welsh Bards* always meet in the open air whilst the Sun is above the horizon, where they form a *circle of stones*, according to the ancient custom; this circle they call *Cylch Cyngrair*, the *Circle of Concord*, or of *Confederation*. In these days, however, it is formed only of a few very small stones, or pebbles, such as may be carried to the spot in one man's pocket; but this would not have been deemed sufficient by those who formed the stupendous *Bardic Circle* of *Stone-henge*.[5]

As well as reverting to ancient usage, the modern Gorsedd circles provide visible evidence of the widespread posthumous popularity of the multi-layered bardic vision of Wales which is the focus of this book; for it is the Bards, Ovates and Druids of Iolo Morganwg's devising who graced these particular bardic circles. Their impressive dimensions betoken the interest of the Victorians in pageantry and in establishing a permanent institutional identity for the Gorsedd.

Finally, the notion of bardic circles may be applied to the intersecting discursive circles of this volume: Iolo's projection of national, regional and personal image and identity. Elijah Waring's hagiographical account of Iolo in his biography set a pattern for all subsequent writers, many of whom argued that Iolo and his bardic system were *sui generis*.[6] While this present study acknowledges that bardism was, indeed, a highly subjective system, the first chapter explores bardism as a novel instrument of self-identification, a channel for the bardic persona which Iolo constructed for himself. The bardic persona was by far the most dominant persona adopted by Iolo because it enabled him, posing as an eccentric bard, to negotiate London's literary

[5] Williams: *PLP*, II, p. 39.
[6] *RAEW*, p. 34.

salons and networks by transcending both his Welshness and his inferior social standing. This opening chapter traces the parallel development of the bardic persona and bardism, revealing how the bardic package conferred upon him autonomy and authority, while also providing much-needed succour in the midst of hardship and disappointment.

Iolo gained considerable confidence from his self-proclaimed status as an 'Ancient British Bard'. He not only claimed this role for himself, but also reclaimed the bardic heritage, together with the prestige associated with it, for the Welsh nation at large. In this context Damian Walford Davies has observed that, 'one might say of Williams, as Blake said of himself, that he created a system to avoid being enslaved by another man's – or another nation's'.[7] The second chapter turns to this broader, national context in which Iolo, assuming the traditional role of the Bard as a custodian of Welsh historical consciousness and Welsh nationhood,[8] championed the ancient refinement and uniqueness of the Welsh nation. His response had a distinctly Celtic dimension, for he had discerned this model in the work of Irish antiquaries, to whom the bard was also 'the cultural guardian of the Gaelic heritage, whose task it was to guarantee historical continuity, to legitimize the present in terms of past history'.[9] This purportedly shared Celtic heritage provided bardism with its intellectual framework. But while Iolo was eager to assert the superiority of the Welsh poetic tradition, he also appreciated the value of the primitivist approach adopted by apologists for an essentially bardic Irish national identity, a form of cultural nationalism which Katie Trumpener has aptly termed 'bardic nationalism'.[10]

The conceptual framework and lexicon which Iolo borrowed from primitivism was malleable enough to withstand a shift in emphasis from national to regional. The third chapter traces the transformation of Iolo's natural love of his native county of Glamorgan into an overriding obsession, motivated primarily by the collapse of his relationship with his friends and patrons from north Wales, William Owen Pughe and Owen Jones (Owain Myfyr). Iolo's regional infatuation is reflected in his calculated attempt to weave the tension between north and south Wales into the very fabric of bardism, and to explain it in primitivist and druidic terms. However, behind the personal, and indeed interpersonal, imperatives of Iolo's obsession with the imputed

7 Damian Walford Davies, *Presences that Disturb: Models of Romantic Identity in the Literature and Culture of the 1790s* (Cardiff, 2002), p. 160.

8 Glanmor Williams, *Religion, Language and Nationality in Wales* (Cardiff, 1979), pp. 127–8.

9 Joep Leerssen, *Mere Irish and Fíor-Ghael: Studies in the Idea of Irish Nationality, its Development and Literary Expression prior to the Nineteenth Century* (Cork, 1996), p. 153.

10 Katie Trumpener, *Bardic Nationalism: The Romantic Novel and the British Empire* (Princeton, NJ, 1997), p. xii. See also Andrew Davies, '"The Reputed Nation of Inspiration": Representations of Wales in Fiction from the Romantic Period, 1780–1830' (unpublished University of Wales Ph.D. thesis, 2001).

superiority of Glamorgan lies a valid critique of how the London Welsh and their cultural agenda were perceived by native Welsh antiquaries.

The interplay between the discursive bardic circles is the overarching theme of the fourth chapter. Iolo's national agenda for bardism and the Gorsedd was clear, but both the vision and the wherewithal which sustained it did not achieve truly national status until after his death. By that stage the institution had overtaken its institutor and Iolo was considered merely a link in a chain which stretched back over the millennia. Although the personal and regional appeal proved to be the more enduring, Iolo's image of a morally upright, Christian and anciently civilized nation was perfectly timed to meet Welsh needs following the indictment of the nation by the 'Treachery of the Blue Books' in 1847.

In keeping with the overall aim of the research project currently under way at the University of Wales Centre for Advanced Welsh and Celtic Studies, the second part of this volume includes a selection of Iolo's writings on bardism. As well as illustrating the personal, regional and national dynamics of Iolo's bardic vision, these documents also give a clear sense of Iolo's own convictions and the saliency of his message. Since much of Iolo's writings still remain in manuscript, it is hoped that the reader and the researcher will be drawn to discover Iolo Morganwg's archive for themselves.

2

Personal Image and Identity in Bardism

> I do not intend to make my own dear self the great hero of my Tale, I shall relate of myself however as much, and in as few wor[ds] [as] possible, of myself as may be necessary for the Truth of my History, for informing the world of some particulars in [my] life that are not yet publicly known, and which being unknown, would leave room for misrepresentations of my ch[aracter] a few, not many, letters, and extracts of letters from some with whome I have corresponded will be given.[1]

Here, in an outline of a pamphlet entitled 'The History of My Life' which he proposed to publish in 1805, we hear the voice of a man acutely concerned with himself and with his self-image. Iolo Morganwg had first proposed undertaking this task in 1791,[2] and the proposal was still on the drawing board in 1810 when he discussed it with his long-suffering London publisher, Evan Williams of the Strand. By now in his fifty-ninth year, Iolo was determined to appraise his achievements and, more importantly, colour the way in which he would be remembered by posterity.[3] Iolo's sense of the self is the starting point for this discussion of bardism's competing agendas. The national, regional and personal forces at work within bardism should not be considered as discrete entities because their complex interaction within the system suggests that, for Iolo, the boundaries between them were highly permeable. Indeed, when he discussed the autobiography seven years later, his false modesty notwithstanding, the extent to which Wales's story had become a part of his own individual story becomes clear:

> I have written a great part of the History of my Life. I endeavour to make it the vehicle of such remarks as I may be able to make on Welsh Literature, ancient and modern; on the Welsh Language, and its several Dialects; on Welsh History, Manners, Habits of Living, Various Popular Antiquities, &c. &c. I endeavour, as much as possible, to avoid frivolous egotism, – a thing rather difficult for one to accomplish handsomely, who writes his own history. I have sometimes thought of writing it, like Julius Caesar, in the third person: this will cost me no great trouble

1 NLW 13221E, Letter no. 24, p. 122, Iolo Morganwg to William Owen Pughe, 20 July 1805. Iolo's letters and manuscripts abound with examples of false modesty. See also *Cambrian Register*, 3 (1818), 174–9, Iolo Morganwg to Evan Williams, 16 January 1810; Williams: *IM*, pp. xxvi–ii.

2 See NLW 21285E, Letter no. 797, Iolo Morganwg to Margaret (Peggy) Williams, 19 February 1791. See also ibid., Letter nos. 822, 848, 850; NLW 13221E, pp. 111–14.

3 *Cambrian Register*, 3 (1818), 174–9, Iolo Morganwg to Evan Williams, 16 January 1810.

> in preparing press-copy. My great object in this work is to illustrate the Literature, History, and Manners of the Welsh Nation: these are the topics that will render it interesting, and not the mere incidents of the life of such an obscure and insignificant person as I am.[4]

But if any one part of his bardic agenda can be considered more forceful than the others, it is Iolo's own personal identity: he was not only bardism's self-appointed public mediator but also its creator. As a result, his own personal foibles and wide-ranging intellectual interests as much as his national and regional concerns determined bardism's shape. In turn, bardism lent an important dimension to the public persona which he adopted. He identified intimately with both Wales and Glamorgan, and passionately defended them against slights as if he himself had suffered a personal affront. Bardism's most subjective element was the primacy which Iolo gave to Glamorgan, a partiality which was fuelled by his feelings of inadequacy as a south Walian amid the primarily north Walian members of the Gwyneddigion Society in London, and which was intensified by his increasingly bitter interpersonal difficulties with William Owen Pughe and Owain Myfyr. Nevertheless, Iolo Morganwg was the glue which held this exceedingly diverse and idiosyncratic bardic system together, and he clearly used it as a vehicle for his own personal image and identity.

Iolo's correspondence reveals that his bardic persona represented only one facet of his personality.[5] A consummate social and literary chameleon, he was able to change his colours according to the needs of his associates or implied readers; his fictions of the self, whose very construction was one of the main features of the art of letter-writing,[6] satisfied the varied social, cultural and political expectations of his correspondents. Among the personas conjured up in his correspondence are the irresponsible yet loving paterfamilias, the versatile stonemason, the poor labouring poet, the patriotic antiquarian, the political radical, the Rational Dissenter, the agricultural commentator and the champion of the poor.[7] Faced with such an array of personas, his letters and the many ideological positions he adopted within them present nuanced responses at one end of the scale and contradictory opinions at the other: the authentic Edward Williams held fast to all of these

4 Ibid. It was also to be a vehicle for conveying his hatred towards William Owen Pughe and Owen Jones (Owain Myfyr), and for establishing the primacy of Glamorgan.

5 David Ceri Jones, 'Fictional Selves in the Life and Writings of Edward Williams (Iolo Morganwg, 1727–1826)' in Tim Burke, Steve Clark and Katherine Turner (eds.), *Romanticism in the Eighteenth Century* (forthcoming).

6 Janet Gurkin Altman, *Epistolarity: Approaches to a Form* (Columbus, Ohio, 1982); Rebecca Earle (ed.), *Epistolary Selves: Letters and Letter-Writers, 1600–1945* (Aldershot, 1999), pp. 1–12. For the fictional use of the letter form, see Thomas O. Beebee, *Epistolary Fiction in Europe 1500–1850* (Cambridge, 1999), pp. 1–22.

7 Most of these aspects are discussed in *Rattleskull Genius*.

things. Nonetheless, the venerable Bard, 'Iolo Morganwg', is the most prominent and most enduring persona and was often (though not entirely consistently) the point at which the other personas converged.

In terms of content and shape, in its intricate interweaving of fact and fiction, past and present, and in the sheer diversity of its basic elements, bardism was an expression of the complicated and controversial nature of its mastermind, Iolo Morganwg. Wales's genuine poetic tradition and its structures, informed by received learning on druidism, antiquarianism and primitivism, provided its basic framework. But other intellectual interests also shaped bardism: Jacobinism, Freemasonry, orientalism, Unitarian theology, and the history and literature of his native county of Glamorgan.[8] Much like an image viewed through a kaleidoscope, these various elements collided in constantly shifting patterns and combinations throughout Iolo's lifetime, while remaining part of a more or less coherent whole. This, of course, poses innumerable problems for those who seek to organize his ideas and influences into an orderly fashion. Iolo was a contrary and paradoxical figure, and a neat and chronologically accurate exegesis of bardism is difficult to achieve for two reasons: Iolo's methodology and the way in which his archive was collated by his son, Taliesin Williams (Taliesin ab Iolo). A self-pronounced autodidact, Iolo lacked the rigour and discipline required to bring his many and varied ideas to fruition and, as early as 1788, he admitted to William Owen Pughe that his papers lay in disarray: 'the countless disorderly papers (the entangled wilderness, as it is fair to call them').[9] Following his death, the responsibility of collating these was shouldered by his son Taliesin, who arranged the largely undated commonplace books and sheets of paper in a broadly thematic way.

For Iolo, bardism was more than merely a literary and cultural construct which served his proto-nationalist and regional agendas. Throughout his life he was seemingly obsessed by his bardic vision and channelled much of his time and energy into it. He constantly sought to improve upon it, and worked on it at regular intervals throughout the greater part of his life, from the late 1780s until his death in December 1826. As bardism was honed over four decades, Iolo's bardic persona grew in tandem with it. Indeed, of the

8 Williams: *IM*; Lewis: *IM*; Ceri W. Lewis, 'Iolo Morganwg' in Branwen Jarvis (ed.), *A Guide to Welsh Literature c.1700–1800* (Cardiff, 2000), pp. 126–67; Morgan: *IM*; Geraint H. Jenkins, *Facts, Fantasy and Fiction: The Historical Vision of Iolo Morganwg* (Aberystwyth, 1997); idem, 'Iolo Morganwg and the Gorsedd of the Bards of the Isle of Britain', *Studia Celtica Japonica*, 7 (1995), 45–60.

9 NLW 13221E, pp. 11–14, Iolo Morganwg to William Owen Pughe, 12 March 1788: 'yr aneirif bapirau didrefn (yr anialwch dyrus fal y mae'n gymmwys ei alw)'. See also BL Add 15024, Letter no. 3, f. 312, Iolo Morganwg to Owain Myfyr, 26 July 1800: 'My sheets of transcript[s] the labours of many years, are for the most part unbound and in great disorder, like everything else with me . . . I have always had too many Irons in the fire, a llawer un ohonynt yn llosgi'n ulw [and many burning to a cinder].'

many personas which emerge from his extensive writings and correspondence, the bardic persona is the most striking and, without doubt, the most consistent and enduring: he was and still is universally known by his bardic pen-name, 'Iolo Morganwg'. Nevertheless, 'Iolo Morganwg' was not his first incarnation as a bard; he experimented with several pseudonyms from the late 1760s before settling on 'Iolo Morganwg' early in the 1790s. Each one marks a different stage in his bardic career.

'Iorwerth Gwilym' (sometimes spelt 'Gwilim'), a Cymricized version of his Christian name, was his first choice. The fact that Iolo signed himself 'Iorwerth Gwilym' in a letter to his acquaintance, Mrs J. Harrison (née Margaret Spencer) as late as 1794, suggests that this name may not have been an exclusively bardic alias, but rather a Welsh one.[10] It was common practice to use Welsh aliases in everyday contexts, and Iolo's own writings and correspondence concerning neighbours reveal that people were known both by their Welsh and English names. The linguistic make-up of his locality and family was bilingual, but English was the language favoured in his home,[11] and his contemporaries observed that Iolo's English was generally more fluent than his Welsh.[12] The Welsh alias 'Iorwerth Gwilym' was, however, more than the product of this bilingual inheritance since it also corresponded chronologically with the period during which he came under the influence of the cultured clerics of the Vale of Glamorgan (John Walters and Thomas Richards), and a small group of Welsh poets from the uplands of Glamorgan in the late 1760s. Although he may have assumed the Welsh alias earlier, evidence from his correspondence suggests that it was safely established by the early 1770s. Between 1770 and 1773 he signed himself 'Iorwerth Gwilym' and he was addressed in this manner by local poets, many of whom also possessed Welsh aliases: David Richards (Dafydd ap Rhisiart, Dafydd Rhisiart), John Bradford (Siôn Bradford), Edward Evan (Iorwerth ab Ioan) and James Turberville (Iaco Twrbil).[13] Since 'Iorwerth Gwilym' was the name by which he was known within poetic circles in Glamorgan and London

[10] NLW 21285E, Letter no. 831, Iolo Morganwg to Mrs J. Harrison, 8 February 1794. Addressing Iolo in 1793, Davidd ap Hugh or David Pugh in London used the Welsh–English hybrid alias 'Iorwerth Williams'. NLW 21282E, Letter no. 389, Davidd ap Hugh to Iolo Morganwg, 8 January 1793.

[11] 'My first attempts in Poetry were in Welsh, that being in the country *vernaculum*, though English was the language of my father's house', Williams: *PLP*, I, p. xvi; Morgan: *IM*, p. 2.

[12] Williams: *IM*, p. 99.

[13] The following letters use the patronymic 'ap Gwilym' (son of William): NLW 21280E, Letter no. 35, John Bradford to Iolo Morganwg, 15 April 1771; ibid., Letter no. 62, Wil Dafydd to Iolo Morganwg, 1 January 1770; NLW 21281E, Letter no. 282, Siencyn Morgan to Iolo Morganwg, 30 November 1771, refers to him as Nedi William. For further information on these figures and Iolo's involvement with them, see *TLlM* and Ceri W. Lewis, 'The Literary History of Glamorgan from 1550 to 1770' in Glanmor Williams (ed.), *GCH IV*, pp. 608–39.

in the early 1770s, and since it was also the name which he appended to his youthful imitations of Dafydd ap Gwilym's poetry, it clearly operated as a badge of his commitment to his newly discovered Welsh cultural inheritance and to his apprenticeship in Welsh strict-metre poetry and antiquities. Indeed, Iorwerth Gwilym was the alias he appended to his elegy to Lewis Hopkin, his bardic teacher.

By 1779 Iolo had amended his bardic name slightly: Iorwerth Gwilym (Edward Williams) was replaced by Iorwerth Morganwg (Edward of Glamorgan). This time, the impetus for change had come from the club mentality of the Gwyneddigion Society in London, whose members and associates had a penchant for bardic names which reflected the expatriate Welshman's place of origin: Robin Ddu o Fôn (Robert Hughes), Owain Myfyr (Owen Jones), Gwilym o Feirion (William Owen Pughe) and Siôn Ceiriog (John Edwards).[14] Bardic names like these were more than an outward sign of nostalgic patriotism born of exile. Assuming bardic names, especially those which evoked the poet's home or locality, was an act of homage to a long-established tradition observed by medieval Welsh poets and, as such, indicated their involvement with the Welsh cultural renaissance. This subtle amendment to his bardic name reflects therefore the extent to which Iolo's cultural and patriotic interests had been galvanized by his contact from *c.*1773 with the London Welsh.

However, the transformation from Iorwerth Gwilym to Iorwerth Morganwg should not be overstated; it merely served to reinforce his enthusiasm for Welsh strict-metre poetry and antiquities, and may even have signified his growing confidence in these fields. Nor was the change overly significant, since a degree of overlap between both aliases is evident in his correspondence. From 1779 to 1788 his friends in the Gwyneddigion Society, and even Iolo himself, used the names Iorwerth Gwilym and Iorwerth Morganwg interchangeably,[15] and even as late as 1793, when Iolo had established yet another pseudonym, Walter Davies (Gwallter Mechain) addressed a letter to him as 'Iorwerth Gwilym, Bardd wrth fraint a defod' (Iorwerth Gwilym, Bard according to right and privilege).[16] If, by adopting the name 'Iorwerth Gwilym', Iolo wished to acknowledge his apprenticeship in Welsh strict-metre poetry and its traditions, his new bardic name, 'Iorwerth Morganwg', was indicative of a more advanced step in his bardic career – Iorwerth Morganwg was a Welsh bard in the making. In view of later revisions to his bardic name (and especially the way in which 'Iolo Morganwg' later

14 See Ffion M. Jones, '"Gydwladwr godi[d]og": Gohebiaeth Gymraeg Gynnar Iolo Morganwg', *LlC*, 27 (2004), 140–71.

15 NLW 21281E, Letter nos. 226, 227; NLW 21282E, Letter nos. 307, 308; NLW 21285E, Letter no. 786; NLW 21389E, no. 15.

16 NLW 21280E, Letter no. 72, Walter Davies to Iolo Morganwg, 16 May 1793.

subsumed Edward Williams and earlier aliases), it should be noted that at this stage Iolo used his bardic names only among those to whom bardic nationalism was a familiar concept: his fellow poets in Glamorgan and within the London-Welsh societies.

The year 1791 marked a significant development in Iolo's career and bardic persona. This was the year in which the name 'Iolo Morganwg' became more or less fixed and in which he began an intermittent, yet highly stimulating, four-year residence in London. Ironically, 'Iolo Morganwg' was a name which he had attributed *c.*1784 to a medieval Glamorgan poet of his own invention, and whose anti-clericalism was an early example of the way in which Iolo's so-called ancient writings projected contemporary radical concerns.[17] But since 'Iolo' (Ned) was a diminutive of 'Iorwerth' (Edward), just how significant in reality was this shift? He arrived in London in February 1791, intent on publishing his English poems and eventually launching a new career as a professional writer. To this end, he presented himself to prospective subscribers and the city's polite society as a labouring-class poet, an impoverished but nonetheless knowledgeable autodidact. But among his old friends at the Gwyneddigion Society he presented himself differently: the apprentice poet they had known and nurtured in the 1770s and 1780s was now a fully fledged (not to mention self-appointed) 'Ancient British Bard'. Moreover, proof of his enhanced status lay in the bardic arcana which he imparted to his former mentors. He had by now developed his own alternative version of the Welsh poetic tradition – bardism – and possessed a wealth of genuine knowledge which he combined with a fabricated metrical system, a spurious bardic alphabet and a bogus bardic lineage. In the light of the transformation from Iorwerth Morganwg to Iolo Morganwg (from apprentice to master), it is astonishing that members of the Gwyneddigion had not quizzed him on his failure to mention bardism and ceremonies associated with the Gorsedd in previous encounters and correspondence over nearly two decades. None of them, for instance, recognized the similarity between Gorsedd meetings and the society which Iolo had invited Owain Myfyr to join as early as 1781, namely 'Brodoliaeth Beirdd Morganwg' (The Fraternity of Glamorgan Bards).[18]

To some extent, Iolo's arrival in London heralded a fresh start in his relationship with the London Welsh, and this might have facilitated the ease with which they accepted his new bardic name and equally new bardic status. A brief hiatus had occurred in his correspondence and relationship

[17] Williams: *IM,* p. 1: 'un o henfeirdd y byd Ioloaidd' (one of the ancient bards of the Ioloic world). See 'The Clerical Shepherd[:] A Monmouthshire Pastoral, Translated from the antient British of Iolo Morganwg, A Bard that flourish'd about the Year 1285', NLW 13170B, pp. 187–91.

[18] Williams: *IM*, p. 378.

with his London-Welsh friends: no correspondence survives for the period from August 1784 to April 1788, at which time William Owen Pughe, with whom Iolo was newly acquainted, wrote to him brokering peace.[19] During these silent years, when the penniless Iolo had been incarcerated in Cardiff gaol, he had been deeply wounded by the lack of attention he had received from Owain Myfyr and Siôn Ceiriog during this humiliating experience. But since he had neglected to inform them of his financial troubles and their sorry outcome, his displeasure towards them was largely unwarranted.[20] However, when Iolo and Owain Myfyr resumed their friendship, their letters became more serious and devoid of the ribaldry and sexual innuendo of earlier years. Their new-found gravity stemmed not only from encroaching middle-age but also from the fact that the Gwyneddigion Society had established the cultural authority it had previously lacked, and had elevated its sights above salacious songs such as 'Cân Morfydd i'r Gyllell Gig' (Morfydd's Song to the Meat Knife).[21] Masterminded by Pughe, and bolstered by Myfyr's financial support, they had begun work on an ambitious and unprecedented programme of publishing medieval Welsh literature.[22] When Iolo resumed his correspondence with Owain Myfyr in 1788, Myfyr and Pughe were focused on the task of preparing and publishing an authoritative collection of the poetry of Dafydd ap Gwilym. Iolo, whose earliest poetic pieces were skilful imitations of the great medieval poet's poems,[23] supplied them with forgeries which were published at the last minute in the now infamous 'Ychwanegiad' (Appendix) included in *Barddoniaeth Dafydd ab Gwilym* (1789).[24] By the time of his arrival in London he had perfected bardism and, judging by the content of *The Heroic Elegies of Llywarç Hen* (1792) and *The Myvyrian Archaiology of Wales* (1801–7), he had grasped the opportunity of insinuating his own bardic ideas into the publishing programme of the Gwyneddigion Society. By adopting the bardic name 'Iolo Morganwg' at this crucial time for the Gwyneddigion Society and their enterprise of cultural renewal, Iolo abandoned the persona of the genial, smutty and misogynistic poet and prose-writer known to the Gwyneddigion as both 'Iorwerth Gwilym' and 'Iorwerth Morganwg'. With a new alias to match both a new agenda and a new identity, 'Iolo Morganwg' had reinvented himself as a serious bard and as bardism's sole mediator.

19 Jones, '"Gydwladwr godi[d]og": Gohebiaeth Gymraeg Gynnar Iolo Morganwg', 168–9.

20 Geraint Phillips, 'Forgery and Patronage: Iolo Morganwg and Owain Myfyr' in *Rattleskull Genius*, pp. 403–24.

21 NLW 21390E, nos. 22, 23.

22 G. J. Williams, *Agweddau ar Hanes Dysg Gymraeg*, ed. Aneirin Lewis (Caerdydd, 1985), pp. 239–44.

23 Huw Meirion Edwards, 'A Multitude of Voices: The Free-Metre Poetry of Iolo Morganwg' in *Rattleskull Genius*, pp. 97, 106, 107, 112, 120.

24 Owen Jones and William Owen Pughe (eds.), *Barddoniaeth Dafydd ab Gwilym* (Llundain, 1789). These forgeries were exposed by G. J. Williams in *IMChY*.

To modern readers, the multiplicity of names may appear confusing and even suggestive of an identity crisis rather than a crystallization of identity, but in eighteenth- and nineteenth-century Wales multiple aliases were not unusual. Pughe, for example, was variously known as 'Gwilym Owain' (William Owen), 'Gwilym Dawel' (Silent William), Gwilym o Feirion (William of Merioneth) and 'Idrison' (son of Idris).[25] Iolo himself, however, favoured the name 'Iolo Morganwg' as an expression of his bardic persona and, until the 1810s, he tended to use it in two narrow contexts: among fellow poets in Glamorgan and the literary-minded and radically engaged Gwyneddigion. Even though both Iolo and others used the appellation 'Edward Williams' as frequently as 'Iolo Morganwg', his bardic name was certainly a badge of individuality. In later life, his comments about the 1823 eisteddfod at Carmarthen reveal that he did not take kindly to having a 'presumtious Namesake', the younger poet Edward Williams (Gwilym Fardd Glas) of Cowbridge and Merthyr Tydfil.[26] Iolo jealously guarded his name and reputation, and his lifetime achievement, bardism, was truly that of Iolo Morganwg. By reviewing the main texts that express the bardic vision, we gain a clear chronological sense of the parallel development of bardism and Iolo's bardic persona and also an appreciation of the ebb and flow of his ideas and personal prejudices.

The first public pronouncement of Iolo's truly bardic status appeared in the *Gentleman's Magazine* in 1789. In this pen-portrait, using the initials 'J.D.' to conceal his identity, Iolo introduced himself to the metropolitan literary scene: 'Besides Edward Williams, there is, I believe, now remaining only one regular Bard in Glamorgan, or in the world . . . These two persons are the only legitimate descendants of the so-long-celebrated *Ancient British Bards*.'[27] The overall emphasis of the piece focuses on how his poetic or bardic persona was rooted in history and druidism, and may have been an attempt to stimulate interest in his bardic vision. In terms of propagating bardism, the letter to the *Gentleman's Magazine* was perfectly timed to coincide with the Gwyneddigion Society's attempts to revive the eisteddfod, and may therefore have constituted an artful attempt to inveigle himself into their plans after an absence of over a decade in their midst and in correspondence. In the same year the London Welsh published many of his fabrications alongside the genuine poems of the fourteenth-century poet Dafydd ap Gwilym in *Barddoniaeth Dafydd ab Gwilym*. Although these are

[25] *WOP*, p. 91.

[26] NLW 21286E, Letter no. 994, Iolo Morganwg to Taliesin Williams, 22 September 1823.

[27] *Gentleman's Magazine*, LIX, part 2 (1789), 976–7. The letter is reproduced in full in Williams: *IM*, pp. 464–5. See also the autobiographical material in NLW 21387E, nos. 9–10.

not ostensibly bardic, since they stake Glamorgan's claim to the canonical bard they provide an early indication of the significant role which Glamorgan and Dafydd ap Gwilym would play in bardism and, indeed, in Iolo's own bardic persona.[28] By leaving Wales for London, he hoped to enhance his literary reputation as both a Welsh bard and an English-language poet of the labouring class.[29] But strictly speaking, these were not discrete entities for Iolo since, as part of a movement that would later be termed 'the Celtic revival', his aim was to use his native Welsh poetic tradition to revitalize English poetry.[30] The portrait in the *Gentleman's Magazine* was a ploy to stimulate interest in his forthcoming volume of poems and, although it contained no detail on bardism, it set the scene for the parallel development of Iolo's bardic vision and persona in the politically charged atmosphere of the metropolis in the 1790s.

Iolo arrived in London in 1791 armed not only with his English poems but also with a manuscript entitled 'Cyfrinach Beirdd Ynys Prydain' (The Secret of the Bards of the Island of Britain). It is with 'Cyfrinach Beirdd Ynys Prydain' that bardism's story begins and ends, for it was the first significant text he composed on the subject and also the very last bardic text he put to press. He did not live to see it through the press, however, for *Cyfrinach Beirdd Ynys Prydain* (1829) was eventually published posthumously. His obsession with the text also reminds us that the proper preservation of Welsh strict-metre poetry was bardism's main priority. He had intended the treatise to be the 'Crown' of his proposed 'History of the Bards', in which 'it would appear as the most brilliant Jewel',[31] and, as will become clear, its fate was intertwined with that ambitious, unrealized project which he had begun planning as early as 1791.[32] Written mainly during the year he spent in Cardiff gaol from August 1786, the manuscript's genesis during a time of extreme personal stress and financial difficulty marked the beginning also of the safe haven which bardism as a whole would offer Iolo throughout the rest of his life.[33] A highly original metrical treatise, 'Cyfrinach Beirdd Ynys Prydain' reveals that Iolo, through his antiquarian researches into the ancient and medieval poetry and bardic grammars of Wales, had become the main authority of his generation on Welsh metrics.[34] In this treatise he combined

28 Gwyneth Lewis, 'Eighteenth-Century Literary Forgeries, with Special Reference to the Work of Iolo Morganwg' (unpublished University of Oxford D.Phil. thesis, 1991), pp. 167–203.

29 For the cultural phenomenon of the labouring-class poet, see William J. Christmas, *The Lab'ring Muses: Work, Writing, and the Social Order in English Plebeian Poetry, 1730–1830* (London, 2001).

30 Lewis, 'Eighteenth-Century Literary Forgeries', pp. 168–70, 173.

31 NLW 13221E, Letter no. 30, pp. 143–6, Iolo Morganwg to William Owen Pughe, 12 January 1806.

32 The earliest sketch of 'The History of the Bards' was in 1791: NLW 13144A, pp. 391–2.

33 Williams: *IM*, pp. 376, 377, 423; Lewis: *IM*, p. 50.

34 Williams: *IM*, pp. 128–9; Lewis: *IM*, pp. 14, 217.

authority with ingenuity, for John Morris-Jones was able to demonstrate in his celebrated study of Welsh metrics, *Cerdd Dafod* (1925), that Iolo structured his peculiar classification along guidelines established by the botanist Linnaeus.[35] The Welsh metres which had been classified and standardized by Dafydd ab Edmwnd (*fl.*1450–97) and accepted at the eisteddfod hosted by Gruffydd ap Nicolas at Carmarthen *c.*1453[36] had became renowned for their technical demands and complexity in subsequent centuries. But in 'Cyfrinach Beirdd Ynys Prydain' Iolo rejected Dafydd ab Edmwnd's standards and reclassified the Welsh metrical system; to this end he reinstated some ancient strict-metre forms and fashioned new ones which were imaginative fusions of existing strict- and free-metre forms.[37] He also forged supporting examples which he attributed to Glamorgan bards, both real and imagined.

This alternative metrical system was part of the declared aim of eighteenth-century cultural revivalists both to recover the Welsh poetic tradition and to marry it to their own Augustan literary tastes in order to create new poetic models of great sublimity and taste.[38] One of the foremost practitioners was Goronwy Owen, whose comments on Dafydd ab Edmwnd's stringent amendments – particularly 'Gorchest y Beirdd' (the Feat of the Bards), the most notorious of the so-called improvements – had been read by Iolo in the Morris papers housed at the Welsh Charity School.[39] Iolo's alternative metrical treatise must be understood in this context of experimentation and innovation. In 1780, as a member of the short-lived 'Brodoliaeth Beirdd Morganwg' (the Fraternity of the Bards of Glamorgan), he wrote enthusiastically to Owain Myfyr, informing him of the society and its aims: 'the few Bards that are in Glamorgan (I mean those who know any thing of our old poetry) have established a yearly association at Llantrisaint. We . . . intend to make some new regulations in our *BARDDONIAETH* [poetry]'.[40] Furthermore, he argued, their innovations included authorizing Goronwy Owen's scheme of *tawddgyrch gadwynog* and the *cadwyn fer*, and the utter rejection of Dafydd ab Edmwnd's scheme, including the notoriously difficult *Gorchest y Beirdd*, which they had 'as far as our authority can effect it, banish'd entirely

35 *CD*, pp. 376–8; Lewis: *IM*, p. 16.

36 D. J. Bowen, 'Dafydd ab Edmwnd ac Eisteddfod Caerfyrddin', *Barn*, 142 (1974), 441–8; G. J. Williams, 'Eisteddfod Caerfyrddin', *Y Llenor*, V, no. 1 (1926), 94–102.

37 Williams: *IM*, pp. 371–8; Edwards, 'A Multitude of Voices' in *Rattleskull Genius*, p. 99.

38 Saunders Lewis, *A School of Welsh Augustans* (Wrexham, 1924); Williams: *IM*, p. 375, 377; Lewis: *IM*, p. 66. See also Taliesin Williams (ed.), *Cyfrinach Beirdd Ynys Prydain: ys ef Llwybreiddiaeth ag Athrawiaeth ar y Farddoniaeth Gymraeg a'i Pherthynasau, yn ol Trefn a Dosparth y Prif Feirdd gynt ar y Gelfyddyd wrth Gerdd Dafod* (Abertawy, 1829), pp. 11–21, 23–34.

39 For Goronwy Owen's comments, see J. H. Davies (ed.), *The Letters of Goronwy Owen (1723–1769)* (Cardiff, 1924), p. 111.

40 BL Add. 15024, Letter no. 2, ff. 188–9, Iolo Morganwg to Owain Myfyr, 10 July 1780.

from our Language for ever'.[41] The treatise was born of a revisionist impulse, and in its initial stages it was not employed as evidence of Glamorgan's cultural superiority over Gwynedd, or as evidence of the druidic inheritance of Wales. It was, rather, an engagement with Wales's very own dispute between Ancients and Moderns and constituted a 'modern' alternative to the 'ancient' standard classification of Welsh metrics.[42] Only when his wider bardic system had crystallized fully in his mind did Iolo backtrack, and disguise Goronwy Owen's influence by contending that Owen's metrical innovations had not been innovations at all: Owen had merely stumbled upon bardism's druidic metrics (see Document IX).[43]

The metrical innovations which Iolo described in 1780 also point to the regional dimension of 'Cyfrinach Beirdd Ynys Prydain', for the treatise was also known as 'Mesurau Beirdd Morganwg' (Measures of Glamorgan Bards) and, more commonly in later years, 'Dosbarth Morganwg' (Glamorgan Measures or Classification):

> Rhai hen fesurau yr ydym wedi adferu, ar gynghanedd yr oesoedd diweddarach. ag hefyd wedi rhyfygu Llunio mesurau newyddion, a gwneuthur dull newydd ar amryw or hên fesuron, y rhain a alwasom Mesurau Beirdd Morganwg. os byddai dda gennych eu gweled mi a'u danfonaf attoch yn fy llythyr nesaf.[44]

> (We have restored some old measures, in the *cynghanedd* of later ages, and have dared to create new measures and have made a new style from the old measures, which we have called *Measures of Glamorgan Bards*. If you would like to see them I shall send them to you in my next letter.)

One of its most daring interpretations was that of Glamorgan's characteristic tradition of free-metre poetry in relation to bardism.[45] Since free-metre poetry – the hallmark of *clêr y dom* (dunghill poets) – was considered beyond the pale by members of the professional guild of poets, Iolo needed to form a tenable link between it and Wales's ancient and rich poetic inheritance. His reading of the role and duties of the *bardd teulu* (domestic bard) in medieval bardic grammars and triads helped him achieve this. The precise meaning of the term *bardd teulu* (domestic bard) still eludes modern scholars, but Iolo developed the notion that the domestic bard was ostensibly a poet in the free-metres, in contrast to the *prydyddion* (poets/bards), the proponents of the prized strict-metres. His observations on the gradual development of

41 Ibid. No English translations exist of these indigenous metres. They are, however, described in *CD*, pp. 344–8, 350–2.
42 Williams: *IM*, p. 377.
43 NLW 13114A, pp. 250–1.
44 BL Add. 15024, ff. 188–9, Iolo Morganwg to Owain Myfyr, 10 July 1780.
45 Williams (ed.), *Cyfrinach Beirdd Ynys Prydain*, pp. 159–71.

cynghanedd also facilitated this reading of events, for it later allowed him to argue in favour of a direct link between the primitive poets Aneirin and Taliesin and the free-metre poetry of Glamorgan. Despite the spurious spin he placed on it, Iolo had accurately recognized the antiquity of Welsh *cynghanedd*-free poetry, which also represented a separate strand from the tradition of free-metre poetry which had been introduced in Wales from England in the seventeenth century.[46]

Iolo had indeed brought his manuscript version of 'Cyfrinach Beirdd Ynys Prydain' to London so that he could engage in the debate on strict- and free-metre poetry, but he was also bent on settling old scores – both personal and regional – with members of the Gwyneddigion Society who, in the 1770s, had derided the Glamorgan colloquialisms of his own strict-metre poetry.[47] By 1791 the Glamorgan Classification lay at the heart of Iolo's bardo-druidic vision of the past, and conferred ancient authority (not to mention superiority) on the literary tradition of his native county. He now argued that the Glamorgan Classification contained in 'Cyfrinach Beirdd Ynys Prydain' was the product not of the Fraternity of Glamorgan Bards established in 1780 but of a quarrel between the bards of north and south Wales at the definitive eisteddfod held at Carmarthen in *c.*1453 at which Dafydd ab Edmwnd's metrical classification had been authorized. Iolo's new narrative account of the genesis of 'Cyfrinach Beirdd Ynys Prydain' locates the Carmarthen eisteddfod as a point of bifurcation in the Welsh bardic tradition: by embracing the innovations, the poets of north Wales fell away from the bardic path and descended into barbarism, while the genuine tradition of bardism prevailed in south Wales under the aegis of Glamorgan bards who had rebelled against 'The Pretender', Dafydd ab Edmwnd (see Document IX). He argued that, following the Carmarthen eisteddfod, the bards of Glamorgan undertook a search for the metrics which correctly reflected Welsh bardism. 'Cyfrinach Beirdd Ynys Prydain' was the culmination of that research: collated by various *penceirddiaid* (master poets) – Edward Dafydd, Meurug Dafydd, Dafydd Llwyd Mathew, Dafydd Benwyn and Llywelyn Siôn – it had been confirmed at a phantom eisteddfod held at Beaupre in 1681.[48] This narrative captivated the London-Welsh and their associates in Wales. David Thomas, whose initial curiosity in time turned to suspicion, wrote to Iolo in 1791 in awe of the *gwybodaeth ryfeddol* (wonderful knowledge) which he possessed,[49] while William Owen Pughe was sufficiently

46 Lewis: *IM*, pp. 106, 214; Edwards, 'A Multitude of Voices' in *Rattleskull Genius*, pp. 107–09.

47 See Robin Ddu's comments on Iolo's 'Cywydd y Daran' in NLW 21285E, Letter no. 772, Iolo Morganwg to Thomas Williams, 26 August 1774; ibid., Letter no. 784, Iolo Morganwg to Owain Myfyr, 1 March 1776; ibid., Letter no. 785, undated draft in Iolo Morganwg's hand.

48 Williams (ed.), *Cyfrinach Beirdd Ynys Prydain*, p. 1; the spurious provenance of the manuscript is outlined in a fictitious letter attributed to Edward Dafydd, ibid., pp. 2–6.

49 NLW 21283E, Letter no. 473, David Thomas to Iolo Morganwg, 1 November 1791.

impressed to preface his *Heroic Elegies of Llywarç Hen* with a 'sketch' of bardism drawn from information related to him by Iolo, and based on the very first Gorsedd meetings over which Iolo had presided in London in 1792.

The information on bardism contained in William Owen Pughe's *Heroic Elegies of Llywarç Hen* represents another stage in the evolution of bardism, namely its dynamic engagement with the radical Dissent of the 1790s.[50] The political climate in the city was electric and, located at the periphery of Joseph Johnson's wide circle of authors, the easily side-tracked Iolo swiftly allied himself with the radical cause and applied his newly acquired credo to his bardic vision and persona. At one level at least, his bards and Druids became democrats and republicans masquerading in ancient garb. The complex matrix of cross-currents which constituted the radicalism of the 1790s, and the way in which Iolo accessed and absorbed it, make the radical element of bardism and Gorsedd ceremonial the most complex aspect of his vision. Iolo was not a neat, systematic thinker, and he appears to have derived and developed his radical ideas within his own social networks, from contemporary events in London, and from the popular press that saturated the market.[51] A *bricoleur* and an intellectual opportunist by nature, there is every reason to believe that he deliberately radicalized bardism. It not only suited his idealistic version of Welsh history but also enhanced its appeal among members of the Gwyneddigion Society whose fundamental rationale, according to its founder member Owain Myfyr, was 'Rydd-did mewn Gwlad ac Eglwys' (Freedom in State and Church).[52] The ideals of the French Revolution had fired the imagination of several of the London Welsh and it is significant that bardism's overt radical content did not materialize until Iolo arrived in the metropolis in 1791.[53] There is nothing in the article which he published in the *Gentleman's Magazine* in 1789 that anticipates the

50 For Iolo's radicalism, see Gwyneth Lewis, 'Eighteenth-Century Literary Forgeries'; Damian Walford Davies, *Presences that Disturb: Models of Romantic Identity in the Literature and Culture of the 1790s* (Cardiff, 2002); idem, '"At Defiance": Iolo, Godwin, Coleridge, Wordsworth' in *Rattleskull Genius*, pp. 147–72; Jon Mee, *Dangerous Enthusiasm: William Blake and the Culture of Radicalism in the 1790s* (Oxford, 1992), pp. 109–11, 119–20; idem, '"Images of Truth New Born": Iolo, William Blake and the Literary Radicalism of the 1790s' in *Rattleskull Genius*, pp. 173–93.

51 Marcus Wood, *Radical Satire and Print Culture 1790–1822* (Oxford, 1994); Michael T. Davis (ed.), *Radicalism and Revolution in Britain, 1775–1848* (London, 2000).

52 NLW 1806E, f. 665, Owain Myfyr to Walter Davies, 31 October 1789.

53 By 1795 Iolo proposed to publish the following items: 'Dissertations on the *Rights of Man*, or an attempt to ascertain the true Principles of Liberty, natural and political, and the *Duties of Man*, as a member of society'; 'Christianity versus Kingcraft. with a plan proposed for Abolishing the Christian religion as inimical to the Rights of Tyrants'; 'A new plan for civilizing the American Indians and other Barbarous Nations; addressed [to] the British Protestant Dissenters'; 'A new and equitable plan for the Abolition of Slavery in the West Indies. addressed to the British Parliament'; 'The History of the Ancient British Bards'; 'A Search after Political Truth', NLW 21400C, no. 9.

crypto-republicanism which characterized the bardic meetings held in London in 1792 and 1793.

A further complication in any discussion of the relationship between bardism and Iolo's politics lies is the nature of bardism itself. It was essentially an antiquarian construct, a system firmly rooted in the past and subject to the prevailing didactic attitude towards history. Its confidence in history and historical precedence was incongruous with, and furthermore militated against, the anti-historical spirit of Painite radicalism which held that terms of governance should be dictated by the rights of the living rather than the traditions of the dead and that public consent should not bow to historical precedence.[54] Since bardism and bardic gorseddau were essentially vehicles for perpetuating historical precedents – both real and invented – and relied for their authority on resurrecting the traditions of the dead, it seems incongruous that Iolo should have sought to graft revolutionary values onto such a traditional framework. But such considerations did not present themselves as inherent contradictions to Iolo. He was determined to portray the ancient civilization of Wales and the Welsh in terms which contemporary audiences could understand and develop, and radicalism thus added further grist to his mill. It reflected the beginnings of a lifelong pattern of constant evolution and incessant revision to the detail of bardism without reconciling each new element to the existing whole.

Iolo's commitment to radicalism is discernible in the many embellishments he made to bardism and in its language and rationale. Gwyneth Lewis has drawn attention to the fact that Iolo's strident, undeferential and direct style matches that of Tom Paine, and the simple language of the triads made them a perfect tool in his eyes not only for disseminating subversive sentiments, but also (equally controversial in a post-revolutionary world) for educating the largely illiterate populace.[55] In terms of language, the term *gorsedd* itself was also transformed by Iolo's encounter with *sans-culottes* and republicans: in his manuscripts he translated the word as 'convention', 'bardic convention', 'national convention', 'voice conventional' and 'national legislative convention'. These examples occur in assorted material devoted to the triad form and within numerous drafts of 'A Short Account of the Ancient British Bards'.[56] In his published poems he used both a 'convention' and the less politically loaded 'congress'.[57] His use of the term 'convention' evokes

[54] James E. Epstein, *Radical Expression: Political Language, Ritual, and Symbol in England, 1790–1850* (Oxford, 1994), p. 5.

[55] Lewis, 'Eighteenth-Century Literary Forgeries', p. 214.

[56] NLW 13087E, pp. 251–8 (dated 13 August 1817); NLW 13088B, pp. 66–7; NLW 13089E, pp. 438, 442; NLW 13093E, pp. 189, 191; NLW 13097B, pp. 244, 267–8; NLW 13103B, p. 107; NLW 13158A, p. 187. Iolo even referred to the eisteddfodau at Caerwys as 'Caerwys conventions': NLW 13089E, p. 461.

[57] For 'convention', see Williams: *PLP*, II, pp. 220–1, 230. For 'congress', see ibid., p. 70n.

Paine's *Letter Addressed to the Addressers on the Late Proclamation* (1792) and that letter's revolutionary insistence that a constitution could only be formed by a democratically elected convention of people. In the light of the way in which members and supporters of English and Scottish conventions were persecuted in 1792 and 1794, this was a daring evocation. *A Convention the only Means of Saving us from Ruin* (1793) figures among the books which Iolo had in his possession in September 1795.[58] Its author, Joseph Gerrald had, like Paine, advocated a British Convention, and for his pains had been transported in 1793 for sedition, after attending the 1792 Scottish Convention as a delegate of the London Corresponding Society. Gerrald's concept of the convention was highly idealized: he considered it the only way of reviving the Anglo-Saxon constitution.[59] Echoes of this can be discerned in the democratic and anti-monarchic nature of bardism, and in Iolo's proposal that the Gorsedd meeting might provide an ideal administrative framework for a proposed Welsh colony in America.[60] But while the language of bardism and Gorsedd ceremonies bore unmistakable overtones of radical ideology, the most striking emphasis was on strict-metre poetry and its survival.

The Heroic Elegies of Llywarç Hen provided the most concise description of Iolo's version of bardism, even if its inconsistencies bore witness to William Owen Pughe's credulity. It contained none of the technical metrical detail of 'Cyfrinach Beirdd Ynys Prydain'; pseudo-historical, it concentrated on the rationale and ceremonial of the ancient Welsh bards and Druids, their maxims, tenets of religion, the discipline of the bards, the qualification to their ranks, and a selection of pertinent triads. It was trumpeted as a system whose principles derived from the patriarchs: 'a system embracing all the leading principles which tend to spread liberty, peace and happiness amongst mankind'.[61] Its leading maxims were peace, the free investigation of matters which attained to truth and wisdom, the equality of members, and the transparency of Gorsedd activity.[62] The extent to which Iolo had been stimulated by the political climate in London were also elaborated in the radical undertones of the bardic mottos and robes, and in the rubric of bardic meetings. Peace, Truth and Learning were represented by the blue, white and green robes of the Bard, Druid and Ovate respectively.[63] More specifically, one of the overarching themes of bardism and bardic meetings was 'truth', a watchword which resonated with both Jacobinism and Rational

58 NLW 21407C, no. 1.

59 Epstein, *Radical Expression*, p. 18; David Worrall, *Radical Culture: Discourse, Resistance and Surveillance, 1790–1820* (London, 1992), pp. 13–14, discusses the trial for sedition of Joseph Gerrald, William Skirving and Maurice Margarot, who had called for a British Convention.

60 Lewis, 'Eighteenth-Century Literary Forgeries', pp. 181–2, 212; NLW 13104B, pp. 87–91.

61 William Owen, *The Heroic Elegies of Llywarç Hen* (London, 1792), p. xxiv.

62 Ibid., pp. xxv–xxvii.

63 Ibid., p. xxxvii.

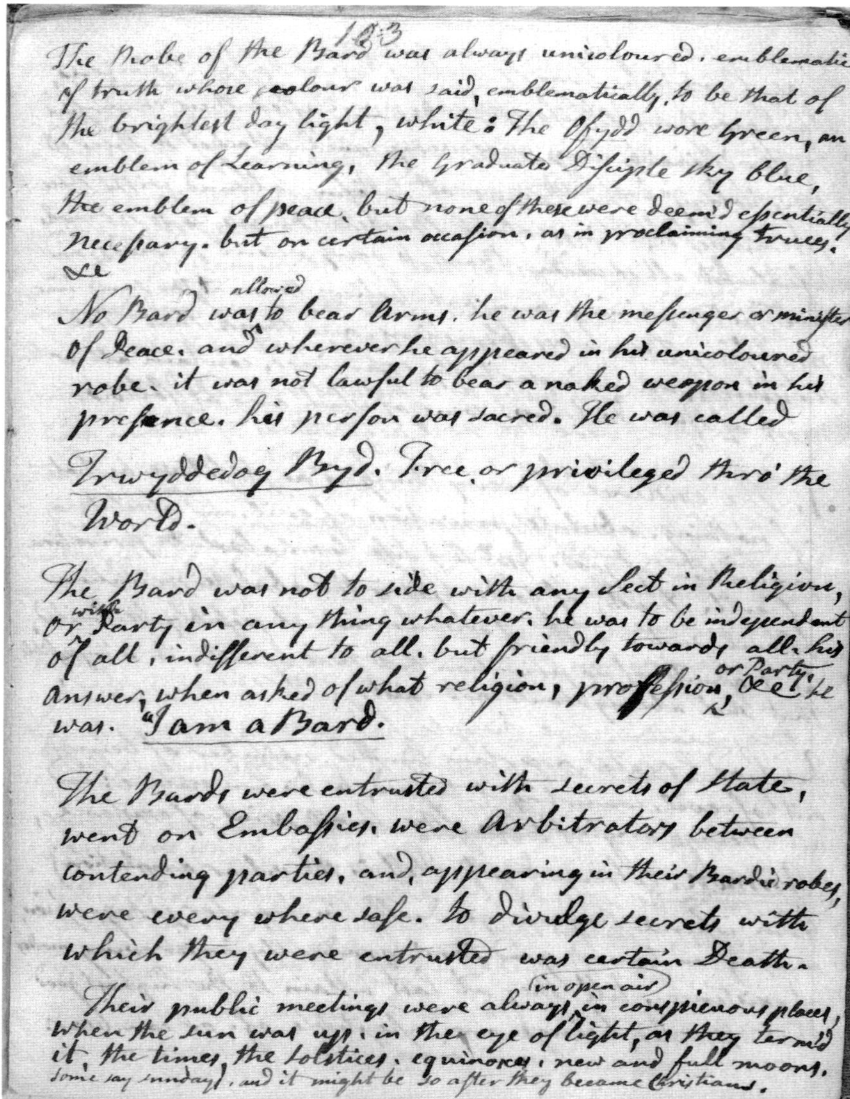
103

The Robe of the Bard was always unicoloured, emblematic of truth whose colour was said, emblematically, to be that of the brightest day light, white: The Ofydd wore green, an emblem of Learning, the Graduate Disciple sky blue, the emblem of peace, but none of these were deem'd essentially necessary, but on certain occasions, as in proclaiming truces, &c.

No Bard was allowed to bear Arms, he was the messenger or minister of Peace, and wherever he appeared in his unicoloured robe, it was not lawful to bear a naked weapon in his presence, his person was sacred. He was called Trwyddedog Byd, Free, or privileged thro' the World.

The Bard was not to side with any Sect in Religion, or with Party in any thing whatever, he was to be independent of all, indifferent to all, but friendly towards all, his answer when asked of what religion, profession, or Party, &c. he was, "I am a Bard.

The Bards were entrusted with secrets of State, went on Embassies, were Arbitrators between contending parties, and, appearing in their Bardic robes, were every where safe. to divulge secrets with which they were entrusted was certain Death.

Their public meetings were always in open air in conspicuous places, when the sun was up, in the eye of light, as they term'd it, the times, the solstices, equinoxes, new and full moons. Some say sundays, and it might be so after they became Christians.

Fig. 1 In spite of bardism's radical undertones, this page from 'A Short Account of the Ancient British Bards' proclaims the non-partisan status of the bard.

Dissent,[64] and which was encapsulated in the celebrated motto of the Bards of the Island of Britain: 'Y Gwir yn erbyn y Byd' (The Truth against the World). In terms of its rationale, bardism and Gorsedd ceremony owe much

[64] J. Anne Hone, *For the Cause of Truth: Radicalism in London, 1796–1821* (Oxford, 1982); D. Elwyn J. Davies, 'Astudiaeth o Feddwl a Chyfraniad Iolo Morganwg fel Rhesymolwr ac Undodwr' (unpublished University of Wales Ph.D. thesis, 1975), *passim*.

to the political climate of the early 1790s during which bardic meetings were held for the first time. Its democratic ethos was conveyed in the equal rank of all three bardic orders, a facet which also echoed Freemasonry but differed from it in its openness to scrutiny:

> The Bards held their Gorsedd meetings, always in a conspicuous place, in the open air, when the sun was above the horizon, for every thing must be done, (to use the Bardic expressions) publickly under the eye of the Sun &c in the face of light; darkness, privacy, and secrecy were absolutely forbidden in all their proceedings, nothing in their Bardic capacity could be done, but what the world could be witness of, there was nothing in their proceedings as corporate Society, or order of people, to be withheld from public observation.[65]

The mixture of received learning on the Druids and contemporary concerns was most clearly seen in William Owen Pughe's rapturous description of the religious tenets of bardism: as an essentially bardo-druidic system, it was claimed that the bards believed in metempsychosis,[66] that they had retained the pure Christian religion throughout the centuries of Roman Catholicism,[67] and that Quaker teachings had also left their imprint upon them.[68]

Although much of the material related by Pughe in this sketch of bardism echoed Iolo's own later writings on the subject (the various drafts of 'A Short Account of the Ancient British Bards' in particular), one suspects that Pughe's influence accounts for the more esoteric material, such as the musings on metempsychosis. Iolo sometimes sought Pughe's approval by confirming his speculations in suitably pleasing detail, as in the following example in which Pughe could hardly contain his enthusiasm for bardism's eastern parallels revealed to him by Iolo:

> An account of the religious worship of the Natives in Circles of Stones, and identifying it with the worship of the Hindus, &c &c. Don't you think this wonderful news? – It is a favourite idea with you, and I like it – that there will be a recovery of all things revealed to Mankind. – This is a happy instance of such a work going on. – Your bardic History will be the most important part, which the Cymry will be able to furnish therein.[69]

65 NLW 13089E, p. 451. See also pp. 456–7: a Gorsedd must be held in open air, in 'the eye of the sun, and the face of light'; it must be impartial on religious and political issues and all opinions must be deduced from Reason and Nature.

66 Owen, *Heroic Elegies*, p. xxx.

67 Ibid., p. xxxii.

68 Ibid., pp. liv–ix. For the levelling subtext of bardism as expressed in *Heroic Elegies*, see Davies, '"At Defiance": Iolo, Godwin, Coleridge, Wordsworth' in *Rattleskull Genius*, p. 160.

69 NLW 21282E, Letter no. 366, William Owen Pughe to Iolo Morganwg, 18 September 1805. See also NLW 13221E, pp. 55–8, Iolo Morganwg to William Owen Pughe, 20 December 1798.

The lexicographer John Walters, Iolo's friend and mentor, clearly believed that bardism as it appeared in *Heroic Elegies* was a collaborative effort, a 'made Dish':

> cooked up from obscure scraps of the ancient Bards, and the Cabala (the pretended *arcana*) of the modern ones; a superficial acquaintance with the Metempsychosis; and these ingredients spiced with an immoderate quantity of wild Invention. It is a species of Free Masonry . . . All that I shall further say on the Subject is that Mr Owen and his Coadjutor have not clubb'd their wits for nothing.[70]

It was William Owen Pughe who kept Iolo abreast of contemporary theories, both in person during Iolo's sojourns in London and through their correspondence once Iolo had returned to Glamorgan.[71] But the dynamic which charged their relationship was never one-sided, and this sketch was undoubtedly the product of lively conversation and speculative exchanges on the bards and the Druids between both men. Yet it is significant that Iolo allowed Pughe to announce bardism to the world. Iolo may have been wary of the potential trouble which the thinly veiled political text might attract. Moreover, as Geraint Phillips has argued in the context of Iolo's literary forgeries, affixing another name to his own work was a strategy he developed in order to blunt the pain of potential criticism.[72] However, Iolo was hardly absent from the sketch: his voice frequently interjected in the lengthy footnotes which cut across the more esoteric material with historical and practical detail about the British bards, their mottos, and the legitimate line of bardic descent to which Iolo allegedly belonged. By allowing William Owen Pughe to take the credit for introducing bardism to the literary world, was Iolo testing the waters to see how receptive the metropolis might prove to his revelations?

1792 was, however, a mixed year for Iolo. The relative success of his Gorsedd meetings and the interest which his bardic vision evoked was countered by the disappointments which accompanied his poetic publishing enterprise. The slow progress which *Poems, Lyric and Pastoral* (1794) made through the press, together with Iolo's own growing reputation as a Jacobin, alienated many wealthy potential subscribers,[73] and his low spirits

[70] Cardiff 3.104, vol. 6, Letter no. 3, John Walters to Edward Davies, 3 May 1793.

[71] NLW 21282E, Letter no. 340, William Owen Pughe to Iolo Morganwg, 30 June 1800; NLW 21282E, Letter no. 342, William Owen Pughe to Iolo Morganwg, 28 August 1800. A copy of the *Bagavat Geeta* was in Iolo's possession in London in 1794: NLW 13136A, p. 141. But his scattered notes on Sanskrit and Hinduism all date from the first decade of the nineteenth century: NLW 13108B, pp. 12–13; NLW 13144A, pp. 359–62; NLW 21419E, no. 51.

[72] Phillips, 'Forgery and Patronage: Iolo Morganwg and Owain Myfyr' in *Rattleskull Genius*, pp. 408–9.

[73] See the draft letter to Mrs Nicholls, NLW 21426E, no. 50; NLW 21285E, Letter no. 862, Iolo Morganwg to Miss Barker, 26 March 1798.

and increasing frustration were further compounded by the guilt he felt on being unable to provide financial support for his wife and children. By July 1792 a mentally and physically exhausted Iolo fell into a depressive, even suicidal, state.[74] The preface to his poems and its various manuscript drafts refer to the perceived obstacles he faced: these included 'the mean machinations of Envy', injury from 'some that I once thought my friends',[75] and the inadvertent inclusion of errors 'occasion'd by what I have experienced of mental distress and confusion during the course of this wildernessed business of publication'.[76] But the persona of the labouring poet which he employed in London's literary marketplace proved both enabling and disabling in equal measure: it initially proved useful in gaining access to networks of patronage, but since it was constructed around the rigid class dynamics of eighteenth-century polite society it was a persona which, as Iolo discovered to his cost, only reinforced the social inequality of its proponents. Iolo experienced the same corrosive effects of class antagonism implicit in the complex patron-client relationship which had constrained Stephen Duck and Ann Yearsley.[77] In a letter to an unknown recipient, Iolo, who never deferred gracefully to his social superiors, railed against the class antagonism he had experienced in his efforts to acquire subscribers in his guise as a labouring-class poet:

> To their inferiors (as we must be called) the Gentry &c (as they call themselves) behave with the most unfeeling cruelty (I was going to use the word indifference but it was too mild). How many hours have I shivered at the doors of great and opulent names waiting for the paltry sum of four shillings.[78]

Frustrated by the closed elite circles, and humiliated by his failure to gain access to them, he resolved to 'subject myself no more to their superciliousness'.[79] As his position in the conservative English literary scene became increasingly fraught, and as his reputation was compromised by his radical allegiances, he positioned himself even more closely to Jacobinism and Rational Dissent by retreating further into the more successful Welsh bardic persona which had excited the attention of the London Welsh and others.

74 NLW 21285E, Letter no. 810, Iolo Morganwg to Margaret Williams, 20 July 1792; ibid., Letter no. 812, Iolo Morganwg to Margaret Williams, 27 October 1792; 'Suicide': NLW 21433E, no. 5a.

75 Williams: *PLP*, I, pp. xi, xii, xxii. See also Morgan: *IM*, p. 38.

76 NLW 21387E, no. 11.

77 Anne Stott, *Hannah More: The First Victorian* (Oxford, 2003), pp. 72–3.

78 NLW 21286E, Letter no. 1025, Iolo Morganwg to an unknown recipient, undated. See also Anna Seward's condescension towards Iolo: NLW 21282E, Letter no. 459, Anna Seward to Iolo Morganwg, 12 July 1792.

79 NLW 21285E, Letter no. 811, Iolo Morganwg to Margaret Williams, 9 August 1792. See also ibid., Letter no. 809, Iolo Morganwg to Margaret Williams, 20 June 1792.

Bardism and the bardic persona were the props which Iolo's waning confidence and self-esteem required, and in the strange, slightly incongruous content of the second volume of *Poems, Lyric and Pastoral* we see the gradual encroachment of the bardic Jacobin persona onto that of the labouring-class poet.[80] Initially, he introduced bardism in a scholarly guise, declaring that the aim of the bardic poems was to set the record straight in terms of British history.[81] He played down his bardic status, even though he mentioned his bardic name,[82] and by pandering to racial stereotypes – Welsh 'warmth' accounted for his radicalism – he distanced himself slightly from the radical viewpoint, thereby ensuring that the dominant persona of the preface was that of the journeyman mason. The personas and opinions voiced in the poems themselves do not form a neat harmonious whole. Yet, as Mary-Ann Constantine has pointed out, there remained an underlying element of continuity in the volume's radical tone.[83] Poems such as 'Ode, on converting a Sword into a Pruning-hook' and 'Ode on the Mythology of the Ancient British Bards' and their 'rambling excursus of footnotes',[84] were both stylistically and ideologically different from the more conventional pastoral poems included in the less politically charged first volume. Indeed, it was the radical content of the footnotes to the bardic poems and triads which attracted the most negative response from reviewers.[85] Iolo was not aware at the time that he had injured his reputation with his 'Kingflogging Notes', and explained them away as 'a weak endeavour to abet the cause of truth, Justice, and humanity', adding somewhat immodestly that it was 'a cause to which I long to be a martyr'.[86] The stigma was not easily removed and it prejudiced his later application to the Royal Literary Fund in 1805.[87]

Poems, Lyric and Pastoral was finally published to relative acclaim in January 1794, and a buoyant and relieved Iolo returned (albeit temporarily) to his family in Glamorgan. Returning to the metropolis in August that year, he laboured over what would have been (had he ever completed it) his *magnum opus*: the comprehensive exposition of bardism, 'The History of the Bards'. A handwritten title-page which notes it as a forthcoming publication

80 He was encouraged by the Unitarian printer Joseph Johnson to include radical pieces in the volume. Mary-Ann Constantine, '"This Wildernessed Business of Publication": The Making of *Poems, Lyric and Pastoral* (1794)' in *Rattleskull Genius*, p. 135.

81 Williams: *PLP*, I, p. xix.

82 Ibid., I, pp. xxiii.

83 Constantine, '"This Wildernessed Business of Publication"' in *Rattleskull Genius*, pp. 139, 141. The chronological development of the volume only partially explains 'the conflict of voices' contained within the finished book, ibid., p. 145.

84 Morgan: *IM*, p. 37.

85 Lewis, 'Eighteenth-Century Literary Forgeries', pp. 176–8.

86 NLW 21285E, Letter no. 826, Iolo Morganwg to John Walters, 21 January 1794.

87 NLW 21280E, Letter no. 87, William Thomas Fitzgerald to Iolo Morganwg, 18 October 1805.

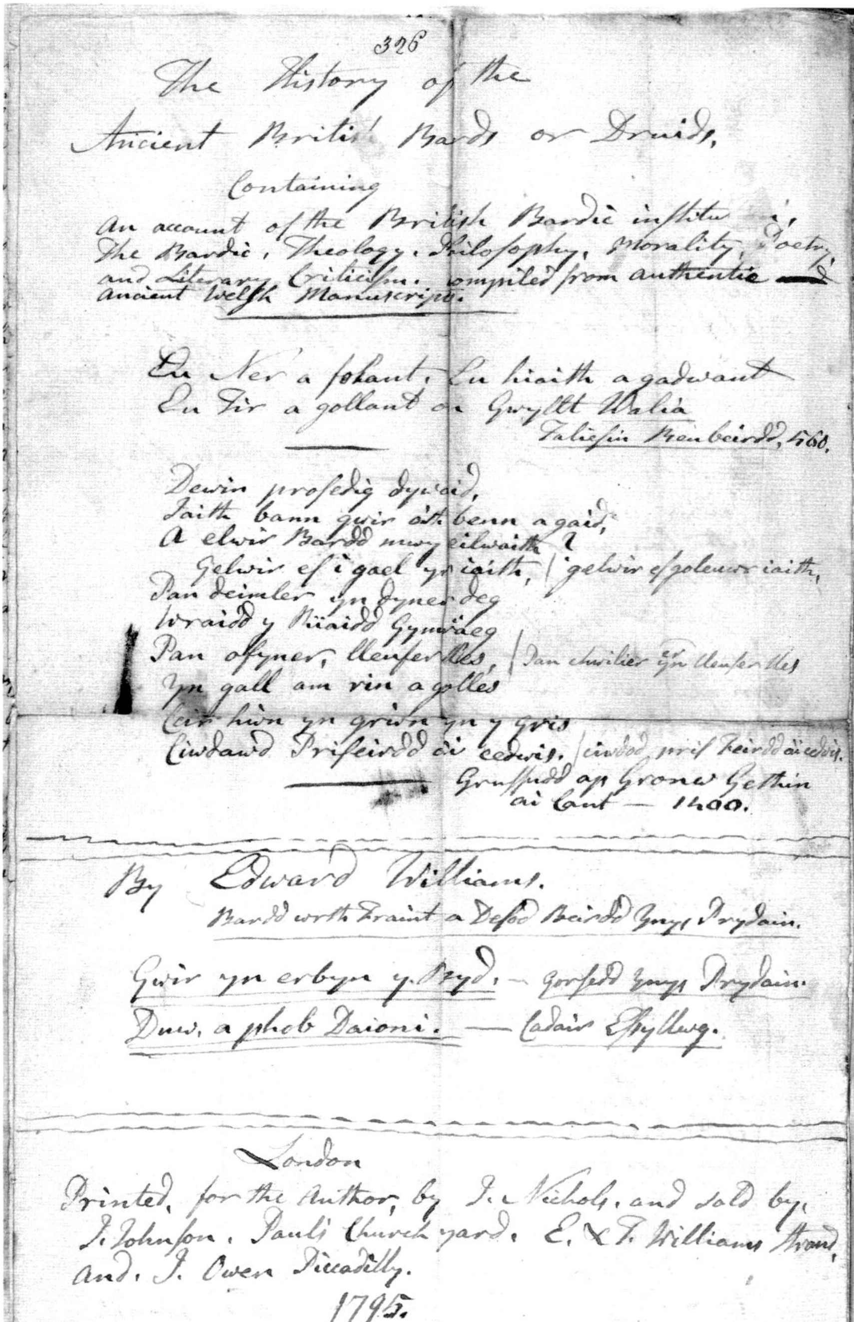
326

The History of the
Ancient British Bards or Druids,
Containing
An account of the British Bardic institution, The Bardic, Theology, Philosophy, Morality, Poetry, and Literary Criticism. compiled from authentic and ancient Welsh Manuscripts.

Eu Ner a folant, Eu hiaith a gadwant
Eu Tir a gollant ond Gwyllt Walia
Taliesin Penbeirdd, 560.

Dewin prosedig dywaid,
Iaith bann gwir ath benn agaid,
A elwir Bardd mwy eilwaith?
Gelwir ef i gael yr iaith, | gelwir ef goleuwr iaith,
Pan deimler yn dyner deg
Wraidd y Prifardd Gymraeg
Pan ofyner, llenferthes, | Pan chwilier yn llenferthes
Yn gall am rin a golles
Cair hwn yn gwirion yn y gwir
Cinwawd Prifeirdd ai cedwis. | Cinwad prif feirdd ai cedwis.
Gruffudd ap Grono Gethin ai Cant — 1400.

By Edward Williams.
Bardd wrth Fraint a Defod Beirdd Ynys Prydain.

Gwir yn erbyn y Byd. — Gorsedd Ynys Prydain.
Duw, a phob Daioni. — Cadair Essyllwg.

London
Printed, for the Author, by J. Nichols, and sold by J. Johnson, Pauls Church yard, E. & T. Williams Strand, and J. Owen Piccadilly.
1795.

Fig. 2 This handwritten title-page for Iolo's uncompleted *magnum opus*, 'The History of the Bards', belongs to 1795 when he was able to work energetically on the project.

in 1795 made the venture concrete for Iolo.[88] His letters to Walter Davies and Margaret (Peggy) his wife reveal that he was engaged in collecting material at the British Museum and the Welsh Charity School during this period.[89] His approach was professional, systematic and thorough, and in a letter of appeasement to his wife, he explained the importance of remaining in London to complete the scholarly groundwork that was vital to the integrity of the volume:

> you seem to be angry with the Muse[um] but it was absolutely necessary for me to consult the Manuscripts there for the History of the Bards. History is not like Poetry a thing of invention and imagination. It must have authority, and the best authorities must be consulted, otherwise the work will acquire no credit.[90]

He worked with manic energy, seldom pausing to eat or pass water, and unsurprisingly he developed kidney stones and eye strain during this period of intense study.[91] Undeterred by painful past experience of the publishing business, his hopes of becoming an established writer were pinned on 'The History of the Bards': 'this work', he earnestly told his wife, 'must be a substitute for my trade, and it would be ruinous not to pursue it.'[92]

A table of contents which he drew up reveals that he was now ready to pin his own name to bardism, and the introduction especially was to be a platform for him to assert his own unrivalled authority on the subject: 'Introduction, pointing out the Errors of the Ancient Romans, the modern English, French, & Welsh, as [Henry] Rowlands, Edward Jones, L[ewis] Morris, Edward Llwyd, Edward Davies &c &c.'[93] This was simply one plan among many, all of which, despite superficial differences, reveal that 'The History of the Bards' was to be a comprehensive exegesis of bardism, incorporating dissertations on the following topics: the Welsh language, the origin of letters among the Welsh, the bardic alphabet, the origin and principles of the bardic institution, theology and mythology, various triads (religious, ethical, philosophical, historical and the Moelmutian triads Iolo attributed to Dyfnwal Moelmud), the introduction of Christianity and its effects on bardism, the ancient principles of government and law of the Welsh, the national manners of the Welsh, and Welsh music. It was also to contain a

88 NLW 13091E, p. 326. For relevant material, see Documents V–XI.

89 See NLW 1895Ei, Letter no. 78, Iolo Morganwg to Walter Davies, 26 August 1794; NLW 21285E, Letter no. 841, Iolo Morganwg to Margaret Williams, 27 August 1794; ibid., Letter no. 843, Iolo Morganwg to Margaret Williams, 1 October 1795.

90 NLW 21285E, Letter no. 847, Iolo Morganwg to Margaret Williams, 9 December 1794.

91 NLW 21285E, Letter no. 841, Iolo Morganwg to Margaret Williams, 26 August 1794; ibid., Letter no. 843, Iolo Morganwg to Margaret Williams, 1 October 1795.

92 NLW 21285E, Letter no. 843, Iolo Morganwg to Margaret Williams, 1 October 1795.

93 NLW 13138A, p. 122. For other plans, see NLW 13144A, pp. 292, 391–4, 396–7; NLW 13158A, p. 103.

detailed study of the development of Welsh versification, the schools of Welsh poetry, as well as the full text of the Glamorgan Classification which was contained in the manuscript 'Cyfrinach Beirdd Ynys Prydain'. Iolo's first biographer, Elijah Waring, noted that oral communication was Iolo's preferred and most accomplished means of communication,[94] and the subtle degree of variation in the various plans for 'The History of the Bards' appears to confirm that Iolo often had great difficulty in structuring his all-encompassing themes and topics. Yet, this want of clarity and direction was only one factor which accounted for his failure to complete his *magnum opus*.

An appreciable amount of the material which Iolo produced for 'The History of the Bards' was either poorly organized or diffuse, or was siphoned off into *The Myvyrian Archaiology of Wales*. Very few of the dissertations which he planned for 'The History of the Bards' may be adequately described as complete. Several incomplete drafts of 'A Short Account of the Ancient British Bards' survive,[95] and these provide a more elaborate account of 'Bardism' than that supplied by William Owen Pughe in *The Heroic Elegies of Llywarç Hen*. They include, for example, further speculation on bardism's Christian inheritance, though little further light was shed on esoteric detail such as metempsychosis. A sketch of his 'Analytical Dissertation on the Welsh Language' survives, but only scattered material on the *Coelbren y Beirdd* (Alphabet of the Bards) and the use of letters are extant.[96] His manuscripts abound with seemingly endless series of triads (both genuine and spurious), and a draft version of a dissertation on the 'Moelmutian Triads'.[97] The main sources for his analysis of the history of Welsh versification and *cynghanedd* are two lengthy essays in which the leading narrative drive was bardism's contentious north–south dynamic.[98] Assorted material, such as bardism's Arthurian and oriental elements survive in scraps of paper, jottings and short musings *in vacuo*, and appear to have been later additions which he was never able to incorporate fully into his writings on the overall vision. Much of the fabricated bardic material which was published in the second and third volumes of *The Myvyrian Archaiology of Wales* had originally been

94 *RAEW*, p. 68.

95 NLW 13089E, pp. 422–9, 434–67; NLW 13097B, pp. 97–111, 123–52, 239–63. See Documents VII–VIII.

96 For the 'Analytical Dissertation on the Welsh Language', see NLW 13121B, pp. 423–40; NLW 13131A, p. 364. For *Coelbren y Beirdd*, see NLW 13087E, pp. 15–36; NLW 13089E, p. 315; NLW 13093E, pp. 155–6, 157–65; NLW 13097B, pp. 177–80, 200–09, 212–14; NLW 13123B, pp. 104–5, 263–5, 286; NLW 13128A, pp. 293, 392; NLW 13138A, pp. 42–4; NLW 13144A, pp. 35–44, 135–6, 143; NLW 13150A, pp. 95–6; NLW 21428E, no. 6.

97 NLW 13088B, pp. 55–78.

98 NLW 13130A, pp. 188–92, 196–9, 258–9; NLW 13138A, pp. 45–96. See Documents X–XII.

intended for 'The History of the Bards', and so in this sense *The Myvyrian Archaiology* and the breakdown of Iolo's relationship with William Owen Pughe and Owain Myfyr played an instrumental part in its non-appearance.

The fate of 'The History of the Bards' was thus inextricably bound up with his friendship with leading London Welshmen and their antiquarian aspirations. Iolo returned to Wales in 1795, set up a bookshop in Cowbridge, resumed his work as a stonemason, turned his attention to writing agricultural and topographical accounts of his native Glamorgan, and consequently devoted less time to his 'History of the Bards' than before. Meanwhile, although Owain Myfyr and William Owen Pughe zealously supported his aim of publishing this work, their main efforts were devoted to publishing the three-volume compendium of Welsh medieval poetry and prose, *The Myvyrian Archaiology of Wales*, an enterprise which was largely financed by Owain Myfyr himself. Pughe began work on it in 1798, but Owain Myfyr feared that Iolo's other interests meant that he was not pulling his weight. His frustration was compounded by Iolo's apparent reluctance to return to London and by his failure to honour his promises of providing them with material for the volumes. Struggling to make ends meet and make sense of the mass of literary material which he had assembled over time, Iolo despaired of ever being able to set aside adequate time to work through his ideas in a consistent and sustained manner:

> my materials lay in great confusion, owing to the necessities of my being obliged to leave off my studies for other occupations, to work at my trade for bread, &c, and owing to such things and the frequent and long interruptions of my studies, my chain of ideas and arrangement were so broken and all their connections so broken, as to escape my memory, so that on returning to those studies and not recollecting what I had previously written, I wrote the same again over again and again and in other things only added more and more to my mass of confusion, so that I found myself more and more obstructed in my progress rather than going on.[99]

William Owen Pughe, who frequently assumed the role of peacemaker, rightly noted Iolo's procrastinatory habits:

> I believe that I know your fault: and it is the aiming at a perfection that is unattainable, you run out into too much detail, ever to bring the work to a conclusion: and thus we shall lose the whole. Such details would be highly valuable to us as Welshmen, if the spirit of cultivating our antiquities were in any degree extensive: but a comprehensive view of the subject, suitable for the world at

[99] NLW 21285E, Letter no. 880, Iolo Morganwg to Owain Myfyr, 5 April 1806.

> large, might have been already finished, if it had been possible to keep you to that point: Would it not, think you?[100]

To appease an increasingly uneasy Owain Myfyr, in 1799 Iolo toured north Wales collecting materials for *The Myvyrian Archaiology* in private libraries. Yet, his failure to send a regular flow of transcripts and to travel to London vexed Owain Myfyr considerably.

It was at this stage that Iolo began dipping into the forged texts he had intended to include in 'The History of the Bards'. The second volume of *The Myvyrian Archaiology of Wales*, published in 1801, included a series of triads, two forged chronicles, 'Brut Aberpergwm' and 'Brut Ieuan Brechfa', which followed the rubric of the authentic medieval Welsh chronicle, Brut y Tywysogyon.[101] 'Doethineb y Cymry' (The Wisdom of the Welsh), first offered to an initially sceptical Owain Myfyr in 1800,[102] was included in the third volume published in 1807. Iolo even toyed with the notion of including 'Cyfrinach Beirdd Ynys Prydain' in *The Myvyrian Archaiology of Wales*, exclaiming in a letter to William Owen Pughe in 1804: 'I wish it was printed by somebody.'[103] Iolo, of course, was anxious to please his collaborators, but the highs and lows which he experienced also suggest that he suffered from manic depression.[104] When his spirits were low, he despaired of ever completing 'The History of the Bards': a loss of nerve in 1800 prompted him to inform William Owen Pughe that he planned to let it rest.[105] But when his spirits soared, his ambitions knew no bounds: 'What I have resolutely assigned of time to the history of the Bards shall never be broken upon by any study whatever, not [even] to save every member and servant of the Board of Agriculture from the Gallows.'[106] By this stage Iolo's self-esteem had been bolstered by seeing his work appear in print in the first two volumes of *The Myvyrian Archaiology of Wales*, both of which were published in 1801. In addition to the fabricated ancient bardic texts published in the

100 NLW 21282E, Letter no. 357, Iolo Morganwg to William Owen Pughe, 20 June 1803. Here, and in other letters, Pughe displayed an uncanny sensitivity and adeptness for dealing with Iolo, wishing that he 'had as many hands as the Indian deity' to ensure that all these projects were completed.

101 *TLIM*, p. 3. See G. J. Williams, 'Brut Aberpergwm: a Version of the Chronicle of the Princes' in Stewart Williams (ed.), *Glamorgan Historian*, Vol. IV (Cowbridge, 1967), pp. 205–20.

102 BL Add. 15024, f. 310, Iolo Morganwg to Owain Myfyr, 10 April 1800; *MAW*, III, pp. 1–144.

103 NLW 13222C, pp. 181–4, Iolo Morganwg to William Owen Pughe, 9 November 1804. See also BL Add. 15027, ff. 79–80, Iolo Morganwg to Owain Myfyr, 21 September 1805; NLW 13221E, pp. 139–42, Iolo Morganwg to William Owen Pughe, 6 February 1806.

104 Phillips, 'Forgery and Patronage: Iolo Morganwg and Owain Myfyr' in *Rattleskull Genius*, p. 407.

105 NLW 21282E, Letter no. 342, William Owen Pughe to Iolo Morganwg, 28 August 1800.

106 NLW 13222C, pp. 181–4, Iolo Morganwg to William Owen Pughe, 9 November 1804.

second volume, the well-informed 'A Short Review of the Present State of Welsh Manuscripts', which prefaced the first volume, was mostly penned by Iolo himself.[107] The publication of these first two volumes also brought about a rapprochement between Owain Myfyr and Iolo, and in March 1802 Iolo paid a brief visit to London. Recounting events four years later in a draft letter, Iolo claimed that Owain Myfyr had promised him an annuity of £50 in order that he might 'never fag any more at your Trade', thus allowing him, finally, to complete 'The History of the Bards'.[108] During this visit, however, a chain of events drove the two men irrevocably apart and caused Owain Myfyr, two years later, to retract his generous financial offer. Myfyr believed that Iolo had neglected his work on the third volume of *The Myvyrian Archaiology of Wales* in favour of promoting the Unitarian cause in south Wales. This was a claim which Iolo strenuously denied, but he certainly played an instrumental role in establishing and promoting the South Wales Unitarian Society from 1802 onwards.[109] As these events unfolded, Owain Myfyr's business suffered financial losses, and this only deepened his suspicion that Iolo was taking advantage of his generosity. Exasperated, but not without humour, William Owen Pughe wrote:

> From seeing these last documents of antiquity and others before, I more and more wish that Pair Dadeni [the cauldron of rejuvenation] were in Dyffryn Goluch, and for some of your brother bards to throw you in, and then I might look for the History of the Bards completed, to astonish the world.[110]

March 1806 marked the end of their collaboration and, to all intents and purposes, their friendship: Iolo's relationship with Owain Myfyr ceased altogether, and his friendship with Pughe finally petered out in 1808. However, a letter which Iolo drafted to Owain Myfyr in April of that year reveals an alternative interpretation of events. Certain that he had indeed supplied them with material (albeit fabricated) for *The Myvyrian Archaiology of Wales*, Iolo seems to have understood that they had wished him to concentrate his efforts on 'The History of the Bards'. He felt wounded that the promise of financial assistance had not been honoured: he had not only travelled far and wide to transcribe bardic material, but had also laboured at his trade in order to support his family. All of this had proved an insurmountable obstacle to which he had often referred in his earlier letters to them. It was with some feeling that he wrote to William Owen Pughe shortly before relations broke down irreparably: 'it is for Wales, for the Welsh nation, for the Welsh language

107 *MAW*, I, pp. ix–xxi.

108 NLW 21285E, Letter no. 880, Iolo Morganwg to Owain Myfyr, 5 April 1806.

109 Geraint H. Jenkins, '"Dyro Dduw dy Nawdd": Iolo Morganwg a'r Mudiad Undodaidd' in idem (ed.), *Cof Cenedl XX: Ysgrifau ar Hanes Cymru* (Llandysul, 2005), pp. 65–100.

110 NLW 21282E, Letter no. 370, William Owen Pughe to Iolo Morganwg, 4 March 1806.

and literature . . . [that] I have sacrificed all the comforts of life'.[111] Iolo thus believed that he had been the unwitting victim of Owain Myfyr and William Owen Pughe's deception. In the final letter he drafted to Owain Myfyr in April 1806 he justified his position by quoting extensively from their correspondence, before concluding bitterly: 'all this was nothing but a coolly premeditated plan of delusion carried on for almost three years'.[112]

Without doubt, the break with William Owen Pughe and Owain Myfyr was a painful wrench for Iolo and it coloured all aspects of his work, not merely bardism. Since his allegiance to the Unitarian cause played a large part in this split – Iolo considered Owain Myfyr's 'unreasonable enmity against Unitarians' as 'a pretence' for breaking off their friendship[113] – it is not unusual that Iolo should have concentrated his efforts on promoting Unitarianism. In the introduction to his collection of Welsh Unitarian hymns, *Salmau yr Eglwys yn yr Anialwch* (1812), he cryptically referred to William Owen Pughe and Owain Myfyr as the 'infallible ones', whose prejudiced response to the volume he already anticipated.[114] Iolo may have perceived his success and recognition in Unitarian circles as a victory over his enemies, since he had gained these independently of them and their fickle patronage. Indeed, thanks to the support he had received from the likes of John Aikin, Andrew Kippis, Theophilus Lindsey and John Prior Estlin, Unitarianism provided Iolo with a sense of self-esteem which his associates in London could no longer provide. His introduction to his hymns resonated with themes associated with bardism: it included a lengthy section on metrics and on the pre-eminence of his chosen language register, namely his regional dialect.[115] Just as elements of Iolo's Unitarian convictions were expressed within the fabric of bardism,[116] so did the latter appear in publications which he penned on behalf of the South Wales Unitarian Society. In these he wrote, not as Edward Williams, but as 'Iolo Morganwg B.B.D.', and he even introduced the subtle trappings of bardism, dating the prefaces to his hymns and primer 'Alban Hefin' (Summer Solstice). Moreover, his bardic insignia, the *nod cyfrin* or secret insignia /|\, appeared in print for the first time on the title-page of his collection of hymns. In the Welsh

111 NLW 13221E, pp. 147–50, Iolo Morganwg to William Owen Pughe, 1 March 1806.

112 NLW 21285E, Letter no. 880, Iolo Morganwg to Owain Myfyr, 5 April 1806. See also NLW 21286E, Letter no. 967, Iolo Morganwg to Evan Williams, 12 December 1818.

113 NLW 21285E, Letter no. 880, Iolo Morganwg to Owain Myfyr, 5 April 1806.

114 Edward Williams, *Salmau yr Eglwys yn yr Anialwch* (2nd edn., Merthyr-Tydfil, 1827), p. iv. He referred also to false friends ('twyll gyfeillion') whom he assumed were ready to strike him most treacherously ('bradergydio drach fy nghefn').

115 Ibid., pp. vi–vii.

116 D. Elwyn J. Davies, 'Astudiaeth o Feddwl a Chyfraniad Iolo Morganwg fel Rhesymolwr ac Undodwr', pp. 113–14, 188, 363–412; Geraint H. Jenkins, 'The Unitarian Firebrand, the Cambrian Society and the Eisteddfod' in *Rattleskull Genius*, pp. 269–92; idem, '"Dyro Dduw dy Nawdd": Iolo Morganwg a'r Mudiad Undodaidd', *passim*.

primer he described himself as 'Bardd Cymdeithas Dwyfundodiaid Deheubarth Cymru' (Bard of the Society of the Unitarians of South Wales), thereby extending the bardic role he had created for himself within bardism. In a short preface to this Unitarian catechism, for example, he styled himself 'Minister of the Scourge' and appeared more concerned with the linguistic integrity of Unitarian publications than with the spiritual edification of congregations.[117]

His self-esteem restored, Iolo resumed work on 'Cyfrinach Beirdd Ynys Prydain' in 1813.[118] In August the following year he also revived Gorsedd meetings at *Y Maen Chwŷf* (the Rocking-stone) at Pontypridd.[119] The passage of time had renewed his confidence but had done little to soothe his wounds, and as he resumed work on 'Cyfrinach Beirdd Ynys Prydain' it becomes clear that he had increasingly come to perceive his rejection by Owain Myfyr and William Owen Pughe in terms of antagonism between north and south Wales. This was a theme which had emerged earlier in his letters to Pughe as their relationship gradually unravelled, and he had also become convinced that Owain Myfyr 'disapproved of its being introduced in the History of the Bards in preference to the System that has for almost 400 years prevailed in North Wales'.[120] Just two months before the final split the north–south tension came to the fore in a letter which placed the 'Glamorgan Classification' within a context of metrical reform and, most tellingly of all, within the context of its unfavourable reception by the Gwyneddigion Society on the grounds of regional bias. It is worth quoting at length since it demonstrates that events which had occurred fifteen years earlier still rankled:

> Gronwy Owen, Lewis Morris, Evan Evans, and, as echoes to them, Mr Owen Jones, and m[any] North Walians besides bitterly complained of the defects of the commonly received System of Versification. When I brought Cyfrinach y Beirdd with me to London in 1791, or –92, I imagined that it would be considered as a valuable acquisition amply supplying the defects of the common System, but so far from this did I find that [?] Sion Ceiriog, several others, even Mr Jones himself, exhibited the clearest sy[?] marks of their prejudice against it, why I

117 Edward Williams, *Holiadur, neu Addysgiadau Cyffredin, Hawl ac Atteb, yn Athrawiaethau Dyledswyddau Crefydd* (Merthyr Tudfil, 1814), p. 2.

118 NLW 21284E, Letter no. 643, Taliesin Williams to Iolo Morganwg, 7 August 1813.

119 See Chapter 4, pp. 147–50.

120 NLW 13221E, pp. 143–6, Iolo Morganwg to William Owen Pughe, 12 January 1806: 'I intend indeed that it should appear in competition with that, but not to the exclusion of a single Iota of the Northwalian System, for I have by me a great variety of Systems that have in different ages prevailed, and so far from be[ing] inclined to suppress either of them am I, that nothing could prevail with me to do [so] I would not upon any account do it, I would not so violate the fidelity of History.' See also NLW 13222C, pp. 181–4, Iolo Morganwg to William Owen Pughe, 9 November 1804. For Iolo's general observations on the rivalry between north and south Wales, see EL 15027, ff. 79–80, Iolo Morganwg to Owain Myfyr, 21 September 1805.

know not. They never gave any rea[son] indeed they knew not of any reasons or grounds of objection. Unless that it was So[uth] Walian, or perhaps because it militated powerfully and successfully against th[e] System that the Gwyneddigion were then, and are still, warmly but blindly patron[ising]. In ninety nine when I went to Northwales, I took the whole with me, first [?and] second books, shewed them to Wms. of Llanrwst, but he expressed a rancou[rous] prejudice against them asking me this question. 'do you think that your Systems in Southwales are as perfect as ours?' Wms. is thoroughly ignor[ant] of either, of all systems whatsoever. but that Dafydd Ddu Eryri, and [?] several others who being perfectly masters of the common System and [?] previously, as I had intentionally led them to do so, acknowledged its gre[at] defects in the least objectionable parts of it, and its glaring absurdities in other parts, that they should when produced to them reject our South Walian System, with openly and rancourously expressed and professed prejudice, made me greatly wonder: It is obvious Envy, they felt their own idolized System melt into nothing before it, like a slight sprinkling of [?] before the sun of a clear midsummer noon very few can endure the discovery of their own ign[orance]. it was in vain that I propo[sed] to prove from authentic examples from old Venedotian Bards, prior to the d[ays] of Davydd ap Edmwnd, that what they called the Southwalian System was as ancien[t] as their own as much at least as it was the system of Southwales, but National Provi[?] and every kind of local prejudices are very blind and always very stupid thi[ngs] but enough of this – Whether it shall be printed in the Archaiology o[r] not, I will prepare a Copy for you in the course of the approaching summ[er] I cannot promise it sooner.[121]

Against this personal and regional backdrop, 'Cyfrinach Beirdd Ynys Prydain' became a symbol of Iolo's humiliation at their hands. He had perceived its rejection in terms of the north–south antagonism, and since he was emotionally ill-equipped to differentiate between criticism of his work and criticism of his person, he internalized his viewpoint and began to conceive of his own alienation within this framework of regional rivalry. This partly explains the transformation of the primacy of Glamorgan from the subtext in its earliest manuscript manifestation to the main thesis in the printed text of *Cyfrinach Beirdd Ynys Prydain*. Convinced of the validity of his own position, he turned the symbol of his rejection and humiliation into a means of retaliation. Through *Cyfrinach Beirdd Ynys Prydain*, he planned to upbraid his detractors publicly:

I received some Scurrilous but anonymous letters on this occasion from north Wales; by which I understand that the North Walians are all in an uproar against me. I resolved to print Tudur Aled's tract . . . and this will, at a needless expense of about 30s, or 40s, to me, silence the North Walian clamour; having for 3 or 4 centuries boasted their superiority over the Hwyntwyr, as the Deudneudwyr call

121 NLW 13221E, pp. 143–6, Iolo Morganwg to William Owen Pughe, 12 January 1806.

us South Walians. They will be maddened to find that all their great knowledge of which they so loudly brag, consists in nothing but what every man of sense will confess to be disgraceful to Human Reason. I shall feel another Swarm of wasps about me for the ridicule with which in many of my Marginal notes I have treated the Owenpughian or Southcottian Dialect, formed on Hottentotic principles. I am ready and prepared to meet them all.[122]

Yet, in spite of their prominence in the story of the making and unmaking of 'The History of the Bards', William Owen Pughe and Owain Myfyr do not feature as heavily as might have been expected in the scathing footnotes to *Cyfrinach Beirdd Ynys Prydain*. Rather, it was David Thomas (Dafydd Ddu Eryri) who became the butt of criticism:

> Y mae'r Bardd mawr! mawr! mawr! a mawr iawn! Ni wyr neb pa mor fawr ond efe ei hunan ardderchog, DAFYDD DDU o'r Eryri yn dywedid . . . i Ddafydd ap Edmwnd ddysgu dau fesur i Feirdd Deheubarth, odid nad gorchestion Pwll Gweppra y mae'n ei feddwl: rhyfedd a rhyfedd yw rhinweddau cwrw da; a phwy a wyr hynn yn well na Dafydd Ddu?[123]
>
> (The big Bard! big! big! and very big! No-one knows how big but his own excellent self, BLACK DAVID of Snowdon says . . . that Dafydd ap Edmwnd taught two measures to the Bards of South Wales, he most likely had in mind the feats of Pwll Gwepra: strange and stranger are the qualities of good beer; and no-one knows this better than Black David.)

Since David Thomas, who did indeed battle against the bottle, not only cut an influential figure in eisteddfodic circles and the Cambrian Society, but had a faithful following of bardic disciples, Iolo may have considered him a more immediate threat to his bardic authority in the 1820s than the deceased Owain Myfyr (d.1814) and the much-derided William Owen Pughe, who had become embroiled in the mission of the prophetess, Joanna Southcott. Moreover, Iolo's financial reliance on Owain Myfyr meant that their friend-

122 NLW 21286E, Letter no. 989, Iolo Morganwg to the Revd D. Jones, 6 May 1822.

123 Williams (ed.), *Cyfrinach Beirdd Ynys Prydain*, pp. 172–3, 183. See also NLW 21286E, Letter no. 986, Iolo Morganwg to Evan Williams, Strand, 15 November 1821: 'I understand that many of those pupils of ignorant selfconceit the Bardlings of Snowdon, or Eryron [Eagles] as they presumptuously style themselves are spitting their venom at me. Poor Devils! one of their Topics of Malevolence is my publishing a System of Poetical Critici[sm] and versification different from what they call their own System, which they borrowed from South Wales and the Carmarthen Eisteddfod of 1461, bedaubed as it was by Dafydd ap Edmund, with the offensive mud of Gwepre pool. Another is that I faithfully retain the orthography of my original MS, and its Gwenhwyseg (Silurian) idiom, I have always been more disposed to cheerfullness than to sullenness, and those Eryron supply me with exitements to mirth and laughter rather than to anger or resentment: Eryron do they call themselves? Gwyddau [Geese] would be a more proper term; for Geese are of low and heavy flight, of feeble wing; and they always scream horridly as they Fly.'

ship was never equally poised, and so to publish *Cyfrinach Beirdd Ynys Prydain* without his financial support would assert his independence of both men. Ironically, too, it was the Welsh literary parsons who had approached Iolo about publishing the volume; this avowed Unitarian had not been required to beg for their financial support.[124] The upshot was that the manuscript he had taken with him to London in 1791 was published posthumously, under the title *Cyfrinach Beirdd Ynys Prydain* (1829). With this publication we have come full circle. Since it had been intended as the cornerstone of 'The History of the Bards' and since it was also one of the few completed components of that ambitious project, *Cyfrinach Beirdd Ynys Prydain* may at one level be considered a 'History of the Bards' *manqué*. Indeed, the final volume was not as comprehensive as Iolo had originally intended, for it did not include the proposed definitive discussion on *Coelbren y Beirdd*.[125]

Having reviewed the parallel development of Iolo's bardic persona and the main texts of his bardic vision, we must now ask what did he gain from bardism in terms of self-definition and self-validation? The answer is two-fold. Firstly, it provided him with a sense of authority and legitimacy which did not rely on the rigid class-bound and fickle market-driven forces of the metropolitan literary scene. Secondly, it provided him with an anchor in the midst of his turbulent life. Like many autodidacts, Iolo was so sensitive about his lack of university education that he considered it 'a means of acquiring an unjust ascendancy over those whose fortune in life never enabled them to reside there, or whose early acquaintance with truth became an invincible obstacle to their own admission at any college whatever where any religious articles of human manufacture must be assented to'.[126] His status as Bard, therefore, was a means of confirming his public credibility: to this end he frequently appended the qualification of his own making to his name: 'B.B.D.', 'Bardd Braint a Defod Beirdd Ynys Prydain' (Bard according to the Rights and Privileges of the Bards of the Island of Britain). Because of its home-grown quality, after Iolo's days this suffix developed into an important status symbol and a badge of Welshness in cultural circles. Since he believed that other scholars, past and present, could not rival him in terms of knowledge and wisdom, he peppered his manuscripts with caustic remarks about the ignorance displayed by the likes of Edward Lhuyd, Lewis Morris and Edward Jones. But rather than retaliate with scholarly rigour, he assumed a

124 NLW 21282E, Letter no. 413, Richard Rees to Iolo Morganwg, 6 November 1809; NLW 21286E, Letter no. 986, Iolo Morganwg to Evan Williams, 15 November 1821; ibid., Letter no. 989, Iolo Morganwg to David Lewis Jones, 6 May 1822; ibid., Letter no. 992, Iolo Morganwg to David Davis, 3 January 1823.

125 Williams: *IM*, pp. 375–8.

126 NLW 13089E, p. 288. See also NLW 13174A, pp. 2^v, 3^v, 4^r.

subjective stance and used his self-appointed role as the heir and preserver of bardism to reveal their alleged ignorance. In numerous drafts of 'A Short Account of the British Bards', he argued that no writer on the Welsh poetic tradition (except himself) had properly understood it:

> A good History of the Welsh Bards, with proper extracts from their works, would be a very interesting work but when will it appear? All that has hitherto been imposed on the World, under pretentions of this kind, is only a crude jumble of Absurdities, falsehoods, and misconceptions, and may as well be called the History of the Man in the Moon, as that of the Ancient British Bards.[127]

In effect, he presented himself as a piece of living archaeology, the embodiment of centuries of accumulated bardic wisdom: 'a regular Welsh Bard can in a few minutes give them a much better account than all the cobweb'd rolls of antiquity of the Druidic Mythology'.[128] Iolo was that 'regular Welsh Bard', though he sometimes unwittingly overstated his position to ironic effect, as in this thinly veiled allusion to William Owen Pughe and Edward Jones in a draft of 'A Short Account of the Ancient British Bards':

> many, who either knew nothing of the ancient Bardic Institution, or having romantic notions of their own to palm on the World for true History, have so distorted and misrepresented every thing that has been said of the British Bards, that this, once celebrated Institution seems such an absurd meaning thing as would be a disgrace to the rudest nation upon earth.[129]

Since the technical term 'Bard' referred to someone who had inherited the accrued bardic knowledge of distant centuries,[130] Iolo could, with some justification, rail against those whom he accused of misinterpreting not only the genuine bardic tradition but also the tradition as he presented it to the world. His verbal swipes were utterly devoid of irony and suggest that Iolo the Bard was wholly convinced (as those who act out personas frequently are) of the veracity of his own interpretation and the palpable inadequacies of that of his rivals.[131] Having read Edward Jones's *The Bardic Museum* (1802), he deemed his druidic writings as insulting, not least because he had failed to introduce Iolo's more reliable bardic interpretations into his writings.[132]

127 NLW 13097B, p. 125. See also NLW 13087E, p. 22.

128 NLW 13089E, p. 423.

129 NLW 13097B, p. 138.

130 Williams: *IM*, p. 304.

131 Erving Goffman, *The Presentation of Self in Everyday Life* (Harmondsworth, 1990), p. 28; Robert C. Elliott, *The Literary Persona* (London, 1992), p. 151.

132 NLW 21285E, letter no. 841, Iolo Morganwg to Margaret Williams, 27 August 1794. For Jones's suspicions regarding Iolo's bardic alphabet, see NLW 21280E, Letter no. 72, Walter Davies to Iolo Morganwg, 16 May 1793, and for his view of the unnecessary severity with which Iolo judged north Walian poets, see NLW 13121B, p. 445.

'Humstrum Jones' was perceived as a threat to his own authority and thus became a frequent target for Iolo's sarcasm:

> To fill up the jumble, musicians have been added. They have been said to be of the Bardic Orders. This is to say that in order to be a parson it was necessary to be a fiddler. A Parson certainly the Bard originally was, but there are laws, still extant in many of our old Manuscripts, and oldest printed books, that expressly forbid the Bard to thrum the harp or scrape the fiddle. In short there was a strict injunction that a Bard should not practice or profess music – and, by the same Law, it was impossible for a Musician to be a Bard . . . Those heterogeneous characters, properly coddled together, make up, in many modern writers their imaginary character of the Ancient British Bard. It seems to me that Geoffrey of Monmouth will never die as long as the pregnant pen of Welsh History, boldly brandished in defiance of Truth, is secured in its assumed privileges.[133]

Similar 'professional' jealousy prompted him to undermine Edward 'Celtic' Davies by dubbing him a 'Smatter-dasher'.[134]

The authority inherent in the bardic persona exposed Iolo's irrepressible egotism, the intensity of which may have been partly attributable to his long addiction to laudanum.[135] He was more than bardism's mediator and last legitimate proponent: he was its centre of gravity because, short of admitting to forgery, laying claim to being the only rightful inheritor of Wales's ancient lineage of bards was his only means of justifying his own personal importance. For this purpose, he created a bogus line of descent in which his own bardic lineage could be traced back to Trahaearn Brydydd Mawr (Trahaearn the Great Poet).[136] More audacious than the brand new 'ancient lineage' which Iolo constructed for himself was the way in which he also wrote himself into his bardic narrative. Ostensibly he achieved this by claiming descent, albeit tongue-in-cheek, from the fourteenth-century poet Dafydd ap Gwilym

133 13097B, pp. 139–40. On hearing that the prolific Jones was to publish yet another book on Welsh music, Iolo hissed: 'the Harpist, I hear, is going to harp again upon Harpinistism': BL Add. 15030, Letter no. 2, ff. 3–4, Iolo Morganwg to William Owen Pughe, 13 August 1799. See also NLW 13130A, p. 221: 'Humstrum Jones may have some wit at his finger's ends, he may also, for ought I know have a trifle at the lower extremities of his carcase, but at the upper he certainly has not a single atom.' Iolo was also appalled by Jones's impudence in assuming the title 'Bard and Harpist to the Prince of Wales': NLW 13108B, p. 114. For the druidic context of Iolo's dealings with Jones, see Tecwyn Elis, 'Bardd y Brenin, Iolo Morganwg a Derwyddiaeth', *NLWJ*, XIII (1963–4), 147–56, 224–34, 356–62; XIV (1965–6), 183–93, 321–9, 424–36; XV (1967–8), 177–96.

134 Moira Dearnley, '"Mad Ned" and the "Smatter-Dasher": Iolo Morganwg and Edward "Celtic" Davies' in *Rattleskull Genius*, pp. 438–40.

135 Geraint Phillips, 'Math o Wallgofrwydd: Iolo Morganwg, Opium a Thomas Chatterton', *NLWJ*, XXIX, no. 4 (1996), 391–410.

136 These are listed in a (substantial) footnote in Owen, *The Heroic Elegies of Llywarç Hen*, pp. lxii–lxiiii. The list's provenance is spuriously traced to John Bradford's manuscript collection.

and Wil Tabwr, a fictional poet from the Interregnum period whom Iolo upheld as the finest proponent of the popular verse (and ultimately druidic) characteristic of Glamorgan:

> a llyma fal y mae arwydfeirdd Llundain ar goreu ynghymru yn tynnu fy acheu i Iorwerth Morganwg, ab Iorwerth ab Thomas ab Gyttyn garpiog ab Will Tabwr, ab Hywel Gorngam, ab Deio fardd y blawd, ab Ifor ben gwydd, ab Ianto lygadwyrdd, ab Hittyn Bendew, ab Llywelyn folwag, ab Iolo drwy'r berth un o fastarddiaid Dafydd ab Gwilym o forfydd, ag felly drwy bymtheg llwyth Gwynedd hyd Gadwaladr Fendigaid, ag o hynny hyd Brutus ab Sylfus.[137]

> (and this is how London's heraldic bards and the best ones in Wales chart my pedigree: Iorwerth Morganwg, son of Iorwerth son of Thomas son of ragged Gyttyn son of Will Tabwr, son of Hywel crooked horn, son of Deio poet of flour, son of Ifor goose head, son of green-eyed Ianto, son of fathead Hittyn, son of empty-bellied Llywelyn, son of Iolo through the bush one of Dafydd ab Gwilym's bastards by Morfydd, and thus through the fifteen tribes of Gwynedd to Cadwaladr the Great, and from thence to Brutus son of Sylvus.)

The creation of such a link was not merely an act of egotism; it was a means of defending his spurious forgeries to himself: by virtue of his familial and bardic connections, he could quite legitimately add links to the long chain of tradition. Elsewhere, he rooted himself firmly in the literary history of Glamorgan by claiming descent from one of the seven poetess sisters of Tŷ Talwyn (White Gable House), from whom all the poets of Glamorgan were supposedly descended, and by claiming that the poet Edward Williams of Middle Hill was his godfather as well as his poetic tutor.[138] His fanciful claim to be descended from the mythological Rhitta Gawr (Rhitta the Giant), whose cloak was fashioned from the beards of despots,[139] strengthened his radical and republican profile.[140] Through these assorted connections, Iolo's own bardic identity became inextricably bound up with the protagonists and ideology of his bardic vision, and bardism, as well as Glamorgan, may justly be considered an extension of his own ego.

Its enduring presence suggests that the bardic persona meant a good deal to Iolo and served as an anchor during his many trials and tribulations. Both

137 NLW 13089E, p. 137. This mock pedigree belongs to prose squibs, in the form of letters from the dead to the living, which Iolo proposed to publish in a quarterly magazine called 'Dywenydd Morganwg' (The Delight of Glamorgan). For Iolo's creative use of Dafydd ap Gwilym, see also *IMChY*; Lewis, 'Eighteenth-Century Literary Forgeries', pp. 145–62.

138 For the sisters of Tŷ Talwyn, see NLW 13141A, pp. 363–4; NLW 13144A, pp. 181–6; Williams: *IM*, p. 89.

139 NLW 21323B, p. 41; NLW 21398E, no. 9.

140 Iolo also claimed a distant kin relationship with Oliver Cromwell through his father's family, the Williams family of Whitchurch and Llanishen. Williams: *IM*, pp. 83–5; Davies, *Presences that Disturb*, p. 152.

G. J. Williams and Ceri W. Lewis have argued that Iolo's romantic and bardic fantasies began life as a place of refuge (*dinas noddfa*), especially during the troubled 1780s when he became burdened by domestic responsibilities and financial hardship. Williams argued convincingly that much of the manuscript version of *Cyfrinach Beirdd Ynys Prydain* was composed during the year which Iolo spent in Cardiff gaol in 1786–7.[141] Bardism and the bardic persona thus began as a temporary and pragmatic form of escapism but, as we have seen, they became a more permanent refuge whenever Iolo felt threatened by poverty, criticism and perceived betrayal. It was into the bardic persona that Iolo retreated from 1792 onwards, a process which is clearly visible in the bardicism of his hymns and published poems, and confirmed by his intention in 1803 to strengthen the bardic element in a proposed second edition of *Poems, Lyric and Pastoral*.[142]

This brings us to the final consideration: bardism's role in the manner in which Iolo envisaged his legacy in the face of death, the ultimate dissolution of the self. Iolo was clearly concerned about how he would be perceived after his days. He not only considered writing an autobiography, 'The History of my Life', at different points in his career, but also, in keeping with a man who made a living by engraving epitaphs on other people's gravestones, he fashioned several epitaphs for himself. The earliest dates from 1795:

> The above Edward Williams was born March 10th, and registered April 00th 1747 in the Parish of Lancarvan – he died and lies buried here (at Nootka Sound) June 00th 1795, aged 48.[143]

That this mock epitaph was written on the same page as an elegy for his daughter Lilla, who died in 1793, indicates Iolo's unbalanced state of mind at the time. Yet the fact remains that he identified himself with the radical cause: Nootka Sound was the focus of the patriotic 'Madoc fever' of the 1790s.[144] Elsewhere, too, he asserted his wish to be a martyr to the radical cause,[145] and so this grand gesture – death while in search of the Madogwys in America, the land of freedom – indicates a deep-seated wish for heroic recognition. In an altogether lighter vein, in 1805 Iolo 'commissioned'

141 Williams: *IM*, p. 342.

142 NLW 13221E, pp. 111–14, Iolo Morganwg to William Owen Pughe, 1 August 1803.

143 NLW 13141A, p. 111.

144 Gwyn A. Williams, *Madoc: The Making of a Myth* (London, 1979), pp. 2–3. For Iolo's involvement with the Madoc myth, see ibid., pp. 99–105, 108–11, 115, 118, 122, 123, 125–9, 132–6, 140–4. See also the *Gentleman's Magazine*, LXI, part 2 (1791), 612–14, Iolo Morganwg to Mr Urban, 16 June 1791; The National Archives 30/8/190/83LH, Iolo Morganwg to William Pitt, 4 February 1793. In NLW 13123B, p. 73, Iolo referred to the curious 'caps of Nootka Sound' as an example of how 'arts, very often exist where in other respects the greatest barbarity and savagism prevails'.

145 NLW 21285E, Letter no. 826, Iolo Morganwg to John Walters, 21 January 1794.

(through William Owen Pughe) a mock elegy from John Jones (Jac Glan-y-Gors): 'I wish Glan y Gors would write a funeral hymn for me, ar fesur triban [triplet] in his usual humorous manner. Tell him that I expect this last token of friendship and old acquaintance from him, and that before I die if possible.'[146] Here again, he was eager to maintain his allegiance to Jacobinism and seek vicarious glory on its coat-tails. But timing is all important in these particular expressions of black humour: they all belong to the stressful final stages of his long friendship and association with Owain Myfyr and William Owen Pughe, and their morbid tone hints at the low spirits which accompanied their acrimonious split.[147] Another body of mock epitaphs give a physical form to the acute sense of failure which haunted him during these years. They are less self-aggrandizing, and evince a metaphorical meaning associated with his bardic persona. Fittingly for a stonemason, he employed the image of a dilapidated house as a metaphor for the collapse of his own bardic construction in three Welsh versions of this mock epitaph:

> Er cof am Iorwerth Gwilym o'r Plwyf hwn Maensaer. Ty pa un a syrthiodd yma'n garnedd ar yr 21 dydd o Fawrth 1805, Er hynny cesglir etto mewn amser priodol yr holl ddefnyddion ynghyd, ag au hadgysylltir gan y Pensaer mawr yn adeiliad hardd, ail waith yn dra chywrain, wedi ei seilio ar Graig yr oesoedd a byth mwy ni syrth, a byth mwy ai welir arno'r adfeiliad lleiaf.
>
> Ty Newydd hardd bardd y bydd iw godiad
> Yn gadarn a chelfydd.[148]
>
> (In memory of Iorwerth Gwilym of this Parish, stonemason, whose house fell here in a heap on 21 March 1805. However, the whole materials will be gathered together at an appropriate time and will be reconstituted by the great Master builder for a second time, very skilful, into a beautiful building, founded on the rock of ages and never more will it fall and never more will the least decay be seen on it. The new house will be the beautiful edifice of a poet, solid and artful.)

Two of the epitaphs are dated 1805 and coincided with the breakdown of his friendship with William Owen Pughe and Owain Myfyr. The hope of 'rebuilding' proved prophetic since, by the time he had penned the third

146 NLW 13221E, pp. 119–22, Iolo Morganwg to William Owen Pughe, 20 July 1805.

147 See also: 'I thought of writing this evening but my spirits fail me greatly. I have been attempting a Cywydd Marwnad Iolo Morganwg [Iolo Morganwg's Elegiac Ode] by way of amusement during a late little ramble, If I can finish it tolerably to my mind I will send you a copy of it.' NLW 13221E, pp. 143–6, Iolo Morganwg to William Owen Pughe, 12 January 1806.

148 NLW 13159A, p. 184. Iolo also penned two English versions, one undated and the other dated 1817, ibid., p. 190. The epitaphs also combine several biblical references: 2 Corinthians 5:1; 1 Corinthians 3:9–11; Hebrews 11:10.

version in 1817, Thomas Williams had already renewed a general interest in bardism through the Rocking-stone Gorseddau held at Pontypridd, and the decisive eisteddfod at Carmarthen was only two years away.

Following the low point of 1792, Iolo does not appear seriously to have considered taking his own life. Nonetheless, because of the respiratory problems which affected him, he retained a morbid preoccupation with death. In addition to these numerous mock epitaphs, his letters are replete with qualifications such as 'if I live'. Twenty-six letters by Iolo contain this lugubrious phrase, sixteen of which belong to the period 1792–1806 which encompassed his over-commitment to various antiquarian projects and the messy split with William Owen Pughe and Owain Myfyr. The remaining ten belong to his dotage, from 1814 until shortly before his death in 1826. The certainty of death often prompts individuals to evaluate their life and achievements,[149] and by 1810 Iolo had once more turned his attention to 'The History of my Life', an autobiography which Evan Williams of the Strand had encouraged him to write. Williams had also expressed an interest in publishing a selection of Iolo's letters.[150] The letters to Evan Williams on the subject may be seen as exercises in self-justification, for in them he rehearsed the familiar list of personal *bêtes noires* – Pughe and Myfyr, as well as the north–south conflict – which reveals that old age had not soothed the bitterness of the Glamorgan Bard.

[149] Philippe Ariès, *At the Hour of our Death*, trans. Helen Weaver (London, 1981); idem, *Western Attitudes Toward Death*, trans. Patricia M. Ranum (London, 1976); Ralph Houlbrooke, *Death, Ritual and the Family in England, 1480–1750* (Oxford, 2000).

[150] Three letters from Iolo to Evan Williams were printed in the *Cambrian Register*, 3 (1818), 174–9, 372–4, 381–5.

3

Wales: A Civilized Nation

We now turn to explore the way in which Iolo Morganwg, through the concept of bardism, upheld the linguistic, literary and cultural reputation of Wales against the deeply entrenched prejudices of the imperial mentality of his day. Although his bardic nationalism was largely a natural corollary of his antiquarianism, it was also deeply coloured by the negative images of Wales which prevailed in both high and low culture in England. Since specific themes – linguistic, cultural and moral inferiority – which belonged to this complex image of 'barbarous Wales' were strenuously repudiated by him, we must first understand this context and consider the colonial mindset that informed the derogatory images and assumptions about the nature of Britishness and Celticism in the eighteenth century.

A disparaging view of Wales and the Welsh had been prevalent long before the loss of Welsh independence at the close of the thirteenth century. In his writings on Wales and Ireland, the ambitious Norman-Welsh cleric, Gerald de Barri (Giraldus Cambrensis, *c.*1146–1223), had deliberated at length about the barbarity of the natives. By contrasting Celtic barbarity and English refinement in order to assist his advancement in English courtly and ecclesiastical circles, he unwittingly established what became an unbroken tradition of anti-Celtic prejudice which survived until the Romantic period and beyond.[1] By the time Wales had been assimilated administratively into England following the Acts of Union (1536–43), the English conquerors had, according to Prys Morgan, inherited 'a long tradition of defining themselves as a civilized people, superior to the neighbouring Welsh'.[2] This powerful binary opposition of Welsh barbarism and English civility permeated all social and cultural strata throughout the early modern period and,

1 E. D. Snyder, 'The Wild Irish: A Study of some English Satires against the Irish, Scots, and Welsh', *Modern Philology*, XVII (1920), 152, 162, 183; R. R. Davies, 'Buchedd a Moes y Cymry', *WHR*, 12, no. 2 (1984), 155–79; idem, '"Sweet civility" and "barbarous rudeness"' in *The First English Empire: Power and Identities in the British Isles 1093–1343* (Oxford, 2000), pp. 113–41. Joep Leerssen, however, argues that Giraldus was merely reinforcing existing attitudes towards the Welsh and the Irish. Joep Leerssen, *Mere Irish and Fior-Ghael: Studies in the Idea of Irish Nationality, its Development and Literary Expression prior to the Nineteenth Century* (Cork, 1996), p. 35.

2 Prys Morgan, 'Wild Wales: Civilizing the Welsh from the Sixteenth to the Nineteenth Centuries' in Peter Burke, Brian Harrison and Paul Slack (eds.), *Civil Histories: Essays Presented to Sir Keith Thomas* (Oxford, 2001), p. 266.

by the eighteenth century, lampoons and caricatures of the Welsh landscape, people, customs and language were commonplace in both high and low literary and visual cultures in England.[3]

Much like that of the Irish and Highland Scots, the received image of the provincial Welsh was one of marked difference from the English centre or core.[4] Their otherness was intensified by their indigenous languages whose very survival undermined the supposed homogeneity of the British nation-state under whose 'contractually formed superstructure' they were increasingly marginalized and regarded with suspicion.[5] Nation-building, as Murray Pittock has shown, dictated that xenophobia during the eighteenth century was more commonly directed internally within the British Isles than externally towards France.[6] Despite much commonality between these Celtic stereotypes, images of the Welsh were in fact less malicious than those of the Irish: on balance, the stereotypical Welshman was portrayed as a comical rather than a repulsive figure, possibly because Protestant Wales had never posed a political or religious threat to the English centre.[7] Prys Morgan has demonstrated that the Romantic period, and the Celtic revival in particular, constituted a brief interlude of civility and acceptability for the Welsh in a history of otherwise unremitting barbarism.[8] But this was arguably a respite only in select Romantic circles, for it was a legacy which died hard. After all, most of the travellers who were drawn by the natural allure of 'wild Wales' from the 1770s to the 1830s had pored over Giraldus Cambrensis, Leland and Camden, and had subsequently reinforced the same long-held chauvinist

3 Peter Lord, *Words With Pictures: Welsh Images and Images of Wales in the Popular Press, 1640–1860* (Aberystwyth, 1995).

4 For national stereotypes in Ireland and Scotland, see Leerssen, *Mere Irish and Fior-Ghael*, pp. 32–76, 77–150. For Scotland, see Richard J. Finlay, 'Caledonia or North Britain? Scottish Identity in the Eighteenth Century' in Dauvit Broun et al. (eds.), *Image and Identity: The Making and Re-making of Scotland Through the Ages* (Edinburgh, 1998), p. 148; Peter Womack, *Improvement and Romance: Constructing the Myth of the Highlands* (London, 1989). For more general studies, see Linda Colley, *Britons: Forging the Nation 1707–1837* (London, 1994), pp. 105–17; Murray Pittock, *Inventing and Resisting Britain: Cultural Identities in Britain and Ireland, 1685–1789* (London, 1997), pp. 13–15; idem, *Celtic Identity and the British Image* (Manchester, 1999).

5 Pittock, *Celtic Identity*, p. 23. See also Snyder, 'The Wild Irish', 162, 178–9.

6 Pittock, *Celtic Identity*, p. 25.

7 While the alleged characteristic laziness of the Irish was considered a feature of their adherence to Catholicism and the Scots were distrusted for their Jacobinism, the Protestant Welsh were spared. Although they were sometimes branded as 'superstitious' and as irreligious as their Hibernian cousins, they were redeemed in English eyes by their speedy embrace of Protestantism following the Reformation, and only with the emergence of Methodism in the mid-eighteenth century did religion become a viable theme for satire of the Welsh. See Alun R. Jones, '"Vermin [who] creep into all corners through the least crevices": Lewis Morris and the Methodists', *THSC*, 5 (1999), 24–35.

8 Morgan, 'Wild Wales', p. 266. This change of heart also mirrored the Romantic admiration for all that was close to nature.

attitudes in their own travel narratives.[9] And even in supposedly sympathetic Romantic circles the kudos which Iolo commanded as a self-proclaimed Ancient British Bard did not shield him from the mild condescension of his English friends such as Robert Southey, who described him in the following terms:

> The most eccentric man I ever knew, in whose eccentricity there was no affectation, and in whose conduct there was nothing morally wrong. Poor fellow! with a wild heart and a warm head, he had the simplicity of a child and the tenderness of a woman.[10]

Southey's description of 'Old Iolo', immortalized in *Madoc*, is characteristic of the nineteenth-century predilection for taming the Celts by both infantilizing and feminizing their national traits.

The landscape which so attracted later Romantic travellers in search of authentic, untamed nature in Wales's non-industrialized interior had held little charm for previous generations of writers. By the late seventeenth and early eighteenth centuries, the inhospitable landscape had become the established backdrop of visual and literary satires of the Welsh. Gibson's 1696 edition of Camden's *Britannia,* for example, derided its craggy, hostile landscape,[11] and since the inhabitants of Wales were considered a natural product of their rough and forbidding environment, they too were deemed in need of cultivation:

> For when we consider the *soil* from whence they *sprang*, and the *Deserts* and Mountains wherein they *wander*, we cannot but think that greater pains should be taken in cultivating and manuring, in disciplining and taming them.[12]

This assumed correlation between the savagery of the people and the landscape had also informed Sir Benjamin Rudyerd's sneer in 1628 that 'Wales is scarce in Christendom'.[13] Ned Ward's dehumanizing attitude towards the Welsh as 'noxious vermine' is also typical of this stance since, in view of the

9 W. J. Hughes, *Wales and the Welsh in English Literature from Shakespeare to Scott* (Wrexham, 1924), p. 87.

10 Quoted in Damian Walford Davies, *Presences that Disturb: Models of Romantic Identity in the Literature and Culture of the 1790s* (Cardiff, 2002), p. 135.

11 Keith Thomas, *Man and the Natural World: Changing Attitudes in England 1500–1800* (London, 1983), p. 258.

12 [William Richards], *Wallography or the Britton describ'd* (London, 1682), p. 81. See also ibid., pp. 81–2: 'if we compare this Kingdom to a *Man*; (as some do *Italy* to a Man's Leg) they inhabit the very *Testicles* of the Nation. And I pray what are those but the vilest of Creatures that breed as well in the *Privities* of the *greater* Brittish World, as those that are hatcht in the *Pudenda* of the lesser?'

13 Quoted in Morgan, 'Wild Wales', p. 270.

custom of housing people and livestock under the same roof, it was 'hard to say, which are the greater Brutes'.[14]

The Welsh temperament and language were also routinely employed as an alienating tactic. This 'hot cholerick'[15] people spoke an unintelligible tongue which sounded 'more like the Gobling of Geese, or Turkeys, than the Speech of Rational Creatures'.[16] In another example, William Richards's satire, *Wallography* (1682), was imbued with unintentional irony because the gradual Anglicization of the middling sorts which he depicted was one of the more insidious effects of the prolonged attack on Welsh civility instigated by work such as his own:

> Their Native *Gibberish* is usually pratled throughout the whole *Taphydome*, except in their Market Towns, whose Inhabitants being a little rais'd, and (as it were) pufft up into *Bubbles* above the ordinary *Scum*, do begin to despise it. Some of these being elevated above the common Level, and perhaps refin'd into the Quality of having *two Suits*, are apt to fancy themselves above their Tongue, and when in their *t'other Cloaths*, are quite asham'd on't. 'Tis usually cashier'd out of Gentlemens Houses, there being scarcely to be heard even one single Welch Tone in many families; their Children are instructed in the *Anglican* Ideom, and their Schools are *Pædagogu'd* with Professors of the same; so that (if the Stars prove lucky) there may be some *glimmering* hopes that the Brittish *Lingua* may be quite extinct, and may be *English'd* out of *Wales*, as *Latin* was barbarously *Goth'd* out of *Italy*.[17]

The Welsh language and the culture it sustained also came under attack in learned circles. John Pinkerton, one of the most frequently abused figures in Iolo's writings, held that the Celts who had inhabited western Europe were not only 'in a state of barbarism and primeval habitation, when science had attained the highest perfection in the east', but that they continued in that lamentable state,[18] and in his *Letters to the People of Great Britain on the*

14 Ned Ward, *A Trip to North-Wales: Being a Description of that Country and People* (London, 1701), p. 3. Similar portrayals of the Irish as subhuman persisted into the nineteenth century, and their imputed simian quality was framed in Darwinian terms., L. Perry Curtis Jr., *Apes and Angels: The Irishman in Victorian Caricature* (London, 1997); R. F. Foster, 'Paddy and Mr Punch' in idem, *Paddy and Mr Punch: Connections in Irish and English History* (London, 1995), pp. 171–94.

15 Ward, *A Trip to North-Wales*, pp. 5, 7.

16 Ibid., p. 3. See also Richards, *Wallography*, pp. 121–4.

17 Richards, *Wallography*, pp. 123–4. For a critique of *Wallography*, see Michael Roberts, '"A Witty Book, but mostly feigned": William Richards' *Wallography* and Perceptions of Wales in Later Seventeenth-century England' in Philip Schwyzer and Simon Mealor (eds.), *Archipelagic Identities: Literature and Identity in the Atlantic Archipelago, 1550–1800* (Aldershot, 2004), pp. 153– 65.

18 John Pinkerton, *Ancient Scotish Poems* (2 vols., London, 1786), I, p. xxi. See also Richard M. Crowe, 'Diddordebau Ieithyddol Iolo Morganwg' (unpublished University of Wales Ph.D. thesis, 1992), p. 188.

Cultivation of their National History nothing could persuade him of the value of Welsh and Irish antiquarian 'phrenzy'.[19]

Viewed in colonial terms, the prejudices of the English centre against the Celtic nations on its peripheries outlined above were a means both of rationalizing and asserting the authority and inherent superiority of every aspect of English life over those of the nations they had conquered and assimilated into the British state. Language, culture, customs and manners were identified as markers of otherness which ultimately justified the so-called 'civilizing' influence of the conqueror. The perceived racial and cultural inferiority of the Welsh was reinforced by coupling them with other so-called barbarous cultures and races, notably the Jews and the Turks.[20] In an age of intense interest in the history of the Ancient Britons for 'British' nation-building purposes, satires of the Welsh often contested or mocked the validity of their traditional claims to be the original inhabitants of Britain, sometimes through the unflattering lens of hard primitivism:

> I had no sooner passed the *River Dee*, but I began to grow sensible I was not in *England*; for the Country I was got into, look'd no more like it, than if a Man had been in *America*, or the most uninhabited parts of *Arabia*. There was a savage Air in the Face of every body I met, that plainly told me, These must be Descended from Brutus, *the Nephew of* Virgil's *Heroe*.[21]

Subtextual references of this kind point to the sensitivity of the terms 'Briton', 'Britain' and 'British': dissenting or competing notions of Britishness were either scoffed at or suppressed in order to maintain the veneer of unity of the burgeoning British empire, and even English communities such as the south-east and the Midlands which lay outside the London core were deemed barbarous.[22] Indeed, these images produced a twin effect when internalized by the Welsh populace. On the one hand, they greatly facilitated the assimilation of the Welsh into Great Britain by eroding the esteem in which they held their indigenous culture and language and thus contributed greatly

19 'Philistor', *Letters to the People of Great Britain on the Cultivation of their National History*, Letter V, *Gentleman's Magazine*, LVIII, part 1 (1788), 500–1.

20 Ward, *A Trip to North-Wales*, pp. 3, 5. For some strikingly similar motifs in eighteenth- and nineteenth-century anti-semitism, see Michael Ragussis, *Figures of Conversion: 'The Jewish Question' and British National Identity* (London, 1995); Carol Margaret Davison, *Anti-Semitism and British Gothic Literature* (Basingstoke, 2004), pp. 4, 7, 15–33.

21 Ward, *A Trip to North-Wales*, p. 7. 'They are (doubtless) the true Off-Spring of the Antient Britains; and having crept into an obscure Corner of the Land, no ways able to recompence the toyl of Conquest; They liv'd for many Ages undisturb'd . . . till our first *Edward*, with much ado, Cudgell'd 'em into Humanity, and persuaded 'em (fore against their wills) to live a little like the rest of their Neighbours', ibid., p. 3. See also [Richards], *Wallography*, pp. 81–2. For similar analogies between Native Americans and the Irish, see Pittock, *Celtic Identity*, p. 49.

22 Pittock, *Inventing and Resisting Britain*, pp. 2, 24; Colley, *Britons*, *passim*.

to the inferiority complex of the Welsh. On the other, as in Iolo's case, the negative images ultimately strengthened the sense of Welsh identity they had sought to impede. In an age when cultural achievements and heroes were considered representative of national character, an attack on Welsh literature constituted an attack on the Welsh themselves. We therefore now turn to Iolo's response to the multilayered image of 'barbarous Wales'.

As a Welsh stonemason who had lived and worked in the west of England and in London in the 1770s and early 1790s,[23] Iolo Morganwg had more experience of England and English society than the majority of the Welshmen of his day. He was no stranger to anti-Welsh prejudice and the bardic persona which he adopted was a highly original attempt not only to overcome his lowly social standing but also to counter the snobbery that his provincial Welshness elicited among potential patrons and subscribers.[24] Conscious that identity is defined and constructed in opposition, Iolo sometimes retaliated in kind. For example, in a series of over fifty mostly bogus triads, 'Trioedd y Sais' (The Englishman's Triads), which he located in the period of the English civil wars, he attacked the deceit, ostentation, immorality, warmongering and general incivility of the English:

> Tair Cenedl ormes Ynys Prydain, y Gwyddyl Ffichtiaid, Ciwdawd y Coraniaid, a Chenedl y Sais.
>
> (The three tyrannical nations of the Island of Britain, the Irish Picts, the Coraniaid and the English nation).
>
> Tri pheth anwadal, Lleuad, Ceiliog Gwynt, a meddwl Sais.
>
> (Three fickle things, the moon, a weathercock, and an Englishman's mind).
>
> Tri pheth nid oes eu caletach, Maen Cellt, Torth haidd Cybydd a chalon Sais.
>
> (Three things of which there is nothing harder, adamant, a miser's barley loaf and an Englishman's heart).
>
> Tri pheth goreu pa leiaf o honynt yng Nghymru, Tlodi, Pechod a Sais.
>
> (Three things all the better for being rare in Wales, poverty, sin and an Englishman).

23 Iolo's work as a stonemason is discussed by Richard Suggett, 'Iolo Morganwg: Stonecutter, Builder, and Antiquary' in *Rattleskull Genius*, pp. 197–208.

24 For example, Iolo's alleged encounter with Dr Samuel Johnson in a London bookshop, *RAEW*, pp. 26–7.

Tri gelyn Cymro y sydd, ei galon hygred ei hun, Cythraul o Uffern, a Charn Sais.

(The Welshman has three enemies, his own amiable heart, a Devil from Hell, and an arch-Englishman).

Tri Dyn a fawr gerir gan Gymro, Bardd wrth fraint a Defod Beirdd Ynys Prydain, Deifiwr Barf Cybydd, a Chrogwr Sais.

(Three men much loved by a Welshman, a Bard according to the rights and privileges of the Bards of the Island of Britain, he who scorches a miser's beard, and he who hangs an Englishman).[25]

The first triad cited above is a genuine bardic triad, and the series as a whole provides an excellent example of the way in which genuine bardic material could stimulate bardic flights of fancy in Iolo. He also penned a corresponding series of 'Trioedd y Cymro' (the Welshman's triads), attributed to Hopcin Twm Philip of Gelli'r-fid, in which he exalted the morals, habits, religiosity and cultural refinement of the Welsh.[26] These jovial and mildly xenophobic triads are typical of the anti-English, misogynist and bawdy humour which Iolo and fellow members of the Gwyneddigion Society often enjoyed,[27] but they were more than just a puerile riposte to the imperial mindset which had constructed the familiar dynamic of barbarous Wales and civilized England in the first place. Whenever Iolo discussed Wales, England was a perennial presence, a constant cultural paradigm; and so these rather crude triads articulated the oppositional discourse of civilized Wales and uncivilized England which formed the basic premise of bardism. Its prevalence, however, should not be overstated, for while the antagonism towards England was a constant feature of bardism, it was not consistently sustained. Unlike the later north–south antagonism that he systematically wove into the fabric of bardism, the basic opposition between England and Wales was fluid, and the range and intensity of Iolo's direct comparisons of Wales with England fluctuated greatly. This ambivalence is perhaps analogous to the personal dilemma he faced within London's literary scene: a desire for Welsh acceptance within the British state and an equally strong desire to resist its cultural hegemony.

25 NLW 13124B, pp. 304–14; *MAW*, III, pp. 253–6. See also a short list of proverbs which he concocted about other nations, including Spain, Portugal, Italy, France, Scotland and Ireland. These include the following anti-English sentiments: 'Rho fodfedd i Sais ac efe a gymmer filltir' (Give an Englishman an inch and he will take a mile) and 'Tri Sais, dau'n lladron a'r trydydd yn wrthryfelwr' (Three Englishmen, two are thieves and the third a rebel): NLW 13122B, pp. 281–2.

26 NLW 13124B, pp. 300–4; *MAW*, III, pp. 251–3.

27 Cathryn A. Charnell-White, 'Women and Gender in the Private and Social Relationships of Iolo Morganwg' in *Rattleskull Genius*, pp. 379–80; Glenda Carr, 'Bwrlwm Bywyd y Cymry yn Llundain yn y Ddeunawfed Ganrif' in Geraint H. Jenkins (ed.), *Cof Cenedl XI: Ysgrifau ar Hanes Cymru* (Llandysul, 1996), pp. 59–87.

Iolo's antiquarian researches gave him an insight into the historical processes which had led to the subjugation of the Welsh nation and people. In the prefatory essay on Welsh manuscripts in *The Myvyrian Archaiology of Wales*, he considered the social, cultural and political implications for Wales of the Acts of Union, and identified two particular ills: Anglicization and the absence of state support for the Welsh language.[28] He recognized that the Welsh defined themselves by their common history, culture and language, and also that it was the fate of the conquered to see their culture denigrated. In this respect he was especially sensible of the fact that the English centre's method of measuring the cultural value and civilization of the Celtic peripheries by its own values and experience was a form of cultural oppression. In the following excerpt from a brief note on the pre-Roman refinement of the Welsh, he applied a colonial paradigm to Wales's situation by conflating the Welsh and Native American experience:

> The great Error of English writers when they write any thing about Wales arises from their viewing most things thro' false mediums. Thus the Welsh Language is viewed in a light similar to that wherein they would view the Cherokee Language, the Welsh MSS in the same lights in which the pretended MSS of Ossian are now justly viewed, the present state of Society in Wales thro the medium of antiquated authors, for instance Giraldus, who wrote what was most probably True in his own days, one author views things thro' what a preceding Author has said, a Welsh custom is viewed thro the medium of an English usage which is something similar, or conceived to be so. and a great number of things are viewed thro the mediums of long continued prejudices, thro' some false medium or another every thing is view'd.[29]

References to Ossian and Giraldus Cambrensis in this outburst also demonstrate Iolo's intuitive understanding of the self-perpetuating nature of anti-Celtic prejudices which, as we have seen, did not originate entirely with Giraldus Cambrensis but were nonetheless successfully propagated by him and reinforced in the angry backlash against Macpherson's Ossian texts. This insight proved empowering insofar as Iolo's own defence of the culture and language of the Welsh nation offered an alternative, workable paradigm with which the English republic of letters could measure Welsh literature without finding it wanting. His chosen paradigm was primitivism.

28 *MAW*, I, p. x; NLW 13112B, p. 12. See also Geraint H. Jenkins (ed.), *The Welsh Language before the Industrial Revolution* (Cardiff, 1997), *passim*.

29 NLW 13121B, p. 486. Compare this with Iolo's response to an item which appeared in the *Monthly Review* in May 1805: 'It appears from this, and many similar things in other English writers that the Welsh are considered as an uncivilized people similar probably to an American Indian Nation, that their Language is not a literary one, But the fact is that it is by far the oldest literary and at the same time living language in Europe.' Ibid., pp. 473–4.

A recognized intellectual discourse since the seventeenth century, primitivism already had strong associations with the Druids when Iolo first embraced it.[30] With its origins in Enlightenment philosophy, Platonic mysticism and the philosophical school of moral sense, primitivist discourse considered primitive man, in whom the immutable and universal laws of nature and reason were innate, to be inherently inclined towards goodness, wisdom and benevolence.[31] From this a theory of progressive degeneration developed, in which civilized man was considered corrupt and insensate to nature and the moral law.[32] Judging by the chronology of Iolo's bardic writings and interests, he derived his knowledge of primitivism almost exclusively from the Ossian debate and its satellite issue, literary historicism.[33] Ossian's spectre was raised in 1760 with the publication of Macpherson's *Fragments of Ancient Poetry* (1760), but the earliest reference to Macpherson in Iolo's correspondence occurs in 1774 in a letter to John Walters regarding etymology rather than the ongoing Ossian debate itself.[34] Iolo derived much of his early views on language from Walters – he often echoed Walters's *Dissertation on the Welsh Language* (1771) – and it is likely that Walters, as well as Evan Evans, provided him with important introductions to the debate and its ideology. In addition to the relevant information he gleaned from reviews and abridgements in contemporary magazines such as the *Gentleman's Magazine* and the *Critical Review*, he also absorbed much from lively exchanges on the subject in literary and cultural circles in London. By the 1790s his ideas had come to fruition. William Owen Pughe, who from 1788 had published specimens of ancient Welsh poetry in the *Gentleman's Magazine* to counter Pinkerton's attack,[35] was a vital channel of the latest scholarship for Iolo, and was also another sounding board on this matter. Their collaborative projects, particularly the introduction to *The Myvyrian Archaiology of Wales*, in which the intellectual climate surrounding Ossian was a significant frame of reference, was indebted to the language of primitivism.[36] The variety of first-hand and second-hand sources from which Iolo acquired the conceptual vocabulary of primitivism illustrates his nature as an intellectual magpie. This tendency, together with the unstable and fluid nature of eighteenth-century primitivist

30 Stuart Piggott, *The Druids* (London, 1999), pp. 20, 91–3; Sam Smiles, *The Image of Antiquity: Ancient Britain and the Romantic Imagination* (London, 1994), pp. 75–112.

31 Lois Whitney, *Primitivism and the Idea of Progress in English Popular Literature of the Eighteenth Century* (New York, 1973), pp. 7, 10–12, 14, 22.

32 Ibid., pp. 11, 14, 20, 42. Rationalism also led to an anti-primitivist view of progress, ibid., p. 17.

33 For an analysis of Iolo's engagement with Macpherson, see Mary-Ann Constantine, *The Truth Against the World: Iolo Morganwg and Romantic Forgery* (Cardiff, 2007).

34 NLW 21285E, Letter no. 777, Iolo Morganwg to John Walters, 18 September 1774.

35 Moira Dearnley, '"Mad Ned" and the "Smatter-Dasher": Iolo Morganwg and Edward "Celtic" Davies' in *Rattleskull Genius*, p. 426.

36 *MAW*, I, pp. ix, xviii, xix.

thinking,[37] thwarts attempts to see anything but a loosely knit primitivist framework in bardism.

As the defensive introduction to *The Myvyrian Archaiology of Wales* reveals, Ossian was the issue which inflamed contemporary scholarly prejudices against the Welsh language and its literature. Crucially, however, as M. M. Rubel has shown, the debate was also a platform for an emerging school of historical literary criticism which used primitivism as a serious critical tool for the first time outside the field of antiquarianism:

> Critics of the historical school utilized the historically-loaded concepts of Savage and Barbarian in their analysis and appraisal of the poems of Ossian and Homer, which they thought to represent the artistic and moral values of savage and barbarous societies respectively.[38]

More recently, Joep Leerssen has taken this argument a step further by arguing persuasively that Macpherson's Ossianic texts 'influenced and even shaped European literary historicism, which involved giving precedence to the particular context and cognitive framework of the past'.[39] Moreover, the dismissive, ill-informed condescension it sparked in scholarly circles regarding the validity of Welsh manuscripts and poetic tradition roused the ire of patriotic Welsh scholars and antiquaries.[40] The debate was an important formative influence on Iolo's antiquarian imagination, for the issues raised by the controversy and the growing historicism of literary criticism would become salient themes in his interpretation of the literary tradition of Wales. Macpherson's Ossianic poems and their reception demonstrated that primitivist discourse and the validation of national identity were compatible bedfellows. Blinkered by Ossian's subversive evocation of Scottish independence, many contemporary Scottish historians and critics were loath to acknowledge its inauthenticity:

> Ossian was for the Scots a unique chance for a kind of national revenge. Unsuccessful militarily and politically, unable to derive honour or glory from their contemporary circumstances, they could here at least beat an honourable retreat to the memory of their once glorious past that indeed extended

37 The eighteenth century witnessed the transmission from a rationalistic primitivism to a more emotional form that resonated with the cult of sensibility. Whitney, *Primitivism*, p. 69.

38 M. M. Rubel, *Savage and Barbarian: Historical Attitudes in the Criticism of Homer and Ossian in Britain, 1760–1800* (Oxford, 1978), p. 22. See also Pittock, *Inventing and Resisting Britain*, p. 153.

39 Joep Leerssen, 'Ossian and the Rise of Literary Historicism' in Howard Gaskill (ed.), *The Reception of Ossian in Europe* (London, 2004), pp. 110, 113.

40 See also his engagement with Dr Johnson's contribution to the Ossian debate regarding the barbarism of the Highlanders. NLW 13104B, p. 127; Mary-Ann Constantine, 'Ossian in Wales and Brittany' in Gaskill (ed.), *The Reception of Ossian in Europe*, pp. 67–90.

> much further back than any English history could reach, and announce proudly to all that the Scots had in fact been already a civilized nation at a time when the English were still a gang of Scandinavian or German marauders.[41]

Such was the power of nationalistic sentiment stimulated by the Ossian texts that those like William Shaw, who had doubted their authenticity, were labelled traitors to the national cause.[42] In the light of the miserable reputation of Welsh learning, and the equally wretched reputation of Wales in general, it is easy to see why the subtextual nationalistic possibilities of primitivism appealed to ardent Welsh patriots such as Evan Evans, William Owen Pughe and especially Iolo Morganwg.

Macpherson's evocation of an independent Scotland and Iolo's barely disguised Jacobin bards point towards the link between primitivism and historicism and the creation of national identity: the language of civilization and barbarism was liberally employed when the remote past was used to validate contemporary concerns by Scottish, Irish and Welsh antiquaries.[43] Literary historicism placed a greater emphasis on the past origin of texts than on their availability or relevance in the present,[44] but this did not preclude writers from enacting the most daring projection onto the past, in which contemporary relevance was paramount. This process of self-definition and justification could also be used to promote British loyalty as well as Celtic difference and, as Sam Smiles has shown, it dominated the way in which the Ancient Britons, between 1750 and 1850, regularly masqueraded as instructive models for contemporary Britain and notions of Britishness in antiquarian writing, creative literature and the visual arts:

> In reviewing the varying constructions of Ancient Britain, ranging from disavowal and suppression to celebration and espousal, we are, of course, witnesses of a process of self-validation, where present concerns are projected into the past to produce the desired image of antiquity.[45]

John Pinkerton articulated the didactic and patriotic importance of the past in a series of twelve *Letters to the People of Great Britain, on the Cultivation of their National History*. Writing under the pseudonym 'Philistor', he published

41 Rubel, *Savage and Barbarian*, p. 51; Gwyneth Lewis, 'Eighteenth-Century Literary Forgeries, with Special Reference to Iolo Morganwg' (unpublished University of Oxford D.Phil. thesis, 1991), pp. 9, 22–32.

42 Rubel, *Savage and Barbarian*, p. 51n; Fiona Stafford, *The Sublime Savage: A Study of James Macpherson and the Poems of Ossian* (Edinburgh, 1988), pp. 158, 164, 170.

43 Leerssen, *Mere Irish, Fior Ghael*; idem, 'Ossian and the Rise of Literary Historicism', pp. 109–25; Clare O'Halloran, 'Irish Re-creations of the Gaelic Past: the Challenge of Macpherson's Ossian', *Past and Present*, 124 (1989), 69–95.

44 Leerssen, 'Ossian and the Rise of Literary Historicism', p. 111.

45 Smiles, *The Image of Antiquity*, pp. 1, 129–93. See also Rosemary Sweet, *Antiquaries: The Discovery of the Past in Eighteenth-Century Britain* (London, 2004), pp. 119–53.

them in the *Gentleman's Magazine* during 1788. His most important argument was that a nation could not properly conceive of its cultural and political identity without first acquiring a complete understanding of its history:

> The history of Greece and Rome all seek for in the fountains: and why should not the history of Great Britain obtain even greater attention from every native? As the study of our history has declined, true patriotism has declined; and to attempt its revival may, it is hoped, be regarded as a service both to patriotism and to literature.[46]

Knowledge of history, he argued, was not necessary in itself, but was certainly necessary to understand the modern state of the nation.[47] Significantly, the letters and their appeal to the patriotic duty of antiquaries and historians of early British history made an impact on Iolo at precisely the time when bardism was crystallizing in his mind. He knew very well the true identity of 'Philistor',[48] and responded to Pinkerton's denunciations of the languages, manuscripts and indigenous scholarship of the Celtic nations[49] as if he himself had been personally wounded. He responded to the challenge by utilizing early British history to the patriotic ends which Pinkerton had never anticipated: resistance to Great Britain! 'British' was synonymous and interchangeable with 'Welsh' in Iolo's vocabulary, while Pinkerton, a Scot and a spokesman for the burgeoning Anglo-Saxon historiography, and a writer who subscribed to the 'Norman Yoke' school of thought, considered it in terms of the British nation state.[50] Pinkerton can claim the dubious virtue (alongside Macpherson) of being one of Iolo's earliest and most detested bugbears. By nicknaming Pinkerton 'the rude Goth',[51] Iolo consciously echoed the opprobrium heaped on the Scot in the periodical press, notably by John Tudor in *Celtic Animadversions on John Pinkerton's Gothic Reflections*, a work which was reprinted in the *Gentleman's Magazine* in 1790.[52] Iolo's manuscripts are replete with references to letters and reviews

46 *Letters to the People of Great Britain on the Cultivation of their National History*, Letter I, *Gentleman's Magazine*, LVIII, part 1 (1788), 127. Also quoted in Smiles, *The Image of Antiquity*, p. 9.

47 *Gentleman's Magazine*, LVIII, part 1 (1788), 405.

48 NLW 21282E, Letter no. 310, William Owen Pughe to Iolo Morganwg, 1 October 1788. See also NLW 21419E, nos. 5–6, 8.

49 *Gentleman's Magazine*, LVIII, part 1 (1788), 500–1. For Pinkerton's view that Scotland's Celtic population hindered the nation's progress, see Pittock, *Celtic Identity*, p. 56.

50 *Letters to the People of Great Britain on the Cultivation of their National History*, Letter IV, *Gentleman's Magazine*, LVIII, part 1 (1788), 404: Pinkerton considered it a 'mortifying reflection' that Englishmen 'should seem to think England of no account till it became a prey to Norman ravagers!'.

51 NLW 13089E, pp. 425–1.

52 Tudor denounced 'the Goth Pinkerton' for insulting 'all the descendants of ancient Britons in all three kingdoms', *Gentleman's Magazine*, LX, part 2 (1790), 601. See also Dearnley, '"Mad Ned" and the "Smatter-Dasher"' in *Rattleskull Genius*, pp. 426, 435.

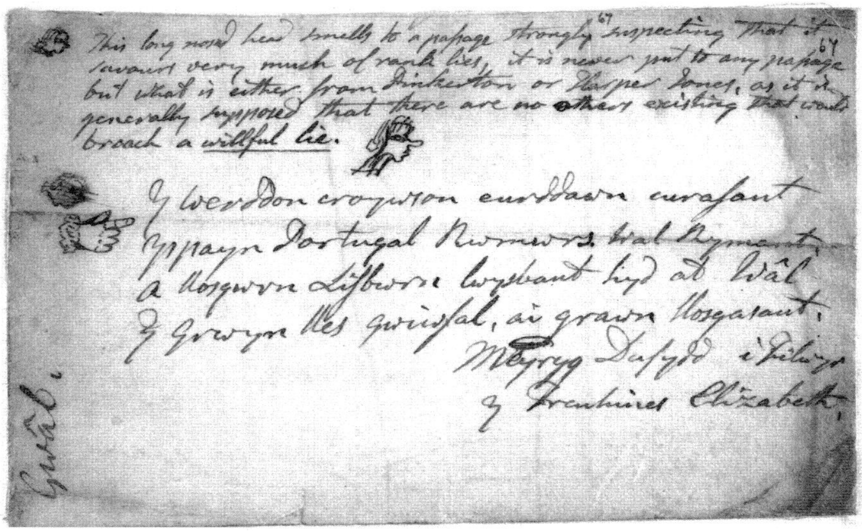

Fig. 3 A sketch of a 'long-nosed head' for sniffing out the lies of John Pinkerton.

of Pinkerton which he collected between 1788 and 1803,[53] and he also owned a copy of Pinkerton's *Dissertation on the Origin and Progress of . . . the Goths*.[54] Pinkerton was an obsessive concern in the numerous drafts of 'A Short Account of the Ancient British Bards', essays which indicate that Iolo was unable to distinguish the man from his ideas, and the general mentality whence those ideas arose. In Pinkerton's case, Iolo's intense hatred for him narrowed to focus entirely on the man, thus providing an example of the complex intersection of Iolo's personal and nationalistic agendas within bardism.

The Scots were not the only Celtic nation to use primitivist vocabulary to nationalist effect: both Gaelic and Ascendancy writers of the eighteenth century swiftly realized its value in presenting a self-image of a civilized and refined Gaelic-speaking Ireland.[55] In her preface to *Reliques of Irish Poetry* (1789), Charlotte Brooke paid homage to the 'laurelled champions of my country' – Sylvester O'Halloran, Charles Vallancey and 'the elegant and faithful' Charles O'Conor – and made an effective show of solidarity in a common cause 'to throw some light on the antiquities of this country, to vindicate, in part, its history, and prove its claim to scientific as well as to military fame' by positioning her own work alongside them.[56] The message

53 NLW 21419E, nos. 3–4; NLW 13104B, p. 127; NLW 13108B, pp. 12–13; NLW 13138A, p. 40.

54 NLW 13136A, p. 142. By 1804 he had mislaid his copy. NLW 21407C, no. 5.

55 Leerssen, *Mere Irish and Fior-Ghael*, pp. 294–376; O'Halloran, 'Irish Re-creations of the Gaelic Past', 69–95.

56 Charlotte Brooke, *Reliques of Irish Poetry* (Dublin, 1816), p. cxxxix.

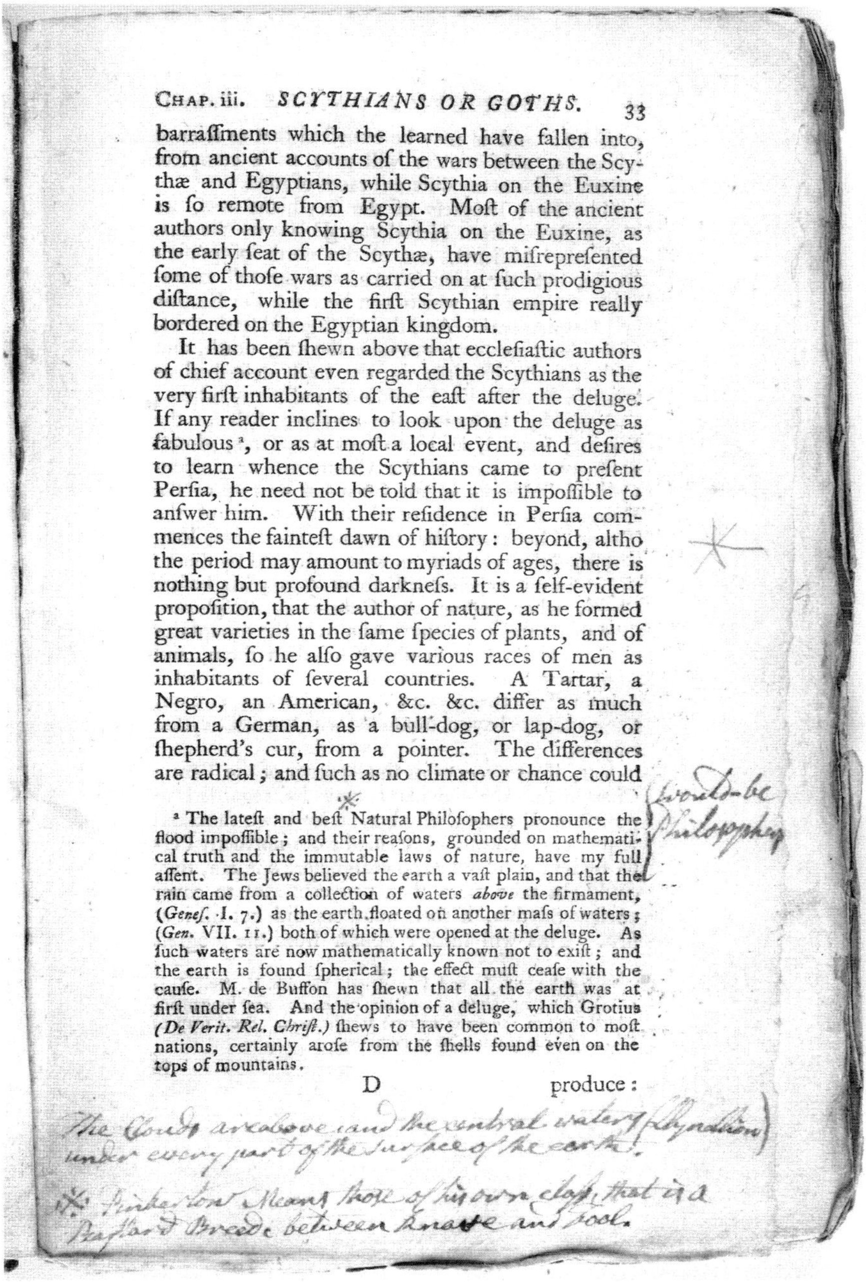

CHAP. iii. *SCYTHIANS OR GOTHS.* 33

barraſſments which the learned have fallen into, from ancient accounts of the wars between the Scythæ and Egyptians, while Scythia on the Euxine is ſo remote from Egypt. Moſt of the ancient authors only knowing Scythia on the Euxine, as the early ſeat of the Scythæ, have miſrepreſented ſome of thoſe wars as carried on at ſuch prodigious diſtance, while the firſt Scythian empire really bordered on the Egyptian kingdom.

It has been ſhewn above that eccleſiaſtic authors of chief account even regarded the Scythians as the very firſt inhabitants of the eaſt after the deluge. If any reader inclines to look upon the deluge as fabulous[a], or as at moſt a local event, and deſires to learn whence the Scythians came to preſent Perſia, he need not be told that it is impoſſible to anſwer him. With their reſidence in Perſia commences the fainteſt dawn of hiſtory: beyond, altho the period may amount to myriads of ages, there is nothing but profound darkneſs. It is a ſelf-evident propoſition, that the author of nature, as he formed great varieties in the ſame ſpecies of plants, and of animals, ſo he alſo gave various races of men as inhabitants of ſeveral countries. A Tartar, a Negro, an American, &c. &c. differ as much from a German, as a bull-dog, or lap-dog, or ſhepherd's cur, from a pointer. The differences are radical; and ſuch as no climate or chance could

[a] The lateſt and beſt Natural Philoſophers pronounce the flood impoſſible; and their reaſons, grounded on mathematical truth and the immutable laws of nature, have my full aſſent. The Jews believed the earth a vaſt plain, and that the rain came from a collection of waters *above* the firmament, (*Geneſ.* I. 7.) as the earth floated on another maſs of waters; (*Gen.* VII. 11.) both of which were opened at the deluge. As ſuch waters are now mathematically known not to exiſt; and the earth is found ſpherical; the effect muſt ceaſe with the cauſe. M. de Buffon has ſhewn that all the earth was at firſt under ſea. And the opinion of a deluge, which Grotius (*De Verit. Rel. Chriſt.*) ſhews to have been common to moſt nations, certainly aroſe from the ſhells found even on the tops of mountains.

D produce:

Fig. 4 These personal and scornful comments are typical of the marginal notes which Iolo added to his personal copy of John Pinkerton's *A Dissertation on the Origin and Progress of the Scythians or Goths* (1787): 'Pinkerton Means those of his own class, that is a Bastard Breede between Knave and Fool.'

of Irish antiquaries bears striking analogies with Iolo's own writings and also the second wave of Welsh antiquaries which centred on the London-Welsh societies in the late eighteenth century. Iolo was certainly aware of the work of Charles Vallancey and Joseph Cooper Walker, and he may have read a review of O'Halloran's work.[57] It is likely that he learned about Vallancey through David Samwell, and a brief letter to the Revd Hugh Maurice in 1805 reveals that he knew of Vallancey's interest in alphabets – he enquired whether Maurice had given his example of the bardic alphabet to Vallancey.[58] The links with Walker are frustratingly vague. Walker's *Historical Memoirs of the Irish Bards* (1786) received short shrift from Iolo in drafts of 'A Short Account of the Ancient British Bards',[59] despite Walker's encouraging remarks about Iolo in the pages of the *Gentleman's Magazine* in 1790.[60] Iolo did not engage fully with Walker's ideas, but he had clearly read his work on the Irish bards, and had therefore seen how champions of another Celtic literary language had employed the powerful discourse of primitivism to challenge the barbarous image imposed on it from the English centre. Instances in which Iolo shows an appreciation for the comparable situations of the Celtic languages and learning are rare,[61] but in a 'first rude sketch' of his uncompleted 'History of the Bards' (dated 1791) he planned to discuss 'Irish Bards and Druids' and 'Highland Bards' separately.[62] The prominence of the *Gentleman's Magazine*, the *Critical Review* and the *Monthly Review* in the footnotes to this section reinforce Rosemary Sweet's point that the periodical press played an invaluable role in the diffusion and exchange of current ideas in antiquarian and learned circles.[63] The constant, and rapid, turnover of reviews, abridgements and letters available in periodicals meant that interested parties such as Iolo could keep abreast of developments in a way, and at a pace, that was not even conceivable for his predecessors, who had depended heavily on private correspondence and word of mouth.

While we should not discount the interest of Welsh antiquaries like Evan Evans and Edward Davies in primitivism, it is important to place Iolo in this

[57] An edition of Sylvester O'Halloran's *An Introduction to and an History of Ireland*, published in 1803, was reviewed in the same volume as Edward Davies's *Celtic Researches* (1804): *Monthly Review*, XLVI (1805), 75–84.

[58] NLW 21285E, Letter no. 875, Iolo Morganwg to the Revd Hugh Maurice, 28 June 1805. I am grateful to Dr Martin Fitzpatrick for drawing my attention to Iolo's links with Charles Vallancey through David Samwell.

[59] NLW 13089E, p. 456: 'Mr Walker, in his account of the Bards and Druids has tacitly charged them with all fopperies of human vanity and all the insolence of modern Parsons.' See also NLW 13108B, pp. 102, 114; NLW 13120B, p. 115.

[60] *Gentleman's Magazine*, LX, part 2 (1790), 801–2.

[61] NLW 13089E, p. 303.

[62] NLW 13144A, p. 391.

[63] Sweet, *Antiquaries*, pp. xvi, 90. By the 1790s the *Gentleman's Magazine* in particular had become a locus for airing differences and settling personal disputes. Ibid., p. 109.

Celtic context not only because bardism and its primitivist framework constituted one of the most imaginative responses to the Celtic revival, the Ossian debate and literary historicism, but also because, through the pages of the notoriously conservative *Gentleman's Magazine,* the antiquaries of the Celtic peripheries had access to, and could exercise, the same conceptual vocabulary of dissent and resistance to the English core. In the poems of Ossian, the writings of the Irish antiquaries, and the critical responses to both in the periodical press, Iolo found a tried and tested pattern with which to project a positive national self-image, as well as an intellectual framework conducive to bardic traditions and the ancient Druids. The primitivist framework and the lexicon which Iolo gleaned from these sources from the late 1780s onwards were present in bardism from the early 1790s onwards, as the manifesto of late eighteenth-century Welsh antiquaries – the introductory essay to *The Myvyrian Archaiology of Wales* – reveals:

> These books are venerable monuments of enlightened periods of literature amongst the Britons, while scenes of barbarity were acted over Europe, and darkened the light of our island: a literature whose origin was not borrowed, but matured at home, under the extraordinary system, the Bardic Institution; concerning which, under the name of Druidism, much has been written, much misunderstood, and of which the world yet knows but very little.[64]

In terms of identifying the Welsh as the aboriginal inhabitants of Britain, the enlightened nature of their indigenous and precocious cultivation, as well as confirming Iolo's own position of authority, this passage sets the tone for the second half of this chapter which shows how primitivism informed Iolo's idiosyncratic bardic antidote to the notion of 'barbarous Wales'.

In order to demonstrate the inherent civility of the Welsh nation, Iolo celebrated the native poetic tradition as a relic or, in contemporary parlance, a 'monument' of its past brilliance; indeed, as an exemplar of the enlightened character of the Britons/Welsh and their society, culture and language 'a noble spirit of Liberality, genuine morality, and Liberty runs through it, and it does very considerable honour to the Nation that gave it existence, its great leading principle was that of civilizing the community'.[65] By using their antiquity and Celtic, rather than Trojan descent, as markers of individuality, Iolo argued that the Cimmeri (the ancestors of the Britons) and their wise men were considered to be one of the few 'Nations who appear to have attained to a considerable degree of civilization in the very infancy of the

64 *MAW*, I, p. v.
65 NLW 13121B, p. 306. See also NLW 13088B, p. 76; NLW 13144A, p. 390; *MAW*, I, p. v.

world, or who rather had retained the primeval civilization'.[66] The logic of Iolo's system was simple: such a rational and moral system could not have been produced by the supposedly uncivilized nation which had been etched on the popular imagination. He presented the primitive origins of Welsh society and the culture it sustained as inherently good, wise and benevolent. This gave him scope for projecting contemporary radical ideology into the remote British past. Four broad themes emerge in which the Welsh identity was validated in primitivist terms: Wales's home-grown civility, the Welsh language, its religion and its morality. The polarization of Welsh/Britons and English/Saxons, so typical of contemporary historical and antiquarian writing and literary criticism which dealt with ancient civilization and refinement, remained a persistent undercurrent throughout: the Welsh/British were 'civilized', 'enlightened' and 'natural', while the English/Saxons were 'barbarous', 'rude' and 'savage'.

Iolo insisted that bardism was a thoroughly indigenous phenomenon: 'the Institution of the Bards originated in *Britain* and they are emphatically called Beirdd Ynys Prydain' (The Bards of the Island of Britain).[67] Because of their unique status he planned to discuss 'the Ancient British Bards and Druids' independently of the bards and poets of other Celtic and European nations in 'The History of the Bards'.[68] Indeed, according to one of the patriotic triads quoted earlier, bardism figured among the accomplishments for which the Welsh nation was said to excel: 'Tri pheth y sydd o Genedl y Cymry yn oreuon o'u rhyw yn y Byd. Barddas, Rhaith, a Cherdd dant' (Three things emanating from the Welsh nation that are the best of their sort in the world. Bardism, Law, and instrumental music).[69]

One aspect of Iolo's insistence on the non-contingent nature of Welsh cultural refinement was his eagerness to prove that it predated those of other nations. In this respect, the Romans, Saxons and Normans provided a useful benchmark against which Welsh civilization could be measured.[70] Civilizing Norman influence within bardism was limited to south Wales and, since it was cited by him as proof of Glamorgan's superiority over Gwynedd, it will be dealt with in the next chapter on bardism's internal regional hierarchy. Despite the fact that a good deal of bardism's ideology was indebted to contemporary Augustan literary taste and English radicalism, Iolo was wary of admitting that any English influence could be detected in either bardism

66 NLW 13159A, p. 149. The bards embraced only what they recognized in nature. NLW 13097B, pp. 101–2.

67 NLW 13089E, p. 458; William Owen, *The Heroic Elegies of Llywarç Hen* (London, 1792), p. xxv.

68 NLW 13144A, p. 391. Iolo discussed the exclusive British origins of the Bards and Druids at length in ibid., pp. 227–30.

69 NLW 13124B, p. 303.

70 Cathryn Charnell-White, *Barbarism and Bardism: North Wales versus South Wales in the Bardic Vision of Iolo Morganwg* (Aberystwyth, 2004), pp. 12–13.

or the language of bardism. The Saxons or the English were an undercurrent which ranged in prominence and intensity, and was less systematic and pointed than the Welsh regional hierarchy he wove into bardism. As many of the pieces quoted in this chapter demonstrate, Iolo peppered his writings with invective against the Saxons and their supposed inferiority. For example, he boasted of the purity of the Welsh language which, he erroneously claimed, contained no borrowings from Old English because it was an uncultivated tongue, inferior in cultivation to the Welsh: the Saxons, by contrast, 'were barbarous, their language not formed, and probably ignorant of the use of Letters'.[71]

On the other hand, Roman culture or civilization offered a more fruitful and profitable vein in bardism (see Document IV), even if they occupied an ambiguous position within it. This ambiguity arose from Iolo's need to maintain a fine balance between deriving vicarious prestige from Roman links without actually compromising the indigenous bardic culture he was at pains to uphold. As a result, his views on the Romans were confusing, and were thoroughly representative of the increasingly fractured coherence of the Roman vision of antiquity that was a corollary of the emergence of competing histories of national origins within the British Isles during the eighteenth century.[72] Despite the powerful images of the Romans as instruments of the destruction of the Druids in Anglesey and as an imperial threat to British liberty, Iolo was keen to take advantage of their civilizing reputation. He thus wove them into the bardic narrative. Having recognized that the Welsh included some Latin loan-words, he claimed that this was not a sign of the poverty of the Welsh language but rather of its cultural sophistication: it provided evidence that the Ancient Britons or Welsh were conversant with classical learning.[73] As well as providing models and principles with which the Welsh could cultivate their language, poetry also exhibited Roman influence, notably in the good taste and style of the 'Ancient School of Taliesin'.[74] But this also raised questions about the extent of Roman influence, an anxiety he surmounted by arguing that in south Wales the Romans had encountered a refined people, polished by their self-civilizing system:

> What Druidism was in its primeval I should perhaps have said crude state before the roman invasion may be pretty clearly collected from the many intimations of Greek and roman Writers, by which it will appear that it was rather polished than altered in ages of greater refinement.[75]

71 NLW 13123B, p. 183.
72 Sweet, *Antiquaries*, p. 187.
73 NLW 13146A, p. 218; NLW 13094E, p. 59.
74 NLW 13108B, pp. 32, 97–8, 116. See also NLW 13103B, p. 136.
75 NLW 13087E, p. 205.

Wales's indigenous language had already achieved a level of sophistication comparable to Latin, and the spurious bardic alphabet, *Coelbren y Beirdd*, which he had invented, proved that the Welsh were already a literate people.[76] Iolo boasted that, following the fall of Rome, the Welsh had no need of Latin for literary purposes since in bardism the Welsh language had been used as a medium of learning long before the arrival of the Romans on British soil.[77] Always careful not to overstate bardism's debt to Roman learning, he insisted that they had merely introduced Christianity to Britain:

> There is something in a rational and sublime Theology that gives a noble grandeur and elegance to the mind, gives a cast of great rationality to every act and sentiment, from it we derive the truest ideas of justice, of Benevolence and in general of whatever is beautiful proper, and dignified. The refinement which Bardism acquired under the roman civilization seems from its peculiar character to be more immediately derived from Christianity than from any thing else. We may however naturally conclude that the Pythagorean Philosophy had peculiar charms to the Bards as Strikingly coinciding with their own sentiments.
>
> The Bards were professedly the cultivators of wisdom and justice when they were first discovered. Of course when the Roman sources of knowledge became known to them they would not be treated with that contempt which has often been [the] experience from Nations in an absolute state of nature.[78]

The Romans served his primitivist purpose well, for the inferred colonial paradigm of the final sentence quoted above is that bardism's 'Noble Savages' were regarded more sympathetically by their Roman conquerors than were the native peoples of the New World, and indeed the Celtic minorities of Britain by the English (and Spanish). According to Iolo, Roman and Norman presences were not in themselves considered civilizing, for the cultural sophistication they encountered upon their arrival in Britain was part of his broader strategy of proving that all refined facets of Welsh culture had predated them.

As an indigenous Welsh product, bardism's much maligned language lay at the heart of Iolo's construct of the national identity of Wales:

> The Welsh with their Language, retain in its words and phrases . . . a tolerable history of their progress in arts, literary knowledge, and civilization. They are, I believe, the most tenacious, the Jews, perhaps, excepted, of ancient customs and

76 NLW 13144A, pp. 223–38; NLW 13108B, p. 5.
77 NLW 13104B, pp. 127–8; NLW 13151A, pp. 179–80.
78 NLW 13087E, p. 205.

usages and national peculiarities, of any civilized people in Europe, and the English the least so.[79]

In *Cyfrinach Beirdd Ynys Prydain* (1829) he described it as an ingenious language which surpassed all other languages under the sun.[80] The prominence which Iolo gave to the Welsh language was in keeping with the chief responsibilities of the poets as preservers of the national memory. According to the traditional lore of the genuine guild of medieval poets, the 'tri chof' (three memorials) placed the preservation of the indigenous language alongside the history of the deeds of British and Welsh kings and the pedigrees of the native aristocracy, and broadly corresponded to the branches of learning that their Irish counterparts were required to master.[81] In this sense, Iolo kept alive the potent sense of linguistically defined nationality which was part of the inheritance of Wales's medieval poetic tradition on which bardism was founded, and which had been perpetuated by the Welsh humanists.[82] A note on 'Original Traditions' underlined bardism's dependence on the Welsh language. Preserved in the very fabric of the language, often in nuanced ways, was the memory of key events, myths and characters, memorials which would disappear if the Welsh language ever ceased to exist:

> Events of such a description [the Triads of Dyfnwal Moelmud] must have taken place unavoidably in the early ages of every Nation, and such must have been very striking and very beneficial events, and must have made very great very general, and very indelible impressions on the national memory, such as would never, so long as the nation retained its original language, be obliterated.[83]

Iolo's ideas on the antiquity, purity and copiousness of the language which he believed to have been the first and original language of Britain were probably derived from the work of the lexicographers Thomas Richards and

79 NLW 13097B, p. 207. See also NLW 13087E, p. 22. See also Iolo's attempts to persuade Owain Myfyr of the importance of publishing the wisdom of Catwg Ddoeth: 'When we consider the dark middle ages when no People in Europe besides the Welsh wrote in their own language, but in Mon[kish] Latin, our literary remains, however in some things inferior to modern literature will do infinite credit to our ancestor[s] nation, and our posterities will allow infinite credit to you for thus preserving them from utter destruction which one century more would have effected.' BL Add. 15024, Letter no. 18, ff. 299–300, Iolo Morganwg to Owain Myfyr, 27 November 1799. See Document I.

80 Taliesin Williams (ed.), *Cyfrinach Beirdd Ynys Prydain* (Abertawy, 1829), p. 14: 'yn ei thrylen athrylith, y mae hi'n rhagori, ag yn blaenori ar bob Iaith arall dann Haul ag wybren'. See also pp. 11, 15.

81 G. J. Williams, 'Tri Chof Ynys Prydain', *LlC*, III, no. 4 (1955), 234–9.

82 Glanmor Williams, *Religion, Language and Nationality in Wales* (Cardiff, 1979), pp. 127–8; R. Geraint Gruffydd, 'The Renaissance and Welsh Literature' in Glanmor Williams and Robert Owen Jones (eds.), *The Celts and the Renaissance: Tradition and Innovation* (Cardiff, 1990), pp. 17–39.

83 NLW 13088B, p. 89.

John Walters. When he claimed that the Welsh language held the key to bardism and the bardic mythology, he merely echoed sentiments expressed by his mentor John Walters in *A Dissertation on the Welsh Language* (1771).

Despite his attempts to dignify the Welsh language through its symbiotic relationship with bardism, Iolo believed that the language was worthy of merit in its own right. Next to the inherent rationality, perfection and genius of the indigenous language (and the bardic culture it sustained) was the related theme of its precociousness. The antiquity of the Welsh language was a great source of pride: following humanist learning, Iolo believed that it shared similarities with other ancient languages such as Greek, Hebrew, Latin, Teutonic, Persian and Sanskrit,[84] and that it had remained structurally robust since its inception four, if not five, thousand years earlier.[85] He followed the premise that all literary languages (including dialects) pass through a 'due course' of cultivation and that the state of a language's cultivation was clear from its structure, regularity, syntax, rationality of analogies and antiquity of vocabulary. Most importantly, Iolo was able to use bardism to embellish the ancient cultivation of the Welsh language. Furthermore, his ambitious timescale could be employed to provide proof of the home-grown cultivation of the language, thereby countering Camden's arguments that it was the Romans who had brought civilization to the uncouth Britons. Anxious also to dispel the prejudices of contemporary critics of the Welsh language, Iolo maintained that a language retained within it the 'abstract ideas and principles of science' known to its speakers, and that for a language to possess appropriate philosophical and arithmetical terms proved 'that those nations that spoke it were self-civilized to a degree corresponding with the science or knowledge that such a set of terms and phrases express and indicate'.[86] On the other hand, he considered that for a language to borrow from other languages was 'undoubted proof that the speakers of this borrowing language had never any science of their own, and that of course that they were in a state of Barbarism'.[87] He concluded that, had the likes of Pinkerton compared the richness and perfection of the Welsh and Irish languages with the 'rude and barren' English, they would have realized that Pinkerton's notions of barbarism and civility were heavily skewed: 'surely the language that has within itself the most ample stores and resources on all occasion is not so barbarous as that which begs borrows and steals from all others'.[88] For Iolo, Welsh was truly the language of genius.

[84] NLW 13121B, p. 425.

[85] NLW 13121B, pp. 383–4, 423–4. In another source the timescale was estimated at two thousand years: NLW 13151A, p. 179. Iolo cited the preponderance of names for God as further proof of the antiquity of the Welsh language: NLW 13121B, p. 436.

[86] NLW 13089E, p. 303. See also ibid., p. 426.

[87] NLW 13089E, p. 303.

[88] Ibid.

Both poetry and prose testified to the polish of the Welsh language and to the sophistication of the Welsh. Since bardism was essentially a reworking of Wales's genuine poetic tradition, poetry – in which druidic learning, maxims and mythology were enshrined – was given precedence. The poetic tradition of Wales had been a focus of patriotic zeal for Iolo's humanist predecessors but, by the Romantic age, scholars believed that poetry and national consciousness had been inextricably entwined since antiquity. Indeed, poetry provided a mirror to the Welsh past and civilization:

> for, besides frequent instances of beautiful poetry, it will be found that from our old bards new and great lights on history are obtained; they exhibit lively pictures of primitive manners, afford curious anecdotes of our ancient knowledge, especially of the very beautiful ethics of our remote ancestors; who seem to have penetrated farther into the knowledge of human nature than the world can be easily brought to believe; and on these occasions we see the Welsh piercing into depths that are almost unfathomable to other languages.[89]

Iolo's emphasis on the cultural significance of poetry reveals his indebtedness to Joseph Ritson, and among miscellaneous notes and memoranda in his manuscripts he noted the following quotation on this subject from the 'Essay on National Song' prefixed to Ritson's *English Songs* (1783): 'Their Songs were chiefly designed to transmit to posterity the National History.'[90] However, Iolo also noted that the Welsh language was 'almost exclusively the Nursling of Poetry'.[91] It was *almost* exclusively so because, in order to bolster Welsh civility and indeed the primacy of the culture of the inhabitants of south Wales, he needed to enlist the aid of the Welsh prose tradition.[92] Although poetry formed the backbone of bardism, the importance of prose in contemporary debate regarding its cultural significance meant that he could not afford to omit it from his narrative of Welsh cultural superiority. Some of his commonplace books are a quarry of pertinent quotes on the subject, many of them culled from the writings of Denina, Gregory, Mallet, Percy and Ritson.[93] From these 'authorities' Iolo learned that poetry, which was intimately linked with oral modes of transmission, represented the primary stage in the process of civilization, the 'first effort of genius' in every

89 *MAW*, I, p. xix.
90 NLW 13107B, p. 66.
91 NLW 13128A, p. 179.
92 Charnell-White, *Barbarism and Bardism*, pp. 15–16.
93 NLW 13107B, pp. 36–63, 66–70 offers a list of authorities and the main thrust of their arguments. Hugh Blair's dissertation on the poems of Ossian, George Gregory's essay on the life of Chatterton in idem, *The Works of Thomas Chatterton* (3 vols., London, 1803), Susan Dobson, *The Literary History of the Troubadours . . . collected and abridged from the French of Mr. de Saint-Pelaie* (London, 1779), Thomas Percy, *Reliques of Ancient English Poetry* (3 vols., London, 1765), William Warrington, *The History of Wales* (3rd edn., 2 vols., London, 1791) and Joseph Ritson, *A Select Collection of English Songs* (3 vols., London, 1783).

nation.[94] Prose, on the other hand, was intimately linked with written transmission and literacy, and thus indicated a more advanced stage in the development of a nation's literature and civilization. This notion served two purposes for Iolo. Firstly, he used it to prove precocious development: the Welsh had developed prose before they had encountered the Romans (Christianity) and Saxons,[95] and secondly, since Iolo accepted Evan Evans's view that Glamorgan was the cradle of prose in Wales,[96] he could also weave it into bardism's internal hierarchy.

The association of prose with written forms of language meant that Iolo could enhance his nation's reputation for civilization by drawing attention to its standards of literacy and the early development of Welsh as a written literary language. Several writers influenced his view on this subject. The debate surrounding Ossian had taught Iolo that critics of Macpherson considered orally transmitted material to be deeply suspect. He had also noted Samuel Johnson's comments in *A Journey to the Western Islands of Scotland* (1775), which attributed the perceived ignorance of the Highland Scots to their illiteracy.[97] Keen to avoid such condemnation of his own fellow bards, Iolo retorted valiantly that 'our old Bards were not Barbarians amongst Barbarians. They were men of Letters, we possess authentic documents that inform us in what seminaries they were educated'.[98]

Moreover, Paul Henri Mallet, whom Iolo had read in Thomas Percy's translation, cited illiteracy and the absence of an alphabet as outright proof of the barbarity of the Celtic nations compared with the refined and literate northern or gothic nations.[99] For this reason Iolo included literacy and writing in his game of cultural one-upmanship, supporting the pre-Saxon and pre-Roman achievement of Welsh letters with a purpose-built bardic alphabet, *Coelbren y Beirdd*.[100] This audacious invention allowed him to capitalize on early literacy as proof of the profound civilization of the Welsh, without undermining the historically proven fact that the Welsh poetic guild had adhered to a predominantly oral mode of transmission until the mid-sixteenth century, when it was superseded by transmission through written

94 NLW 13107B, p. 41. See also NLW 13098B, p. 101.
95 NLW 13098B, pp. 95–6. In January 1816 Iolo wrote a proposal for the publication of 'Specimens of ancient Welsh Literature in Prose and Verse, Translated into English from ancient Welsh Manuscripts. By Edward Williams', which was designed to prove this theory. NLW 21400C, no. 15. That the Irish were literate before the arrival of Christianity in Ireland was central to Charles O'Conor's *Dissertations* (1753). See O'Halloran, 'Irish Re-creations of the Gaelic past', 76.
96 *TLIM*, p. 174.
97 NLW 13104B, pp. 127–8.
98 Ibid., p. 128; *MAW*, I, p. xviii.
99 Mallet, *Northern Antiquities*, I, pp. xvii–xviii.
100 NLW 13087E, pp. 15–36; NLW 13089E, p. 262.

manuscripts.[101] *Coelbren y Beirdd*, whose provenance and make-up he described at length in a drafted letter to the *Gentleman's Magazine* in 1792,[102] was presented as a long-held bardic secret dating back to the time of Taliesin, if not earlier.[103] His inspiration came from contemporary interest in linguistics, orthography, inscriptions and alphabets, especially runic letters,[104] and from Robert Plott's Staffordshire clogg, which he had read about in the *Gentleman's Magazine*.[105] He argued retrospectively that its basis was the bardic insignia which represented the three ineffable utterances of the creator. This ushered in an eclectic cabbalistic element to the mythological origins which Iolo created for bardism by involving the fictional Menw Teir-gwaedd, whose three cries are represented by the three-pronged bardic insignia /|\.[106] Perhaps the most remarkable individual creation in bardism – the *Coelbren*'s potential as an emblem of national identity – was not fully realized until the nineteenth century, thanks to the publications of Iolo's son, Taliesin Williams, and John Williams (Ab Ithel), as well as the growing eisteddfod movement.[107] In the final analysis, Iolo believed that the nation's poetry, prose and bardic alphabet all bore witness to the glittering past of the Welsh language, which had surpassed the defunct Latin in its glory:

> The Welsh have thro' all ages, from the remotest antiquity, cultivated their own language, and thro' all the Periods of their history have (almost exclusively) used it for every purpose of Literature, and in those periods called properly enough, the dark ages, they wrote in their own vernacular tongue, which appears to have attained to such high degrees of genuine refinement as will probably secure it from that kind of Death which has befallen all or most of the Ancient Literary languages, a few only of which still live a torpid life as it were, in Books but in the vernacular use of any nation now living: of all the Languages of the vast Roman Empire the Welsh is the only one now living and we may venture to say that it is living in a state of renovated youth having fairly recovered all the features

101 Daniel Huws, *Medieval Welsh Manuscripts* (Aberystwyth, 2000), pp. 89–93; idem, *Cynnull y Farddoniaeth* (Aberystwyth, 2004), p. 6.

102 NLW 13087E, p. 17. See also ibid., pp. 15–36; NLW 13089E, p. 315; NLW 13093E, pp. 155–6, 157–65; NLW 13097B, pp. 177–80, 200–9, 212–14; NLW 13123B, pp. 104–5, 263–5, 286; NLW 13128A, pp. 293, 392; NLW 13138A, pp. 42–4; NLW 13144A, pp. 35–44, 135–6, 143; NLW 13150A, pp. 95–6; NLW 21428E, no. 6.

103 NLW 13121B, pp. 423–30; NLW 13089E, p. 315.

104 See NLW 13121B, pp. 419–20 regarding runes and the magic of Odin, taken from Mallet, *Northern Antiquities*, II.

105 NLW 13087E, p. 13.

106 For Menw Teirgwaedd, see NLW 13093E, p. 156; NLW 13097B, pp. 56, 212; NLW 13121B, p. 439; NLW 13141A, p. 334. Iolo had probably been inspired by William Jones the Orientalist. See BL Add. 15030, ff. 12–13, Iolo Morganwg to Owain Myfyr, 17 June 1800. See also Caryl Davies, *Adfeilion Babel: Agweddau ar Syniadaeth Ieithyddol y Ddeunawfed Ganrif* (Caerdydd, 2000), pp. 277–84.

107 Taliesin Williams, *Traethawd ar hynafiaeth ac awdurdodaeth Coelbren y Beirdd: yr hwnn a Ennillodd Ariandlws a Gwobr Eisteddfod y Fenni, 1838* (Llanymddyfri, 1840); *HGB*, pp. 124, 134, 353.

of its pristine beauty, not a wrinkle of its periods of sickness remaining, (and it will ere long cast away all the false ornaments with which some of late endeavour to trick it out).[108]

Not merely a romantic idealist, Iolo also had a pragmatic side which was reflected in his belief that the anciently cultivated Welsh language was sufficiently resilient to withstand the depredations of contemporary linguistic development. Motivated by a deep love of his native language, his desire to defend Welsh and its ancient literature against scholarly condescension was also supplemented by a pedantic concern for the preservation of linguistic purity. He complained about the poor quality of the 'scribblers enough pouring upon us from the Press', a defect he attributed to the absence of a Welsh-language 'elementary treatise on the principles of good writing'.[109] In one sense, therefore, the section on the Welsh language in *Cyfrinach Beirdd Ynys Prydain* was an attempt to remedy this situation. In later life especially, he railed against the Anglicized syntax of the 'very barbarous and truly ridiculous' contemporary Unitarian publications:

modern Lexicographers, grammarians &c have attempted to dress powder and paint it in such a style as to render it in the writing of some of our modern writers in prose and verse a most uncouthly dressed Bedlamite, more particularly so in the writings of most of the Unitarian would be authors, who have most ridiculously caricatured it. But it will ere long escape from under their paw[s] out of their polluting clutches.[110]

He directed similar accusations against the London Welsh,[111] particularly William Owen Pughe, whose 'Cockney and Southcottian Dialects' had 'pernicious effects on the practice of recent Scribblers who adopt the barbarisms and hobby horsisms of those Jargons',[112] and who 'if not murdered our Language, [had] given it such dreadful stabs which can not be with speed

108 NLW 13151A, p. 179.
109 NLW 13121B, p. 478.
110 NLW 13151A, pp. 179–80. See also NLW 13121B, p. 435; NLW 13128A, p. 502; Edward Williams, *Holiadur, neu Addysgiadau Cyffredin, Hawl ac Atteb, yn Athrawiaethau Dyledswyddau Crefydd. Gan y Parchedig I. P. Estlin* (Merthyr Tudfil, 1814), p. 2.
111 NLW 13146A, p. 265. In February 1806 he warned William Owen Pughe: 'by all means be most attentive of the language of the *Greal* it is but very little to the purpose that every word is in itself etymologically Welsh, whilst the Construction and idiom is nothing but rank Hottentotic.' NLW 13221E, pp. 139–42, Iolo Morganwg to William Owen Pughe, 6 February 1806; NLW 21286E, Letter no. 992, Iolo Morganwg to David Davis, 3 January 1823.
112 NLW 13121B, p. 430; NLW 13128A, p. 502. He was particularly dismissive of the standard of Welsh used in *Seren Gomer* and *Y Greal*. NLW 13117E, p. 136; BL Add. 15029, ff. 143–5, Iolo Morganwg to Owain Myfyr, 1 March 1806.

or with ease cured'.[113] His animus against Pughe as well as his general prejudice against the regional dialects of north Wales coloured his language, but Iolo nonetheless correctly identified the threat which Pughe's orthographical innovations posed to the purity and integrity of the Welsh language. Pughe's quirks were based on his belief that every language was a combination of monosyllabic root-words derived from the primitive mother-language, which spawned inordinately long neologisms – such as *dibechddoeth* (unsinfully wise) or the virtually unpronounceable *gogoelgrevyddusedd* (some degree of superstition) – and imposed historically fanciful contortions on the orthography of the language.[114] Iolo's objections to Pughe's orthographical innovations were based on contemporary orthoepic theories of language: he dismissed them as being 'made on principles of the most grating and horrid cacophony'.[115] While many of Iolo's attacks on Pughe are entertaining, they also had a serious edge since they revealed a keen awareness of linguistic change, the dangers of which he planned to expose in a section entitled 'Analytical Dissertation on the Welsh Language' in 'The History of the Bards'.[116] But the harmful effect of Pughe's ideas on Welsh orthography were not fully recognized until a scientific approach to linguistic research was established by John Rhŷs and John Morris-Jones in the latter decades of the nineteenth century.[117]

Far from representing a savage, uncouth stage in the development of the Welsh nation, Iolo believed that bardism represented the height and purity of its civilization. In his eyes, the triad form was the druidic form par excellence and he forged a prodigious number of bardic triads to attest the 'Patriarchal Simplicity' of the society from which they emanated (see Document III). His essay on the 'Moelmutian Triads' contextualized them within bardism and a British society whose adherence to democratic and rational principles of government enabled them to live in liberty and happiness:

> The term Barbarism should by no means be applied to the Patriarchal simplicity which appears to have been the character of our ancestors, whose institutions were calculated to do justice to those who were subject to them, to act with humanity towards Aliens, and to patronize all the learning and arts that were known to them. After they had been ruined, and their fine institutions destroyed by their invaders, it is no wonder that they fell into a state of Barbarism out of which they have but very imperfectly emerged. Nor will they till a better order of

113 NLW 13088B, p. 83.

114 G. J. Williams, 'William Owen [-Pughe]' in idem, *Agweddau ar Hanes Dysg Gymraeg*, ed. Aneirin Lewis (Caerdydd, 1985), p. 245; *WOP*, pp. 70–99, chapter IV; Davies, *Adfeilion Babel*, pp. 267–94.

115 NLW 13121B, p. 424. See also BL Add. 15024, ff. 273–5, Iolo Morganwg to William Owen Pughe, 29 September 1798.

116 NLW 13121B, pp. 423–30.

117 Williams, 'William Owen[-Pughe]', pp. 232–3.

things takes place and prevails in the World. The objects of True Civilization is to patronize and enforce true morality, Rational Religion, truly beneficent Arts and Sciences and that Equality which Genuine and properly restrained Liberty demands, to distribute justice, to secure competency to every member of the Community, and to curb with an invincible Bridle the arrogancies and Tyrranies of Power, Rank, Title, and illgotten Wealth that at present enslave every part of the world, the whole race of mankind.[118]

The contemporary resonance of justice, humanity and the 'Tyrranies of Power, Rank, Title' in this neat summary of Welsh civility were thinly disguised and constituted a harsh indictment of the guiding principles of William Pitt's government. It also highlighted two themes enshrined in bardism which not only formed a counterpoint to the contemporary state of affairs but also militated against the general image of barbarous Wales: its 'Patriarchal simplicity' and 'true morality'.

Since the charge of atheism still carried associations of immorality and madness in the eighteenth century,[119] Iolo was careful to guard against charges of either atheism or religious heresy, and he duly mocked those who deemed the Bards 'Deists, Atheists, and some even deem them Turks, and I know not what, every thing that is bad'.[120] He insisted on the Christian, and specifically Protestant, orthodoxy of bardism. Echoing William Stukeley, he maintained that the Britons/Welsh and their bards ('the Christian Divines of the Ancient Britons') had held fast to the patriarchal religion: 'the primitive religious opinions of the Bards are purely Patriarchal'.[121] He defended the native purity of bardism by associating 'corruptions' (presumably of a pagan nature) with Saxon influence, but he also quickly asserted that these had been rectified following the introduction of Christianity proper to Britain, when 'Bardism, or, as it is called, Druidism (perfectly congenial to the Gospel Doctrines) was restored to its ancient purity'.[122] He provided conflicting

118 NLW 13088B, p. 76. See also ibid., p. 75: 'The principles of Government and legislation exhibited in Triad 64, by which the Nation and its Territories were united into one, tho subdivided into several independent states or subsovereignties, were admirable. What a noble Institution the *Rhaith Gwlad a Chywlad* was? What a Check upon Monarchy at the same time retaining all its advantages. It is certain that much may be urged in favour of Monarchy strongly and effectually bridled, Whilst unbridled or feebly restrained Monarchy is the superlative degree of Infernality.'

119 D. P. Walker, 'Ways of dealing with Atheists: A Background to Pamela's Refutation of Cecropia', *Bibliotheque D'Humanisme et Renaissance*, XVII (1955), 252–77; James Thrower, *A Short History of Western Atheism* (London, 1971), pp. 99–100; David Berman, *A History of Atheism in Britain: From Hobbes to Russell* (London, 1988), pp. 118, 121, 155, 163–5.

120 NLW 13097B, p. 99. See also ibid., p. 151; NLW 13089E, p. 453.

121 NLW 13097B, pp. 124, 128. The Bards functioned 'as Pagan Priests (as it seems they must be called, tho' they worship'd the true God, as much as Abraham did)'. Ibid., p. 128. See also ibid., p. 252.

122 NLW 13097B, p. 124. The druidism typical of Taliesin's age and Christianity were described as 'so congenial in their main doctrines', ibid., p. 116.

accounts of the introduction of Christianity into Wales, ranging from a Roman source to a spurious, but nonetheless original, story regarding St Paul's Christian legacy to the Britons.[123] Implicit in this confusion was the thoroughly Protestant religious identity of the Ancient Britons and modern Welsh, a feature more fully developed in bardism's virulent anti-Catholic component.

Anti-Catholicism was admittedly rife in the late eighteenth century, especially following the Gordon Riots of 1780, but bardism's animus against Rome was also an artistic necessity. Iolo identified the 'Celtic Druids' with a small, select number of tribes – the Jews, the Persian Guebres, the Indian Brahmins, 'and a few others' – who had escaped from the descent into barbarism which accompanied the destruction of the Tower of Babel and which had retained 'ancient morality, justice and happiness' of the patriarchal religion.[124] In Iolo's eyes, these tribes had been oppressed by the nations of the 'Grand Apostacy', that is Roman Catholicism.[125] Since Wales's Roman Catholic past and the vast corpus of medieval literature which sustained its ideology proved problematic to this hypothetical identification with the pure patriarchal religion, much of Iolo's anti-Catholicism stemmed from his need to maintain the Protestant orthodoxy of his vision:

> It is worthy of remark, that thro' the long and dark ages of Popish Superstition, the Bards in general, retained the Christian religion, (which is only a brighter manifestation of ancient Bardism, or Patriarchal Religion) in its original purity and simplicity, violently opposing the depravity and absurdity of the Popish Doctrines.[126]

Writing Roman Catholicism out of his bardic narrative proved so challenging that it entailed flights of fancy which further complicated an already abstruse system. In order to maintain the patriarchal, Protestant religious integrity of both the Ancient Britons and their descendants, Iolo invented an alternative institution of bards, 'Beirdd Beli' (the Bards of Beli), who had been established by Beli Mawr (Beli the Great), a prince from north Wales,

123 NLW 13121B, p. 425; NLW 13087E, p. 205.

124 NLW 13088B, p. 76. They retained 'pure notions of Religion and morality, correct maxims of Justice and Benevolence, Rational principles of Government, and a proper sense of the great importance of Peace and reciprocal good will amongst mankind', ibid., pp. 76–7. These notions were supposed, rather than asserted, in NLW 13159A, p. 149.

125 NLW 13088B, p. 77. See also Document IV.

126 NLW 13097B, p. 125. See also ibid., p. 246: the bards retained their priestly function following the introduction of Christianity into Britain, 'and were not deprived of it till the Pope to whom they were never friendly, imposed his Clergy on Britain'. Various drafts of 'A Short Account' also claimed that the priestly function of the bards was usurped by the Roman Catholic clergy. NLW 13097B, pp. 100, 247.

to whom he attributed the introduction of Roman Catholicism into Welsh poetry.[127] Beli, so Iolo claimed, had initially persecuted St Germanus, but had ultimately been converted by him from 'the plain simple Christianity' of bardism to a form of Christianity 'much corrupted of pompous Episcopacy'.[128] That 'Beirdd Beli' were an afterthought rather than an integral part of the bardic vision from its inception is revealed by the fact that they are never satisfactorily explained; Iolo never named any individuals, and failed to work this theme into the bardic narrative.[129] Indeed, from *c.*1806 onwards, 'Beirdd Beli', who might have added a controversial religious dimension to Iolo's main theme of southern suavity and northern barbarity, had seemingly been forgotten.

Roman Catholicism was also an expedient for explaining the diminished status of bardism and the straitened circumstances of the Welsh nation because, according to Iolo's chronology, the medieval (Roman Catholic) era of Welsh literature corresponded roughly to the era in which Wales and bardism were barbarized: 'Superstition' was the first item listed under the heading 'Gothick or middle ages' in his outline of the 'Characteristics of ancient Welsh Literature in its several ages or periods'.[130] This decline into barbarism, he asserted, was through no fault of the Welsh. Harassed by savage nations, it was their pacifism which had led to their downfall: 'They were not sufficiently ferocious or infernalized to make an effectual stand against the incursions of Brutish Lords that surrounded them, the Caisariaid (Romans), Gwyddyl (Irish), Ffichty (Picts), Saeson (English), Eingl (Angles) &c.'[131] But if the destruction of bardism by invading forces had caused the decline in Welsh civility, the restitution of this system held the key to their rehabilitation as a civilized nation:

> after they had been ruined, and their fine institutions destroyed by their invaders, it is no wonder that they fell into a state of Barbarism out of which they have but

[127] NLW 13091E, p. 299, offers a variant on the name Beli Mawr: Benlli Gawr (Benlli the Giant). Beli was in fact a mythological character whom Iolo had plucked from Nennius' *Historia Brittonum*, or Geoffrey of Monmouth's *Historia Regum Britanniae*, or from medieval prose-tales. See Peter C. Bartrum, *A Welsh Classical Dictionary: People in History and Legend up to about A.D. 1000* (Aberystwyth, 1993), pp. 38–9.

[128] NLW 13091E, p. 299. For 'Beirdd Beli', see also NLW 21401E, no.14; NLW 13089E, p. 439; NLW 13097B, pp. 149–51; NLW 13100B, p. 277; NLW 13101B, pp. 159–60; NLW 13141A, pp. 121, 123.

[129] An early draft contained a tentative outline of the story which was later conveyed as fact: 'perhaps that Beirdd Beli were no more than those who were regulated by a new Institution founded by some Beli who was probably a Prince, about the time the Bards ceased to be the Ministers of Religion, but were retained in a character, and official avocations something different from the ancients'. NLW 13097B, p. 151.

[130] NLW 13131A, p. 508.

[131] NLW 13088B, p. 75.

imperfectly emerged. Nor will they till a better order of things takes place and prevails in the world.[132]

This 'better order of things', however, was tantalizingly ambiguous, and may be interpreted either as the restoration of bardism and the 'True Civilization' it represented or a radical revolution of the false civilization of his day.

Welsh historians have emphasized the key role played by Christianity in the formation of a sense of Welsh identity since the Romano-British period,[133] and this trend was revitalized with the beginnings of print culture in post-Reformation Wales when it adopted a distinctly Protestant character.[134] The complex interrelationship between language, religion and nation was summed up in a stanza from the canon of poetry attributed to the sixth-century poet Taliesin, a figure who plays a cameo role in bardism's formation, and which Iolo planned to quote on the title-page of 'The History of the Bards':

> Eu Nêr a folant, Eu hiaith a gadwant,
> Eu tir a gollant ond Gwyllt Walia.[135]
>
> (They will praise their God,/They will keep their language,/
> They will lose their land except Wild Wales).

In terms of expressing a sense of Welsh identity, this evocative stanza already had a distinguished pedigree before Iolo adopted it: John Walters had used it for the same purpose in his *Dissertation on the Welsh Language* (1771) and, before him, John Davies of Mallwyd had cited it in his preface to *Antiquae Linguae Britannicae . . . Rudimenta* (1621). Thus, while the strong Protestant flavour which Iolo had imprinted on bardism appears to have been consonant with Linda Colley's thesis of an overarching British identity unified by a shared Protestant faith, he did not publicize Wales's Protestant credentials in order to strengthen its loyalist position within the British state. Rather, it provided yet another example of Iolo's determination to defend the precocious flowering of civilization in Wales.

Finally, we turn to the theme of the innate morality of the Welsh. This emerged in bardism's insistence on both individual and collective moral integrity. On an individual level, Iolo echoed the insistence of medieval

132 Ibid., p. 76.

133 See, for instance, John Davies, *The History of Wales* (new edn., London, 1994), p. 72.

134 Williams, *Religion, Language and Nationality in Wales*, p. 135; Geraint H. Jenkins, *Literature, Religion and Society in Wales, 1660–1730* (Cardiff, 1978), *passim*; E. Wyn James, '"The New Birth of a People": Welsh Language and Identity and the Welsh Methodists, *c.*1740–1820' in Robert Pope (ed.), *Religion and National Identity: Wales and Scotland c.1700–2000* (Cardiff, 2001), pp. 14–42.

135 NLW 13091E, p. 326; NLW 13093E, p. 189.

bardic grammars that 'unimpeachable morals' were the principal requisite for admission into the class of 'Awenyddion' (bardic disciples), for the bard was to be 'above all things, a good man'.[136] A bard's wisdom and veracity were taken for granted, and although Iolo did not articulate this explicitly we may infer a gentle reproach towards Freemasonry in his assertion that, for this very reason, bards were not required to take oaths: 'it was a peculiar privilege of a Bard that, "Gair ei air ef ar bawb", his word was admitted before that of any other man whatever'.[137] In more general terms, bardism worked on the premise that all knowledge was useless and that happiness was unattainable without 'genuine morality': 'the wisdom derived from pure morality was the grand and ultimate object of ancient British Bards and Bardism'.[138] He considered 'the bardic morality' to be 'the glory of our ancient Literature'.[139] If Iolo is to be believed, moral rectitude was a national trait that was enshrined in bardism and was encapsulated in its philosophy, and the moral cast of all songs and verses associated with bardism meant that Welsh peasants were morally superior to those of other countries:

> Language and manners are improved and amusement far more innocent as well as elegant is obtained, greatly superior to the ruder diversions of the peasants in most other countries.
>
> The English have never have any such custome, and for the want of it, they to this very day have cause of lamentation.[140]

England's perceived inadequacy in this respect provided potential for comparison. Since Iolo argued that bardism and its ideology constituted the ideal civilization, any society or nation which was not party to this civilizing ideology was by definition uncivilized. The best-argued example of this thesis is found in an essay which showed how the irascible Iolo could be prompted by specific events or arguments as much as by general attitudes (see Document XIII). Benjamin Malkin's *The Scenery, Antiquities, and Biography of South Wales* (1804), in which Iolo made a fleeting appearance,[141] was

136 NLW 13097B, p. 126; NLW 13089E, p. 436. This prerequisite of bardic apprenticeship appears in every draft version of 'A Short Account of the British Bards'. The traditional poetic grammars, 'Gramadegau'r Penceirddiaid', dictated that the professional poet should be faithful, generous, chaste, full of spiritual love, moderate in the consumption of food and drink, geniality and godliness to avoid the seven deadly sins which corrupted the poetic Muse. G. J. Williams and E. J. Jones, *Gramadegau'r Penceirddiaid* (Caerdydd, 1934), p. 35. I am grateful to Barry J. Lewis for this information.

137 NLW 13097B, p. 249. For bardic secrecy, see also NLW 13121B, p. 439; NLW 13138A, pp. 201–2. NLW 13100B, p. 182, mocked the secrecy associated with Masonic meetings.

138 NLW 13089E, p. 287.

139 NLW 13221E, p. 123, Iolo Morganwg to William Owen Pughe, 14 February 1805.

140 NLW 13089E, p. 324.

141 Benjamin H. Malkin, *The Scenery, Antiquities, and Biography of South Wales* (London, 1804), pp. 126–30.

serialized in the *Monthly Review* in 1805. The abridger sandwiched the following remark between an extensive quote about the scenery of Cardiganshire and a description of the Hafod estate:

> Mr M. states that this part of South Wales [Cardiganshire] to be the strong hold of the antient British language. He enters into an interesting disquisition on the advantages and disadvantages of its retention: but, if knowledge and civilization be beneficial, there can be no doubt that its disuse is to be desired.[142]

Even a passing remark of this kind could cause offence and trigger a passionate response, but Iolo's riposte, a strident essay 'On the Welsh Literature', for all its specificity, summarized the arguments at the heart of bardism because the definition of civilization – or, more tellingly, 'true civilization' – which he proposed followed strict bardic precepts:

> True Civilization then signifies Such a System of things, of really usefully learning arts, sciences, &c that are of real utility and comforts to Mankind, and supply his real wants; above all such a System of Morals, and whatever the advocates of the above system may think of me, I will say Religion, as may be effectual [to] subdue the malignant and foolish passions and propensities of human Nature.[143]

Proceeding from this definition of 'True Civilization' Iolo argued that literature alone could not (and did not) actually constitute civilization; it was merely a civilizing tool empowered either to promote or destroy civilization. Echoing ideas that either he or, less probably, William Owen Pughe had promulgated in *The Myvyrian Archaiology of Wales*,[144] Iolo argued that, in its latter function, literature had become the 'Herald of Immorality, the Champion of infidelity' and was no better than 'the scalping knife of the Savage, the dagger of the Assassin'.[145] Furthermore, since Welsh literature could not offer authors either wealth or power, it was immune to the 'knaves of fortune, of the fools of fashion' who bedevilled the English literary scene:

> And it is for this very reason that it is so effectual in improving the minds and morals [of] those to whom it dictates, softening their manners, and superinducing

142 *Monthly Review*, XLVII (1805), 45.
143 NLW 13121B, p. 471.
144 *MAW*, I, pp. xiv–xv.
145 NLW 13121B, p. 472. This was an argument which Iolo had rehearsed briefly in a response to Mallet's characterization of barbarous Celts and civilized Scandinavians: The Ancient Britons conveyed the 'arts of peace' through poetry, and used it to inculcate principles of religion and morality. In contrast, the ancient Scandinavians had used poetry 'To perpetuate, as far as inflaming the worst passions and propensities of the human heart . . . it does not appear to have been applied to any purpose whatever of ameliorating the character or condition of man, but rather to infernalize him.' NLW 13098B, p. 101.

> a suavity and rectitude of disposition and conduct that must be obvious to every eye but that of prejudice. It has nothing in view but pure mental improvement, has it not in its power to be ostentatious and arrogant, has no means of so exalting itself over the head of humble poverty, has nothing to trample upon. It is acquired from no other motive than that of becoming better acquainted with the most important Truths, for no purposes but those of morality unsophisticated virtue, and that of all others the most fundamental principle of true civilization, Religion. In addition to those most important objects, it has attained to the means [of] acquiring the knowledge of many of the most truly important arts of life, and thus of being useful to man in enabling him to supply his natural wants without creating artificial wants.[146]

By applying bardism's moral centre to the apparatus of literary production, Iolo ensured that Welsh literature held the moral high ground, in stark contrast to English literature.

Received learning on civilization, exemplified in the ideas of Hugh Blair, John Pinkerton and Adam Smith, considered the course of history as linear and uniform, moving forward stage by stage: from hunter-gathering to pastoralism and agriculture, and finally culminating in commerce.[147] Iolo rejected this in favour of the primitivist model, preferring to interpret the commercialism of the English literary scene as a sign not of English advancement but of English barbarism, and in effusive prose that barely pauses to draw breath, he enumerated its defects:

> English Literature has hardly any thing in view but improvement of fortune, the sordid acquisition of wealth, not the attainment of virtue and pure morality. Its objects are those of avarice, ambition, power, the means not of instructing those who are destitute of knowledge, but of trampling upon them, and of more effectually holding them in that state of degradation, slavery and mental blindness that best suits its own superciliousness, arrogance, and self-conceit, that best answers the purposes and gratifies the wishes of avarice and Pride, calling to its aid the numerous Artifices of Pedantry, self-interest and vain glory, things of all others the most abhorrent of Genuine Civilization, and stifle it in every thing but outward and fallacious appearances, render it a whitened sepulchre, fair without, but all filthy corruption within. It wishes to hold all in the thraldom of ignorance, and consequently, in every other species of slavery, but those of a class that has been created by itself, never by nature or the God of Nature.[148]

146 NLW 13121B, pp. 472–3.

147 Rubel, *Savage and Barbarian*, p. 42; Stafford, *The Sublime Savage*, p. 158.

148 NLW 13121B, p. 473. NLW 13123B, p. 73 includes scathing comments on the process of industrialization: 'and if we step into the shops of many London artists – or visit the manufactories of Birmingham, Manchester &c we shall find in those places the greatest degree of barbarity of manners that can be conceived'. For Iolo's contradictory views on urbanization and industrialization, see Geraint H. Jenkins, 'The Urban Experiences of Iolo Morganwg', *WHR*, 22, no. 3 (2005), 463–8.

In the views expressed here we glimpse a nexus between bardism's personal and national bardic circles: the criticisms of the mercenary and immoral English marketplace and its superficial air were informed as much by contemporary abhorrence – held, for example, by the satirist Bernard Mandeville and the moral philosopher Richard Price – of the false refinements of civil society as the perils of luxury exemplified by Iolo's own bitter experience of guiding *Poems, Lyric and Pastoral* (1794) through the press.[149]

Pursuing his theme of bardism's moral legacy for contemporary Welsh culture, Iolo cited the strong moral content of Welsh-language books printed in Wales, though he conveniently omitted any reference to the large corpus of licentious literature, mostly ballads, which was an integral part of the eighteenth-century literary landscape:

> It has no loose immoral books, of any kind, none that fewel the unruly passions, none that inculcate the pernicious doctrines of infidelity, none that lead the understanding into those labyrinths of scepticism that lead never to return the public mind into the depths of immorality.[150]

Although this statement was not necessarily true, it was in keeping with bardism's pedagogical dimension which he cited as further evidence of its self-civilizing nature. Because it lacked ancient bardic origins, English literature could not do 'real good, of instructing the ignorant, of improving the heart and enlightening the mind'.[151] Furthermore, in a spurious bardic document, 'Llafar Gorsedd Beirdd Ynys Prydain' (The Voice Conventional of the Gorsedd of the Bards of the Island of Britain), which purported to be one of the primary sources for Iolo's writings on the bards, he described the role of the bard as a 'bridge' (*pont*) which offered guidance and education to the lower classes.[152] Elsewhere, in a draft version of 'A Short review of the present state of Welsh MSS', included in *The Myvyrian Archaiology of Wales*, he expressed a democratic animus in his praise of the 'humbler classes' for not perverting Welsh literature while it remained in their hands.[153] However, this was less a testimony to the ability of the lower classes than to the inherent civilizing power of Welsh literature and the Welsh language:

[149] Whitney, *Primitivism and the Idea of Progress*, pp. 44, 46–51; Constantine, '"This Wildernessed Business of Publication"' in *Rattleskull Genius*, pp. 123–46; Phillips, 'Forgery and Patronage: Iolo Morganwg and Owain Myfyr' in ibid., pp. 403–24.

[150] NLW 13121B, p. 474.

[151] Ibid., p. 473.

[152] NLW 13097B, p. 29. 'Llafar Gorsedd Beirdd Ynys Prydain' was allegedly a document copied by Llewelyn Siôn from Meurig Dafydd's manuscript, once housed in the library of Raglan castle: NLW 13097B, p. 7.

[153] NLW 13112B, p. 17.

> Wales will never become truly civilized but by the Literature of its own language, English learning may make us Coxcombs, knaves, and fools, but so many temptations in its hands held out to seduce us, will never in any valuable degree truly civilize us. It may make us richer, prouder, and what is the acme of its attainments atheistically philosophical, and thus uncivilize us. But our own native Literature has no other tendency than to make us wise and better . . . There can be no doubt but that the preservation and retention of the Welsh Language will be [the] greatest blessing of all others to Wales. In this Language and in no other can civilization and truly useful, free from baleful knowledge be advanced and sustained amongst the Welsh. Compare the Lower classes in England with those of the same order in Wales, and let impartiality decide. I will venture to say that the first are mere savages compared to the last.[154]

The language of primitivism was thus used to startling effect to validate the age-old native culture.

In conclusion, bardism, as well as the civilizing druidic past and the living inheritance it sustained, was designed to reconfigure the Anglocentric notion of 'barbarous Wales, civilized England'. To this end, Iolo directed his message to an English-speaking audience: he wrote the greater part of his writings on bardism, both published and unpublished, in English; and in the first Gorsedd held in 1792 he justified the use of English as his medium in order to maximize interest in his ideas and their dissemination.[155] Bardism was a *bricolage* of remarkable ingenuity: its all-encompassing scope left scarcely a chink in the armour of the Welsh nation against prevailing contemporary prejudices. It was also breathtaking in its audacity: Iolo's defence of the language, literature, culture and national character of Wales was a wholly self-conscious enterprise, both in the way that he served as its mouthpiece and in the way that his own personal bugbears were frequently brought into play. But was it the confident, buoyant response that Prys Morgan has described?[156] And how truly challenging was his use of primitivist structures and vocabulary in negotiating the minefield of 'British' identity at the end of the eighteenth century?

Iolo's claims of Welsh superiority and cultivation in terms of linguistic and literary antiquity, precocious knowledge of letters, literacy and home-grown civilization were clearly remarkable for their passionate sense of assurance. Bardism represented a romantic inversion of the pernicious image

154 Ibid., pp. 473–5.

155 *Morning Chronicle*, 26 September 1792; *HGB*, pp. 28–9.

156 Morgan, 'Wild Wales', p. 265: 'Iolo Morganwg's was a confident view of the superiority of Welsh culture at the time of Romanticism, when English sympathy for things Welsh rose to a high point.'

of 'barbarous Wales' which prevailed in both high and low culture. The language of civilization and barbarism in Iolo's day was notoriously slippery. The theory of progress viewed the people, language and literature of the Celtic peripheries as savage and uncouth, but in primitivist terms, Irish and Welsh antiquaries could appropriate the lexicon of cultural superiority and turn it against the English centre, thereby transforming the early stages in a nation's cultural development into a Golden Age, 'a touchstone of grandeur and heroism'.[157] In this Iolo, like Irish antiquaries, was placed in a difficult position, for in order to challenge and break existing prejudices he had, to a certain degree, to collude with them: if the past was a Golden Age, then the present was indeed a pale, degenerate reflection of it. A similar dilemma was posed by Britishness, which casts doubt on Linda Colley's assertion that Iolo was 'binational just as he was bilingual'.[158] The union of England and Wales with Scotland in 1707 was hardly equitable, and while bardism voiced resistance to this unequal partnership by upholding the uniqueness of the Welsh – the original 'Britons' – Iolo also desperately sought affirmation of a place for Wales within Great Britain. An earlier generation of Welsh antiquaries had exhibited similar ambivalence, but Iolo's adherence to the terms 'Britons' and 'Ancient Britons' was less of a compromise than the hyphenated identity 'Cambro-Briton' favoured by the luminaries of the Cymmrodorion Society, whose Welsh patriotism was coloured by their Whig politics and loyalty to the Hanoverian throne. But Iolo's scathing attacks on England, English literary circles and various individuals reflect an obsessive, paranoid mind rather than a wholly confident protagonist. His indignation sometimes bordered on blind rage. Unlike the more measured defences of other Welsh and Irish antiquaries, Iolo was a stranger to scholarly footnotes and citation, and he often resorted to defamation instead.

Iolo's frequent use of England and the English as a cultural and moral point of reference demonstrates that his was a reactionary and defensive mechanism. Although the primitivist framework was not employed to the same devastating effect as his strategy for pitting north Wales against south Wales, a sense of one-upmanship remains in the petty sideswipes and lengthy diatribes aimed at England. Primitivism provided bardism with a ready-made framework which was also flexible enough to sustain the increasingly ego-centric tenor of Iolo's vision as it evolved in the early nineteenth century. It was also rigorous enough to accommodate a shift in emphasis from the national to the regional when, from around 1806, he used the oppositional language of primitivism to construct an internal hierarchy within bardism: that of 'civilized' south Wales and 'barbarous' north Wales.[159] In a wonder-

157 Anthony D. Smith, *Myths and Memories of the Nation* (Oxford, 1999), p. 65.
158 Colley, *Britons*, p. 373.
159 Charnell-White, *Barbarism and Bardism*, *passim*.

ful example of the rambling, stream-of-consciousness style of his dotage, Iolo maintained that, as long as the Welsh language existed, it would articulate all the past glories of the Welsh nation and, in a nod to the next chapter on the tension between national and regional identity, he insisted that the bards of Glamorgan would 'maintain the memory of it all':

> [Yr] Iaith Gymraeg, yn ei llawn dyfiant cyn Amser Inachus, yn cofio Llong Nefydd Naf Neifion. yn cofio'r Greadigaeth, yn cofio ei hun yng Ngwlad yr Haf Deffrobani (Deffrofanau). yn cofio ei hun yn y lle y mae Constantinoblis yn Awr, yn cofio ei phlant yn Llychlyn amser Urb ab Erin. [Yr iaith Gymraeg] wedi Gweled ymerodraethau Cynteifion a mwyaf er hynny hyd yr Awr hon a fu yn y Byd: Brenhiniaeth Newmrwth Gawr, – y groegiaid, Rhufeiniaid, Rhufain Babaidd, Siarly Maen, Y Sawdeniaid, Diwygiad – wedi cadw gafael Cadarn ar y ffydd yng Nghrist a gafodd ag a garodd er amser Pawl, Ilid a Bran Fendigaid. – yn cofio ei hen wyddoniaid Beirdd Derwyddon – Prydain, Dyfnwal, Tydain, Alawn, Gwron, Plennydd ap Hu Lawnwaith, a Hu Gadarn gydag aradr a Chan a Choelbren i Ynys Prydain. Gwelodd awr Geni mawredd mwyaf a fu erioed, hyd yn awr gwelodd awr angau miloedd ond y hi ei hunan er hynny yn fyw fyth, ag yn ei blodau, heb un crychyn henaint ar ei thalcen heb un blewyn gwynn ar ei phen, yn ymiachau o'i holl ddoluriau, yn canu mor loyw ei llafar ag erioed. – Dinas Cedyrn tyrrau beilchion. Muriau ar ymgais cyrchu uchelderau'r Nef, wedi malurio yn un a llwch y llawr. Cestyll Gorthrymder gydag eu perchenogion, dim ond rhyw ychydig ou hesgyrn megis yn ymddangos. Beirdd Morganwg yn cynnal cof am y cwbl. Bydd fyw i weled y Byd yn bwrw ymaith ei holl Swrwd ai fudreddi, ag i dderchafu Can Gorfoledd . . . a hithau yn un o'r Anfarwolion!!! Poed felly y bo.[160]
>
> ([The] Welsh Language, in full growth since before the time of Inachus, remembering the Ship of Nefydd Naf Neifion, remembering the Creation, remembering herself in the Summer Country of Deffrobani . . . remembering herself in the place where Constantinople is now, remembering her children in Scandinavia in the time of Urb son of Erin. [The Welsh language] has seen the first and largest empires in the world since then until now: the Kingship of Nemrwth Gawr, the Greeks, the Romans, Popish Rome, Charlemagne, the Sultans, the Reformation – has kept a firm grip on the Christian religion which she had and loved since the time of Paul, Ilid and Bran the Blessed. – remembering her old wise men, Bards Druids – Prydain, Dyfnwal, Tydain, Alawn Gwron, Plennydd son of Hu Lawnwaith, and Hu Gadarn with a plough, a song and Coelbren coming to the Island of Britain. She saw the birth of the greatest glory that ever was, until now she saw the death of thousands, but she herself, nonetheless, still living, in her flowers, without a single wrinkle of old age on her brow or a white hair on her head, recovering from all her wounds, singing as brightly as ever. – City of the Mighty proud towers. Walls built to attempt to reach the heights of Heaven, ruined as dust. Castles of Oppression and their owners, only some of whose bones are

160 NLW 13120B, p. 393.

> visible. The Bards of Glamorgan maintain the memory of it all. She [the Welsh language] will live to see the World throw away all its Dross and filth, and uphold the Song of Joy . . . and she will be one of the Immortals!!! May it be so.)

The past, present and future were interconnected: the past glory of Wales not only coloured the way in which its present should be perceived but also offered a paradigm for the way in which its future could be realized. Iolo depicted not a barbarous Welsh nation, but a bardic one which encapsulated 'True Civilization'.

4

Internal Conflict: The Primacy of Glamorgan and Regional Identity in Bardism

Primitivism was also a convenient and malleable means of expressing regional as well as national loyalty. Implicit in Iolo's bardic narrative was the notion that Wales as a whole owed a debt of gratitude to Glamorgan for preserving bardism, the vehicle of its rehabilitation. As well as providing a framework for Iolo's patriotic ardour, primitivism accommodated bardism's internal hierarchy which elevated 'civilized' south Wales over 'barbarous' north Wales, or, more precisely, 'civilized' Glamorgan over 'barbarous' Gwynedd. However, this antagonism between north and south, Gwynedd and Glamorgan, represents just one discursive strand in Iolo's vision of Glamorgan and its primacy, not least because it developed in middle age and provided an aggressive counterpoint to the joyful Glamorgan of Iolo's more youthful imagination. This chapter thus examines the roots of Iolo's regionalism and its changing dynamics throughout his lifetime, from the romantic vision of the Glamorgan of his youth to its later transformation into an unrelenting clash between 'civilized' Glamorgan and 'barbarous' Gwynedd.

In terms of geography, Iolo's Glamorgan matched not the contemporary county boundaries but, rather, its pre-Norman boundaries, which extended from the river Tawe to the river Wye, and included the hundreds of Erging, Ewias and Ystrad Yw in Herefordshire, which had previously been part of Gwent.[1] While these nostalgic boundaries hint at the romantic disposition of Iolo's vision of Glamorgan's past, they also served the antiquarian dimension of his bardic vision well. In his notes on the antiquity of bardism, he observed that these parameters formed the original kingdom of Esyllwg, known to the Romans as Siluria,[2] a kingdom which comprised Glamorgan, Gwent, Brecknockshire, Maelienydd, Radnorshire, and the land between the rivers Wye and Severn:

> That this district was anciently called Essyllwg (Siluria) is evident from what we find in the Roman writers as well as in our own MSS. Caractacus is said to have been Prince of the Silurians but that it was at that period also called Gwent is also

1 *TLlM*, p. xv. See also Ceri W. Lewis, 'The Literary Tradition of Morgannwg down to the Middle of the Sixteenth Century' in T. B. Pugh (ed.), *GCH III* (Cardiff, 1971), p. 452.

2 NLW 13141A, p. 30.

as evident, the Venta Silurium wherein both these names are united . . . Gwent and Essyllwg being nearly synonymous and both equally common in the time when this Island was first discovered by the Romans.[3]

Glamorgan's existence as a pre-Roman entity lent some legitimacy to bardism's alleged antiquity, and this allowed Iolo to refer to the wide and historically recognized domain of bardism's epicentre, the bardic 'Cadair Morganwg, Ewias, Erging ac Ystrad Yw'.

Glamorgan, 'the Garden of Wales',[4] was the main subject of much of Iolo's poetic juvenilia and verses which he attributed to poets who peopled Glamorgan's imagined past. He wrote in a wide range of genres: love poetry, nature poetry, occasional verses, ballads in strict- and free-metre, and also the *triban* and *cwndid* forms traditionally associated with Glamorgan.[5] Many were the product of *hiraeth* (longing) for his home county while working at his trade as a stonemason in the West Country, Kent and London in the 1770s:

O'r holl wledydd is y nen,
A goris heulwen olwg,
Gorau gwlad a gaf yn wir
Yw gwiraidd dir Morgannwg.
. . .
Bûm yn hir yn Llundain gawr
Lle gwelais mawr drythyllwg,
Pechod, ffoledd, ffug a brad,
Nid fal yng ngwlad Morgannwg.[6]

(Of all the countries under the heaven,/and under the sun's purview,/I find that the best country indeed/is truly the land of Glamorgan.
. . .
I was long in London grey/where I saw much lust,/sin, foolishness, falseness and treachery,/not like in the county of Glamorgan.)

He praised the natives for their unsurpassed morals and goodness, and in poems such as 'Bedwen Cefnpennar' (The Maypole of Cefnpennar) and 'Cân y Porfelwr' (The Pasturalist's Song) we catch a glimpse of contemporary

[3] NLW 13121B, pp. 375–8.

[4] In an untitled poem, he wrote as follows: 'Gardd Cymru'n dra chymwys y'i gelwir, fro gulwys,/Gwlad irlwys, paradwys tir Prydain' (She, beautiful region, is appropriately called the garden of Wales;/lovely, fertile country, Britain's paradise). *CRhIM*, p. 2.

[5] Tegwyn Jones (ed.), *Tribannau Morgannwg* (Llandysul, 1976); Lemuel J. Hopkin-James (ed.), *Hen Gwndidau, Carolau a Chywyddau* (Bangor, 1910).

[6] *CRhIM*, pp. 28–9. *CRhIM* contains a selection of Welsh poems extolling Glamorgan's natural beauty, while *Poems, Lyric and Pastoral* (London, 1794), also includes many pastoral poems which refer to Glamorgan's scenery, such as 'Banks of the Daw' and 'Davona's Tale', Williams: *PLP*, I, pp. 40–4, 109–16.

folk-life.[7] But this vision of an Edenic Glamorgan, with its incomparable scenery, flora, and fauna, also reflects the longing for an ideal primitive simplicity which was a common feature of the pastoral genre which enjoyed renewed interest in the mid-eighteenth century,[8] and which bears comparison with the verses of Robert Burns, John Clare and William Shenstone.[9] Iolo also described with relish the unrivalled beauty of his county's landscape in travel journals, agricultural notebooks, and correspondence. He spent June 1796 touring south Wales on a fact-finding mission for a proposed report for the Board of Agriculture.[10] As the journey drew to a close, Iolo was greatly relieved to return to familiar territory, the village of Llangynwyd. This village was the epicentre of both the genuine and the bardic 'Tir Iarll' (Earl's Land), and he depicted the region both as a model of natural pastoral simplicity and as a willing participant in innovation:

> It was not till I came to Llangynwyd that I felt myself fairly returned to Glamorgan, with whose manner and habits, upon the whole, I am better pleased than with those of more than thirty Counties that I have seen, this may be partiality, even prejudice, but it is very natural and quite harmless. Philosophy does herself no credit by endeavouring to reason us out of those innocent prepossessions and dear sensibilities that are incidental to human nature.
> This County has made considerable progress in modern improvements, and at the same time retains in tolerable purity the ancient Welsh manners and simplicity, and the ancient proverb of
>
> Mwynder Morganwg
> i.e.
> The Suavity of Glamorgan.
>
> may still be retained with considerable propriety, every where, excepting a few of our Vale Towns, Cardiff, Cowbridge &c that, aping they know not what, have acquired much of the Monkey character, with a smack of the Fox, sly, cunning, and thievish, on a plan that keeps clear of the Law.[11]

'Mwynder Morgannwg' was a common topos in Iolo's writings, and it was reflected, so he argued, in the healthy climate, superior living conditions and

7 *CRhIM*, pp. 24–5, 73–6.

8 John Goodridge, *Rural Life in Eighteenth-Century English Poetry* (Cambridge, 1995), p. 3. For pastoral poetry in general, see Judith Haber, *Pastoral and the Poetics of Self-Contradiction: Theocritus to Marvell* (Cambridge, 1994); David Fairer, *English Poetry of the Eighteenth Century 1700–1789* (London, 2003), pp. 79–101.

9 Daniel Huws, *Caneuon Llafar Gwlad ac Iolo a'i Fath* (Cymdeithas Alawon Gwerin Cymru, 1993).

10 David Ceri Jones, 'The Board of Agriculture, Walter Davies ("Gwallter Mechain") and Cardiganshire, *c.*1794–1815', *Ceredigion*, XIV (2001), 79–100; idem, '"Mere Humbug": Iolo Morganwg and the Board of Agriculture, 1796–1815', *THSC*, 10 (2003), 76–97.

11 NLW 13115B, pp. 115–16.

habitations of the Vale,[12] which contributed towards the extraordinary longevity of the inhabitants: 'all this Country has a very salubrious air, and 100 years of age is not uncommon'.[13] Having seen the grave of Jane Jenkins at Llangynwyd, who reputedly lived to be 110, he mused:

> if he will content himself with wholesome Welsh mountain fare, drink often from the fine fountains that will serve him for a mirror, and hear often a Welsh Bard, and Welsh harp, he may stand a fair chance of living to the age of Jane Jenkin.[14]

This general wholesomeness even extended to the morality of Glamorgan people. Recounting a conversation with 'a sensible drover' regarding the relative virtues of their respective counties, Iolo referred to the alleged higher incidence of illegitimacy in Carmarthenshire with some satisfaction:

> I asked his opinion of the Carmarthenshire manners and morals, he said that he was pleased with their simplicity and hospitality; and in many things he prefer'd the morals of Carmarthen to those of Glamorgan: but he says (and he knows, seemingly, much of the Country) that female seduction prevails greatly there, as much nearly (for so he observed) as in England, half the women that mar[r]y, he says, are previously pregnant, – He observed that the Glamorgan neatness in houses, is not often seen in Carmarthenshire, and I had thought so myself, from what I had an opportunity of observing, nor have I seen it in any other part of the Kingdom, this is not partiality I am certain.[15]

But the defensive and greatly exaggerated account of Glamorgan's primacy revealed in Bardism was more than a natural affection or 'partiality' for his locality; it grew from his involvement with the antiquaries of his native county and the exiled Welshmen of the London-Welsh societies from the 1770s onwards. The 'Grammarians' (*Gramadegyddion*, men of the grammar books) were a group of poets who initiated a cultural revival in Glamorgan in the mid-eighteenth century through their poetry and through occasional eisteddfodau which they modelled on those held in north Wales in the early

12 Ibid., pp. 29–44. See also NLW 13091E, pp. 317–20; NLW 13114B, p. 69. He attributed the architectural sturdiness of Glamorgan cottages to the influence of local Norman castles and mansions. NLW 13150A.

13 NLW 13115B, p. 10. See also ibid., p. 114. Longevity was of interest to the *Gentleman's Magazine*. In NLW 13112B, 348–9, Iolo copied examples from the 1789 issues, and in 1791 and 1793 he contributed to the debate himself: *Gentleman's Magazine*, LXI, part 2 (1791), 1000; ibid., LXIII (1793), 106. For longevity, see NLW 13116E, p. 142; NLW 13120B, pp. 171–4 (a list of 'Ages of Literary and Studious Men'); NLW 21413E, no. 14; Williams, *PLP*, II, p. 157n.

14 NLW 13115B, p. 115.

15 Ibid., p. 113. See also NLW 13221E, pp. 87–90, Iolo Morganwg to William Owen Pughe, 25 October 1802.

part of the eighteenth century.[16] Based largely in the uplands of Glamorgan, members of the group later played both key and cameo roles in Iolo's version of bardism: they included John Bradford of Betws, Rhys Morgan of Pencraig-nedd, Edward Evan of Aberdare, Dafydd Nicolas of Aberpergwm, and Iolo's tutor in strict-metre poetry, Lewis Hopkin of Llandyfodwg.[17] The clergymen and lexicographers John Walters and Thomas Richards, residents of the Vale of Glamorgan, also played a vital role in the cultural revival in the region and in nurturing Iolo's poetic and antiquarian interests.[18] They maintained links with both the Grammarians and the London Welsh. Richards's dictionary was partly financed by the Cymmrodorion Society,[19] and Owain Myfyr ensured the publication of Walters's dictionary.[20] Like their north Wales and London-Welsh counterparts, the poets, lexicographers and antiquarians of Glamorgan depended on books published by Welsh humanists and contemporary revivalists in order to learn anew the poetic skills of the defunct medieval professional poetic guild.[21] In fact, they called themselves Grammarians in deference to the published poetic grammars which had enabled them to reclaim their poetic heritage: Siôn Dafydd Rhys's *Cambrobrytannicae Cymraecaeve Linguae Britannicae . . . Rudimenta* (1592), William Midleton's *Bardhoniaeth, neu brydydhiaeth* (1593) and, to a lesser degree, John Rhydderch's *Grammadeg Cymraeg* (1728). Iolo himself, despite his insistence in later years that the Grammarians were not 'book taught', acknowledged that Siôn Dafydd Rhys's grammar was the text most frequently studied by local poets.[22] In his autobiographical material Iolo also claimed that around 1763 he had received a copy of Siôn Rhydderch's grammar from William Robert, Yr Ydwal, a blind poet and sexton at Llancarfan.[23]

16 Williams: *IM*, chapter 1; *TLlM*, pp. 228–318; Brian Ll. James, 'The Welsh Language in the Vale of Glamorgan', *Morgannwg*, XVI (1972), 16–36; Morgan: *IM*, pp. 3–5; Lewis, 'The Literary History of Glamorgan from 1550 to 1770', pp. 608–29; Jones, '"Gydwladwr godi[d]og": Gohebiaeth Gymraeg Gynnar Iolo Morganwg', 140–71.

17 Other members of the *Gramadegyddion* included Dafydd Hopcyn of Coety, Dafydd Thomas of Pandy'r Ystrad and, perhaps, the poet who became a romantic figure in local folklore, Wil Hopcyn of Llangynwyd. Iolo composed an elegy to Lewis Hopkin, Edward Williams, *Dagrau yr Awen neu Farwnad Lewis Hopcin fardd, o Landyfodwg ym Morganwg* (Pont-y-fon, 1772).

18 Brian Ll. James, *Thomas Richards of Coychurch* (Coychurch, 1990); Richard M. Crowe, 'Thomas Richards a John Walters: Athrawon Geiriadurol Iolo Morganwg' in Hywel Teifi Edwards (ed.), *Llynfi, Afan, Garw ac Ogwr* (Llandysul, 1998), pp. 227–51.

19 Crowe, 'Thomas Richards a John Walters', p. 235.

20 Ibid., pp. 235, 242–6. Richards perused the manuscripts of John Bradford and other Grammarians while preparing his dictionary.

21 Lewis, 'The Literary History of Glamorgan from 1550 to 1770', p. 622.

22 Ibid., p. 611. In NLW 13154A, p. 438, Iolo claimed that he was fifteen when he saw Rhydderch's grammar for the first time and the work is listed in a catalogue of his books in London in 1794: NLW 13136A, p. 148.

23 *TLlM*, p. 265; G. J. Williams, 'William Robert o'r Ydwal', *LlC*, III, no. 1 (1954–5), 47.

The Grammarians established links with the London-Welsh society, and it was they who introduced Iolo to Welshmen in the metropolis. Iolo's long partnership with the London-Welsh had far-reaching repercussions for bardism because they not only stimulated his ardent sense of Welsh patriotism and provided outlets for its expression but also exerted an immeasurable influence on bardism's regional dimension. Moreover, their own activities demonstrate clearly that regionalism was a concept which could develop into nationalism.[24] The patriotic impulse of the eighteenth-century cultural revival was expressed in the bilingual constitution of the Cymmrodorion, published in 1751, in which they outlined specific aims for the cultivation of the Welsh language and research into its antiquities:

> There is implanted in the Nature of Mankind, a strong Attachment to that Country which gave them Birth, and a laudable Curiosity to acquaint themselves with the genuine History and Antiquities of the People from whom they are immediately descended . . . To this End, a considerable Number of Persons, Natives of the Principality of *Wales*, now residing in and about *London*, inspired with the love of their common Country, and consulting the honour of the *British* Name, propose to establish a general Monthly Society, distinguished by the Name and Title of *Cymmrodorion* (or *Aborigines*).[25]

However, the deeds and declarations of leading members of the society – Lewis Morris, his brothers Richard and William, and their protégé, Goronwy Owen – reveal an ambiguity between national and regional pride, for their correspondence displayed a blatant partiality for their native Anglesey. Anglesey was a potent topos in the poetry of Goronwy Owen. In a poem reminiscent of John Pomfret's 'The Choice', he set out his desire to live a measured, moderate life in Anglesey: 'Ym Môn araul, a man orau – yw hon,/Llawen ei dynion, a llawn doniau' ('In serene Anglesey, the best place – is this,/her men are merry, and full of talents').[26] An even clearer regionalist strain emerges in the correspondence of the Morris circle, but their bias in favour of the language and literature of Anglesey was neither as fully

24 M. A. Heslinga, *The Irish Border as a Cultural Divide: A Contribution to the Study of Regionalism in the British Isles* (Assen, 1962), p. 17: 'Nationalism is, generally speaking, activated, intensified and magnified regionalism. It can be distinguished from regionalism in so far that it implies a theoretical justification and a development of political demands.' See also Thomas Crawford, 'The View from the North: Region and Nation in *The Silver Darlings* and *A Scots Quair*' in R. P. Draper (ed.), *The Literature of Region and Nation* (London, 1989), p. 109. Regarding the shared characteristics of nationalist and regionalist discourse, see John Hutchinson and Anthony D. Smith (eds.), *Nationalism* (Oxford, 1994), p. 4.

25 *Gosodedigaethau Anrhydeddus Gymdeithas y Cymmrodorion* (Llundain, 1755), pp. 5, 13.

26 Goronwy Owen, 'Gofuned Goronwy Ddu o Fôn' (The Wish of Black Goronwy of Anglesey) in A. Cynfael Lake (ed.), *Blodeugerdd Barddas o Ganu Caeth y Ddeunawfed Ganrif* (Llandybïe, 1993), p. 88. See also his boasts regarding Anglesey's poetic tradition in 'Cywydd i'r Awen' (*Cywydd* to the Muse), ibid., p. 87; 'Cywydd yn Ateb y Bardd Coch o Fôn' (A *Cywydd* answering the Red Poet from Anglesey), ibid., p. 113.

developed or as fully systematized as Iolo's pro-Glamorgan bias. Iolo, however, might have argued that, through the activities of the Cymmrodorion and Gwyneddigion societies, bias towards the poetry and poets of north Wales had been thoroughly institutionalized. Having read the correspondence of the Morris brothers in the Welsh Charity School during the 1770s, and again in the early 1790s, he was familiar with their derogatory attitude towards south Wales and of the deep-rooted rivalry between the two regions. Writing to Owain Myfyr in 1805, he claimed that 'at present each entertains the strangest and most mistaken prejudices with respect to the other. The Deudneudwyr [northerners] and the Hwyntwyr [southerners] treat each other as aliens. Even Gronwy Owain . . . entertained those prejudices of Vulgar and ignorant minds'.[27] Iolo copied salient excerpts from these letters and added comments to his own transcriptions, sometimes responding to them with the directness more often seen in face-to-face interaction. One striking example of this tendency was his savage retort to Goronwy Owen's assertion that the dialect of Gwynedd was eminently superior to that of south Wales. Here, he deployed auxiliary verbs, a feature which he observed in the dialects of north Wales, to undermine northern hubris:

> [Goronwy Owen] Nid yw'r Hwyntwyr ond hanner Cymry, gan eu bod gan mwyaf yn hanfod o Stad pobyl Fflandrys a Normandi, a rhyfedd yw allu o naddynt gadw maint yn y byd o'u hen Iaith, ac o'r achos hwnnw yn bendifaddau mi fynnwn iddynt adael ymgeleddu'r Iaith i'r sawl a fedrant yn orau wneuthur hynny sef Pobl Wynedd, – na feiddient roi na llaw na throed yn y gwaith rhag ei ddiwyno a'u llediaith ffiaidd.
>
> (The Southerners are only half Welsh, because they hail, in the main, from the people of Flanders and Normandy, and it is surprising that they have kept their old language at all, and for that reason, verily, I wish they would leave the succouring of the [Welsh] language to those who can do it properly, namely the People of Gwynedd. – may they not dare to put hand or foot in the work lest they soil it with their vile patois.)
>
> [Iolo] Mwy ffiaidd yw llediaith y Deudneudwyr, pam yr arferaist lediaith yr Hwyntwyr, sef, a fedrant yn lle a wnant fedru fal y dylassai fod. Canys felly y mae'r Deudneudiaith yn gwneud deudyd. Da tithau gwna ddeudyd gwirionedd, a thithau ddeudneudiwr gwna fyned i Wlad yr Hwyntwyr lle y cei weled a chlywed beth yw ei hiaith a dos a Thaliesin a Gwalchmai a Chynddelw yn dy law yno, a thi a gei weled pa un ai Hwyntwr ai Deudneudiwr au deall hawsaf. Da dywaid Sippyn Cyfeiliog ynghylch 1350.
> Gnawd yngwyned focsedd eiriau
> Bocseddus oeddynt erioed y Deudneudwyr a bocseddus ydynt fyth.[28]

27 BL Add. 15027, ff. 79–80, Iolo Morganwg to Owain Myfyr, 21 September 1805.

28 NLW 13131A, pp. 412–13. Elsewhere, Iolo's attitude towards Goronwy Owen was more conciliatory and he blamed Lewis Morris for poisoning his disciple against the literature of south Wales: NLW 13112B, p. 368.

Fig. 5 Even though long buried, the poet and antiquary Lewis Morris (1701–65) was the target for much of Iolo's personal and professional jealousy. He also played a significant role in the development of Iolo's regional bias in favour of Glamorgan.

(The patois of the North Walians is viler. Why did you [Goronwy Owen] use the corrupt speech of the Southerners, namely, 'a fedrant' instead of 'a wnant fedru' as it should. Because that is how the language of North Wales says 'to say'. For goodness sake, tell the truth, and you, North Walian, go to the South where you will see and hear what their language is and take there [the poems of] Taliesin and Gwalchmai and Cynddelw in your hand, and you will see whether a South Walian or a North Walian understands them best. Well did Sypyn Cyfeiliog say around 1350.

Boastful words are customary in Gwynedd

The North Walians have always been boastful and they still remain boastful.)

Goronwy Owen reiterated this theme of the superiority of 'the People of Gwynedd' in his sarcastic comments about the attention which the 'poor plodding' lexicographer Thomas Richards had paid to the Silurian dialect in his dictionary: 'what has *Glam.* words to do with Welsh?', he asked. 'I had rather he had made use of any Gibberish, and authoriz'd it with a *Hottentoticê*'.[29] Indeed, responses to his dictionary bring the tension between regionalism and patriotism into sharp focus: as a corresponding member of the Cymmrodorion, Richards had received their assistance to publish his dictionary. Richard Morris described him to a rather uninterested Lewis as 'a poor Welshman, but eat up with zeal for ye language! Was last year [1760] initiated member of Cymrodorion: the most friendly man alive'.[30] The other brother William, ensconced in Anglesey, clearly revealed the extent of their intellectual jealousy and their inflated sense of their own importance:

> Wale, wale, fe fu dydd pan allai Wynedd ymffrostiaw oi 'scolheigion Cymroegaidd, a bâs a fai gan y Gwenhwysiaid glywed sôn fod neb un Ddeaudiryn yn rhyfygu dodi allan na geirlyfr, na gramadeg, na'r cyffelyb, ac yn awr pwy ond y Dr Richards a Gambold, a bagad o'r cyfryw sydd yn llenwi ein celloedd au llediaith?[31]

> (Woe, woe, there was a day when Gwynedd could boast of its Welsh scholars, and the Silurians had little hope of hearing that a single knave from the South dared to put out a dictionary, or a grammar, or anything similar, and now who but Dr Richards and Gambold, and a host of the same ilk, are filling our studies with their corrupt speech?)

Although Iolo was aware of this unpleasant aspect of their regionalism, it does not appear to have had an adverse effect on him at this early stage in his career. After all, he had been smitten by the conviviality of the London Welsh, among whom a patriotic zeal for Welsh letters and antiquarianism coexisted with ribald sociability and, for the time being at least, this overrode the undercurrent of regional bias which he encountered in their company and in the letters of their predecessors. At this stage, Iolo was still the apprentice, and his relationship with them was characterized by feelings of awe and admiration: they exchanged ideas and poetry, and Iolo even solicited their criticism of his own poetic works. Indeed, he thrived in an atmosphere of cultural vitality and soon gained confidence by participating in debates over strict-metre poetry, by upholding the Welsh-language rule, by contributing to their impressive publication programme, and even by

29 J. H. Davies (ed.), *The Letters of Goronwy Owen (1723–1769)* (Cardiff, 1924), p. 68.

30 J. H. Davies (ed.), *The Letters of Lewis, Richard, William and John Morris, of Anglesey, (Morrisiaid Môn) 1728–1765* (2 vols., Aberystwyth, 1909), II, p. 420.

31 Ibid., II, p. 460. See also Lewis Morris's disparaging remarks, ibid., p. 443.

changing his name to 'Iorwerth Morganwg'.[32] If anything, their regionalism exerted a positive influence on Iolo, stimulating him to complement their focus on Gwynedd with a healthy interest of his own in the literary fortunes of Glamorgan. This is made clear by his involvement with two early literary enterprises: 'Brodoliaeth Beirdd Morganwg' (The Fraternity of Glamorgan Poets) and the proposed publication of a quarterly magazine, 'Dywenydd Morganwg' (The Delight of Glamorgan). He mentioned these in a letter to Owain Myfyr in 1780 in which he described the Fraternity of Glamorgan Poets as a society which received every man 'proficient in the [Welsh] language', regardless of his poetic gifts.[33] Their rules and regulations, so Iolo claimed, were few and simple. They assembled in Llantrisant for an annual eisteddfod in order to reform and develop strict-metre poetry: 'we (for I am one of the meanest) intend to make some new regulations in our BARDDONIAETH [poetry], but with what success must be left to the determination of the Judicious when they are made public'.[34] The 'Measures of the Poets of Glamorgan' which he described were his Glamorgan Classification (*Dosbarth Morganwg*) in embryo. Iolo was undoubtedly inspired by earlier literary activity centred around Llantrisant. He had attended informal poetic meetings in the town in the late 1760s and early 1770s,[35] and he was a central figure in the Society of *Gwrth-Hengistiaid* (Anti-Hengistians), which had been established in 1771 to support Welsh poets and authors as well as to sustain the Welsh language.[36] However, the society described by Iolo in 1780 was more preoccupied with the external form and stylistics of poetry, particularly the reform of strict-metre poetry as proposed by Goronwy Owen.[37] The letter also referred to disputes which had arisen over the relative merits of strict- and free-metre verse that surrounded the awarding of a prize by the

32 Jones, '"Gydwladwr godi[d]og": Gohebiaeth Gymraeg Gynnar Iolo Morganwg', 156–9.

33 BL Add. 15024, ff. 188–9, Iolo Morganwg to Owain Myfyr, 10 July 1780: 'y mae Brodoliaeth Beirdd Morganwg yn derbyn attynt bob cywraint yn yr iaith, ai Bardd ai amgen, a gwych a fyddai ganthynt alw brawd ar y Myfyr, nid rhaid i un Brawd, os mynn, fod yn gyndrychol yn yr Eisteddfod flynyddawl, eithr ysgrifennu yno a wasanaetha'r un cystal, y mae'r ychydig iw dalu'n flynyddawl cyn lleied fal nas ceisier gan y neb na fo drigiannol yn ddigon agos i ddyfod ei hun i'r Eisteddfod.' (The Fraternity of Glamorgan Poets accept anyone proficient in the [Welsh] language, be he a Poet or not, and they would consider it excellent to call the Myfyr a brother. No brother, if he so wishes, must be present in the annual Eisteddfod, but it would suffice just as well to write to it. The little to be paid annually is so small that it is not requested from those who live close enough to come to the eisteddfod in person.)

34 Ibid.

35 See NLW 13141A, p. 93 (1767); NLW 13094E, p. 35 (1769); NLW 13134A, p. 199 (1770). Iolo had been invited by Siencin Morgan of Penrhiw-fer to the 1771–2 eisteddfodau at Llantrisant. Williams: *IM*, p. 371.

36 Williams: *IM*, p. 373. See also Siencin Morgan's suggestion that the young Iolo was one of their most valued members. NLW 21281E, Letter no. 282, Siencin Morgan to Iolo Morganwg, 30 November 1771.

37 BL Add. 15024, ff. 188–9, Iolo Morganwg to Owain Myfyr, 10 July 1780.

Cymmrodorion for an elegy to Richard Morris in 1780.[38] The adjudicators, Owain Myfyr and Robert Hughes (Robin Ddu), awarded the prize to Richard Jones of Trefdraeth, Anglesey, for a strict-metre *awdl*, but it was a decision which proved unpopular among Cymmrodorion members who had preferred the free-metre elegy submitted by John Edwards (Siôn Ceiriog).[39] Iolo invited Owain Myfyr, along with other London-Welsh associates (Robin Ddu, Siôn Ceiriog and, possibly, Richard Jones, Trefdraeth), to join the fraternity as a corresponding member for a small annual fee. Surviving members of the Grammarians, such as John Bradford, Edward Evan and William Davies, may also have been involved, and Iolo implied that Evan Evans was already a member.

G. J. Williams believed that this fraternity was an attempt to create a society in Glamorgan which could rival those of the Cymmrodorion and the Gwyneddigion.[40] But it never posed a serious challenge to the hegemony of the London-Welsh societies, not least because it lacked financial support as well as a critical mass of interested and committed members in Glamorgan. Unlike the bitterness which characterized Iolo's attitude towards the Gwyneddigion in later life, any rivalry inherent in the fraternity of the 1780s was of a healthy nature and reflected the esteem in which Iolo held the London-Welsh societies in the early years. That he envisaged a similar institution in Glamorgan is a tribute to the influence of the London-Welsh societies, and the letter in which Iolo introduced the fraternity to Owain Myfyr provides an excellent example of the ethos of these societies. The zeal for antiquities was palpable, as was the spirit of exchange, mutual encouragement and collaboration: Iolo could hardly contain his enthusiasm for the fraternity's metrical innovations and eagerly enquired after a poem by an Anglesey poet which Robin Ddu had showed him:

> cofiwch mi'n garedig filwaith at y Du o Fôn, y Ceiriog, Sion Collen, a phawb eraill o'r hên Gyfeillion. Pan fum yn Llundain e ddangosodd y DÛ imi Owdl ar y pedwar mesur ar hugain a brydodd rhyw fardd Ieuangc o Fôn. A ellir cael yr owdl honno? A oes y fath beth a chael hysbysrwydd o drigfa'r Bardd, a chael cyfeillach llythyrol ag ef? Ai bydd gwiw gan y Du, y Ceiriog ag ynteu fod yn aelodau ym Mrodoliaeth Beirdd Morganwg? Y mae Ieuan Fardd ag Offeiriad ynawr yn Weinidog Maesaleg, eithr nid oes yno un Ifor Hael.[41]

> (remember me kindly a thousand times to Robin Ddu, the Ceiriog, Sion Collen and all of the other old friends. When I was in London, Robin Ddu showed me

38 Helen Ramage, 'Eisteddfodau'r Ddeunawfed Ganrif' in Idris Foster (ed.), *Twf yr Eisteddfod* (Abertawe, 1968), pp. 17–18; Alan Llwyd, *Gronwy Ddiafael, Gronwy Ddu: Cofiant Goronwy Owen* (Llandybïe, 1997), pp. 348–50.

39 Llwyd, *Gronwy Ddiafael, Gronwy Ddu*, pp. 348–9.

40 Williams: *IM*, pp. 373–4.

41 BL Add. 15024, ff. 188–9, Iolo Morganwg to Owain Myfyr, 10 July 1780.

an ode on the twenty four metres that some young poet from Anglesey composed. Could I have that ode? Could I possibly learn the whereabouts of that Poet and have a correspondence friendship with him? Would Robin Ddu, Ceiriog and he like to be members of the Fraternity of Glamorgan Poets? Ieuan Poet and Priest [Evan Evans] is now a minister at Basaleg, but there is no Ivor the Generous there.)

Although Owen Myfyr responded favourably to Iolo's invitation to join the fraternity,[42] since Iolo never mentioned it in subsequent letters the venture must have stagnated. However, throughout the 1780s Iolo developed the ideas first propounded here and, convinced perhaps that his reforms would be taken more seriously if presented in an ancient guise, he introduced the Glamorgan Classification into the manuscript 'Cyfrinach Beirdd Ynys Prydain' a decade later. Indeed, bardism's druidic associations and alleged antiquity proved much more appealing to the London-Welsh when Iolo arrived on the scene in 1791 with his 'ancient' manuscript in his knapsack.

'Dywenydd Morganwg' was broached as a joint venture between Iolo and his younger brother Thomas. In two draft letters to the 'natives of Glamorgan' ('brodorion Morganwg'), they announced their intention of publishing a quarterly literary magazine for a readership restricted to Glamorgan and London, 'for your benefit and entertainment' ('er lles a diddanwch i chwi').[43] It was to contain medieval poetry and prose, contemporary criticism, correspondence, contemporary poetry and prose squibs: 'amryw bethau godidog gan awduron yr oes hon' (various excellent things by authors of this age). In this, as in his antiquarian work, Iolo was influenced by Lewis Morris's example, and he was clearly determined to generate a body of entertaining and urbane prose in Welsh. Lewis Morris's *Tlysau yr Hen Oesoedd* (1735) provided a suitable model. As a compendium of both poetry and prose by ancients and moderns, 'Dywenydd Morganwg' was also an attempt to counter the strong bias in favour of the poets of north Wales, which he had perceived in the work of the Gwyneddigion and in the anthologies of poetry published in Wales during the eighteenth century, among them *Dewisol Ganiadau yr Oes Hon* (1759), *Blodeu-Gerdd Cymry* (1759), *Diddanwch Teuluaidd* (1763) and *Gorchestion Beirdd Cymru* (1773). Although 'Dywenydd Morganwg' was advertised as a diverse magazine, the proposals encouraged contemporary satire, specifically letters from the dead to the living:

Bid hyspys i bawb
Fod dau o brif ddoethion Cymru wedi adgyfodi o farw i fyw, wedi gorwedd yn y bedd dros gannoedd o flynyddoedd. Un yw Sion Cent . . . Fe ddychwelodd i'r

[42] NLW 21281E, Letter no. 227, Owain Myfyr to Iolo Morganwg, 22 August 1780.
[43] NLW 21414E, no. 5a.

> Byd i drin ei gysefin swydd . . . sef yw hynny ich addysgu mewn pob daioni, ach ceryddu am ddrygioni.[44]

> (May it be known to all
> That two of Wales's foremost wise men have been raised from the dead, having lain in the grave for hundreds of years. One is Siôn Cent . . . He returned to the World to fulfil his original office . . . namely to educate you in all goodness, and to chastize you for wrongdoing.)

The combination of the letter form, the otherworldly backdrop and the promise of exposing human folly, was in keeping with the satirical genre practised earlier by Tom Brown and Ned Ward,[45] and also by Lewis Morris.[46] Iolo's protagonists included stock characters such as Siôn Gŵr y Tŷ (John the man of the house), Gweni Law Egor (open-handed Gweni), Twm Pen Berman (Tom yeast head), Yr Hen Geiliog (the old cockerel), Hen Wrach Eisingrug (the old fawning witch) and Wil Tabwr (Will the striker). Historical and legendary characters also featured: Hen Gyrus o Iâl (Old Cyrus of Yale), Morgan Mwynfawr (Morgan the Rich), Catwg Ddoeth (Catwg the Wise), Y Bardd Glas o'r Gadair (The Young Poet of the Chair) and Yr Hen Saffin (Old Saffin). Not a single issue of 'Dywenydd Morganwg' was ever published, but because some of the characters Iolo had envisaged for this purpose were too intriguing to abandon, they were resurrected within bardism: Catwg Ddoeth, Bardd Glas y Gadair and Wil Tabwr, for example, became key figures in his bardic vision and exemplified the civilized and sophisticated Glamorgan that was integral to it. Indeed, that Iolo chose to recycle in bardism characters whom he had originally intended to include in a corpus of entertaining prose throws valuable light on the intersection between his original, creative work and his antiquarian forgeries. His exposure to the aims of the largely London-based promoters of the eighteenth-century cultural revival invigorated his Welsh patriotism and also provided channels through which he could express his love for Glamorgan and enhance the literary and cultural profile of his native county. The Fraternity of Glamorgan Poets and 'Dywenydd Morganwg' were the products of this positive influence, but in these ventures, too, we find Iolo

[44] Ibid., no. 5ch.

[45] Benjamin Boyce, 'News from Hell: Satiric Communications with the Nether World in English Writing of the Seventeenth and Eighteenth Centuries', *Publications of the Modern Language Association of America*, LVIII (1943), 402–37; H. W. Troyer, *Ned Ward of Grub Street* (London, 1968); Pat Rogers, *Grub Street: Studies in a Subculture* (London, 1972).

[46] See 'Llythyr Mari Benwen' [Mary Whitehead's letter] in Saunders Lewis, *A School of Welsh Augustans* (Wrexham, 1924), pp. 146–50. See also Alun R. Jones, *Lewis Morris* (Caerdydd, 2004), pp. 45, 53–5, 56, 147.

rehearsing ideas and experimenting with characters whose potential he would fully realize within bardism.

However, the undercurrent of regional rivalry which he had experienced also shaped the literary contours of Glamorgan and its position within the bardic vision. The romantic Glamorgan he depicted was, despite its exuberance, essentially a defensive construct designed to combat the prejudice he had encountered in the Morris correspondence and had experienced at first-hand among the London-Welsh.

That Glamorgan had a special role to play in the preservation and transmission of bardism was clearly fixed in Iolo's mind from the time of its inception. In the anonymous portrait of himself which he published in the *Gentleman's Magazine* in 1789 he presented himself (in the third person) not as a poet, but as a bard: 'His first poetical productions were in the Welsh language. About the age of twenty he was admitted a bard in the ancient manner; a custom still retained in Glamorgan, but, I believe, in no other part of Wales.'[47] He argued that only he and Edward Evan of Aberdare were steeped in the mysteries of the art of the ancient British bards. His aim was twofold: to tantalize the London literary scene with his novel poetic qualifications and establish a lineage for himself which included his fellow Grammarians, whose very title was an act of homage to their 'book-taught' learning. Since he needed to prove the ancient credentials of his invention, he never used the appellation 'Gramadegyddion', preferring instead an epithet of his own making, 'Gwŷr Cwm y Felin' (The Men of the Valley of the Mill) to describe this group of independently minded artisans and craftsmen.[48] His early antiquarian and linguistic pursuits had enabled him to familiarize himself with received wisdom on druidism. Having visited Stonehenge and Avebury in the early 1770s, he became fascinated by the supposed druidical monuments of Wales,[49] and the megaliths of Glamorgan became valuable proof in his later claims that his home county, rather than Wiltshire or Anglesey, was the authentic seat of the Druids in Britain. Having visited Anglesey and the sites detailed in *Mona Antiqua Restaurata* (1723), he dismissed the 'groundless conjecture' of its author, Henry Rowlands,[50] and argued that Glamorgan's landscape was dotted with much more compelling proof of its ancient druidic inheritance, such as the supposed bardic circle at

47 *Gentleman's Magazine*, LIX, part 2, 976. Reproduced fully in *Williams: IM*, pp. 464–5.

48 NLW 13089E, p. 453; NLW 13097B, pp. 99, 151; NLW 13121B, pp. 335–8; NLW 13130A, p. 224; NLW 13138A, pp. 104–7.

49 NLW 13130A, p. 252. See also references to the rocking-stones of Glamorgan: NLW 13128A, p. 50.

50 NLW 13130A, p. 292.

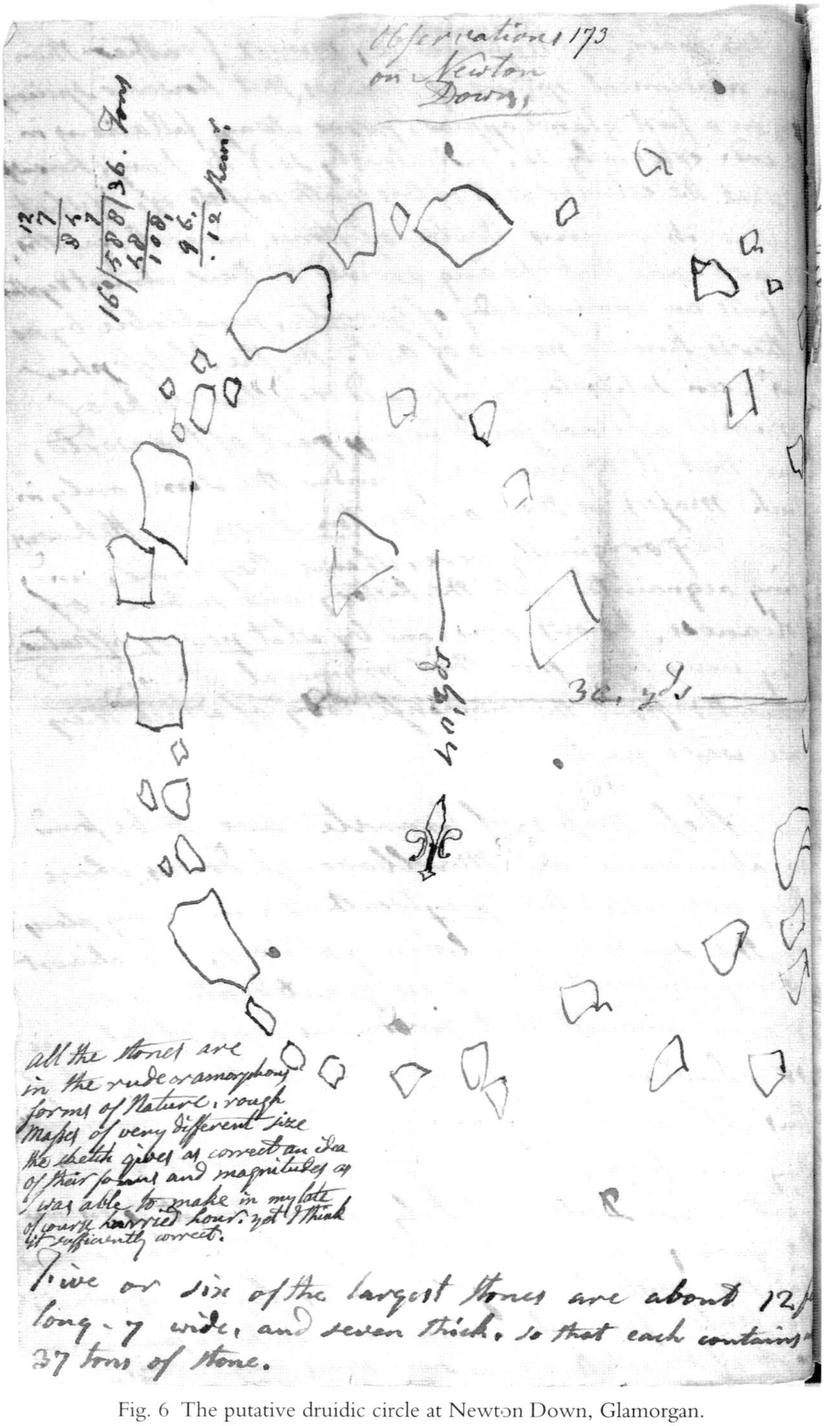

Fig. 6 The putative druidic circle at Newton Down, Glamorgan.

Newton Down,[51] and the vestiges located in the Golych valley, a valley whose etymology bore the imprint of the ancient Druids:

> Dyffryn Goluch (Anglice Vale of Worship) a good house modern built in a fine little vale the gentle rising hills prettily chequer'd with woods, in the fields adjacent are two very large Cistfaens [kistvaen] and may be reckoned amongst the noblest of Druidical antiquities in this Island. This vale was formerly famous for orchards & cyder and there are in it still several good orchards. The pretty village of Dyffryn stands a little southward of Mr Price's seat, and is a good addition to the prospect.[52]

Ystrad Owain, near Bryn Owain (Stalling Down), the location of Gorsedd meetings in the late 1790s, was presented as 'the place where in Glamorgan, from time immemorial, the Bards met. There is a large Tumulus, and in an adjoining field the remains of an ancient Gorsedd'.[53] Such fantasies added a sense of purpose and significance both to bardic meetings and to the ancient locations where they were held, and provide yet another example of the way in which, according to Richard Suggett, his archaeological interest 'linked history and literature in a meaningful way in Iolo's bardic vision'.[54] Many other locations in the county were similarly transformed within bardism, among them Llantwit Major and Beaupre castle.

Sometime between 1794 and 1795 Iolo added marginal notes to a transcript of Lewis Morris's unpublished manuscript, 'Celtic Remains'. These notes and interpolations related mainly to Glamorgan and included valid corrections as well as spurious claims. For instance, Iolo added the following note on Llantwit Major:

> Llanilltud Fawr. This is the name of the Parish. Boverton (not Boviarton) is a large Village in this Parish and gives its name to the Lordships. It is the Bovium of Anton. Here is still standing a very ancient seat of the Lords Marchers of Glamorgan, in the Town of Llanilltud or Llantwit stand in Ruin, the College of Iltutus, in the Church and church yard are more ancient British inscriptions than are to be found any where else in Wales. There are in the neighbouring fields

51 'And out of one stone there now standing (it may be asked by what miraculous powers lifted up) on three pillars, might be had, could we cut or break it, as many stones, and equal in Magnitude, as compose the whole of Stone Henge. There are on Newton Down many that are above twenty feet long, fifteen wide and eighty thick, and these in several places appear to have been brought together (surely not by Nature and we know not by what art) to form circles of about thirty yards diameter.' NLW 13089E, p. 170.

52 NLW 21413E, no. 7. The vestiges were the burial chambers located at St Lythan's and Tinkinswood. See also NLW 13128A, p. 50; NLW 13130A, p. 252.

53 NLW 13144A, p. 429. See also NLW 13153A, pp. 286–7, 290.

54 Richard Suggett, 'Iolo Morganwg: Stonecutter, Builder, and Antiquary' in *Rattleskull Genius*, p. 226.

> four or five Roman and British Camps. The place is famous for the longevity of its Inhabitants, stands in the Vale of Glam on the sea shore. Iolo.[55]

This short piece included several features of Llantwit Major's antiquity which had seized Iolo's imagination and which formed the foundation of Glamorgan's cultural primacy in general: Roman and Norman presence, ancient inscribed stones and a tangible link with early Christianity in Wales.[56] Iolo is credited with having discovered Samson's Pillar at Llantwit Major *c.*1789 and, on the basis of this discovery and his reading of *Bucheddau'r Saint* (The Lives of the Saints), he came to believe that Llantwit Major was the most important Christian centre in Glamorgan and, in his national pedigree, he yoked together disparate characters such as Illtud, the town's eponymous saint, Caradog, Ilid, the mythological Brân Fendigaid and the ancient bards Aneirin and Taliesin.[57]

Beaupre also underwent a radical transformation in his bardic vision of Glamorgan. The seat of the Bassett family had already been abandoned by the time Iolo visited the site in the company of Daniel Walters.[58] Iolo created a romantic tale about Beaupre's elegant porch which involved the Twrch brothers, whose fraternal love and romantic rivalry enabled Iolo to celebrate native Glamorgan genius: he claimed that it was these natives of Glamorgan who had introduced the classical style of architecture into the kingdom rather than Inigo Jones, who was traditionally associated with Denbighshire in north Wales.[59] But Beaupre also emerged as a defining moment in the development of bardism: Iolo posited it as the locus of one of bardism's most illustrious eisteddfodau, in which the so-called Glamorgan Classification, later published in *Cyfrinach Beirdd Ynys Prydain* (1829), was authorized by the bards of Glamorgan.[60] Allegedly held at Whitsun 1681,

[55] NLW 1735D, p. 324. For other descriptions, see NLW 13158A, pp. 270–80; NLW 13123B, p. 289. For Roman connections and Llantwit's alleged ancient name 'Caerworgorn', see NLW 13129A, p. 527; NLW 13114B, p. 105, Iolo Morganwg to David Thomas, 20 October 1798; NLW 21413E, no. 2, Iolo Morganwg to Mr Urban, 1 January 1796.

[56] See NLW 13114B, p. 105, Iolo Morganwg to David Thomas of Bath, 20 October 1798, in which Iolo discussed Samson's Pillar in detail and appeared intent on publishing on the subject: 'Antiquities of Lantwit Major, in the County of Glamorgan. Collected from various Documents. By Edward Williams. 1800.'

[57] Suggett, 'Iolo Morganwg: Stonecutter, Builder, and Antiquary' in *Rattleskull Genius*, p. 222.

[58] The Bassett family was one of many Royalist families in Glamorgan to be ruined by losses in the civil wars. Philip Jenkins, *The Making of a Ruling Class: The Glamorgan Gentry 1640–1790* (Cambridge, 1983), p. 68.

[59] Cardiff 3.216, Iolo Morganwg to Richard Hoare, 17 August 1797; NLW 13116B, pp. 134–7, Iolo Morganwg to Richard Hoare, 17 August 1797; Williams: *IM*, pp. 272–3.

[60] Williams (ed.), *Cyfrinach Beirdd Ynys Prydain* is also a valuable source for the Beaupre eisteddfod. NLW 13100B, pp. 234–7, contains *englynion* allegedly sung at Beaupre and elsewhere. NLW 13095B, p. 78 contains two triads 'discovered' at the castle: 'Llyma drïoedd a gafwyd yn y Bewpyr, a golles rhywun yno, neu fallai mai rhywun oi fodd au dodes ar y llawr lle au cespwyd' (Here are triads discovered at Beaupre, that someone lost there, or perhaps someone wilfully placed them on the floor where they were found).

the eisteddfod had been led by Edward Dafydd and his disciple, the priest Dafydd o'r Nant. Poetic fact lay at the heart of Iolo's bardic fictions, for he knew that Edward Dafydd had been regularly patronized by the Bassetts of Beaupre and that he was one of the last poets in Glamorgan to live by his craft.[61] But it was Iolo's imagination which created the epoch-making eisteddfod at Beaupre and transformed Edward Dafydd from a nonentity into a leading bardic personality.

The phantom eisteddfodau which Iolo concocted were loosely associated with what he had discovered about the literary traditions of Glamorgan. He was familiar with the details surrounding the eisteddfodau of the poetic guild held at Carmarthen *c.*1453 and at Caerwys, Flintshire, in 1523 and 1567. He was also aware of their regulatory function: to confirm poetic rights, safeguard the professionalism and elite quality of the guild, and confirm and revise rules of *cynghanedd* and strict-metre forms.[62] If bardism was to convince as a concept, it needed bardic congresses such as those held by the professional medieval poetic guild and attested in manuscripts. Prior to the eighteenth century, only one recorded eisteddfod had been held in Glamorgan: the Llandaf eisteddfod of 1564 commissioned by William Evans, chancellor of the cathedral. Iolo added to this tradition by claiming that Evans had in fact established the 'Chair of Llandaf' in 1558 and that an annual eisteddfod was held there on the feast of Teilo and on the Monday of Whitsuntide.[63] That the Llandaf eisteddfod was not mentioned in the commonplace book, which he filled with material associated with the history of the Carmarthen and Caerwys eisteddfodau, suggests that this was an early work and that the Llandaf eisteddfod was a later elaboration.[64] Using the precedent set by Llandaf, and fuelled with nostalgia for what he believed to be the numerous eisteddfodau held in Glamorgan during the early eighteenth century, Iolo invented the defining eisteddfod of bardism, the Beaupre eisteddfod of 1681.

Iolo also supported his claims that Glamorgan was the principal home of the druidic tradition in Wales by peopling its landscape with an array of bards and poets, literary patrons, scholars, lawgivers and heroes. They comprised historical and mythological characters from Glamorgan's past and were marshalled to form a lineage of ancient origin which concealed bardism's

61 NLW 13116B, p. 259.

62 G. J. Williams, 'Eisteddfod Caerfyrddin', *Y Llenor*, V (1926), 94–102; D. J. Bowen, 'Dafydd ab Edmwnd ac Eisteddfod Caerfyrddin', *Barn*, 142 (1974), 441–8.

63 NLW 13120B, p. 72; NLW 13127A, p. 165; NLW 13089E, p. 320 lists the poets who attended the eisteddfod.

64 NLW 13099B, pp. 1–80: 'Cynnulliadau Tuag att Hanes Eisteddfodau Caerfyrddin, Caerwys, ag eraill Casgledig (gan mwyaf) yng Ngwynedd gan Iolo Morganwg' (Collections towards a History of the Carmarthen, Caerwys and other Eisteddfodau, collected (mainly) in Gwynedd by Iolo Morganwg).

novel beginnings: they included Gildas, Caradog of Llancarfan, Catwg, Llywelyn Siôn, Meurug Dafydd and John Bradford. He also invented new characters and furnished them with verses of his own making in order to prove the authenticity of the essentially bardic tradition of sophisticated and lyrical *canu teuluaidd* (domestic poetry) in the region: Geraint Fardd Glas o'r Gadair, Rhys Goch ab Rhicert and Wil Tabwr. Iolo also appropriated figures from north Wales, such as Dafydd Ddu Hiraddug[65] and Siôn Mowddwy[66] in order to bolster Glamorgan's bardic credibility. Most memorably, he appropriated the canonical poet Dafydd ap Gwilym into the narrative of Glamorgan's primacy, thereby enhancing his reputation as 'Dafydd Morganwg' (Dafydd of Glamorgan) in the forgeries unwittingly published by William Owen Pughe and Owain Myfyr in *Barddoniaeth Dafydd ab Gwilym* (1789).[67] From the Old North he transported Aneirin and Taliesin, the earliest extant poets to have composed verse in the Welsh language, and located them at the bardic seminary at Llantwit Major. In accordance with local traditions about the saints in south Wales, he linked the Old North ruler Urien Rheged with the Gower peninsula in south Wales,[68] claiming that, following the death of King Arthur, 'The Chair of the Round Table' had been moved from Caerleon to Gower, to be governed by Urien.[69] But whatever their provenance, the characters in Iolo's cultural genealogy bore witness to Glamorgan's ancient civilization and reflected a romantic taste in Britain and western Europe for ancient heroes who represented the virtues of a nation and who could be used to channel nascent nationalist sentiments.[70] He wove endless sub-plots around these enchanting places and characters. In addition to information about bardism in his correspondence and in his sketches for the unfinished 'The History of the Bards', he forged a huge body of secondary material to corroborate his vision of bardic Glamorgan: dialogues, bardic declarations, ritual formulae, verses, triads, anecdotes and cultural events such as eisteddfodau.[71] He not only forged material pertaining to be of ancient provenance but also fabricated anecdotes, poems and correspondence from

65 NLW 13098B, p. 92.

66 NLW 13100B, p. 140; NLW 13089B, p. 330.

67 NLW 13098B, p. 291. See *IMChY*; Charnell-White, *Barbarism and Bardism*, pp. 13–14. For traditions pre-dating Iolo which associate Dafydd ap Gwilym with Glamorgan, see Lewis, 'The Literary Tradition of Morgannwg down to the Middle of the Sixteenth Century', pp. 490–3.

68 William Owen, *The Cambrian Biography: Or Historical Notices of Celebrated Men Among the Ancient Britons* (London, 1803), p. 338.

69 NLW 13087E, p. 72.

70 Sam Smiles, *The Image of Antiquity: Ancient Britain and the Romantic Imagination* (London, 1994), pp. 26–45; Rosemary Sweet, *Antiquaries: The Discovery of the Past in Eighteenth-Century Britain* (London, 2004), p. 197.

71 Mary-Ann Constantine, 'Pious Frauds and Perjurers: Iolo Morganwg's Truth against the World' in Peter Knight and Jonathan Long (eds.), *Fakes and Forgeries* (Cambridge, 2004), pp. 119–34.

Glamorgan poets of an earlier generation, including letters from Rhys Morgan, Pencraig-nedd, and Dafydd Nicolas.[72]

Although born of a sense of defensiveness arising from the region's shortcomings, the vision of Glamorgan depicted so far had been predominantly positive. For Iolo, it was a fusion of romantic rural idyll and a strong cultural tradition. However, this celebratory portrait of Glamorgan changed as Iolo approached middle age: the general north–south tension that had lain dormant during his initial encounter with the Gwyneddigion Society in the 1770s was activated during the 1790s and assumed an acrimonious personal dimension. The first stirrings of resentment towards them occurred in a letter to William Meyler of Bath in 1792 in which he dismissed the Gwyneddigion Society as 'at first whimsical, became afterwards ridiculous, and is now detestable'.[73] Reviewing the situation with the benefit of hindsight in a letter to William Owen Pughe in 1806, it is clear that the 'ranco[rous] prejudice'[74] his Glamorgan Classification had received in London in 1791 was one of the root causes of a growing resentment which had simmered throughout the difficult 1790s until his friendship with Pughe and Owain Myfyr finally collapsed. The prominence that he gave to 'National Provi[dence] and every kind of local prejudices' in this letter not only reprised the sense of alienation he felt at the time, but was a clear indication that Iolo perceived his failure in London and his rejection by the Gwyneddigion within this framework of entrenched north–south tension. The north–south rivalry therefore became the focus of Iolo's revenge. It is significant that, from 1806 onwards, Iolo planned to write what he described as 'A complete and Superb History of Glamorgan'.[75] As Rosemary Sweet has shown, Iolo lived in 'the great age of the county history',[76] but his foray into this field was conceived as a form of personal and regional retaliation against the Gwyneddigion. Not surprisingly, Iolo's 'complete and Superb History of the County of Glamorgan' proved to be yet another of his 'castels in the ayre',[77] for it was never completed. Instead, bardism became the instrument of his pain and anger, and from around 1806 onwards the county's primacy in bardism manifested itself in bitter prejudice towards north Wales, a bitterness which mirrored his antagonism towards William Owen Pughe and Owain Myfyr. This aggressive and hostile rendering of Glamorgan's illustrious past offered a direct challenge

72 For Rhys Morgan's letter, see NLW 13089E, pp. 256–7. For Dafydd Nicolas's letter, see NLW 13122B, pp. 165–74. The latter was published as a genuine letter in *Taliesin*, I (1859–60), 92–5.

73 Cardiff 3.99, Iolo Morganwg to William Meyler, 1 January 1797.

74 NLW 13221E, pp. 143–6, Iolo Morganwg to William Owen Pughe, 12 January 1806.

75 NLW 13103B, p. 267; NLW 13116B, pp. 1–51.

76 Sweet, *Antiquaries*, p. xviii.

77 NLW 21283E, Letter no. 608, Margaret Williams to Iolo Morganwg, 10 December 1794.

to the supposed literary and cultural superiority of north Wales which had been sedulously cultivated by the Cymmrodorion and the Gwyneddigion.

Iolo was well placed to dent the pride of Gwynedd and to prove that Glamorgan was the most prestigious county in the history of Wales. Over the years he had steeped himself in the literary and historical traditions of both regions. The bardic grammars, as well as anonymous collections of poetic lore such as 'Trioedd Ynys Prydein' (The Triads of the Island of Britain) and 'Statud Gruffudd ap Cynan' (The Statute of Gruffudd ap Cynan), provided models and formulae for his own bardic forgeries.[78] He was also conversant with the most seminal secondary sources of the age: Siôn Dafydd Rhys's *Cambrobrytannicae Cymraecaeve Linguae Institutiones et Rudimenta* (1592), John Davies's *Antiquae Linguae Britannicae . . . Rudimenta* (1621) and Edward Lhuyd's *Archaeologia Britannica* (1707).[79] This personal research and association with antiquarian and poetic circles ensured that he was familiar with the genuine professional guild and its key figures, the stages in its development and the circumstances and chronology of its eventual demise. He was thoroughly grounded in the stylistic and metrical differences between the Poets of the Princes and the later Poets of the Nobility, the development of *cynghanedd* (the most fundamental element of Welsh strict-metre poetry),[80] as well as the development of the *cywydd* form. He had also grasped that 'The Statute of Gruffudd ap Cynan' was much more recent than its eponymous historical figure and had realized that the professional bards appeared to have developed a standardized idiom which transcended the pronounced regional dialects of Wales. Another important observation was that the Welsh metrical system was not as inflexible in practice as the written bardic grammars suggested. Iolo used these observations to his own advantage: he wove them into his narrative of the primacy of Glamorgan and explained them in terms of bardism. Poring over manuscript anthologies of poetry, bardic grammars and collections of triads had given him the expertise which allowed him to construct a convincing framework, chronology, pedigree, geography and language for bardism which simultaneously upheld Wales and Glamorgan. It enabled him to revise the grand narrative of Welsh poetry emanating from the London-Welsh cultural base in favour of Glamorgan.[81] His mastery of the genuine professional guild of poetry also allowed him, in

[78] Forged versions of the statute were unwittingly published by William Owen Pughe in *Y Greal*, V (1806), 238–9; VII (1806), 300–3.

[79] Williams: *IM*, p. 105.

[80] For the druidic timescale of *cynghanedd*, see NLW 13108B, pp. 120–1.

[81] In a letter to William Owen Pughe in 1806, Iolo expressed reservations about the reluctance of the Gwyneddigion to embrace the 'corrections' to the strict-metre forms suggested in the supposedly ancient regulations contained in a manuscript that was published posthumously in *Cyfrinach Beirdd Ynys Prydain* (1829); NLW 13221E, pp. 143–6, Iolo Morganwg to William Owen Pughe, 12 January 1806.

the last two decades of his life, to fine-tune the detail of bardism in such a way that it excluded the poetry and poets of north Wales from bardism's civilizing inheritance. For this purpose, bardism's primitivist framework was conveniently at hand: the binary opposition that had equated Bardism with civility and non-bardism with barbarism in order to polarize Welsh and English culture worked equally well in polarizing Glamorgan and Gwynedd.

Iolo worked on the simple premise that since Glamorgan was the home of bardism it was necessarily civilized, while Gwynedd, having no part in bardism, was inherently barbarous. In his numerous writings on the subject, ostensibly prepared for 'The History of the Bards', Iolo carefully excluded north Wales poets and schools of poetry from the bardic line of descent. In two protracted essays intended for his *magnum opus* he arranged his materials under 'aera's or periods of time, and peculiarity of characteristics'.[82] He divided Welsh poetry into schools: combining fact and fiction, he also divided north and south Wales in the process. Its druidical element aside, Iolo's categorization of Welsh poetry into schools represents one of the most original aspects of his bardic vision since it revealed a profound understanding of the fortunes of the professional Welsh poetic guild. He began on solid ground by citing the earliest school as the Ancient School or the School of Taliesin in the sixth century, whose poetry was syllabic and rhymed,[83] but lacking the *cynghanedd* which became formally systematized in later ages. But to him, the poetry of this school was patriarchal, a valuable repository of druidic philosophy and mythology:

> The great object of this school was to propagate useful knowledge and to convey effectually from one person, place or age to another, such principles of theology, morality, jurisprudence and whatever had a tendency to forward the progress of civilization, and to ameliorate the condition of society.[84]

It is clear that more than poetry was at stake, for the early material was considered indicative of the Welsh/British past and of national character:

> for, besides frequent instances of beautiful poetry, it will be found that from our old bards new and great lights on history are obtained; they exhibit lively pictures of primitive manners, afford curious anecdotes of our ancient knowledge, especially

[82] BL Add. 15030, ff. 9–10, Iolo Morganwg to Owain Myfyr, 7 August 1798. See Appendices X–XII.

[83] Modern scholars remain divided as to whether these archaic forms were accented or syllabic. See Marged Haycock, 'Metrical Models for the Poems in The Book of Taliesin' in Brynley F. Roberts (ed.), *Early Welsh Poetry: Studies in the Book of Aneirin* (Aberystwyth, 1988), pp. 155–77; Peredur Lynch, 'Yr Awdl a'i Mesurau' in Brynley F. Roberts and Morfydd E. Owen (eds.), *Beirdd a Thywysogion: Barddoniaeth Llys yng Nghymru, Iwerddon a'r Alban* (Caerdydd, 1996), pp. 258–87.

[84] NLW 13108B, p. 2.

> of the very beautiful ethics of our remote ancestors; who seem to have penetrated farther into the knowledge of human nature than the world can be easily brought to believe; and on these occasions we see the Welsh piercing into depths that are almost unfathomable to other languages.[85]

Iolo believed that, following a dearth of manuscript testimony for the period between the ninth and the eleventh centuries, a revival of poetry had occurred in north Wales during the twelfth century. This revival was traditionally associated with Gruffudd ap Cynan, the son of a Welsh prince and an Irish woman.[86] Following Edward Lhuyd, Iolo agreed that *cynghanedd* had been systematized at this time,[87] and that this school produced characteristically heroic poetry. Although Iolo acknowledged the presence of 'a very brilliant constellation of Poets'[88] within the school identified with Gruffudd ap Cynan, he qualified his compliment with a sting:

> The rising of an unclouded sun at the deep moon of the darkest winters night is the one simile that can be used in speaking of the wonderful revival of Poetry (I say poetry rather than Bardism) that blazed out as if it were instantaneously at this time that it can not be referred to any earlier period, nor has it the least appearance of having been the effect of any kind of Gradationary improvement. It is not greatly short of a miracle.[89]

This was no unguarded remark. By differentiating between 'Poetry' and 'Bardism', Iolo effectively denied the genuine poets and the poetic tradition of north Wales an illustrious druidic pedigree. The reference to the 'instantaneous' appearance of this school underlies this point. Aware of the difficulties of untangling the perplexing clues which brought him to this conclusion, Iolo sought to demonstrate that the poets of north Wales were far removed from the purity of the southern patriarchal and druidic school of Taliesin. Alive to Gruffudd ap Cynan's Irish links, he further emphasized this difference by stressing the northern Welsh affinity with the Scandinavian Scalds, whose heroic poetry exhibited the 'same savage sublimity, the same ferocious grandure'.[90] Indeed, he believed that added proof of this affinity could be found in other shared practices, such as the habit of castrating opponents and gouging out their eyes.[91] For all its gruesomeness, Iolo's point was a serious one, echoing Macpherson's assertions in *Fingal* that the Scandinavians were a

85 *MAW*, I, p. xix.
86 NLW 13221E, pp. 99–106, Iolo Morganwg to William Owen Pughe, 7 June 1803.
87 NLW 13108B, p. 84.
88 NLW 13107B, p. 42.
89 NLW 13108B, p. 71. See also NLW 13221E, pp. 147–50, Iolo Morganwg to William Owen Pughe, 1 March 1806, regarding the lost succession of bards in north Wales.
90 NLW 13098B, p. 88.
91 Ibid., pp. 90, 97, 98.

barbarous people and boldly inverting the notion of the civilized Scalds which he had read in Mallet's *Northern Antiquities* (1770), a history which associated northern heroes and northern antiquities with cultivation and the Celts of the south with barbarousness.[92] He expressed this more explicitly in a stray note on 'Gray's Bard', which he considered 'a very inferior thing' on the strength of its gothic influence: 'the barbarous Scandinavian Mythology, as inferior to the Bardic as the Nadir is to the Zenith'.[93] It should be noted, however, that, for Iolo, the 'purity' of the south Wales tradition did not necessarily imply an ethnic or cultural otherness. Indeed, the 'barbarizing' influence of the Scalds on the northern Welsh was matched by corresponding 'civilizing' influences from the Continent in the shape of the Romans and the Normans.

Ignoring assertions that the Romans had eliminated the Druids and ignoring, too, the received image of the bards and Druids as defenders of British liberty against the imperial might of Rome, Iolo incorporated the Romans, civilizers par excellence, into his bardic narrative. These were introduced, not as aggressors, but as a civilizing force within south Wales, though Iolo was at pains to stress that the Romans did not encounter a barbarous people. Bardism, as we have seen, was construed as a self-civilizing institution and, according to Iolo, the Romans would have come face to face with a cultured nation whose language had already reached a high level of sophistication.[94] A major indication of this refinement was the assertion that the Britons/Welsh, unlike the Saxons/English, were a literate nation *before* the arrival of the Romans. Although he conceded that some Roman learning had permeated the ancient school of Taliesin[95] in the guise of good taste and style,[96] he nevertheless insisted that bardism was 'rather polished than altered in ages of greater refinement'.[97] He also boasted that the Britons/Welsh had always used their own language for every literary purpose, while other countries subsequent to the fall of Rome had recourse to Latin, 'their own native languages being yet in their crude incipiencies, like cubs of Bears unlicked into form'.[98] Significantly, illiteracy and the lack of an alphabet

92 Mallet argued that the unconquerable spirit of the people of the North was a remedy to the great evil of the 'Yoke of Rome' in its barbarous later stages. He modified Journandes' comment that north Europe was 'The Forge of Mankind', and asserted instead: 'I should rather call it, the forge of those instruments which broke the fetters manufactured in the south.' Paul Henri Mallet, *Northern Antiquities* (2 vols., London, 1770), I, p. liv. See also I, pp. iv, xvii–xviii, 386; II, p. xx. Iolo copied extracts from Thomas Percy's translation of Mallet in NLW 13121B, pp. 419–20.

93 NLW 13159A, pp. 156–7.

94 NLW 13144A, pp. 223–38; NLW 13108B, p. 5.

95 Both schools are compared in NLW 13108B, pp. 97–8; see also the erroneous remarks about the Roman origin of metres in ibid., p. 32.

96 NLW 13108B, p. 116.

97 NLW 13087E, p. 205.

98 NLW 13104B, p. 128. See also NLW 13151A, p. 179.

were among the barbarities of the Celtic nations cited by Mallet,[99] and Iolo may well have been responding directly to Mallet's imputation when he included one of his most remarkable inventions, *Coelbren y Beirdd* (the bardic alphabet), in the apparatus which would prove the precocious literary capabilities and civilization of Wales.[100]

The ancient school of Taliesin, Iolo then claimed, was succeeded by the early medieval 'School of South Wales'. This school favoured lyrical topics and used a wider variety of metres than had been the case for the north Wales school of Gruffudd ap Cynan, and also maintained the syllabic metres of its druidic forebear. His description of it bears witness to his determination to marginalize the north:

> The southwalian, this is in a great measure, (and much more so than that of north Wales), the offspring, and in many things a continuation of the ancient or Taliesinian school. The variety of its versifications and metres are very great, it seems to delight more in Lyrical than in Heroical Subjects and metres, and all the Pastoral, rural or domestic (Teuluaidd) poetry appears as of this school, less Heroical than the Northwalian, less grand, but more natural.[101]

The druidic link was pure fantasy, but the observations regarding the fluid nature of Welsh metrics and *cynghanedd* remain salient, for it has not yet been fully appraised.[102] Iolo attributed the change of direction towards lyrical poetry to Norman influence in Glamorgan, a hunch that would prove to be more or less correct, though he conveniently ignored earlier north Wales examples of courtly love which did not fit his argument and was thus obliged to cite his own forgeries in order to bolster his claims. Once again Iolo rather surprisingly recruited a foreign and indeed invading force to his south Wales scheme. The 'Norman Yoke',[103] the bane of Anglo-Saxon historiographers and the curse of literary primitivists and patriots alike, was brushed aside by Iolo in a positive interpretation of the post-Conquest

99 Mallet, *Northern Antiquities,* I, pp. xvii–xviii.

100 NLW 13097B, pp. 49, 154–73, 177–80, 200–9, 212–14; NLW 13087E, pp. 15, 243; NLW 13089E, pp. 286, 315. Much in the same way that Mallet elucidated the mythic creation of the runic alphabet by Odin, Mallet, *Northern Antiquities*, I, p. 371, Iolo invented a creation myth for the *Coelbren* and the three sacred symbols on which it was founded. See Richard Crowe, 'Iolo Morganwg – An Eighteenth-Century Welsh Linguist' in Cyril J. Byrne, Margaret Harry and Pádraig Ó Siadhail (eds.), *Celtic Languages and Celtic Peoples: Proceedings of the Second North American Congress of Celtic Studies* (Nova Scotia, 1992), p. 310.

101 NLW 13098B, p. 88.

102 John Morris-Jones did not engage with this matter in his otherwise seminal study of Welsh metrics. For Morris-Jones's damning comments about Iolo's Glamorgan Classification, see *CD* (1925), pp. 372–9.

103 Christopher Hill, 'The Norman Yoke' in idem, *Puritanism and Revolution: Studies in Interpretation of the English Revolution of the Seventeenth Century* (new edn., London, 2001), pp. 46–111.

colonization of Glamorgan. He hailed the exposure of the indigenous people to European and Norman culture as one of the most significant events in Welsh literary history,[104] but was at pains to stress that the Normans did not civilize the inhabitants of Glamorgan; they simply added a layer of sophistication and polish to an already highly civilized language and culture.[105] As with the Romans, Iolo was careful as he uncovered Wales's cultural debt to external influences. The Normans were Cymricized in Iolo's version of post-Conquest Glamorgan: many of them were praised for patronizing local bards,[106] and some of them, like Robert Duke of Normandy, were depicted as accomplished Welsh-language poets.[107]

Iolo also transported Dafydd ap Gwilym into this south Wales school, though he also argued that Dafydd had merely 'polished' an existing tradition of love-poetry established by the Glamorgan-born poet, Rhys Goch ap Rhicert. In fact, Iolo not only composed fifteen of the twenty poems attributed to Rhys Goch but also conjured him up from genuine Glamorgan pedigrees.[108] Graciously, he conceded that Dafydd was the better poet, but nonetheless claimed him for Glamorgan, thus strengthening the county's claim to an ancient tradition of invigorating, gallant poetry.[109] By the end of the eighteenth century Dafydd ap Gwilym had become a recognized cultural icon, with scores of late medieval and early modern manuscripts attesting his canonicity. The inclusion by the Gwyneddigion of Iolo's own forgeries of Dafydd's work in the appendix to *Barddoniaeth Dafydd ab Gwilym* (1789) was only the first stage in Iolo's appropriation of Dafydd as a Glamorgan man. As Gwyneth Lewis has pointed out, by claiming his own descent from an illegitimate child of Dafydd ap Gwilym and Morfudd, Iolo used Dafydd's presence in the bardic lineage of Glamorgan to confer authority on himself.[110] This fanciful genealogy revealed Iolo's determination 'to write himself into the dramatis personae of the Welsh literary tradition'.[111]

Iolo issued another challenge to the superiority of north Wales by separating what he referred to as the 'Newfangled' school of north Wales and the imagined ancient druidic past. This school had approved Dafydd ab Edmwnd's classification of Welsh metrics at the controversial eisteddfod at

104 NLW 13141A, p. 305.
105 NLW 13128A, p. 251.
106 NLW 13087E, p. 124; NLW 13088B, p. 175.
107 NLW 13117E, pp. 121–2; NLW 13151A, p. 98. Iolo even claimed that the Duke had founded the Chair of Tir Iarll: NLW 13151A, p. 113.
108 Ifor Williams, 'Rhys Goch ap Rhiccert', *Y Beirniad*, III, no. 4 (1913), 230–44; G. J. Williams, 'Rhys Goch ap Rhiccert', ibid., VIII, no. 4 (1919), 211–26, 260.
109 NLW 13098B, p. 94.
110 NLW 13089E, p. 137.
111 Gwyneth Lewis, 'Eighteenth-Century Literary Forgeries with Special Reference to the Work of Iolo Morganwg' (unpublished University of Oxford D.Phil. thesis, 1991), p. 150.

Carmarthen *c.*1453, a piece of tyranny, according to Iolo, which exercised a stranglehold over the professional poetic guild and Welsh metrics for centuries:

> that huge Mushroom of a very foggy night, the New North Walian School, or rather the School of Caerwys, whose founder was Dafydd ap Edmwnd, obliterated every trace of antiquity in Northwales. New versification, new Bardic regulations, new orders of Bards, new of every thing that was absurd and irrational took place, and was established to the utter damnation, as I may Justly say, of all our ancient and magnificently rational principles of Bardism, Poetry, moral Discipline and regulations of the Bards in their several orders &c. But more of this Newfangled school when I come [to] treat more particularly of it, or to take it in hand, as we often say of things and persons that merit Castigation.[112]

For Iolo, the eisteddfod at Carmarthen constituted a victory for north Walian metrics over the so-called archaic and druidical metrics of south Wales. His own narrative of events was an attempt to subvert this defeat and, indeed, he never tired of denouncing the narrowness of *cynghanedd* practised under the 'barbarously modified principles of versification',[113] and the 'dogmata [of] Dafydd ab Edmund'.[114]

Undeterred, Iolo insisted that Glamorgan bards had continued to use archaic metres and had not always abided by the over-technical *cynghanedd* prescribed by Dafydd ab Edmwnd. He made this a Glamorgan peculiarity, and exaggerated its significance by viewing it as an index of a direct link with the druidic school of Taliesin and its looser *cynghanedd* and archaic metres. Furthermore, he manipulated the historical account of a revolt by south Wales poets against Dafydd ab Edmwnd at Carmarthen, and used this to justify his own alternative system of metrics – 'The Glamorgan Classification' – which was eventually published in *Cyfrinach Beirdd Ynys Prydain*. As was so often the case, his view of the past on this point was coloured by present concerns. Echoing contemporary debate in Wales regarding the merits and demerits of strict-metre verse in general,[115] he complained that its technical difficulty placed unwarranted restrictions on diction and natural expression before concluding that the dissolution of Dafydd ab Edmwnd's abhorrent, undruidic system could only bode well for bardism and, therefore, civil society:

112 NLW 13108B, p. 59.
113 NLW 13106B, p. 116.
114 NLW 13144A, p. 433.
115 E. G. Millward, *Yr Arwrgerdd Gymraeg: Ei Thwf a'i Thranc* (Caerdydd, 1998), pp. 22–7. Millward takes issue with the eighteenth- and nineteenth-century debate surrounding a suitable metre for the much longed-for Welsh epic poem.

Nature has however since that time been struggling hard to recover her rights but is nature depressed, there are none or very few to patronize, the Right, of nature! the Rights of man, and even the rights of God, are deemed it sadly seems to give way for a little while at least to the rights of fools, of Kings, and of Devils, but things will not remain so for ever. Barbarity with all its tinsel glare is, much faster than is consistent with its own wishes, giving way as the dawn arises. The Glow-worm will disappear – night's tapers will soon burn out.[116]

Iolo thus constructed a system which set the civilization of south Wales against the barbarism of the north, and which contrasted the antiquity, freedom and lyrical quality of south Walian 'bardism' with the novelty, rigidity and limitations of the 'Poetry' of north Wales. Iolo constructed an unbroken line from the ancient school of Taliesin, through the medieval school of poets in south Wales, and eventually to himself as (from 1798) the last surviving authentic Glamorgan bard. The north Wales schools were simply not party to these privileges.[117]

But outlawing the literary history of Gwynedd from bardism had ramifications for the final school in his interpretation of the indigenous poetic tradition, the contemporary school of north Wales: 'For little less than two centuries the lyric Poetry of Northwales has been the most stupid that was ever known in any Country.'[118] Because the northern-biased Gwyneddigion had hailed the refinements of Gruffudd ap Cynan and Dafydd ab Edmwnd as their models, and had rejected the allegedly superior and druidic 'Glamorgan Classification', they, too, were necessarily marginalized from this enviable past:

with the decayed edifice of Dafydd ap Edmunds school greatly dilapidated indeed, but repaired or patched up a little of late by the Gwyneddigion Society of London, who might more laudably and more nobly useful employ themselves in razing every particle of its foundations, and in founding some new structure on either an old or new plan on the site of it, a worse or more uncouth and unserviceable building can never be conceived by a brain the most fertile in stupidity than that which they have been for sometime endeavouring to re-found or re-edify.[119]

116 NLW 13144A, p. 437. For the influence of the theory of nature on the theory of the progress of man, see M. M. Rubel, *Savage and Barbarian: Historical Attitudes in the Criticism of Homer and Ossian in Britain, 1760–1800* (Oxford, 1978), pp. 17, 23–38.

117 NLW 13130A, pp. 198–9. See also Iolo's claims in a letter to William Owen Pughe that 'The succession of Bards has in Northwales been broken.' NLW 13221E, pp. 147–50, Iolo Morganwg to William Owen Pughe, 1 March 1806.

118 NLW 13138A, p. 60. Here Iolo is referring disparagingly to an anthology published *c.*1760, possibly *Dewisol Ganiadau yr Oes Hon* (1759) or *Blodeu-Gerdd Cymry* (1759).

119 NLW 13130A, p. 198. See also NLW 13221E, Iolo Morganwg to William Owen Pughe, 12 January 1806.

If followed to its bizarre logical conclusion, Iolo's line of argument clearly implied that, since it was divorced from bardism (the true bardic tradition of Wales), the whole rationale of the Gwyneddigion Society's literary mission was based on a facile misunderstanding of the professional poetic tradition in Wales and thus deserved nothing but ridicule. Indeed, he dismissed their cultural reforms as 'a laudable attempt on a bad plan and very crude and grossly undigested principles' and, because the true inheritors of bardism in Glamorgan knew better, he added '[it] has nothing in it that will be imitated in South Wales'.[120] This was a far cry from the glorious new era he had sycophantically envisaged for poetry under the aegis of Owain Myfyr and the Gwyneddigion:

> I have been informed some time ago, that you intend publishing our ancient Welsh mss. Mr Owen has told me on what plan. I cannot help greatly admiring and wondering at your Benevolent Patriotism, you have already done more towards the revival of our ancient Bardic Literature than any one living; than any one that ever lived since the commencement of its decline, which was coeval with the commencement of the 17th century . . . The Name of Owen Myfyr must descend to future ages with transcendent fame.[121]

Iolo's account of northern barbarism and southern sophistication revolved mainly around poetry. Poetry was the primary source of patriotic pride for Welsh cultural patriots who, in accordance with contemporary thought on the links between verse and history espoused by the likes of Joseph Ritson, maintained a profound and ancient link between poetry and national consciousness.[122] Nonetheless, Iolo also strengthened Glamorgan's superior position with parallel arguments regarding the development of prose and the regional dialects of the Welsh language. As far as prose was concerned, contemporary theories about the stages in the historical development and cultural significance of poetry and prose provided valuable ammunition. Intimately linked to oral modes of transmission, poetry – 'in every nation . . . the first effort of Genius' – was considered an initial stage in the development of a nation's literature and civilization,[123] while prose was allied with literacy and therefore represented a more advanced stage in the civilizing process. Iolo employed this argument to promote his national agenda, for he argued that prose had flowered in Wales before England.[124] But this basic argument, together with the fact, conveyed to him by Evan Evans, that a

[120] NLW 13130A, p. 190.
[121] BL Add. 13030, ff. 9–10, Iolo Morganwg to Owain Myfyr, 7 August 1798.
[122] This belief related specifically to the ancient poets of Greece. Iolo quoted from Ritson's 'Essay on National Song' prefixed to his *English Songs* (1783): 'Their Songs were chiefly designed to transmit to posterity the National History.' NLW 13107B, p. 66.
[123] NLW 13107B, p. 41.
[124] NLW 13098B, pp. 95–6.

sizeable corpus of Welsh medieval prose had been preserved in manuscripts of south Wales provenance, allowed Iolo to claim that south Wales had progressed from poetry to prose in advance of north Wales:

> But what appears very remarkable in this Period is that whilst Northwales in its Poetry was greatly superior to South Wales, it does not appear that a Single Prosewriter can be found in that part of Wales. All the Prose writers of the Period were South Walians.[125]

In this context, he referred specifically to Geoffrey of Monmouth, Walter Map (to whom he attributed a forged agricultural treatise),[126] Caradog of Llancarfan, the unknown author of the Mabinogion, Blegywryd (compiler of Welsh legal tracts) and the Physicians of Myddfai. In contrast, he claimed that no prose of any note had been produced in north Wales by a native of the region until *c.*1640 [*sic*] when Gutun Owain wrote his metrical treatise. From this he drew some predictable conclusions: 'How can this be accounted for? Is it that the Northwalian Literature was then only in its primary or poetical stage, and had not arrived at that of Prose? This appears to have been the case.'[127] Once more, Iolo created a greater fiction from a small number of facts: during the fourteenth and fifteenth centuries, prose works such as *Chwedlau Saith Doethion Rhufain* and *Ffordd y Brawd Odrig* had indeed been translated from Latin and French into Welsh at the behest of noblemen from Glamorgan and Gower.[128]

For Iolo, the early maturity of prose in south Wales mirrored the linguistic advancement of the people. His manuscripts and letters abound with acerbic comments about the Venedotian dialect: 'a contrary system cacophonous beyond all the usual powers of the organs of speech . . . the man who wishes to preserve his teeth unbroken, and his tongue from being forcibly pull[ed] up by the roots, had better beware of attempting the North Walian Welsh'.[129] Writing with thinly veiled sarcasm, Iolo singled out the dialectal penchant of north Wales for auxiliary verbs as a sign of vulgarity:

> The Northwalian dialect is still in its primitive rude and uncultivated state, its verbs have never been reduced to a regular system of inflection, they use auxiliaries and whence they inflect generally and needlessly add the pronoun, tho it be, as in

125 NLW 13107B, p. 42. See also NLW 13088B, pp. 82–3; NLW 13097B, p. 53; NLW 13098B, pp. 69–75, 94–7; NLW 13108B, pp. 95–6; NLW 13121B, p. 478; NLW 13154A, pp. 359–60; NLW 13162A, p. 144; NLW 21375A, no. 53.

126 NLW 13088B, p. 80; NLW 13098B, pp. 72, 96–7; NLW 13154A, p. 292; NLW 21431E, no. 34a.

127 NLW 13107B, p. 43. See also NLW 13088B, p. 82.

128 *TLlM*, p. 149; Lewis, 'The Literary Tradition of Morgannwg down to the Middle of the Sixteenth Century', p. 488.

129 NLW 21425E, p. 41b.

> the Latin &c involved in the inflection <conjugation>, if such antiquity can add merit to a language the north Walian may boast of it in a degree not greatly inferior perhaps to that of the Hottentots, and it happily has retained this species of excellence from its never having been a written dialect, at least by any remembered writer, however as a curiosity of antiquity.[130]

'Hottentot', which means 'one who stutters', was coined by Dutch missionaries for South African tribes, notably the Khopkoi, because of the characteristic clicks of their language. It became a standard term of denigration, notably among members of the Morris circle, in referring to the dialects of south Wales.[131] By comparing the north Wales dialect unfavourably with the language of the Hottentots, Iolo not only turned their own arguments against them but also adhered to a clearer primitivist agenda, as suggested by his barbed comment about the possible pedagogic use of north Wales dialects: 'it may be worth retaining, as a specimen of original uncultivated Welsh. It may have its use for ought I know as such to those who may wish to trace the progress of language from primeval barbarism to cultivated civilization'.[132]

Statements such as these provide a context for his arguments regarding Welsh as a literary medium. The battle for pre-eminence among the Welsh dialects was central to Iolo's interpretation of the development of the Welsh language as a literary medium. To reinforce the cultural advancement of Glamorgan, Iolo placed the Silurian dialect at the top of the hierarchy of dialects, and linked the paucity of north Wales prose with the feebleness of its linguistic dialect as a literary idiom. In a rough plan for an 'Analytical Dissertation on the Welsh Language', he noted that:

> The Venedotian Dialect notwithstanding its boasted purity, is by far the most corrupt of the Welsh Dialects. It never had any ancient cultivation, written specimens never appeared in it before the 1500 century and even then not very frequent or in all the nakedness of unpolished rudeness.[133]

Here, Iolo moulds the facts regarding the genuine medieval poetic guild around his narrative of Glamorgan's supremacy. The professional medieval poets had indeed developed a standardized poetic idiom, a lingua franca,

130 NLW 13138A, p. 145. A similar belief underpinned his retort to Goronwy Owen's comments about the corruption of south Wales dialects in NLW 13131A, pp. 412–13. See also NLW 13121B, p. 425.

131 Davies (ed.), *The Letters of Goronwy Owen*, p. 68; idem (ed.), *The Letters of Lewis, Richard, William and John Morris, of Anglesey*, II, p. 179.

132 NLW 13138A, p. 145. See also ibid., p. 427.

133 NLW 13121B, p. 426. See also NLW 13107B, pp. 42–3, in which he claimed that the dialect of north Wales did not become a literary language until the mid-sixteenth century. Richard M. Crowe, 'Sylwadau Iolo Morganwg ar Ynganiad y Wenhwyseg', *Cardiff Working Papers in Welsh Linguistics*, 7 (1992), 9.

which, allowing for some regional nuances, transcended the pronounced regional dialects of medieval Wales. This, together with the fact that medieval features had been retained in some south Wales dialects, persuaded Iolo that his own Glamorgan dialect, the *Gwenhwyseg* (Silurian), had been the universal literary and courtly dialect of medieval Wales:

> The Silurian Dialect, however the contrary opinion came to prevail, is certainly the purest by far of the Welsh Dialects; the richest, most copious, most expressive &c of all others. It was that of the Courts of the Welsh Princes, even of that of Aber-ffraw. It is that of all our ancient Writers and Bards, even those of North-wales. This is evident from what remain of the works of our Bards, &c.[134]

He explained the supposed pervasiveness of the Silurian dialect by incorporating Arthur into his bardic narrative, for had not the Silurian dialect been the language of office and government at the court of King Arthur in Caerleon and thereafter spread throughout Wales?[135] Elevating the Silurian dialect was a reaction to those in north Wales – notably the Morris brothers of Anglesey – who believed that their own dialects were purer than those found in the more Anglicized marcher regions of south Wales. He seethed at such conceit:

> The dialect of north Wales is certainly the most remote from either the modern or ancient literary dialects of any, notwithstanding the opinions that prevails to the contrary, which is owing to the Northwalians, so generally arrogating to themselves all philological excellence.[136]

This belief may be traced to the authoritative translation of the Welsh Bible in 1588 which formed the basis of the modern Welsh literary idiom which survives to the present day. The main translator was William Morgan, a native of north Wales, and the priority he accorded to the vocabulary and constructions of north Wales fortified prejudices against the dialects of south Wales. However, since Morgan had used the conservative language of the Welsh guild of poets as his linguistic pattern, Iolo turned this to his advantage by arguing that a combination of the Silurian and Dimetian dialects in the

134 NLW 13098B, p. 99. See also ibid., p. 93; NLW 13107B, p. 43; NLW 13108B, p. 94; NLW 13121B, p. 425.

135 NLW 13121B, pp. 425–6.

136 NLW 13130A, p. 180. See also NLW 13098B, pp. 93, 99; NLW 13107B, p. 43; NLW 13121B, pp. 425–6; NLW 21286E, Letter no. 961, Iolo Morganwg to Evan Williams, 9 February 1818. Richard M. Crowe, 'Diddordebau Ieithyddol Iolo Morganwg' (unpublished University of Wales Ph.D. thesis, 1992); idem, 'Iolo Morganwg – An Eighteenth-Century Welsh Linguist', 305–14; idem, 'Iolo Morganwg and the Dialects of Welsh' in *Rattleskull Genius*, pp. 315–32.

modern literary language accounted for its excellence. Any traces of the Venedotian in the literary language he explained away as corruptions: 'Northwalian Barbarisms', 'Deudneudisms' and 'Deudneudian barbarisms'.[137] The singular noun *Deudneudwr* or *Deudneudiwr* (pl. *Deudneudwyr*), a disparaging epithet coined by Iolo for the people of north Wales, plays with the north Wales pronunciation of the verbs *dweud* (to say, to speak) and *gwneud* (to do): 'as we call them in S. Wales, from Deud and Neud instead of Dywedyd and Gwneuthur, &c'.[138] Far from representing irrelevant tangents, the development of prose and the hierarchy of Welsh dialects were vital constituent parts of bardism's own internal narrative of regional supremacy. Moreover, they bore witness to the intellectual inventiveness of Iolo's prejudice against north Wales.

Finally, although an abiding love for one's native county was certainly not uncommon in eighteenth-century Wales, Iolo's brand of regionalism was unique insofar as it was wilfully woven into the fabric of his interpretation of Welsh literary history. Historical fact became subservient to the narrative of his vision, and in this bardism was both unprecedented and unparalleled. Glamorgan's primacy, though subject to changes in his personal circumstances, was sustained by Iolo in his writings over many decades and assumed both positive and negative forms. By assembling a bardic geography, an elaborate cultural genealogy and a mass of corroborative material around a primitivist framework, Iolo constructed a vision of Glamorgan that became one of the most complex and emblematic creations of the Romantic period in Wales. With its beguiling blend of fact and fiction, it bears comparison with Walter Scott's Scotland.[139] A further comparison may be drawn between Iolo's Glamorgan and Thomas Chatterton's Bristol. Just as Chatterton used the Rowley and Canynge forgeries to create a cultural identity for Bristol that was distinct from that of London, so Iolo enlisted Glamorgan to issue a provincial challenge of his own to London's literary superiority.[140] But the nature of Glamorgan's 'regional' challenge was more complex because bardism's challenge to the metropolitan hegemony was twofold: it constituted both a Welsh challenge to the literary and cultural superiority of the English capital, and a Glamorgan challenge to the literary and cultural superiority of the Gwyneddigion Society who, from their London base, had to a considerable extent dictated the course of the Welsh cultural revival.

137 See NLW 13118B, pp. 17, 21; NLW 13151A, p. 85.

138 NLW 21286E, Letter no. 994, Iolo Morganwg to Taliesin Williams, 22 September 1823. The letter also included many imprecations against William Owen Pughe's linguistic innovations.

139 Williams: *IM*, pp. 270–1, 273; Lewis: *IM*, chapter 15.

140 Lewis, 'Eighteenth-Century Literary Forgeries', pp. 90–1.

When his collaboration with the Gwyneddigion finally ended in 1806, Iolo's regional challenge changed its complexion completely. His obsessive personality and tendency towards paranoia ensured that his exaltation of Glamorgan bards and poetics alienated him from friends in London-Welsh circles and this alienation in turn prompted him to retreat inwards into an increasingly self-conscious and self-centred regionalism. In his study of nineteenth-century Irish identity, Joep Leerssen argued that a sense of historical individuality is the crucial element which distinguishes a province and a nation,[141] that 'a region's sense of history is secondary and incidental to the historical patterns of the nation-at-large', and that a region is typically a-historical, a backwater where metropolitan fashions are slow to permeate.[142] As we have already seen, a degree of parity existed between Iolo's projection of Welsh civilization and the projection of Irish civilization by contemporary Irish antiquaries such as Joseph Cooper Walker, Charlotte Brooke and Sylvester O'Halloran, in which an awareness of its past, its own 'root system' independent of England or Britain was crucial to Irish national consciousness.[143] In terms of regional emphasis, however, Iolo diverges from Leerssen's thesis, for his Glamorgan was by no means a-historical; nor was it a sleepy backwater. On the contrary, Iolo's vision of Glamorgan boasted a vibrant history that was neither secondary or incidental to the historical patterns of Wales as a whole. As the sole preserver of bardism – the vehicle of Wales's precocious and profound civilization – Glamorgan's history was brought to the foreground of Welsh historical consciousness and, as bardism was adopted by literary-minded clerics during the nineteenth century, Glamorgan became ever more deeply rooted in the historical consciousness of the nation. Faithfully transmitted by the likes of Walter Davies (Gwallter Mechain), John Jenkins (Ifor Ceri), W. J. Rees, Casgob and John Williams (Ab Ithel), bardism's fictitious Glamorgan assumed the status of received literary history, and subsequent generations of scholars have been obliged to unpick Iolo's fabrications from the county's authentic poetic tradition.[144] For this, he may justly be charged with having poisoned the waters of Welsh scholarship, but the fact remains that Iolo enjoyed enormous success in overturning the image and fortunes of impoverished, derided Glamorgan. Disregarded by Lewis Morris in the early eighteenth century, and also by a later generation of cultural revivalists based in London, by the nineteenth century scholars shared Iolo's vision of Glamorgan as the most significant region in Welsh history:

141 Joseph Leerssen, *Remembrance and Imagination: Patterns in the Historical and Literary Representation of Ireland in the Nineteenth Century* (Cork, 1996), p. 147.
142 Ibid, p. 187.
143 Ibid, p. 147.
144 See, for example, *TLlM.*

odid na ddywedent mai Morgannwg oedd y dalaith bwysicaf yng Nghymru, neu o'r hyn lleiaf, mai hi oedd y dalaith fwyaf diddorol. Dyma'r wlad a lynodd wrth hen draddodiadau'r genedl, a roddodd i haneswyr ein llên y deunydd gwerthfawrocaf a oedd ganddynt. Llwyd a rhyddieithol oedd y taleithiau eraill o'u cymharu â Morgannwg. Ei beirdd hi a gadwodd afael yn y sefydliad yr oedd pawb yn rhyw deimlo ei fod yn un o'r pethau mwyaf nodweddiadol Gymreig, sef Gorsedd Beirdd Ynys Prydain.[145]

(In all probability, they would say that Glamorgan was the most important region in Wales, or, at least, that she was the most interesting region. This was the county which adhered to the nation's old traditions, that gave our literary historians the most valuable material they possessed. Compared to Glamorgan, other regions were grey and prosaic. Her bards had kept a grasp on the institution that everyone felt was one of the most characteristically Welsh things, that is the Gorsedd of the Bards of the Island of Britain.)

The symbiotic nature of the relationship between national and regional identity brings us to an important question: to what extent, if at all, did the primacy Iolo attributed to Glamorgan in bardism threaten the integrity of his central message of Welsh civilization? Since the primitivist framework and arguments which underpinned the binary opposition of barbarous England/Gwynedd and civilized Wales/Glamorgan are identical, Wales and Glamorgan may be considered interchangeable. Moreover, Iolo's opposition to the metropolitan centre remained constant in both a Welsh/national and a Glamorgan/regional context. While the north Walian barbarism he depicted may have detracted from Wales's overall cultivation, Glamorgan, with its bardic inheritance, more than compensated for this deficiency. However, despite Iolo's regional emphasis, his main focus was always national, and was reflected in the interdependency of the Welsh language (in all its regional variations) and the emblematic Welsh culture it articulated in bardism. Ultimately, for Iolo, the Welsh language transcended its own regional boundaries and, in a forged letter which he composed around 1785 and attributed to Dafydd Nicolas, Iolo, not for the first time in his career, inextricably linked the Welsh language, strict-metre poetry and bardism:

pan y llwyr goller yr hen ffordd o Brydyddu nid hir y bydd hi cyn colli'r iaith Gymraeg. Cyhyd ac y cedwir ac y dyellir yr hen farddoniaeth ai rheolau gorchestol cyhyd a hynny y cedwir yn ddilwgr y Iaith Gymraeg.[146]

(when the old way of versifying is lost entirely it will not be long before the Welsh language is lost. As long as the old poetry and its vaunted regulations are kept and understood, as long as that the Welsh language will be kept uncontaminated.)

[145] Ibid., p. xii. See also Lewis, 'The Literary Tradition of Morgannwg down to the Middle of the Sixteenth Century', pp. 451–2.

[146] NLW 13122B, pp. 165–6. The letter was addressed to Edward Evan, Aberdare, and dated Glyncorrwg, April 1754.

Wales might have been indebted to Glamorgan for preserving bardism, but inherent in bardism's framework was the notion that bardic civilization was within the grasp of other regions in Wales if only they would embrace it and its ideals. This was the 'Age of Taliesin yr Ail [the second] . . . the age of Restitution' that Iolo envisaged for Wales,[147] and following the eisteddfod in Carmarthen in 1819 it became a viable alternative.

In the final analysis, the primacy of Glamorgan and the north–south tension in bardism was symptomatic of the fluid nature of national and regional allegiances rather than of a strict hierarchy in which region was subordinate to nation. In Iolo's case, his was a highly subjective stance, coloured as much, if not more, by interpersonal troubles as by an underlying and ancient rivalry between north and south. In 1822, four years before his death, he was bent on silencing 'the North Walian clamour' by publishing his *Cyfrinach Beirdd Ynys Prydain*. He revelled in the repercussions his arguments would provoke among some of his north Wales detractors: 'they will be maddened to find that all their great knowledge of which they so loudly brag, consists of nothing but what every man of sense will confess to be disgraceful to Human Reason . . . I am ready and prepared to meet them all'.[148] This pugnacious spirit reflected not only the increasingly messianic tone of bardism in Iolo's dotage and of its potency as a form of self-definition, but the way in which his resentment seems to have conflated William Owen Pughe, Owain Myfyr and the Gwyneddigion into one *bête noire*: Gwynedd. Bardism crystallized in Iolo's imagination during a time of considerable stress, and his romantic dreaming about druidic Glamorgan became a 'place of refuge' ('*dinas noddfa*') for him, particularly during the financial troubles he experienced in the mid-1780s[149] and when the close companionship with his London friends broke down. In many ways, bardism had become a permanent place of refuge from life's vicissitudes: it was a parallel world in which all the anti-Welsh and anti-south Wales prejudices and the personal slights he had encountered were avenged within a meaningful intellectual framework. For this reason, it was Iolo's egocentricity, rather than his regional allegiance, which eventually undermined the integrity of his bardic vision. Ironically, therefore, the same primitivist framework which imbued Iolo's passionate objections to anti-Welsh prejudices with intellectual authority was used to support his own anti-north Wales bias with a veneer of scholarly objectivity.

147 NLW 13131A, p. 364.

148 NLW 21286E, Letter no. 989, Iolo to the Revd D. Jones, 6 May 1822. See also *Cambrian Register*, 3 (1818), 174–9, Iolo Morganwg to Evan Williams, 16 January 1810; ibid., 381–5, Iolo Morganwg to Evan Williams, 31 March 1811; ibid., 372–4, Iolo Morganwg to Evan Williams, 23 April 1809.

149 Williams: *IM*, pp. 423–4, 443; Lewis, *IM*, p. 158.

5

The Making of the Gorsedd: A National Pedigree

The Gorsedd of the Bards of the Island of Britain was part of a pseudo-antiquarian system devised and used by Iolo Morganwg to validate the image and identity of Wales, Glamorgan and himself. All three 'bardic circles' came together in the making of the Gorsedd. By resurrecting what he believed to be an ancient model for conveying contemporary messages, Iolo reflected the increasingly symbiotic relationship between domestic antiquarianism and patriotism in a period in which establishing – or more properly, 'constructing' – a national past was exercising antiquaries and cultural patriots within different parts of Britain and Ireland. A complex matrix of historicist, primitivist and patriotic ideas were superimposed on events, material objects, monuments and heroes of the distant past as English, Scottish, Welsh and Irish writers and antiquarians grappled with the ramifications of a supposed British unity, and sought to construct and validate their own distinct national identities. The desired image of Wales presented in bardism was that of an ancient, civilized nation whose proleptic Christianity and republicanism repudiated long-standing popular stereotypes of Welsh barbarism and backwardness. But Iolo's vision was no dry intellectual exercise: he brought his ideas to life by peopling Wales's past with a cast of colourful characters. This was in keeping with his conviction that heroes as well as events and places could encapsulate the qualities and virtues of a nation. With this aim in mind, Iolo applied his imagination in order to create a national pedigree and mythology for a modern institution based on the vestiges of the defunct professional poetic guild of medieval times.

This chapter examines the making of that institution. It focuses on the regional scope of the Gorsedd from its inception in 1792, and the way in which it was gradually embraced as a national institution during the decades after Iolo's death in 1826. The story of the making of the Gorsedd is double-edged insofar as it indicates not only the formation of the institution but also its development and rise to fame as one of the emblems of civilized Welshness. The first part therefore deals with the components of the Gorsedd but, since the human element which gave bardism its narrative drive contributed greatly to bardism's appeal, the discussion focuses on the new but 'ancient' national pedigree Iolo created in bardism. The second part traces the transformation of the Gorsedd from a localized novelty into a national spectacle, and examines the way in which it became a breeding ground for a new generation of patriotic and, indeed, patriarchal bards and Druids once it allied itself with the provincial eisteddfodau from 1819 onwards.

Nowadays, the Gorsedd is considered to be the most familiar and enduring aspect of Iolo Morganwg's bardic vision. It is, and always has been, an essentially public spectacle: its role as an integral part of the cultural festivities of the National Eisteddfod has ensured that it has gained familiarity and authority independently of Iolo's wider bardic vision. During the late eighteenth and early nineteenth centuries bardism was accessible only through Iolo's unpublished manuscripts and limited printed sources. But the Gorsedd subsequently evolved into an institution in its own right and, although its history has been marked by controversy, it remains one of the most popular features of the National Eisteddfod, and to be admitted to the Gorsedd is considered one of the greatest accolades the Welsh nation can bestow.

Iolo fabricated the function, terminology and rationale of the Gorsedd from fragmented and elusive traditions associated with the medieval eisteddfod. But the term Gorsedd, if not the precise meaning he gave it, is genuine. Historically, the common noun *gorsedd* relates to a mound of earth or tumulus, a throne or, more precisely, a repository for weapons in a church or court of law.[1] The most ancient meaning, and the most relevant in Iolo's case, signifies a 'court, hall, dwelling, place; court of law, judicial assembly, tribunal, session, judge's seat; assembly, gathering'. From this, Iolo extrapolated his own peculiar application of the word: for him, it denoted a meeting or a congress of bards and, in his English writings on the subject, he gives the following cognates: presidiality, convention, congress and sedality.[2] Iolo's Gorsedd belongs to the same semantic circle as the word 'eisteddfod', which also means 'assembly, synod, session, council, conference and congress',[3] and from the fifteenth century onwards it acquired a stricter sense: an assembly of poets. In essence, an eisteddfod was an assembly of professional poets, usually supported by an aristocratic patron, for the practice and advancement of strict-metre Welsh poetry.[4] Effectively an exercise in self-regulation, if not self-preservation, it was an occasion for ensuring that the time-honoured rules and practices of strict-metre verse were maintained and that only men properly trained in the craft of poetry were licensed to practise it. Following

1 *GPC*, s.v. 'gorsedd'.

2 See NLW 13089E, pp. 439, 442, 445 and NLW 13150A, p. 113. For 'congress', see also Williams: *PLP*, II, p. 70n; for 'public meetings of Bards', see NLW 13097B, pp. 103, 392; 'Gorseddau or Druidic Temples', NLW 13121B, p. 304; 'Gorsedd (Sedes)', ibid., p. 308. In a letter in which he discussed Avebury and Silbury Hill, William Owen Pughe called the latter a 'mound of the National Assemblies'. NLW 21281E, Letter no. 351, William Owen Pughe to Iolo Morganwg, 8 January 1802.

3 *GPC*, s.v. 'eisteddfod'.

4 Hywel Teifi Edwards, *The Eisteddfod* (Cardiff, 1990), pp. 4–10; Dillwyn Miles, *The Royal National Eisteddfod of Wales* (Swansea, 1977), p. 12. See also Idris Foster (ed.) *Twf yr Eisteddfod* (Abertawe, 1968); G. J. Williams, 'Yr Eisteddfod a'r Orsedd', *Y Llenor*, I, no. 1 (1922), 131–64; Prys Morgan, 'From a Death to a View: The Hunt for the Welsh Past in the Romantic Period' in Eric Hobsbawm and Terence Ranger (eds.), *The Invention of Tradition* (Cambridge, 1983), pp. 56–62.

the dissolution of the indigenous royal court in Wales, the world of patronage in late medieval Wales had become a highly competitive environment in which professional poets could no longer enjoy or expect exclusivity. They were required to compete for increasingly scarce patronage with home-grown amateurs, unlicensed poets, as well as English minstrels and jugglers. For Welsh poets then, the eisteddfod was a means of legitimizing their professional guild and its traditions and also of maintaining their social and cultural standing. The competitive element for which the National Eisteddfod is now famous was introduced in the late eighteenth century when organizers offered medals and financial rewards in order to encourage poets to contribute to the revival of this long-established institution.

The few eisteddfodau for which reliable historical documentation and traditions survive were held in times of crisis for the professional bardic guild and the Welsh nation at large. The breakdown of native patterns of patronage was one of the most detrimental cultural consequences of the loss of political independence in 1282–3. With the demise of the native Welsh princes and Welsh independence, court patronage ceased and the professional guild of poets survived by courting the sponsorship of the Welsh nobility instead. This was the context for the eisteddfod held at Carmarthen *c.*1453, while the eisteddfod held at Caerwys in 1567 was at least partly held as a riposte to the more sinister threat posed to the Welsh language and culture by the so-called 'language clause' of the first Act of Union of 1536. Following the ensuing administrative assimilation of Wales into England the alliance between Welsh poets and the gentry faltered, and poets were discarded by landowners who believed that their own economic interests and social advancement could best be safeguarded by embracing English mores and customs. By the mid-seventeenth century the poetic guild had ceased to exist as a professional body and had become largely the pursuit of amateurs.

Historically, then, eisteddfodau were attempts by the professional guild of poets to put their house in order and maintain a sense of cohesion and identity in times of significant cultural and social change. As a result, when eighteenth-century antiquaries and poets sought to rescue the poetic craft and learning, resurrecting the eisteddfod was a logical step in that process. They, too, were responding to a critical turning point in Welsh culture: the Anglicization of the upper and middle sections of Welsh society was advancing dangerously and, from 1707 onwards, Welsh culture was vulnerable to the encroachment of the expanding British state. Against this backdrop, several small-scale eisteddfodau were held, mainly in taverns, at the beginning of the eighteenth century. Labelled *eisteddfodau'r almanaciau* (almanac eisteddfodau), these boozy, informal gatherings and the poetry they produced were promoted in Welsh-language almanacs. One of the most fervent supporters of the revived eisteddfod was Siôn Rhydderch, a poet and printer whose bardic grammar, *Grammadeg Cymraeg* (1728), which followed the rubric of the medieval 'Statute of Gruffudd ap Cynan', was published to help poets to improve their craft and structure their eisteddfodau effectively. Despite his staunch support for eisteddfodau throughout Wales, Rhydderch's efforts did little to halt the decline of strict-metre verse. By the end of the century, the course of strict-metre verse and the eisteddfod changed when Jonathan Hughes of Llangollen and Thomas Jones of Corwen enlisted the patronage of the Gwyneddigion Society: the first eisteddfod under their auspices was held in Corwen in 1789 and established a blueprint for the National Eisteddfod.[5] It was these eisteddfodau that Iolo's own Gorseddau were intended to rival.

Both the medieval and the revived eisteddfodau became Iolo's model for his Gorsedd, and since both institutions fulfilled similar functions it is not surprising that the words 'eisteddfod' and 'Gorsedd' were used interchangeably by many of Iolo's contemporaries. For example, when he was invited by Iolo to participate in a Gorsedd in Glamorgan in 1798, Thomas Evans (Tomos Glyn Cothi) replied: 'I am not certain whether I can come to the Eisteddfod Alban Elfed or not.'[6] But having usurped the role traditionally associated with the eisteddfod, Iolo simply defined it as something utterly meaningless unless it was accompanied by a Gorsedd.[7] He attempted to circumvent the fact that eisteddfod and Gorsedd were essentially the same phenomenon by using the alleged antiquity and authority of his own invention to weaken the position and prestige of the original on which it was modelled. This, together with his anti-northern animus, accounts for the scribbled invective which he wrote on the margins of a selection of handbills advertising the eisteddfod which the Gwyneddigion Society organized at Caerwys: 'Hah! . . . Awkward attempts at Bardic phrases . . . verbose Jabber . . . inane prolixity and false idioms.'[8]

Iolo's Gorsedd was not only an alternative to the eisteddfod but also a much more sophisticated entity which reflected its roots in antiquarianism. More than a rallying point for the restoration of the Welsh poetic tradition, it also represented the public face of bardism and served to publicize the

5 Edwards, *The Eisteddfod*, p. 12; Helen Ramage, 'Eisteddfodau'r Ddeunawfed Ganrif' in Foster (ed.), *Twf yr Eisteddfod*, pp. 9–27.

6 NLW 21281E, Letter no. 171, Thomas Evans to Iolo Morganwg, 4 August 1798. Thomas Evans made the same association in NLW 21281E, Letter no. 172, Thomas Evans to Iolo Morganwg, 26 October 1798. See also David Samwell to Walter Davies, 17 February 1793: 'Iorwerth Gwilym made our Eisteddfod cut a figure in the newspapers, and that is something', *THSC* (1926–7), 127. Edward Williams of Merthyr also referred to a Gorsedd as an eisteddfod in stanzas inviting Edward Evan to a Gorsedd in 1797. See Edward Williams, *Cyfaill y Cymru, Sef Englynion, Cywyddau, â Chaniadau Newyddion; Ar amryw Desdynau, a Mesyrau* (n.p., 1797), pp. 12–13.

7 NLW 13089E, p. 392.

8 NLW 21403E, nos. 6–8. See also ibid., nos. 4, 5.

historical consciousness and ancient democratic traditions of the Welsh people.[9] Its superiority lay in its abundant detail and rigorously exercised logic, for Iolo not only presented it as an existing tradition, but also as a workable framework in terms which contemporaries could comprehend. Iolo's Gorsedd provided internal evidence that bardic precepts were not decided arbitrarily, but were arrived at by democratic consensus in a series of Gorseddau. In turn, the layered and rigorous process of verification was designed to prove that, contrary to the assumptions prompted by the Ossian controversy, oral transmission was neither unreliable nor disreputable. Reflecting the supposedly druidic penchant for triadic forms, Iolo claimed that there were three types of Gorsedd. *Gorsedd gyfarch* (assembly of request) was the first stage in seeking the judgement of an assembly of bards. This was followed by *Gorsedd hawl* (gorsedd of claim or demand) in which a judgement was honoured. Finally, *Gorsedd gyfallwy* (complete assembly), a national assembly for the entire body of the Bards of the Island of Britain, was the only Gorsedd which could legitimately validate or confirm a precept or tradition:

> Nid oes Bwys na deddf nac awdurdawd ar na chan nac un peth arall, ai cof, ai addysg, ai hysbysrwydd y bo, na pha bynnag onid el wrth farn a nawdd Gorsedd Gyfallwy Beirdd Ynys Prydain.[10]
>
> (There is no importance or law or authority to a song or any other thing, whether it is a memory, or education or knowledge, or whatever else unless it goes before the judgement and patronage of a complete Gorsedd of the Bards of the Island of Britain.)

Both *Gorsedd gyfarch* and *Gorsedd hawl* could be held by regional assemblies of bards, but a *Gorsedd gyfallwy* could only be held by a national assembly. Iolo explained this process in a footnote published in *Poems, Lyric and Pastoral* (1794), in which he invested his 'Ode on the Mythology of the Ancient British Bards' with bardic authority and prestige.[11] Similarly, three types of Gorsedd were necessary for the correct initiation into the bardic orders.[12] Despite Iolo's inordinate attention to detail, in practice these variations proved academic: in his writings pertaining to London and Glamorgan Gorseddau, he rarely noted the specific type held. But Iolo could not refrain from fine-tuning his creation, even though it meant disrupting the druidic resonance of

[9] Geraint H. Jenkins, 'The Bard of Liberty during William Pitt's Reign of Terror' in Joseph Falaky Nagy and Leslie Ellen Jones (eds.), *Heroic Poets and Poetic Heroes in Celtic Tradition: A Festschrift for Patrick K. Ford*, CSANA Yearbook 3–4 (Dublin, 2005), p. 198. See also Gwyn A. Williams, *The Welsh in their History* (London, 1982), pp. 31–64.

[10] NLW 13097B, p. 15; NLW 13098B, pp. 286, 292; NLW 13124B, p. 114; NLW 13128A, p. 93; NLW 13129A, pp. 39–41; NLW 13135A, p. 263; NLW 13144A, pp. 6–7.

[11] Williams: *PLP*, II, p. 193.

[12] NLW 13097B, pp. 22–32; NLW 13106B, p. 13.

the triadic form: other (later) variants include *Gorsedd arddangos* (assembly of demonstration), which was specifically for pedagogic purposes,[13] and *Gorsedd gwsg* (sleeping assembly), an inactive or defunct assembly which could be revived by following a ritual supposedly devised in the time of Prydain ab Aedd Mawr.[14] The latter indicates the frequency with which Iolo's irrepressible personal and regional biases coloured bardism's national agenda, for the 'sleeping assembly' related only to bardic chairs in north Wales, and was one of countless other apparently innocuous details which pointedly excluded the poets of that region from bardism's civilizing inheritance.

Iolo's guidelines for the Gorsedd proceedings are equally replete with detail whose ramifications are more significant than they at first appear. The proclamation of the first Gorsedd held in June 1792 echoed the extant proclamation scroll of the sixteenth-century eisteddfodau at Caerwys and noted that the aim of the proceedings was to appraise every poet who wished to be graded and licensed in music and poetry. It must be emphasized that it was meant to serve as an accrediting body from the outset: a bard could only gain admission into the hallowed ranks through a Gorsedd ceremony.[15] In a Welsh document relating to a Gorsedd held at Bryn Owain (Stalling Down, also occasionally called Bryn Gwyddon, Druid's Hill) in 1795,[16] Iolo set out what Geraint and Zonia Bowen have accurately described as a manifesto for the Gorsedd.[17] Iolo outlined eleven 'considerations' (*darbodau*) which revealed that the Gorsedd reflected and practised the basic tenets of bardism. These considerations or prerequisites may be grouped thematically, though Iolo himself did not arrange them so neatly. He asserted that Gorsedd rituals should be performed in accordance with so-called 'ancient usage', but he was principally concerned with the preservation of the craft of strict-metre poetry and its concomitants. Convinced of the reliability of the oral transmission of poetry, he argued that it was the only accurate method of preserving the Welsh language and its druidic learning. As we have seen, the interdependency of Welsh language and poetry was one of bardism's most fundamental principles. Two further considerations support this, and stress the importance which Iolo laid on maintaining the purity and idiomatic flavour of the Welsh language: 'canys yn anghyfnewidioldeb y gelfyddyd wrth Gerdd y saif anghyfnewidioldeb a chadernyd yr Iaith Gymraeg' (because in

13 NLW 21376A, no. 3a.

14 NLW 13107B, p. 20.

15 The 1792 Gorsedd was proclaimed in David Thomas, *Awdlau ar Destynau Cymdeithas y Gwyneddigion i'r Eisteddfodau Yn B.A. 1789, 1790, 1791. Sef Ystyriaeth ar Oes Dyn, Rhyddid, a Gwirionedd* (Llundain, 1791), p. 46.

16 NLW 13221E, pp. 115–18, Iolo Morganwg to William Owen Pughe, 5 December 1801: William Owen Pughe was under the impression that Gorsedd Bryn Gwyddon was Avebury.

17 *HGB*, p. 34. See also NLW 21286E, Letter no. 1005, Iolo Morganwg to Taliesin Williams, 17 January 1826.

the immutability of the art of poetry stands the immutability and strength of the Welsh language).[18] Clarity of meaning was also paramount and, echoing the Augustan ideals of Goronwy Owen, Iolo warned against 'gorchestion ofergamp a lyffetheiriant iaith a synnwyr' (the feats of vain excellence that fetter language and sense),[19] namely the fiendishly difficult metrical innovations introduced by Dafydd ab Edmwnd in the fifteenth century, which had inspired Iolo to fabricate an alternative metrical system more consonant with the pedagogic aspect of bardism. Two other considerations more explicitly reveal that the north–south tension was maturing gradually by this stage. One upheld the fictional prohibition against the use of Dafydd ab Edmwnd's modifications by the regional assembly of Glamorgan bards, while another entreated Glamorgan bards to demonstrate graciously the superiority of their very own 'manner and consideration' (*dull a darbod*) over visiting poets from other Welsh counties.[20] Yet another relevant consideration in this context was Iolo's injunction that a bard from another region could not declaim his verse in a Gorsedd hosted by the chair of Glamorgan unless a bard of that region had first ascertained that it accorded with proper bardic principles.[21] The remaining considerations revealed his penchant for two associated issues which he believed lay at the heart of bardism: education and morality. In deference to the strand of didactic poetry in Wales, Iolo maintained that a Bard's function was to instruct his nation ('athrawiaethu ei genedl') in the niceties of traditional strict-metre verse and that he should never convey in his poems language and thoughts inappropriate for common people.[22] Moreover, a bard was advised not to recite in a *cadair* (chair) or Gorsedd any poem or song which might contaminate the morals and habits of the Welsh nation, or lead to vain and foolish behaviour.[23] In order to fulfil his pedagogic responsibility, Iolo insisted that a bard was required to be above moral reproach and to be a man of reason and peace ('gwr wrth bwyll a thangnef'). These principles were proclaimed in a Welsh poem on the transmission of knowledge among the Ancient Welsh at a Gorsedd held at Llantwit Fardre in 1797. It reiterated the symbiotic link between the Welsh language, religious knowledge, morality, education and truth, the touchstone of bardism:

Tra fo dy feirdd yn cadw'th iaith
 Na foed eu gwaith yn ofer,
Boed ar eu cerddi o bob rhyw
 Llais deddfau Duw'r uchelder,

[18] NLW 13144A, pp. 13, 14.
[19] Ibid., p. 10.
[20] Ibid., pp. 14–16.
[21] Ibid., p. 14.
[22] Ibid., pp. 10–12.
[23] Ibid., p. 12.

Barddoniaeth yw'th gelfyddyd fawr,
  Bu gynt yn fawr ei lleufer,
O bydded fyth yr hynn a'i gwedd
  Yn addysg hedd bob amser.

A thra bo cynnwrf mawr y byd
  Yn arwain bryd annwyfol,
At waed a rhyfel ymhob mann,
  A sarnu'r gwann cystuddiol,
Bid iaith dy gerddi 'mhlaid y gwir,
  Drwy gyrrau'th dir yn hollol,
Na ddeled byth ond iawnder hardd
  O Benn un Bardd awenol.[24]

(While your [Wales] poets keep your language may their work never be in vain,/ May their myriad verses proclaim the statutes of God on high,/Poetry is your great Art, Her light was once bright,/O may that which befits her forever always [be] the education of peace.

And while the great agitation of the world leads to an ungodly nature,/to blood and war in every place, and trampling on the afflicted [and] weak,/Through all parts of thy entire land, let the language of your poems favour the truth,/Let nothing ever but beautiful justice Come from the mouth of a poetic Bard.)

Only the Bards of the Island of Britain were capable of maintaining these vital links.

The fabricated past of the Gorsedd was supported by a large body of documents which dealt exclusively with its history, rationale, ritual and bardic pedigree. Iolo presented pseudo-historical compositions as copies or transcriptions of genuine bardic lore, sometimes attributing them to specific historical personages, but more often depicting them as received bardic learning, validated by ancient usage.[25] Forgeries such as these were, of necessity, written in archaic Welsh and consisted of metrical guidelines, poems, triads, an occasional 'dialogue' between a bardic disciple and his master, and miscellaneous anecdotes about bards and bardic events. Iolo composed his forgeries with a view to publication, but only a fraction of this material was ever printed during his lifetime. Around 1803 he had intended to publish a volume of 'original' Welsh bardic documents with English translations, an introduction and notes. Entitled 'Collections for the History of the Ancient British Bards &c',[26] like so many of his publishing ventures it never came to

[24] NLW 13141A, p. 29.
[25] *IMChY*; Mary-Ann Constantine, 'Pious Frauds and Perjurers: Iolo Morganwg's Truth against the World' in Peter Knight and Jonathan Long (eds.), *Fakes and Forgeries* (Cambridge, 2004), pp. 119–34.
[26] NLW 13221E, Letter no. 1067, Iolo Morganwg to William Owen Pughe, 1 August 1803.

fruition. However, some of this material was published in the third volume of *The Myvyrian Archaiology of Wales*, which appeared in 1807, and he also duped William Owen Pughe, the editor of the short-lived magazine *Y Greal* (1805–7), into publishing spurious versions of the Statute of Gruffudd ap Cynan which supported his false claims about the druidic superiority of free-metre poetry.[27]

One of the most dynamic and successful elements of the Gorsedd was its inspired use of an authentic bardic pedigree: 'all the Beirdd Ynys Prydain (Bards of the Island of Britain) are representatively and virtually present at a Gorsedd'.[28] As Prys Morgan has shown, Iolo made his 'sublime picture of Welsh history' comprehensible to common people by introducing several colourful and larger-than-life characters, 'all passing in a brilliant pageant, making human and palpable Iolo's weird and wonderful fantasies'.[29] But Iolo's pageant of personalities was not simply intended to bolster his own claims to be the last legitimate 'Ancient British Bard'. His interest in characters and pedigrees was part and parcel of his antiquarian interests,[30] but it also reflected the national obsession with genealogy, a trait often lampooned in satirical tracts in the seventeenth and eighteenth centuries.[31] This national characteristic, however, was deeply rooted in the sense of Welsh nationhood which had been formed in early medieval Wales and which stressed the importance of descent and kindred. In this context, Glanmor Williams observed that 'pedigree was as important to a people as to an individual',[32] and, for the Welsh, their sense of nationhood was founded on the belief that they were descended from the first occupants of Britain, and were therefore its lawful possessors. This ancient historiographical strand first appeared in Gildas's *De excidio Britanniae* in the sixth century and was recycled in the eighteenth century to frame resistance to the burgeoning sense of 'Britishness' propagated by the British state which emerged from the union of England and Wales with Scotland in 1707. Such was the importance of descent and genealogy for Welsh medieval poets – the nation's propagandists – that language and literacy were considered 'secondary tokens of nationality',[33] but although Iolo shared their reverence for lineal connections, in

27 Y *Greal*, V (1806), 238–9; VII (1806), 300–3.

28 NLW 13097B, p. 137. See also ibid., pp. 142, 270.

29 Prys Morgan, *The Eighteenth Century Renaissance* (Llandybïe, 1981), p. 119; idem, 'From a Death to a View', pp. 81–6.

30 The study of genealogy was one of the main preoccupations of contemporary antiquaries, Rosemary Sweet, *Antiquaries: The Discovery of the Past in Eighteenth-Century Britain* (London, 2004), p. 39.

31 W. J. Hughes, *Wales and the Welsh in English Literature from Shakespeare to Scott* (Wrexham, 1924); Peter Lord, *Words with Pictures: Welsh Images and Images of Wales in the Popular Press, 1640–1860* (Aberystwyth, 1995), pp. 38, 68.

32 Glanmor Williams, *Religion, Language and Nationality in Wales* (Cardiff, 1979), p. 5.

33 Ibid.

his own reworking of the medieval poetic tradition in bardism, language and literacy were presented as primary tokens of nationhood (see Document I).

In addition to working within an existing national heritage that prided itself on ancestors and networks of kin, Iolo was also responding to a new situation in which cultural genealogies were assuming an important role in the emergence of nationalist sentiment during the Romantic period. Since the seventeenth century countries in northern Europe had developed an interest in their own cultural origins and had begun marshalling their native heroes to satisfy two ends: to distinguish their own national identities from those of the more influential polities that encompassed them, and to celebrate their individuality.[34] One of the most influential texts in this quest was *Northern Antiquities* (1770), Bishop Thomas Percy's translation of Paul Henri Mallet's comprehensive history of Denmark, a work which furnished Iolo with many of his ideas. Germany embraced Hermann, France found Vercingetorix a useful figure to further Napoleonic propaganda, and many other European countries were eager to include the Druids in their national pedigrees.[35] In England this trend clearly motivated the compilers of the hefty six-volume *Biographia Britannica*:

> [it is] calculated to extend and Support the Reputation of the British People, by preserving the Memories of the most ILLUSTRIOUS PERSONS of all Ranks, and transmitting to Posterity the just Characters of STATESMEN, PRELATES, PATRIOTS, LAWYERS, DIVINES, and whoever else have been eminent among us, for Wisdom, Learning, Valour, and other laudable Accomplishments.[36]

Wales, too, was actively involved in researching its primeval origins, for the late eighteenth and early nineteenth centuries witnessed the transformation of historical characters into national heroes. Iolo's creation of an illustrious cultural genealogy for bardism must be viewed in this context. He was not, of course, alone in fashioning a pantheon of heroes for Wales. The likes of Owain Glyndŵr, Madog ab Owain Gwynedd, Ifor Hael, Dafydd ap Gwilym and Twm Siôn Cati were also elevated to national status by other writers during the eighteenth century.[37] The sterling efforts of Lewis Morris, Evan Evans and William Owen Pughe serve as 'a salutary reminder that the [eighteenth-century] Welsh Renaissance was not a game played by dry-as-dust scholars in their ivory towers, but had a genuinely popular dimen-

[34] Sam Smiles, *The Image of Antiquity: Ancient Britain and the Romantic Imagination* (London, 1994), p. 26.

[35] Ibid., pp. 32–4; Stuart Piggott, *The Druids* (London, 1999), pp. 123–82.

[36] *Biographia Britannica: or, the Lives of the Most Eminent Persons who have flourished in Great Britain and Ireland, From the earliest Ages, down to the present Times: Collected from the best Authorities, both Printed and Manuscript, And digested in the Manner of Mr Bayle's Historical and Critical Dictionary* (6 vols., London, 1747–66), I, p. ii.

[37] Morgan, *The Eighteenth Century Renaissance*, pp. 119–24.

sion'.[38] Evan Evans's poem *The Love of Our Country* (1772) was a roll-call of Welsh cultural champions: informed by antiquarianism and motivated by English aspersions against Welsh history, it included heroes as chronologically distant from each other as Caratacus and Owain Glyndŵr. Lewis Morris had provided a first major building block for constructing a new national pantheon in 'Celtic Remains', an ambitious undertaking which took him forty years to compile and which was eventually published posthumously in 1878.[39] Sometime during 1794–5, Iolo read the manuscript copy transcribed by Richard Morris Jr and added marginal notes of his own to records concerning places and people in Glamorgan. Pughe did not acknowledge his debt to 'Celtic Remains' in the preface, but his *Cambrian Biography* (1803) was similar in intent, if narrower in scope, than that of Morris. Pughe noted in the preface that 'in the first instance it was of importance to bring together all the names deserving of remembrance',[40] and he reiterated the twin concepts of worthiness and remembrance:

> the object in view was to record those characters only, who have rendered themselves eminent as members of the Welsh community, either for their political and social acts, or as writers in the language; and not from their having been merely born in the country, and acquiring their fame amongst other nations; for their memories live in records more ample and more splendid than this humble tablet for the Cymry.[41]

Cambrian Biography may have taken 'Celtic Remains' and *Biographia Britannica* as a blueprint, but it may have been conceived as an antidote to the colonial mindset of the compendious *Biographica Britannica*, which paid only lip-service to Scottish and Irish heroes, and completely ignored their Welsh counterparts.[42] Both 'Celtic Remains' and *Cambrian Biography* were valuable sources for Iolo in the construction of bardism's national pedigree but, as we shall see, Iolo was by the same token an equally valuable source for Pughe. Such was the nature of exchanges between Iolo and Pughe that it is difficult

38 Ibid., p. 124.

39 NLW 1735D is dated 1757 and is in the hand of Richard Morris, Lewis Morris's nephew.

40 William Owen, *The Cambrian Biography: Or Historical Notices of Celebrated Men Among the Ancient Britons* (London, 1803), p. i.

41 Ibid., p. vii. Compare the similar motivation in Edward Jones, *Bardic Museum* (London, 1802), p. v: '*Bardic Songs*, and historic examples of our great and wise progenitors, have always been considered as a most useful and pleasing branch of polite literature. They inform us of the actions, and customs of mankind in former ages, bring the times past into our present view, make us as it were co-eval with the celebrated heroes of former times, and naturally incite us to an emulation with them in glory.' For characters from the bardic pantheon, see ibid., pp. 3, 6, 9, 20–5.

42 The preface was at pains to emphasize that the learned men of Scotland and Ireland were consulted in order to include references to their eminent fellow-countrymen, *Biographica Britannica*, I, p. xiv.

to disentangle the threads of influence which might reveal the true origins of these ideas. Many of these characters were introduced to the public at large in *The Myvyrian Archaiology of Wales*, and may justly be considered an integral part of the volume's aim of elucidating British or Welsh prehistory.

Bardism's pedigree consisted of authentic historical people as well as legendary and imaginary characters. The characters were an integral part of its make-up, for they were often key figures in the mythology which Iolo only tentatively developed within bardism. They were also important to the way in which bardism was presented to the world. The first cohort in the bardic pageant were authentic people, consisting mainly of sixteenth-century poets and professional transcribers, as well as Iolo's contemporaries and near-contemporaries. Without exception, they were Glamorgan men: Llewelyn Siôn, Meurug Dafydd, Dafydd Nicolas, Thomas ab Ieuan, Antoni and Watcyn Powell, Edward Dafydd, Edward Evan and John Bradford. Iolo dressed them in bardic garb and conjured them up in phantom Gorseddau, such as that allegedly held at Beaupre in 1681. Generally speaking, Iolo used authentic people to bolster bardism in two ways: by attributing his own forgeries to them and by using them to legitimize the provenance of his forged bardic material.

Both features are at work in *Cyfrinach Beirdd Ynys Prydain*. Creating a Glamorgan Classification was insufficient in itself, for Iolo needed to legitimize it and invest it with authority and, for this purpose, real figures, past and present, in Glamorgan's literary tradition became invaluable. The traditional and ancient mode of oral transmission in Wales began to decline from the mid-sixteenth century onwards, and by the beginning of the eighteenth century it had more or less ceased.[43] Thus, when Iolo argued that the mythology, institutes, metrical treatises and learning of bardism had been orally transmitted and then collated and committed to paper by Llywelyn Siôn and Edward Dafydd, his bardic fiction was in keeping with historical fact. The version which Iolo presented in *Cyfrinach Beirdd Ynys Prydain* was, so he claimed, fully affirmed in the spurious eisteddfod held at Beaupre castle in 1681. Two forged introductory essays (presented as genuine) precede the text. The first was attributed to the recusant Llywelyn Siôn (1540–?1615), a poet and professional scribe from Llangewydd, Glamorgan, and the second to Edward Dafydd of Margam, Llywelyn Siôn's poetic disciple. The following validation of the bardic secrets contained in the volume derives from the essay attributed to Edward Dafydd:

> Hir o amser, a thros oesoedd, y bu'r pethau hynn dan encudd a choll yn eigion y Tywyllwch; Lewys Morganwg a gafodd i maes lawer o bethau, ond nid y cwbl;

[43] Daniel Huws, *Medieval Welsh Manuscripts* (Aberystwyth, 2000), pp. 89–93; idem, *Cynnull y Farddoniaeth* (Aberystwyth, 2004), p. 6.

Meurug Dafydd a ddatguddiodd lawer o honynt yn y llyfr a wnaeth ef iddei Arlwydd Syr Edward Lewys o'r Fann; Dafydd Benwyn, a Dafydd Llwyd Mathew, a wnaethant Lyfrau, gan ddangos ynddynt o'r newydd rhai bethau hen iawn; a Llywelyn Sion o Langewydd a gasglwys y cyfan yng nghyd iddei Lyfr o'u gwaith hwynt; ag a wnaeth Drefn a Dosparth ar fesurau Cerdd a'r peth oedd berthynraid iddynt . . . am na chanasant y Beirdd ar hanner y cyssefin fesurau er ys cannoedd maith o flynyddau.[44]

(These things were for a long time, and for many ages, hidden and lost in a sea of Darkness; Lewys Morganwg discovered much, but not everything; Meurug Dafydd revealed many of these things in the book he made for his lordship, Sir Edward Lewis of the Van; Dafydd Benwyn, and Dafydd Llwyd Mathew, made Books anew in them, showing some very old things; and Llywelyn Siôn of Llangewydd collected the sum total together in a Book of their work; and imposed Order and Classification on *Poetic* metres and other related things to them . . . because the Poets had not sung on half the original metres for several hundred years.)

The language register was deliberately archaic and mysterious as Iolo sought to distance himself – by two centuries – from his forgeries, but by claiming that the material he presented had passed from one generation to another he created the impression of a genuine bardic succession.

Incriminating innocent poets and scribes appears not to have posed a moral dilemma for Iolo, even if they were, like 'the Bardic Antiquary' John Bradford, close friends and mentors. Iolo's respect for Bradford was genuine, and there was nothing disingenuous about his attempt to give his mentor the national recognition he deserved: he jotted the following statement in one of his manuscripts, 'Siôn Bradford! Ieuan Tir Iarll! Thy name must be remembered.'[45] He also expressed a similar view about Edward Evan:

y Parchedig Edward Ifan o Aberdar ym Morganwg a ddylai gael ei gofio. Nid llai ei ddysgeidiaeth ef nag eiddo Ieuan Bradford a Lewys Hopcin ac yn ben ar y cwbl nid neb yn eu gwlad na hoes yn [haeddu] gwell gair amdanynt am bob campau da a cymmydogaidd a Theuluaidd nag yr oeddynt hwy.[46]

(The Reverend Edward Evan of Aberdare in Glamorgan should be remembered. His learning was no less than that of John Bradford and Lewis Hopkin and, furthermore, no one in their country and time [deserves] a better word for all their good, neighbourly and Domestic deeds than they.)

[44] Taliesin Williams (ed.), *Cyfrinach Beirdd Ynys Prydain* (Abertawy, 1829), pp. 2–3.

[45] NLW 13097B, p. 151. See also NLW 13089E, p. 454 in which Iolo referred to 'the late very ingenious and Bardically learned Mr John Bradford well known in that Country for his uncommon skill in Bardism & Welsh Poetry'. See also love-poems written by Iolo which he attributed to Bradford: NLW 13099B, pp. 114, 124; NLW 21388E, no. 9; *CRhIM*, pp. 76–8.

[46] NLW 13141A, p. 131. See also NLW 13159A, pp. 142–5.

Bradford had introduced Iolo to strict-metre poetry, or as Iolo preferred to call it, his first knowledge of the Ancient British Poetry and bardism, and for this reason perhaps, Bradford's name is the name most frequently tagged to Iolo's forgeries: *Cyfrinach Beirdd Ynys Prydain, Coelbren y Beirdd* (the Bardic Alphabet), 'Llafar Gorsedd' (The Voice Conventional of the Bards of the Island of Britain) and much more. But although Bradford was foremost among the bards in Iolo's bardic world, we never hear *his* voice. Letters which Bradford addressed to William Wynn, Llangynhafal, and Lewis Morris have survived, but in spite of their specific literary and cultural context they contain not even a whisper about bardism or its corollaries.[47] Iolo's false trails, however, succeeded to such an extent that even John Morris-Jones suspected the hapless Bradford of supporting the bardic hoax.[48]

Then there were bardism's legendary characters. Despite the virulent anti-Church and anti-King sentiments which Iolo expressed in his various writings, he revealed an extraordinary affection for ancient kings: Dyfnwal Moelmud, King Arthur and Hu Gadarn. However, Iolo artfully pressed them into service as benevolent models. Hu Gadarn, the ploughman king, was one example in which the republican inferences are clear:

> Hu Gadarn it is true was a King, and one of the Class now called the upper, and he was no Devil. I have searched for another, and am disposed to think a little charitably of Alfred, Hywel Dda, and Caradoc ap Bran, and possibly Bran ap Llyr his father, but was it to save my life, even my soul from Hell, I can think of no other King, the writing of whose name would not, in the eye of real truth, of genuine reason, degrade me to the dirt.[49]

Rachel Bromwich has suggested that a brief note by Lewis Morris in 'Celtic Remains' was Iolo's source for Hu Gadarn, and that further material was provided in Iolo Goch's 'Cywydd y Llafurwr' (The Ploughman's *Cywydd*), in which Hu was depicted as a benevolent emperor and ploughman who used the plough to produce bread by his own labour.[50] Traditionally, Hu Gadarn is recognized as Hugun le Fort, emperor of Constantinople, in the legends surrounding Charlemagne. However, in bardism, and in the series of spurious triads printed in the third series of triads published in *The Myvyrian Archaiology of Wales*, he was portrayed as a civilizing force in Wales: he taught agriculture and other useful arts, and he also established verse as the medium

47 Hugh Owen (ed.), *Additional Letters of the Morrises of Anglesey (1735–1786)* (2 vols., London, 1947–9), I, pp. 48–9; NLW Peniarth 115, ff. 68–9.

48 John Morris-Jones, 'Derwyddiaeth Gorsedd y Beirdd', *Y Beirniad*, I (1911), 71.

49 NLW 13221E, pp. 91–4, Iolo Morganwg to William Owen Pughe, 19 December 1802.

50 Rachel Bromwich, 'Trioedd Ynys Prydain: The *Myvyrian* Third Series', *THSC*, part 1 (1968), 323; A. C. Rejhon, 'Hu Gadarn: Folklore and Fabrication' in Patrick K. Ford (ed.) *Celtic Folklore and Christianity: Studies in Memory of William V. Heist* (Santa Barbara, Calif. 1983), pp. 201–2. For the original note by Lewis Morris, see NLW 1735D, p. 301.

for preserving the history of his people. He earned the title 'patriarch of the Cymry' for bringing the Welsh to Britain from the legendary Deffrobani or 'Gwlad yr Haf' (Land of Summer) and for establishing them peacefully in the island. Iolo was not entirely responsible for transforming Hu Gadarn into a totemic figure, for the legendary king was also one of William Owen Pughe's intellectual interests. In a letter to Iolo in June 1801, Pughe informed Iolo that he planned to depict Hu Gadarn on medals for the Gwyneddigion Society: his plough would be an emblem of arts and peace.[51] Pughe's comments on Hu Gadarn in *The Cambrian Biography* also summed up Iolo's thinking on the ploughman king more succinctly than any of the latter's own writings,[52] and he further developed his ideas in a long *cywydd* in 1822 (with extensive notes). But since their intellectual relationship hinged on the exchange of information, Iolo's influence may be discerned in the closing phrase of *Hu Gadarn* – 'Y Gwir yn erbyn y Byd' (the Truth against the World)[53] – and in cross-references in the poem on Hu Gadarn to other characters also favoured by Iolo: Tydain Tad Awen, Dyfnwal Moelmud and Rhitta Gawr.[54]

One of the most prominent legendary characters in Iolo's bardic forgeries was the fifth-century king, Dyfnwal Moelmud (Dunwallus Molmutius) who, according to Geoffrey of Monmouth's *Historia Regum Britanniae*, was a Cornish king who became supreme monarch of Britain, and achieved fame by establishing the laws of the kingdom and the roads traversing it.[55] Iolo's imprint is evident in the romantic depictions of Dyfnwal in *The Cambrian Biography*, but Iolo had also encountered him in his study of Welsh poetry and triads, and in Lewis Morris's 'Celtic Remains', in which he was also recognized as the first king to wear a golden crown and reduce 'the Pentarchy into a Monarchy'.[56] Morris conflated Dyfnwal with Prydain ab Aedd Mawr, and also seized on his potential as a national British or Welsh hero in a defensive response to Saxon writers who 'have endeavoured to deprive this Monarch of the honour of beginning these roads and would fair have it that they were made by the Romans'.[57] Morris's emphatic tone must have appealed to Iolo, as must his assertion that Dyfnwal's laws predated the laws of the illiterate Saxons and that the British Laws had retained his name even after the island had been overturned by the Saxons. Morris also noted John

51 NLW 21282E, Letter no. 348, William Owen Pughe to Iolo Morganwg, 16 June 1801.

52 Owen, *Cambrian Biography*, pp. 178–80.

53 [William Owen Pughe], *Hu Gadarn, Cywydd o III Caniad: Y Gan Idrison* (Llundain, 1822), p. 79.

54 Owen, *Cambrian Biography*, pp. 179–80.

55 In Welsh law-texts, however, he is remembered as a Cornish earl who measured the island of Britain. He is also associated with North Britain in Welsh genealogies. Morfydd E. Owen, 'Royal Propaganda: Stories from the Law-texts' in Thomas Charles-Edwards, Paul Russell and Morfydd E. Owen (eds.), *The Welsh King and his Court* (Cardiff, 2000), pp. 229–30.

56 NLW 1735D, p. 166.

57 Ibid.

Fig. 7 The frontispiece of William Owen Pughe's *Hu Gadarn* (1803).

Leland's view that Dyfnwal's laws had been translated by Gildas into Latin at the time of the decline of the Roman Empire and that they were eventually incorporated into Saxon and Norman law.[58] Surprisingly, perhaps, in the light of his own highly defensive Welshness, Iolo did not utilize the information about Dyfnwal's influence on Saxon and Norman legislation. Rather, his interest was in Dyfnwal as a lawgiver, a predecessor of the more famous Hywel Dda (Hywel the Good), and in the way in which the fabricated laws in triadic form which Iolo attributed to Dyfnwal chimed with primitivist arguments in favour of early civilization among the Welsh:

> It is much more to the honour of the Welsh that thro the dark ages when no other Country in Europe wrote in its own language, but in a barbarous Latin;

[58] Ibid., pp. 166–7.

> they (i.e. the Welsh) wrote in, and highly cultivated, their own language, had very good grammars in it, their Laws, Histories, works on Agriculture, Physic, Divinity, [?] morality, &c besides their poetry, the versification of which has been five hundred years ago improved to a height that no other nation in the whole world, ancient or modern ever attained to. This I say is much more to our honour than to be considered as the defendants of a gang of vagabond Trojans. It is also much more honourable to have been the primeval possessors of the island in peace and Justice, than to have been depredators that dispossessed, unjustly, the original Inhabitants. What infatuation would urge any one to wish for another origin than that of the most honourable Just and natural, and this no one will deny us. Why must we prefer truth to fiction?[59]

Indeed, Iolo claimed elsewhere that Dyfnwal's laws proved that Welsh laws had been committed to writing long before the days of Hywel Dda.[60] He attributed to him a sizeable series of triads which were published in the third volume of *The Myvyrian Archaiology of Wales* in 1807.[61] For Iolo, the appeal of the triad form lay in its gnomic quality, and he chose to view it as the vestige of an ancient layer of traditional bardic and druidic lore. As a result, he supposed that triads were an integral part of the druidic apprenticeship since they contained the basic moral, theological, historical, medicinal and astrological learning which an ovate was obliged to acquire. The 'Moelmutian Triads' were offered as part of the store of traditional lore retained only in Glamorgan.

Another of Iolo's fictional luminaries was Catwg Ddoeth (Catwg the Wise), whom he dubbed the Welsh nation's Solomon. Copious lists of proverbial sayings, under the heading 'Doethineb Catwg Ddoeth' (The Wisdom of Catwg the Wise), were published in the ubiquitous third volume of *The Myvyrian Archaiology of Wales*.[62] This body of 'wisdom' became extremely popular in Victorian Wales and was quarried, somewhat idiosyncratically, by La Villemarqué, Brittany's answer to Iolo Morganwg, in the 1840s. The bardic entity Catwg Ddoeth is a splendid example of conflation and cultural appropriation at work: he was a composite of native learning (Catwg or Cadog, a recognized Glamorgan saint) and classical learning (Catwn Ddoeth, the Cymricized Latin writer, Cato). A small collection of genuine proverbial wisdom by Catwn Ddoeth (Cato) exists in Welsh manuscripts, but material attributed to Catwg Ddoeth was forged by Iolo, who owned a Latin copy of Cato's *Dionysii Catonis Distich de Moribus ad filius*, and who knew that Catwn (Cato) and Catwg were two separate individuals. Catwn and St Catwg were deliberately conflated in order to enable him, with tenuous legitimacy, to

59 NLW 13221E, pp. 59–62, Iolo Morganwg to William Owen Pughe, 14 November 1799.

60 NLW 13088B, p. 80.

61 *MAW*, III, pp. 199–360.

62 'Doethineb y Cymry' (The Wisdom of the Welsh), *MAW*, III, pp. 1–144.

claim Cato's wisdom for bardism and for Glamorgan. Moreover, Iolo hailed Catwg Ddoeth as the mentor of the sixth-century poet Taliesin and deftly wove them both into the bardic history of Llantwit Major, even though this meant uprooting the latter from the Old North.

The poet Taliesin's traditional links with Arthur provided another layer of intricacy to the interwoven tapestry of facts and fantasy, people and places in the new mythology of bardism.[63] Arthur appealed strongly to the likes of William Owen Pughe and David Samwell, and Iolo may have added him to the bardic *bricolage* to please them: Samwell, for example, founded the short-lived Caradogion Society which met around 'Arthur's Table' in the upper room of the Bull tavern in London. The triangular relationship between Catwg Ddoeth/Catwn, Taliesin and Arthur offers a fine example of the way in which Iolo connected previously unconnected, or even tenuously connected, people and places for the greater good of his bardic vision. It also illustrates beautifully the inspired imaginary leaps which Iolo made in the construction of bardism. Indeed, it is amusing to note that Iolo's disparagement of others for distorting historical characters could just as easily be levied against himself:

> These clearly appear as historical Characters, and have been used as representative or alegorical otherwise mythological character, they were as mythological personages invested most probably with attributes of a higher nature than those now or that have for a thousand years ascribed, but these things have long ago sunk into such depths of oblivion as to be far beyond the reach of rational conjecture. Deranged imaginations may dive in search of them, but will bring nothing up but Phantoms of their own creations.[64]

Finally, imaginary characters also enlivened bardism. These were bards devised by Iolo in order to prove that bardic Glamorgan, unlike barbarous Gwynedd, possessed a long tradition of urbane, lyrical poetry (*canu teuluaidd*). Foremost among them was Rhys Goch ap Rhicert, whom Iolo conjured up from genuine Glamorgan pedigrees,[65] and heralded as the founder of the Chair of Tir Iarll.[66] Iolo composed over a dozen poems in Rhys Goch ap Rhicert's name and used him to prove that Dafydd ap Gwilym had merely refined an existing tradition of love-poetry in Glamorgan.[67] Ieuan Fawr ap y

[63] See NLW 13162A, pp. 73–82.
[64] NLW 13159A, p. 86.
[65] Ifor Williams, 'Rhys Goch ap Rhiccert', *Y Beirniad*, III, no. 4 (1913), 230–44; G. J. Williams, 'Rhys Goch ap Rhiccert', ibid., VIII, no. 4 (1919), 211–26, 260. For poems attributed to Rhys Goch ap Rhicert, see NLW 13127A, pp. 421–54; *CRhIM*, pp. 105–24.
[66] NLW 13120B, p. 69.
[67] NLW 13098B, p. 94. See also NLW 13106B, p. 116.

Diwlith also figured in Iolo's new pantheon of fictional Glamorgan men: according to Iolo's romantic tale, he had been discovered on Diwlith Mound on Margam mountain by bards who had assembled there for a Gorsedd, and he had been duly raised by none other than Rhys Goch ap Rhicert.[68] This association reinforced Ieuan Fawr's importance in bardism as well as the imputed superiority of the Welsh literary tradition in south Wales because Iolo claimed that he had authored the most canonical of medieval Welsh prose, the Mabinogi and The Grail Romances.[69] The earliest extant Welsh prose texts had indeed been preserved by scribes in south Wales but, in the case of Ieuan Fawr, Iolo provided a human, but imaginary, face to supplement a historical fact.

One of Iolo's most playful imaginary characters was Wil Tabwr, a seventeenth-century poet who personified the suave sophistication of Glamorgan poetry whose roots Iolo audaciously traced back to Rhys Goch ap Rhicert. Even though Wil Tabwr was only marginal to bardism proper, he represents the creative impulse which drove Iolo to fabricate a history and genealogy for Glamorgan. Early in his career Iolo had intended to publish in 'Dywenydd Morganwg' fictional characters resurrected from the dead in order to chastise the living in satirical squibs.[70] 'Dywenydd Morganwg' was never published, but Iolo resurrected some of its characters in bardism, notably Catwg Ddoeth, Bardd Glas y Gadair and Wil Tabwr. That he later imported characters from works of fiction into bardism indicates that the boundaries between his original, creative work and his antiquarian forgeries were decidedly blurred. As a result, bardism's vision of Wales, in which plot, characters and events were bound by the bardic narrative, was more akin to the romantic fiction of the period than other antiquarian research. Yet, despite the prevalence of many characters in bardism, there is only one voice: that of Iolo. In this respect Iolo may be compared with Thomas Chatterton and William Blake, both of whom created memorable characters in their poetic worlds. For Blake especially, druidic and mythological characters were an integral part of his poetic vision.[71] But unlike either Chatterton or Blake, who were well camouflaged by the characters in their poetry, Iolo's characters were fated to live forever in the shadow of their maker. Iolo's extensive cast of characters undoubtedly enhanced bardism's appeal. Thomas Williams (Gwilym

68 For information on Ieuan Fawr ap y Diwlith, see NLW 13088B, p. 81; NLW 13098B, p. 72; NLW 13120B, p. 69; NLW 13121B, pp. 164, 427; NLW 13128A, pp. 18–19, 97; NLW 13135A, p. 157. For material attributed to Ieuan Fawr ap y Diwlith, see NLW 13112B, pp. 321–2; NLW 13154A, p. 68. Iolo called him 'Llywelyn Fawr ap y Diwlith' in NLW 13129A, p. 215.

69 Williams: *IM*, p. 271.

70 For the relevant material, see NLW 21414E, no. 5.

71 Jon Mee, *Dangerous Enthusiasm: William Blake and the Culture of Radicalism in the 1790s* (Oxford, 1992), pp. 84–5, 89–100, 121–4, 183–4.

Morganwg) for example, reiterated the Ioloic roll-call in his poem on the ancestors of the Welsh, written for the Llangefni eisteddfod in 1816.[72]

Having considered the composition of the Gorsedd, we now turn to the actual making of the Gorsedd of the Bards of the Island of Britain, its regional beginnings and its protracted rise to national recognition. Since Geraint and Zonia Bowen have already charted in considerable detail the chronological background of each Gorsedd meeting, this discussion focuses on the general stages in its development: the London Gorseddau of the early 1790s, the Gorseddau held mainly in Glamorgan from 1795 onwards, the seminal provincial eisteddfod held at Carmarthen in 1819 which marked a turning point in the popularity and acceptability of the Gorsedd, and the first few decades following Iolo's death, which witnessed the emergence of the Gorsedd as a truly national institution.

By the end of 1791 Iolo had settled in London and, having established his bardic credentials in the metropolis, he persuaded leading members of the Gwyneddigion Society to hold a Gorsedd. Iolo's bardic initiates during the 1790s were drawn from a narrow field: with the exception of Anna Seward, they were mainly members of the Gwyneddigion and their associates: John Jones (Glan-y-gors), Thomas Jones (Y Bardd Cloff), William Owen Pughe, David Samwell (Dafydd Ddu Feddyg), Edward Charles (Siamas Wynedd), Daniel Davies and Walter Davies (Gwallter Mechain). Apart from Davies, these were all men who would have appreciated bardism's radical ideology. But since Iolo's young son Taliesin, Pughe's wife Sarah and their infant son Aneurin were initiated into the order of Ovates in the second Gorsedd of 1792,[73] the colourful new institution may also have been viewed as an enjoyable social occasion for the convivial Gwyneddigion. Yet, they were renowned for their radical leanings and committed themselves to following Iolo's institutional rubric in their own efforts to revivify the traditional Welsh poetic craft in publications such as *Awdlau ar Destynau Cymdeithas y Gwyneddigion i'r Eisteddfodau* (1791) (Odes on The Gwyneddigion Society's Subjects for the Eisteddfodau). In places, this proclamation echoed the 1789 piece in the *Gentleman's Magazine* insofar as Iolo placed himself centre stage and asserted that he was the sole legitimate heir of the Bards of the Isle of Britain and thus the only living person able to confer bardic degrees. Glamorgan's supremacy was also asserted, for the Gorsedd was to be held in

[72] Thomas Williams, 'Haeddedigol Goffadwriaeth am Hynafiaid y Cymry a ymdrechasant y'mhlaid Rhyddid eu Gwlad' (Deserving Memory of the Ancestors of the Welsh who struggled for the Freedom of their Country) in Taliesin Williams (ed.), *Awen y Maen Chwyf, yn cynnwys awdlau, cywyddau, caniadau ac englynion gan y diweddar Dderwyddfardd, Thomas Williams, B.B.D. (Gwilym Morganwg)* (Merthyr Tydfil, 1890), pp. 2–10.

[73] NLW 854D, p. 9; *HGB*, pp. 25–6.

the name of the Chair of Glamorgan and prospective members would be adjudicated under this chair's authority. The first Gorsedd meeting, convened on Primrose Hill on 21 June 1792, was held in the name of 'Beirdd Cyfoeth Morganwg [Bards of the Land of Glamorgan], a Gwent, ac Ergyng, ac Euas, ac Ystrad Yw'. This auspicious setting had also witnessed the inaugural meeting of John Toland's 'The Ancient Druid Order' in 1717.[74] The only record of the first Gorsedd, however, is buried in the footnotes of Iolo's 'Ode on the Mythology of the Ancient British Bards', published in *Poems, Lyric and Pastoral*, which was declaimed on the occasion.[75] Iolo was deeply concerned with the purity of the bardic succession from the outset and in a note, dated 26 August 1792, he wrote out the details of the succession, beginning with Llewelyn Siôn, to whom he attributed the feat of compiling the manuscript version of 'Cyfrinach Beirdd Ynys Prydain', and concluding with 'Iolo Morganwg neu [or] Iorwerth Gwilym'.[76] An addendum to the lineage was more telling because, rather than dwell on bardism's alleged roots, it looked forward, revealing Iolo's position as the transmitter of bardism: 'Iorwerth Gwilym neu Iolo Morganwg . . . Ei ddysgyblion ef oeddynt Dafydd Ddu Feddyg, Gwilym Owen, Gwallter Mechain, Iago Twrbil, Gwilym Ifan ag eraill' (Edward Williams or Iolo Morganwg . . . His disciples were David Samwell, William Owen, Walter Davies, James Turberville, William Evans and others).[77] That Iolo had written this note only two months after the first Gorsedd is a measure not only of its success, but also of his confidence in the new institution and of his own place within it.

The second Gorsedd of 1792 was held at the same location on 22 September and is more widely attested than the first. An account was printed in the *Morning Chronicle* and, since it echoes Iolo's pronouncements on bardism in the various drafts of 'A Short Account of the Ancient British Bards', he was almost certainly its author. Some years later Edward Jones included a brief description in *The Bardic Museum* (1802).[78] The ceremony itself was marked by its simplicity:[79] Iolo created a modest bardic circle from a handful of small stones in his pocket; the sword was sheathed in a symbolic gesture of peace; and the bards wore a coloured armband to denote their rank. A third open-air Gorsedd was planned for 21 December of that year near the British Museum (at which Edward Jones was required to prove his worth), but it is difficult to ascertain whether or not it was held. David Samwell prepared an English ode for the occasion, entitled 'The Resurrection of

[74] Piggott, *The Druids*, pp. 135–6.
[75] Williams: *PLP*, II, p. 193.
[76] Quoted in *HGB*, pp. 26–7, from David Samwell's personal copy of Evan Evans, *Some Specimens of the Poetry of the Ancient Welsh Bards* (London, 1764).
[77] *HGB*, p. 27.
[78] Quoted in ibid., p. 29.
[79] Williams: *PLP*, II, p. 39.

Rhitta Gawr',[80] which illustrated the contemporary relevance of bardism's pantheon of heroes: Rhitta was a 'king-flogging' giant who made a cloak for himself out of the beards of slain kings and tyrants. The following year, 1793, Iolo failed to maintain the momentum, and only one Gorsedd was held in London, during which Anna Seward was made an ovate.[81]

The London Gorseddau enjoyed only limited success: no more than three or four bardic assemblies were held, largely because of the hostile political climate and also because of Iolo's own personal traumas. Early in 1795 he returned to Glamorgan, more convinced than ever before that 'London ruins everyone'.[82] For valid personal and political reasons, he failed to maintain the initial momentum and, despite efforts to publicize them to the wider metropolitan world, the majority of adherents were exiled compatriots who already shared his cultural and political sympathies. Nonetheless, these first Gorseddau set a pattern in terms of the simplicity of the ceremony, a feature dictated perhaps by the contemporary political climate in which overt displays of dissent were considered unwise. Since the Gorsedd was also an essential vehicle of self-promotion, Iolo's own importance to the Gorsedd ceremony was also established at this time, as was his very keen sense of ownership: only he was permitted to initiate members.

If London witnessed the beginning of the Gorsedd, Glamorgan hosted its development. On his return to Wales, Iolo sought to attract a provincial audience by aiming to hold four annual Gorseddau, one on each solstice and equinox. He proclaimed his first Glamorgan Gorsedd of the Chair of Glamorgan, Gwent, Euas, Ergyng and Ystrad Yw, with the resonant motto 'Y Gwir yn erbyn y Byd' (The Truth against the World), in 1795.[83] He invited those who wished to be legitimately enrolled as a Bard of the Island of Britain to convene at Stalling Down and, as was the case at the London Gorseddau, the emphasis of the meeting was on poetry:

> Yn Enw Duw a Phob Daioni
> Bydded hysbys – mae amseroedd defodol cynnal Cadair a Gorsedd wrth Gerdd, yn ol arfer a defod yr hen Gymru ydynt yn gyntaf Gwyl Alban Arthan . . . Gwyl Alban Eilir . . . Gwyl Alban Hefin . . . a Gwyl Alban Elfed . . . ac ar bob un or dyddiau hynn yr ydys yn bwriadu cynnal Cadair a Gorsedd wrth Fraint a Defod Beirdd Ynys Prydain o hyn allan bob blwyddyn ar Ben Bryn Owain ym Morganwg, lle bydd llawen gan bawb Gweled Bardd a charwr Barddoniaeth.[84]

80 'The Resurrection of Rhitta Gawr, being the subject given at a meeting of the Welsh bards on Primrose Hill Sept. 22, 1792'. NLW 21398E, no. 29. Samwell sent the ode to Iolo on 20 October 1792. See also ibid., no. 29a, 'Hints for an Epic Poem on the story of Rhitta Gawr'; ibid., no. 29b, incomplete *englynion* to Rhitta Gawr.

81 *RAEW*, p. 44; *HGB*, p. 25.

82 NLW 21285E, Letter no. 812, Iolo Morganwg to Margaret Williams, 27 October 1792.

83 NLW 13103B, p. 296.

84 Ibid., p. 293.

(In the Name of God and All Goodness
May it be known that the customary times to hold a Chair and Gorsedd of Poetry, according to the custom and ritual of the ancient Welsh are, firstly the feast of Alban Arthan . . . the feast of Alban Eilir . . . the feast of Alban Hefin . . . the feast of Alban Elfed . . . and on every one of these days it is, from now on, intended to hold a Chair and Gorsedd according to the Privilege and Custom of the Bards annually on top of Stalling Down in Glamorgan, where everyone will be pleased to see a Bard and lover of Poetry.)

Although this ambitious programme did not fully materialize, Iolo nevertheless held more meetings in Glamorgan than he had done in London. Between 1795 and 1798 he led Gorseddau on several hilltops: Stalling Down near Cowbridge (1795 and 1796), Garth Mountain, Llantwit Fardre (1797 and 1798), Fforest Mountain, Cowbridge (1797) and Glyn Ogwr (1798). He targeted acquaintances old and new, most of whom were natives of the Vale and Uplands of Glamorgan, though some were drawn from Carmarthenshire. These included the poet and Dissenting minister Edward Evan (Iorwerth Gwynfardd Morganwg) of Aberdare, Edward Williams (Gwilym Fardd Glas) of Merthyr and Cowbridge, William Moses (Gwilym Glan Taf) of Merthyr and Thomas Evans (Tomos Glyn Cothi), the minister of Wales's first Unitarian chapel at Gwernogle, Carmarthenshire.[85]

The spirit of these Gorseddau was vintage Iolo: judging by the nature of the poems and triads which he and others recited, the ideals of the French Revolution were loudly declaimed in Welsh.[86] In the Gorsedd held in 1798 on Garth Mountain, Tomos Glyn Cothi read his 'Cywydd ar Wybodaeth' (*Cywydd* on Knowledge), while Iolo read a poem which outlined the oral dissemination of 'knowledge' among the Welsh.[87] Iolo's poem also made explicit a bard's responsibilities, and served a didactic purpose, educating new members in the rationale and pseudo-history of the Gorsedd, and its political sentiments.[88] In a 1798 Gorsedd, Iolo recited his poem 'Breiniau Dyn' (The Rights of Man), originally written in 1793, perhaps in homage to the second part of Paine's *The Rights of Man*, published in 1792, or perhaps for a London Gorsedd that never transpired. In it, Iolo evoked the spirit of Freedom:

85 Others mentioned include Lewis Williams (Berddyn Bach), Rhys Thomas and Rhys ab Ifan. Plennydd, Alawn and Gwron were also named (for the first time) in this Gorsedd. NLW 13144A, p. xxi. See also Iolo's list of Glamorgan poets in 1798: NLW 13136A, p. 249.

86 NLW 21285E, Letter no. 1032, Iolo Morganwg to David Williams, 1 January 1803. The marginalia of this letter contained a draft proclaiming the Gorsedd meeting at Stalling Down.

87 Extracts from Thomas Evans's 'Cywydd ar Wybodaeth' were published in William Williams (ed.), *Gardd Aberdar, yn cynwys Cyfansoddiadau Buddugol yn Eisteddfod y Carw Coch, Aberdar, Awst 29, 1853* (Caerfyrddin, 1854), pp. 102–3.

88 'Cân Newydd, yn adrodd helynt Gwybodaeth grefyddol ymhlith y Cymry.' NLW 13141A, pp. 17–29.

Clyw'r Brenin balch di râs!
A thi'r offeiriad bras;
  Dau Ddiawl yng nglyn!
Hîr buoch fal dau gawr,
I'r Byd yn felltith fawr,
Gann drochi'n llaid y llawr,
  Holl Freiniau Dyn.
. . .
O! pam Frenhinoedd Byd
y melwch ewyn cyd
  A phoethder gwŷn?
Clywch orfoleddus gainc!
Mae'r gwledydd oll fal Ffrainc
yn rhoddi'r orsedd fainc
  I Freiniau Dyn.
. . .
Gorfoledd! cwyn dy lais!
Cwymp holl deyrnasoedd Trais!
  Mae'nt ar eu crŷn,
Cawn Deyrnas hardd ei gwedd
Dan Farn Tywysog Hedd,
Yn honno cwyn o'r Bedd
  Holl Freiniau Dyn.[89]

(Listen, proud [and] wicked King,/and you, stout priest,/two Devils in the same mould!/For a long time you have been like two giants,/a large plague upon the World,/soiling all the Rights of Man in the mud.
. . .
Oh! Why, Kings of the World/do you exploit for so long/with the heat of lust?/Listen to the joyous melody!/All the countries like France/give the throne/to the Rights of Man.
. . .
Rejoicing! Raise your voice!/Fall, all kingdoms of Oppression!/They are about to fall,/We'll have a Kingdom of Beauty/under the Prince of Peace,/In that kingdom all the Rights of Man/will rise from the Grave.)

On Garth Mountain in the same year, the tone was one of radical Dissent and among the subjects set for the bards were new hymns suitable for the fledgling Unitarian cause.[90]

The relocation of the Gorsedd to Glamorgan, according to Iolo's publicity material, was accompanied by a shift in language. English had been the primary language of the London Gorseddau:

89 NLW 13148A, pp. 299–300: 'Iolo Morganwg ai Cant. 1793. Gerbronn Beirdd Ynys Prydain, yng Nghorsedd Gyfallwy'r Alban Elfen, ar Dwyn Bryn Owain, ym Morganwg, pan oedd Oed Crist 1798. Gwir yn erbyn y Byd.' See also other drafts, ibid., pp. 286–92.

90 NLW 13136A, p. 249.

> The Bardic Tradition, and several Odes were recited. Two of the Odes, one by David Samwell, on the Bardic Discipline, the other by Edward Williams, on the Bardic Mythology, were in English and the first that were ever in the language recited at a Congress of Ancient British Bards. This was with an intention to give the English reader an idea of what, though very common in Wales, has never yet been properly known in England.[91]

But, following Iolo's return to Wales, the Welsh language predominated. Gwyneth Lewis has argued that this language shift was deliberate and that from 1795 Iolo took his Gorsedd underground in Glamorgan in order to avoid the repressive climate he had feared in the metropolis.[92] But on his return, it was surely natural for Iolo to revert to bardism's native tongue and the first language of his fellow-bards. Moreover, bardism's ideology and Gorsedd ceremony remained subversive regardless of the language in which they were voiced. The English language may indeed have rendered Gorsedd activity and its underlying philosophy more accessible and therefore more open to scrutiny and persecution, but in a Welsh-speaking environment Iolo's allegedly dubious politics would not have gone unobserved for being articulated through the medium of Welsh. If anything, given Iolo's status as a local 'character', he would probably have been less conspicuous, if no less paranoid, had he held these meetings in London, for the sheer scale and relative anonymity of the metropolis would have shielded him. The events of 1798 bear this out.

The Glynogwr Gorsedd of 1798 was perhaps the most eventful. Twelve magistrates and the Cowbridge Volunteers were dispatched to observe the proceedings. Iolo related the incident in a letter to William Owen Pughe:

> We (the Bards of Glamorgan) have been as severly persecuted by Church and Kingists as our glorious Predecessors were by Edward the Bardicide. Many of our young disciples have been intimidated and have withdrawn themselves from our Gorsez [Gorsedd]. I am in hopes however that a few will meet on Garth Mountain next Alban Hefin. I intend then to recite some ancient Trïoedd, [?to] deliver a short Araith, to ricite something in verse &c. The Transactions of our Gorsedd I will send to [the] Cambrian Register as an appeal to the Public exhibit[ing] ourselves as Men of Peace and Social order, and not th[e] Seditious persons that some suppose us to be . . . I am threatened, and have been so for some months, wi[th] having my house searched and my books and papers seiz[ed]. How far it is in the power of any one in this County to do s[o] I know not, but I have secured all that might have expos[ed] me to danger by sending them in a strong package to a fri[end] in Pontisel, with such other papers, Manuscripts and Boo[ks] as I greatly

[91] *Morning Chronicle*, 26 September 1792, quoted in *HGB*, pp. 28–9.

[92] Gwyneth Lewis, 'Eighteenth-Century Literary Forgeries with Special Reference to the Work of Iolo Morganwg' (unpublished University of Oxford D.Phil. thesis, 1991), p. 119.

> valued, and which by falling into the tallons of virulent Loyalists might possibly be lost.[93]

Iolo neglected to inform Pughe that, by declaiming his poem on the rights of man, he had actively courted the attention of the very 'Church and Kingists' he had accused of intimidation. The heavy-handedness of the Cowbridge Volunteers reflects the atmosphere of reactionary loyalism of the late 1790s: the revolutionary situation in France had precipitated fears of a revolution on British soil, and war with France had been declared in 1793. A series of repressive laws were passed by William Pitt's government, and although they were very rarely invoked, especially in the provinces,[94] the show trial of Hardy, Thelwall and Tooke in 1794 showed that the authorities were not loath to make an example of prominent radicals and dissidents.[95] The fear of persecution and incarceration which these restrictive laws represented was potent enough and, while Iolo lived in London between 1791 and 1795, the 'terror' of Pitt's administration was very real, as his many anguished letters to his wife reveal.[96] He also experienced at first hand the violence of loyalist 'Church and King' mobs and government spies.[97] In Wales the popular response to the French Revolution was generally more conservative,[98] but the need to silence Welsh republican bards became more pressing when a French fleet landed on the Pembrokeshire coast in February 1797.[99] The surveillance of the Cowbridge Volunteers had the desired effect, for in a letter to Pughe, five years after the event, Iolo turned to the Welsh language to express his fear of persecution:

> Eithr [?nis] gellir, ac nis dylit, gorsedd egored, na dim namyn dan gyfail, yn oes y Crinwas Gwaedgar. Gwr wr[th] ddifrawd ac anrhaith, noeth yw ei gledd ef yn erbyn pob cyfiawnder, pob Gwirionedd, a phob Tangnef[edd].[100]

93 NLW 13221E, pp. 53–4, Iolo Morganwg to William Owen Pughe, 12 May 1798; *Cambrian Register*, 2 (1799), 465.
94 Clive Emsley, 'An Aspect of Pitt's "Terror": Prosecutions for Sedition during the 1790s', *Social History*, 6 (1981), 155–84; idem, 'Repression, "terror" and the rule of law in England during the decade of the French Revolution', *EHR*, C, no. 397 (1985), 822.
95 Pughe and Iolo attended the trial and Iolo published a song celebrating their release, *Trial by Jury, the Grand Palladium of British Liberty* (1795), which was declaimed at 'The Crown and Anchor' in London, 4 February 1795. See also NLW 13221E, p. 1; NLW 21335A, pp. 14–16; NLW 21401E, nos. 32, 32a. For the background to these trials, see John Barrell, *Imagining the King's Death: Figurative Treason, Fantasies of Regicide, 1793–1796* (Oxford, 2000); Alan Wharam, *The Treason Trials, 1794* (London, 1992).
96 NLW 21285E, Letter no. 841, Iolo Morganwg to Margaret Williams, 27 August 1794; NLW 21285E, Letter no. 843, Iolo Morganwg to Margaret Williams, 1 October 1795.
97 NLW 21285E, Letter no. 838, Iolo Morganwg to the Revd Hugh Jones, 4 June 1794; *RAEW*, pp. 85, 104–5.
98 J. J. Evans, *Dylanwad y Chwyldro Ffrengig ar Lenyddiaeth Cymru* (Lerpwl, 1928); Hywel M. Davies, 'Loyalism in Wales, 1792–3', *WHR*, 20, no. 4 (2001), 687–716.
99 Geraint H. Jenkins, 'Glaniad y Ffrancod yn Abergwaun ym 1797' in idem (ed.), *Cadw Tŷ Mewn Cwmwl Tystion* (Llandysul, 1990), pp. 256–72.
100 NLW 13221E, pp. 111–14, Iolo Morganwg to William Owen Pughe, 1 August 1803.

(But one cannot, and should not hold an open/conspicuous Gorsedd, or anything else except under cover/in secret. In the age of the Bloody Miser [George III], unbrotherliness and destruction are seen, his sword is unsheathed against all righteousness, all Truth, and all Peace.)

Fear of further intervention by the authorities may explain why Iolo did not hold the Gorsedd proposed by Thomas Evans and Lewis William in Carmarthenshire for December 1798.[101] Geraint Bowen has claimed that this was a lost opportunity for Iolo to establish (or rather to 're-establish', as Iolo would have it) the Chair of Dyfed, and it illustrates the difficulties which new societies faced at a time when even innocuous voluntary and secret societies were regarded with suspicion.[102] In spite of the fear of government harassment and in spite of bardism's fundamental commitment to transparency, Iolo held a secret Gorsedd on Dinorwig Hill in 1799 while collecting material in north Wales for the forthcoming *Myvyrian Archaiology of Wales*.[103] This was the only Gorsedd he ever conducted in north Wales,[104] and in it he admitted David Thomas (Dafydd Ddu Eryri), as well as two of Thomas's disciples, John Roberts (Ieuan Lleyn) and Griffith Williams (Gutyn Peris).[105] As part of the ceremony Iolo recited a *cywydd*, 'Gorymbil am Heddwch' (Plea for Peace), which confirmed his own, and bardism's, anti-war stance.[106] He held this Gorsedd not simply because he happened to be in the area but also because he was eager to impose his own imprint on the growing interest in eisteddfodau and Gorseddau in north Wales. He was also at odds with the London-Welsh at this time and in low spirits. The Gwyneddigion had arranged to hold a simultaneous eisteddfod at Caerwys, London and Glamorgan in 1798, for which poets were required to translate Gray's 'The Bard' into Welsh. They had planned to hold a Gorsedd in conjunction with the Caerwys eisteddfod, but David Samwell had been called away to Paris and was unable to officiate. In a letter to Pughe, Iolo expressed his disappointment that the former would not be able to attend the Caerwys eisteddfod

101 NLW 21281E, Letter no. 172, Thomas Evans to Iolo Morganwg, 26 October 1798.

102 *HGB*, p. 43.

103 Iolo copied portions of NLW 13129A while at David Thomas's home at Traeth Coch, Anglesey, in 1799. See also transcriptions from Thomas's manuscrips in NLW 13116E, pp. 256, 287; NLW 13122B, pp. 111–16; NLW 13123B, p. 235.

104 In a draft of the essay 'A Short Account of the Ancient British Bards', Iolo recounted a formula for proclaiming Gorseddau, a year and a day in advance. The formula he used suggests that he proclaimed a Gorsedd meeting on the Berwyn Mountain in 1792 in the presence of Walter Davies, William Owen Pughe and Hywel of Eryri, but no corroborative evidence exists. NLW 13097B, pp. 145–6.

105 Albert Evans Jones, 'Tad Beirdd Arfon: Dafydd Tomos ('Dafydd Ddu Eryri') 1759–1822', *THSC* (1969), 7.

106 NLW 13134A, pp. 33–48. It was printed in Edward Williams, *Salmau yr Eglwys yn yr Anialwch*, pp. 220–7.

and Gorsedd,[107] but his tone was less compliant in his private papers.[108] His proprietorial spirit had been sharpened by the fact that the Gwyneddigion had acted without consulting him or seeking his consent.[109] He had been alerted to this by the obsequious Walter Davies, who was similarly dismissive of the bardic formulae of the Gwyneddigion.[110] Geraint Bowen has correctly attributed Iolo's chilly response to the Caerwys eisteddfod to his fear that he was losing hold of the Gorsedd to enthusiasts who were determined to embed it firmly in Gwynedd.[111] This fear may have prompted him to travel in person to north Wales in 1799 to extend bardism's influence by initiating David Thomas, John Roberts and Griffith Williams as bards of the Chair of Gwynedd in the clandestine Gorsedd held on Dinorwig Hill. Thomas's involvement with Iolo is curious because he had rejected an invitation to join Beirdd Ynys Prydain in the first Gorsedd in 1792, and he never disguised his scepticism about Iolo's bardic claims.[112] Nonetheless, independently of Iolo, the status-conscious Thomas held Gorseddau of his own in 1800 and, as an adjunct to the Caernarfon eisteddfod, in 1821.

David Thomas's rival Gorseddau and eisteddfodau are particularly intriguing because they displayed the same enterprising and individualistic spirit as that of Iolo. Iolo was resentful of the precedence the Gwyneddigion gave to the poetic tradition of Gwynedd, past and present, but Thomas was a native of Gwynedd and, despite collaborating with the Gwyneddigion Society in numerous eisteddfodau, he was also openly antagonistic towards their cultural hegemony and took exception to their interference in the poetic tradition, notably by deeming the *cynghanedd*-free metres of Iolo's Dosbarth Morganwg acceptable in an eisteddfod ode. Goodwill between Thomas and the Gwyneddigion was rare from 1804 onwards, and the former made a fervent provincial stand against their willingness to embrace Iolo's spurious metrics:

> Dilys gennyf i y bydd i bob Bardd awenyddol, cadarn, ac effro (ond nid cloffion a chysgadurion) ffieiddio o'i galon ddiweddar farn y Gwyneddigion ar Brydyddiaeth Gymreig, oblegid ei bod yn taflu dirmyg ar yr hên farddoniaeth sydd gymmeredig Ynghymru.[113]

107 NLW 13221E, pp. 53–4, Iolo Morganwg to William Owen Pughe, 12 May 1798.

108 NLW 21403E, nos. 4–8 contains copies of the handbills advertising these events. Iolo covered them with scribbled insults at their 'awkward' and 'inane' phrases.

109 NLW 21281E, Letter no. 158, John Evans to Iolo Morganwg, 22 November 1792; NLW 21282E, Letter no. 325A, printed proclamation of a bardic meeting for 1798; BL Add. 15030, ff. 3–4, Iolo Morganwg to William Owen Pughe, 13 August 1799; NLW 13221E, pp. 87–90, Iolo Morganwg to William Owen Pughe, 25 October 1802; NLW 21280E, Letter no. 67, Revd Hugh Davies to Iolo Morganwg, 8 October 1819. See also NLW 13123B, pp. 262, 267.

110 NLW 21280E, Letter no. 76, Walter Davies to Iolo Morganwg, 19 April 1798.

111 *HGB*, p. 56.

112 Myrddin Fardd (ed.), *Adgof Uwch Anghof: Llythyrau Lluaws o Brif Enwogion Cymru, Hen a Diweddar* (Pen y Groes, 1883), pp. 14–15, 20.

113 Ibid., p. 30.

Fig. 8 Dafydd Ddu Eryri: the poet David Thomas (1759–1822) was wary of the influence wielded by the Gwyneddigion Society over the resurrected eisteddfod movement.

> (I am sure that every inspired, firm and watchful poet (but not the lame and sleepy ones) will despise from their hearts the Gwyneddigion's recent judgement on Welsh Poetry, because it pours scorn on the ancient poetry that is approved in Wales.)

He pursued the theme in a letter to John Roberts, one of his disciples:

> Mae'r iawn bedwar-mesur-ar-hugain yn cynnwys, ac yn rheol i, bob mesur yn yr Iaith Gymraeg; a dilyn yr hen ffordd a wnawn ni, Beirdd Arfon, a gadael i'r Gwyneddigion gymryd y ffordd y fynnont! Nid rhesymol chwaith y gwelaf i roddi Deistiad fel Iolo Morganwg yn feirniad ar Brydyddiaeth Gristnogol, fel y bu gydag Awdl Dewi Wyn.[114]

114 Ibid., p. 33.

(The correct twenty-four metres include, and are a rule for, every metre in the Welsh Language; and we, the Poets of Arfon, will follow the old way and leave the Gwyneddigion to go the way they will! I do not see that it is reasonable either to place a Deist like Iolo Morganwg to judge Christian Poetry, as occurred with Dewi Wyn's ode.)

From 1783 onwards David Thomas was a prominent figure among poetic societies in Gwynedd and was known locally as 'Tad Beirdd Arfon' (the Father of Caernarfonshire Poets). Like Iolo, he had been inspired by the London-Welsh societies (notably the Gwyneddigion Society, of which he became a corresponding member in 1786) to establish similar societies in his own region,[115] and he is credited with having injected greater liveliness into the literary scene in Caernarfonshire.[116] An instinctive conservative, Thomas was profoundly disturbed by the radical bent of the Gwyneddigion and openly flouted their authority by organizing his own educational eisteddfodau in north Wales. Recent scholarship has shown that, as the eighteenth century progressed, the London-Welsh societies became increasingly out of touch with important social and religious changes in Wales, notably the Methodist movement, and that their view of Wales was often coloured by misplaced nostalgia:

Their very departure usually signified an independence of expression, as evidenced by their espousal of events in France, but, paradoxically, they overcompensated for having left Wales with a romantic love of their native land and an overwhelming desire to protect its culture. The Wales they loved was a romantic dream.[117]

The fiercely independent Thomas and his disciples prove that Iolo's was not the only dissenting regional voice within Wales and that, far from being overwhelmingly grateful to the enthusiasm of exiled Welshmen in London, those who lived in Wales sometimes perceived their actions as the meddling of outsiders.

Following David Thomas's induction into the Gorsedd of the Bards of the Island of Britain in 1799, Iolo did not hold another Gorsedd until shortly after Napoleon retreated to Elba in 1814. As well as the incident with the Cowbridge Volunteers in 1798, the trial and incarceration of Tomos Glyn Cothi in 1801 must have stiffened Iolo's resolve to keep a lower profile. He was also overwhelmed by other interests at this time, including completing his report for the Board of Agriculture, collecting material for *The Myvyrian*

115 Jones, 'Tad Beirdd Eryri', 11–12.

116 Thomas Parry, 'Dafydd Ddu Eryri', *THCS*, 41 (1980), 68–9; E. G. Millward, 'Eifionydd y Beirdd', *THCS*, 25 (1974), 42–65.

117 Emrys Jones, 'The Age of Societies' in idem (ed.), *The Welsh in London 1500–2000* (Cardiff, 2001), p. 80.

Archaiology of Wales, and promoting the Unitarian cause in south Wales, for whom he published a selection of hymns, *Salmau yr Eglwys yn yr Anialwch* (1812). But the prospect of peace between France and Britain inspired a revival in Gorsedd activity, and in 1814 Iolo advertised a Gorsedd meeting in the newly founded Welsh-language weekly newspaper, *Seren Gomer*, whose distribution throughout Wales ensured maximum exposure for this initiative. To be held on the Rocking-stone (*Y Maen Chwŷf*) at Pontypridd on 1 August 1814, its fitting theme for bards was 'Adferiad Heddwch' (The Restoration of Peace).[118] The change of location indicates a slight change of direction for meetings, membership and format. Pontypridd was located in north-east Glamorgan, somewhat distant from Iolo's familiar haunts in the Vale and the uplands, and this indicates that a new (and younger) generation of people had became interested in Gorsedd ceremonies, most notably initiates like the rhymesters Thomas Williams (Gwilym Morganwg)[119] and Evan (or Ifan) Cule.[120] Judging by a second-hand account recorded by Owen Morgan (Morien), unlike the semi-clandestine meetings on hilltops in the 1790s which had been restricted to a handful of bards, this proved to be a celebratory and overtly public occasion: led by Iolo, 'the celebrated Welsh antiquary', the bards processed along Taf Street carrying a banner.[121] They met at the New Inn, which was owned by Thomas Williams, an ardent admirer of Iolo and one who became a valuable sponsor. He publicized the Rocking-stone Gorseddau and, although he did not always hold Gorseddau and eisteddfodau concurrently, he encouraged poets to meet occasionally for eisteddfodau at his tavern, meetings which became known as Cyfarfodydd Gwilym Morganwg (William of Glamorgan's Meetings) or Cymdeithas y Maen Chwŷf (The Rocking-stone Society).[122] By 1814 Iolo was nearing his seventieth year, and it is possible that the newly resurrected Glamorgan Gorseddau were driven by the enthusiasm of Thomas Williams rather than Iolo himself. Indeed, Thomas Williams hosted and organized another Gorsedd on 21 December 1814, and set tasks for the bards that were very much in Iolo's mould: The Distinction of Brotherly Love, The Excellence of the

118 *Seren Gomer*, 5 July 1814.

119 For Thomas Williams, see O. V. Williams, 'Gwilym Morganwg', *Glamorgan Family History Society Journal*, 30 (1993), 8–11; 31 (1993), 6–7.

120 For Evan Cule, see Glanffrwd, *Llanwynno* (Caerdydd, 1949), pp. 175–7.

121 Owen Morgan, *The History of Pontypridd and the Rhondda Valleys* (Pontypridd, 1903), p. 6. Owen Morgan (Morien) recorded a second-hand description of the Gorsedd from Lewis Evans, or Lewis y Saer (Lewis the Carpenter), who remembered the event at the New Inn Hotel. Morien commented that 'Ancient ceremonies were performed on the great stone by Iolo in the role of Y Gwyddon or Odin'.

122 *Seren Gomer*, 15 February 1815. Williams, like many others, used the word eisteddfod to describe Iolo's Gorseddau. For the wider context of poetic and druidic circles in Pontypridd, see Huw Walters, *Cynnwrf Canrif: Agweddau ar Ddiwylliant Gwerin* (Llandybïe, 2004), pp. 184–274; idem, 'Myfyr Morganwg and the Rocking-Stone Gorsedd' in *Rattleskull Genius*, pp. 481–500.

Welsh Language, A View of the Bad Heart, Natural Sense, Peace to the World, The Burial of the Sword, The Rocking-stone, The Misers' Fall, God's Goodness and Love.[123] Yet, this second Gorsedd was not held independently of Iolo, without consulting him, for Williams depended on Iolo to dignify the meeting: 'ofni'r wyf mae tra thrwstan a fyddwn i fyned trwy'r gorchwyl, heb eich gwyddfod' (I fear that we will be rather hampered in the undertaking without your presence).[124] Iolo no doubt found the flattery gratifying.

The new location and enhanced membership of the Rocking-stone Gorseddau suggest that Iolo's Gorsedd had become a focal point for literary activity in the area at that time and it certainly remained so throughout the century.[125] Gorseddau were invaluable for budding poets: they provided the initial stimulus to compose and also a public forum to declaim their poetry which, in turn, bolstered their confidence to publish their work in *Seren Gomer* and various anthologies.[126] Further Gorseddau were held at the Pontypridd Rocking-stone in 1815 and 1817,[127] but although these may represent the tip of the iceberg no other records survive of other Gorseddau. The Rocking-stone Gorseddau mark a new direction in several ways. Not only did Thomas Williams and Evan Davies (Myfyr Morganwg) attract a new generation of members for Beirdd Ynys Prydain and their Gorsedd, but the Rocking-stone Gorseddau also marked the involvement of Iolo's son, Taliesin. Taliesin had been initiated *in absentia* as an ovate in London as early as 1792, but he was not properly 'initiated into the arcana of Druidism' until 1814 during a Gorsedd which represented his bardic coming of age.[128] He was clearly being groomed to succeed his father. Thomas Williams's involvement with the new wave of Gorseddau also marked a desire to bring the Gorsedd to the attention of a nationwide audience. In his advertisement for the Gorsedd of December 1814 in *Seren Gomer*, Williams specifically targeted 'Beirdd a Phrydyddion y Dywysogaeth' (Bards and Poets of the Principality).[129]

123 *Seren Gomer*, 12 November 1814. In a subsequent issue Evan Cule's poem on the Rocking-stone was published: *Seren Gomer*, 15 February 1815. See Walters, *Cynnwrf Canrif*, p. 193, for an account of the Rocking-stone printed in *Seren Gomer*, 8 February 1815.

124 NLW 21284E, Letter no. 745, Thomas Williams to Iolo Morganwg, 6 December 1814. He added, 'Mae llawer yn addo dyfod i'r Eisteddfod' (Many have promised to come to the Eisteddfod).

125 Brynley F. Roberts, '"Yn Wladgarol, Iaithgarol a Chenedlgarol": Cymdeithas Cymrodorion Aberdâr' in Hywel Teifi Edwards (ed.), *Cwm Cynon* (Llandysul, 1997), pp. 261–2.

126 *Llais Awen Gwent a Morganwg* (Merthyr, 1824); *Awenyddion Morganwg, neu Farddoniaeth Cadair Merthyr Tudful* (Merthyr, 1826); *Ffrwyth yr Awen: sef Awdlau, Cywyddau, ac Ynglynion, a ddanfonwyd i Eisteddfod Gwent, Medi 1822* (Llundain, 1823).

127 See John Davies, *Blwch y Cantorion* (Merthyr, 1838) for Gwilym Morganwg's poem about the deceit of millers, written for the 1815 Gorsedd. Evan Cule's greeting to the bards who attended the Gorsedd on 21 December 1817 was published in *Seren Gomer*, 17 June 1818.

128 See the introduction to Williams, *Awen y Maen Chwyf*, p. vii.

129 *Seren Gomer*, 12 November 1814; *HGB*, p. 45. Williams used the term 'eisteddfod' rather than 'Gorsedd'.

However, there is little evidence to suggest that poets came from far and wide, though Benjamin Jones (Prif Arwyddfardd Môn; Chief Heraldic bard of Anglesey), a clothier and a staunch Baptist from Holyhead, sent a poem under the pseudonym 'Y Cawr Gwan' (The Weak Giant) to Iolo after reading the advertisement for the second 1814 Gorsedd.[130] Jones's contribution to the institution and his expression of brotherly love between Anglesey and Glamorgan ('o gariad brawdol Môn i Morgannwg') suggest that the regional exclusivity of the Gorsedd was beginning to wane and that the coverage which the Rocking-stone Gorseddau received in the national press created a receptive audience for the Gorseddau that would coincide with the emergence of the provincial eisteddfodau.

The year 1819 proved to be a turning point in the fortunes of the Gorsedd for, in the eisteddfod hosted by the Dyfed Cambrian Society, Iolo held a Gorsedd that set a precedent for every subsequent eisteddfod. Carmarthen was the first in a series of provincial eisteddfodau organized and hosted by the Cambrian Societies which proliferated at this time: Cymdeithas Gymroaidd Dyfed (Dyfed Cambrian Society, 1818), Cymdeithas Gymroaidd Gwynedd (Gwynedd Cambrian Society, 1819), Cymdeithas Cymmrodorion Powys (Powys Cymmrodorion Society, 1819), The Cymmrodorion Society or the Metropolitan Cambrian Institution in London (1820) and Cymdeithas Gymroaidd Gwent a Morgannwg (Gwent and Glamorgan Cambrian Society, 1821).[131] Although there was an element of cross-membership, societies generally worked independently, and often against one another, to achieve their aims. In terms of popularity and respectability, its association with the provincial eisteddfodau proved to be the making of the Gorsedd.[132] It provided a new and wider audience and, since the eisteddfod's cultural programme was sponsored by affluent gentry and was thus much less politically suspect than Iolo's radical Gorseddau of the past, Gorseddau became more acceptable in the public mind.

The first Cambrian society to be established was Cymdeithas Cymreigyddion Dyfed in 1818. The committee, chaired by Bishop Thomas Burgess, who had, in turn, been influenced by literary clerics on the committee, decided to hold an eisteddfod in Carmarthen the following year. However, as Geraint H. Jenkins has shown, radical Dissent was an important context for the venture since Iolo's lone presence as a Unitarian on an otherwise exclusively Anglican committee brought into sharp focus the inherent rivalry between the established church and Rational Dissent and, indeed, the per-

130 NLW 21390E, no. 25, 'Cwymp y Cybyddion'. Jones requested Iolo to submit his poem for publication in *Seren Gomer*. It duly appeared on 19 July 1815.

131 Bedwyr Lewis Jones, *Yr Hen Bersoniaid Llengar* (Dinbych, [1963]); Edwards, *The Eisteddfod*, p. 15.

132 Geraint H. Jenkins, 'The Unitarian Firebrand, the Cambrian Society and the Eisteddfod' in *Rattleskull Genius*, pp. 269–92.

sonal rivalry between Iolo and the prelate. The aim of the Gorsedd, according to the scroll which Iolo composed for the occasion, was to license poets. This was carried out, not in the name of Cadair Morganwg (The Chair of Glamorgan), but in the name of 'Cadair Talaith Dinefwr' (the Chair of the region of Dinefwr).[133] Crucially, this was done in deference to the historical resonance – actual and supposed – of Carmarthen. Not only was the region known to Wales's medieval poets as 'Talaith Dinefwr', but the town had hosted the celebrated eisteddfod *c.*1453 which had become a key event in Iolo's fictional bardic narratives. For Iolo, the auspicious location meant that history had come full circle. Indeed, the famous medieval eisteddfod was evoked in a declaration made by the bards:

> Ac yn yr Eisteddvod hon . . . barnwyd yn unvryd unllais, heb nâg na gwrtheb na llaw na thavawd, bod y Rheithiadau Cerdd a vreiniwyd yn Eisteddfod Caer Vyrddin yn y vl. 1451, dan enw y pedwar mesur ar hugain, yn cyvyngu awen y Bardd o fewn llyffetheiriau rhy gaethion; a bod, yn rhy vynych o yr achaws, synwyr a rhwyddineb iaith yn cael eu hof[f]rwm ar allawr gwag-orchest egwanbwyll a diansawdd.[134]
>
> (And in this Eisteddfod . . . it was unanimously judged, without contradiction or rejection by hand or tongue, that the Rules of Poetry honoured at the Carmarthen Eisteddfod in the year 1451, under the name the twenty-four metres, confine the muse of a Bard in fetters that are too tight; and that, as a result, often the sense and fluency of language are sacrificed on the altar of vain accomplishments that are weak in judgement and lack substance.)

Iolo himself was fully aware of the historical resonance of the event and he invoked the spirit of restitution in his own speech:

> At a period when a dark cloud had involved us in a winter night of ignorance Caermarthen had the highly merited honour of being as it were a morning star preceding the dawn of a glorious Morning that soon afterwards appeared. Some clouds have since appeared, but again at Caermarthen the sky clears up. We see the clouds beginning to disperse, and we hope that a glorious Summers day of Bardic and of every other description of Literature morality virtue and Religion will ensue.[135]

The Carmarthen Eisteddfod and Gorsedd attracted a substantial number of poets,[136] but although some new members (mainly poets from north Wales)

133 NLW 854D, pp. 5–8, 9. A second hand, writing in pencil, has amended this to the region of Gwynedd, ibid., p. 7.

134 *Yr Ymofynydd*, V (1852), 272.

135 NLW 21430E, no. 15.

136 NLW 854D, p. 9.

attended, there was a small element of continuity between the membership in the 1790s and the later stage of its development. Walter Davies remained a stalwart and, despite the total breakdown of his friendship with Iolo, William Owen Pughe's interest was also sustained and communicated to his son, Aneurin, the Recorder (*Cofiadur*) of the bards at the event. Thomas Williams, the veteran of the Rocking-stone Gorseddau in Glamorgan in the years preceding Carmarthen, carried the sword at the Gorsedd ceremony, during which Iolo wrong-footed Bishop Burgess by declaiming radical principles. New members were drawn from the Cambrian societies and included men who would play a significant role in the post-Iolo period: David Richards (Dewi Silin), John Jenkins (Ioan Ceri) and Robert Davies (Robert Nantglyn). Historians of the Gorsedd agree that this eisteddfod was crucial and that bardism and the Bards of the Island of Britain would not have penetrated the national consciousness or awakened the national imagination had not Iolo achieved this 'coup' at Carmarthen. Although provincial eisteddfodau were organized at a provincial level, the Carmarthen eisteddfod of 1819 marked the beginning of the rise of the Gorsedd to national recognition. A not insignificant footnote to the Carmarthen eisteddfod involves David James, who was initiated into the Gorsedd by Iolo at that time. In a neat example of bardism's circular influence, James's volume, *The Patriarchal Religion of Britain* (1836), exercised a profound influence on The Druid Order in England although, by 1849, when he presided over the Gorsedd held in conjunction with the eisteddfod at Aberffraw, he himself was called 'Archdderwydd' (Archdruid), a term borrowed from The Druid Order.[137]

After the 1819 eisteddfod, the Powys Cambrian Society followed suit by holding a Gorsedd at Kerry, Montgomeryshire, in 1821. Those present included Walter Davies and his son, Walter Davies Jr, John Jenkins, W. J. Rees of Casgob, David Richards and his brother Thomas Richards, Robert Davies, Aneurin Owen and John Howel. Walter Davies was one of the few people who had maintained a cordial lifelong friendship with Iolo and, in the latter's absence, the Gorsedd was entrusted to him rather than to Taliesin, who was also present, and this ensured that the pattern established at Carmarthen was properly observed:

> There are now I think a greater number of good poets in N than in S. Wales; they are better patronized and exert themselves accordingly. We had an Eisteddfod and held a Gorsedd; Walter Davies presiding – The ceremonies of the Carmarthen Gorsedd were faithfully observed – You had given Mr Jenkins a copy of the necessary forms which we followed excepting the necessary alterations for the

[137] Geraint Bowen, *Golwg ar Orsedd y Beirdd* (Caerdydd, 1992), p. 21. See also Geraint Bowen, 'Archdderwydd, y Teitl a'r Swydd', *NLWJ*, XXIV, part 3 (1986), 358–88.

> Chair of Powys. Two Bards and 5 or 6 Ovates were Graduated after the manner of Carmarthen.[138]

In 1822 the provincial eisteddfod was held at Brecon. A report of the proceedings was published in *The Cambrian*,[139] and a certificate which William Ellis Jones (Cawrdaf) received upon being initiated by Iolo also survives.[140] Unlike the earlier Gorseddau of the 1790s, those of the early nineteenth century were more concerned with the niceties of poetry and with acting as a body for conferring a legitimate poetic qualification upon aspiring poets. Despite this shift in emphasis, Iolo had lost none of his enthusiasm:

> I was sorely disappointed in not finding you at Brecon: What Demon of the bottomless pit appointed Mr Hughes one of the judges. Never could any man be less qualified, he knows no more of the ancient Welsh versification, than he knows of the Art of spinning monthly new moons out of a clap of thunder; in other respects indeed Mr Hughes is a learned worthy and sensible man. Wm Williams of Dolgethey the successful candidate for the ode certain possesses a good, but very unpolished, genius for Poetry: his language is in a Hottentotic degree barbarous, Cadarnog, llawenog, tawelog, hynodol, parodol &c as if the legitimate adjectives, Cadarn, Llawen, tawel, hynod, parod, required the addition of those Monkey tails of the Southcottian Dialect, og, ol &c so abundantly used by the North Walians [?or] Deudneudwyr, as we call them in S. Wales, from Deud and Neud instead of Dywedyd and Gwneuthur, &cc, but no more of this now. I have noticed a disgusting number of North walian barbarisms in my Welsh introduction to Cyfrinach y Beirdd.[141]

Due to ill health and old age, Iolo had been unable to attend the Gorsedd at Brecon in 1822 and so the heightened passion expressed above may have stemmed from his frustration at having to observe events from a distance.

Nevertheless, this was a period in which Iolo was required to relinquish control, even though he was still able to exert a measure of supervision through Taliesin, his heir apparent, and Walter Davies. At times, one suspects that Iolo was taking advantage of his obedient son, who was utterly ignorant of the fraudulent nature of his father's vision. For example, Iolo drafted a scroll and material to be declaimed at the 1825 Gorsedd held at Twyn-yr-

138 NLW 21284E, Letter no. 684, Taliesin Williams to Iolo Morganwg, 26 January 1821. Taliesin also warned Iolo about Bishop Burgess's objections to Gorsedd meetings: 'I understand that the Bishop of St Davids prevented the G[wallter] holding the Gorsedd at Wrexham, objecting to the ceremonies. Do not mention this to any one, as it may tend to the injury of the persons to whom he expressed his objection – He is more your enemy than friend.'

139 *The Cambrian*, 5 October 1822.

140 Bowen, *Golwg ar Orsedd y Beirdd*, p. 8.

141 NLW 21286E, Letter no. 994, a draft letter to Walter Davies, found in letter to Taliesin Williams from Iolo Morganwg, 22 September 1823.

odyn, Merthyr,[142] at which Taliesin presided. Taliesin was Iolo's eyes and ears and, following the Gorsedd in September 1825, he faithfully reported back to his father. His only concern was that some of the bards had not behaved in the abstemious and exemplary manner required of Bards of the Island of Britain: 'The only alloy to its respectability was the drunkenness of some of those who should have conducted themselves as examples to others.'[143] Perhaps eager to gain his father's approval, Taliesin added that 'unless more temperate habits be observed by them in future, I will relinquish their meetings altogether'.[144] As Iolo's heir, Taliesin was in a position to ensure that the Cambrian Societies abided by Iolo's wishes and that their Gorseddau fulfilled his expectations. He conveyed this reassuring message to his father:

> I will adhere scrupulously to your advice relating to Cadair Merthyr Tudful, Gwaedd uwch adwaedd [cry above resounding cry] &c, and am very glad to receive the information. I wish you would give me the form of a correct 'Gwys' [summons] And also of the Proclamations in opening and closing a Gorsedd together with the mode of conferring Degrees. It is my desire to render our chair as conformable as possible to genuine ancient usages – to divest it completely of the trumpery of modern innovations. If you could come up with safety we should be very happy. If not, I will send you the work from time to time as it comes out. I must now conclude to allow place for Nancy to follow me.[145]

Indeed, Gorsedd meetings became family affairs. Iolo's daughter Margaret (Peggy) was invited to the Brecon eisteddfod in 1822,[146] and in 1825 Ann (Nancy) wrote excitedly to her father at the prospect of taking part in another: 'It is settled upon by some of the bards that I am to dress the chair and hang up the Medals on the back of it in full view there to remain untill every successful bard receives his own.'[147] But even with Taliesin at the helm, Iolo remained loath to let go of his creation, and he continued to make heavy demands on his son:

> You ought never to give the name of Eisteddfod to the Albans [equinoxes and solstices], but Gorsedd. Cadair, or Gorsedd a Chadair – a legally proclaimed Eisteddfod is [without] authority and respectability as a Cadair or Gorsedd. There is no necessity of proclaiming the Albans for the days on which they are held are known and established [since] time immemorial. But an Eisteddfod must be proclaimed, for it is a special meeting on a special occasion or time, and its acts or

142 NLW 21286E, Letter no. 1003, Iolo Morganwg to Taliesin Williams, 28 November 1825.
143 NLW 21284E, Letter no. 696, Taliesin Williams to Iolo Morganwg, 28 September 1825.
144 Ibid.
145 NLW 21284E, Letter no. 698, Taliesin Williams to Iolo Morganwg, 8 November 1825.
146 NLW 21282E, Letter no. 420, W. J. Rees to Iolo Morganwg, 28 January 1822.
147 NLW 21284E, Letter no. 698, Ann Matthews Williams to Iolo Morganwg, an addendum to a letter from Taliesin Williams to Iolo Morganwg, 8 November 1825.

> transactions are of no authority unless legally proclaimed. And if the proclamation is continued uninterrupted for nine (or three times three) years, it may appropriately [be] named an Alban, with an appropriate name or appellations – suppose Alban Merthyr – Alban adwedd, or the Alban of restoration or revival, &c &c.[148]

Old age appears to have deepened his resentment towards the people of north Wales, for while referring to a bound collection of 'Ancient Welsh Poems' in the same letter to Taliesin he warned him in a conspiratorial tone: 'it is a most curious and useful Collection, but you must not shew to any Deudneudian or friend of a Deudneudian, let fools and Coxcombs remain what they are'.[149] One of the last coherent letters he sent to Taliesin, in January 1826, revealed a keen proprietorial spirit, made all the more acute by his awareness of impending death. Because it was one of his last sustained pronouncements on bardism, this letter may be considered Iolo's authoritative last word on the subject. It highlights all the divergent strands of bardism: its national significance, strong regional bias, egocentricity, and the paranoia which consumed him regarding Owain Myfyr and William Owen Pughe. It also has relevance for bardism's line of succession, for Iolo included in the letter a speech, heavily influenced and edited (if not entirely written) by him, for Taliesin to deliver before the newly established 'Cadair Merthyr' (the Chair of Merthyr Tudful). Taliesin's Chair of Merthyr therefore represents an attempt on Iolo's behalf to maintain his hold on his bardic vision in the light of the popularity which Gorsedd meetings enjoyed in provincial eisteddfodau throughout Wales. Ironically, perhaps, considering the significance of this final decree on bardism, he desisted from using his bardic name, Iolo Morganwg, and simply signed himself 'E.W.' Another eisteddfod was held at Brecon in 1826, and was accompanied by a Gorsedd over which William Owen Pughe, one of the adjudicators, presided, in spite of the presence of Taliesin. Iolo was too old and infirm to attend or, indeed, to muster the strength to protest at the presence (and indeed prominence) of a former friend whom he had once likened to Judas.[150]

Following Iolo's days, the Gorsedd, as an accessory to the provincial eisteddfodau, attracted considerable interest throughout Wales, but remained only nominally a national institution. Its organization remained regional in practice and was jealously guarded by a network of Cambrian societies who were mainly interested in furthering their own local programmes. By virtue of his membership of the Cambrian Society of Dyfed, however, Iolo had orchestrated a role for his bards in the 1819 Eisteddfod at Carmarthen. Fortuitously,

148 NLW 21286E, Letter no. 1003, Iolo Morganwg to Taliesin Williams, 28 November 1825.
149 Ibid.
150 NLW 21419E, no. 58.

the various Cambrian societies consisted of men like Walter Davies, John Jenkins, W. J. Rees and Thomas Price (Carnhuanawc) who admired Iolo and who were, to differing degrees, convinced of the veracity of his druidic claims. More important, in terms of maintaining the momentum of Gorsedd meetings after Iolo's days, was the involvement of his son with these societies. As Iolo's only son, Taliesin was considered his father's heir, mediator and interpreter, and he worked tirelessly to edit a comprehensive selection of his father's bardic writings. He had already been groomed for this role during his father's life – the burden of securing the 'second age of Taliesin' had fallen on his shoulders – and it was a role which he took seriously following his father's death.[151]

Taliesin's celebrity status indicates the self-perpetuating nature of bardism and the Gorsedd once the Cambrian societies had embraced them. This impetus was maintained. The 'Cymreigyddion' held a series of successful eisteddfodau in Abergavenny in which Taliesin was heavily involved. Not every eisteddfod arranged by this society included a Gorsedd ceremony, but those that did were significant steps in popularizing the Gorsedd and extending its influence at both national and international levels. The most important in terms of augmenting the international profile of the Gorsedd was the 1838 eisteddfod, which was attended by Theodore Hersart de La Villemarqué who, despite Taliesin's absence, was so impressed by the mysteries of bardism that he superimposed Iolo's ideas on the Breton literary tradition in his *Barzas-Breiz* [The Poetry of Brittany]. The Abergavenny Cambrian Society, more than any other society, sustained bardism's momentum. The Welsh Manuscript Society had been established at the 1836 eisteddfod in Abergavenny by the 'Cymreigyddion' of the town and, following Taliesin's death in 1847, this society, which included Lady Augusta Hall (Gwenynen Gwent) of Llanofer, who became a patron of Taliesin, was heavily involved in organizing eisteddfodau and was also instrumental in publishing Iolo's writings on bardism. Thomas Price completed the editorial work begun by Taliesin, and the *Iolo Manuscripts* was finally published in 1848.[152] For the first time, a wide range of Iolo's bardic writings became accessible in print, and the volume soon became a seminal text for Gorsedd devotees and helped to shape the image of the Gorsedd throughout the nineteenth century. A further step in this self-perpetuating process was the assiduous work of John Williams (Ab Ithel), who later assumed control of the Welsh Manuscript Society and

151 Brynley F. Roberts, 'Mab ei Dad: Taliesin ab Iolo Morganwg' in Hywel Teifi Edwards (ed.) *Merthyr a Thaf* (Llandysul, 2001), pp. 57–93; idem, '"The Age of Restitution": Taliesin ab Iolo and the Reception of Iolo Morganwg' in *Rattleskull Genius*, pp. 461–80.

152 *Iolo Manuscripts: A Selection of Ancient Welsh Manuscripts, in Prose and Verse, from the collection made by the late Edward Williams, Iolo Morganwg; for the Purpose of forming a continuation of the Myfyrian Archaiology; and Subsequently Proposed as Materials for a New History of Wales* (Llandovery, 1848).

continued to publish volumes like *Dosbarth Edeyrn Davod Aur* (1856) and *Barddas* (1862) which would dictate the way in which Iolo and his bardic vision were received and interpreted thereafter.

The development of the Gorsedd and the eisteddfod was such that, once the latter had formed a national body of elected members, it was only a matter of time before the Gorsedd followed suit and formed its own cohesive national governing body. A unified 'national' eisteddfod proper did not materialize until after 1860 when a body calling itself 'Yr Eisteddfod' (The Eisteddfod), consisting of an elected council, was finally formed from the network of regional eisteddfodau and their organizers. John Williams had proposed such a scheme for the Gorsedd in the Llangollen eisteddfod of 1858, but the Society of the Gorsedd, a national body to administer Gorsedd activities, was not formed until 1888. In the same year, the role of archdruid was created. This was an initative which denoted the transition of the Bards of the Island of Britain into an institution proper, even if the new administrative hierarchy contradicted the ideals of its founder. The Gorsedd was finally formally married to the eisteddfod movement in 1937 when both institutions united to form the National Eisteddfod Council. The arrangement was revised in 1952 and, under a new constitution, the Council became known as the National Eisteddfod Court.

Latterly, the word Gorsedd has gained currency as a proper noun requiring a definite article: 'The Gorsedd' denotes the institution and its body of members. For Iolo, a Gorsedd was merely a meeting of bards, and The Bards of the Island of Britain constituted the broader national body. This semantic shift has subsequently modified the way in which the assembly itself is recognized: no longer simply a Gorsedd, it is qualified as 'a Gorsedd meeting' or 'a meeting of the Gorsedd'. Far from representing a break with its origins, these subtle linguistic and semantic changes reflect the organic growth of Iolo's vision. 'Beirdd Ynys Prydain' was neither accurate nor tenable once 'The Gorsedd' had gained national and institutional status, and its ranks had been swollen, not simply by poets, but also by ordinary Welsh men and women committed to the promotion of the Welsh language and its culture.

Documents

Editorial note

The documents which follow have been relatively lightly edited in order to preserve Iolo's idiosyncratic voice and energetic turn of phrase. Punctuation, capitalization, italicization and English spelling have mostly been standardized, with the exception of some of Iolo's quirks. For example, his inconsistent orthography with respect to proper names: Morris/Morys/Morrys and Owen/Owain. Three dots [. . .] denote that extraneous examples have been excised, but Iolo's own unorthodox markings which denote his own omissions have been retained: six dots [......] and four crosses [++++]. Writings which Iolo left untitled have been allotted titles which are enclosed in square brackets; all other titles were chosen by Iolo.

Ancient British Bards and Druids

I: [The cultivation of the Welsh language] (NLW 13144A, pp. 223–38)

This short essay, possibly written with the 'Dissertation on the Welsh language' in mind, was designed to establish the importance and prestige of the Welsh language. Since Iolo believed that the truths of bardism were enshrined in the language, he was quite certain that the Welsh language itself was inherently civilized. Here he raises some of the broad themes pertaining to Welsh civilization and identity: Wales's pre-Roman polish, its ancient national pedigree, and the Celtic, rather than Trojan, origins of the nation.

It appears from the names of persons, places &c that were found amongst the Britons by their first Roman invaders, that prior to that time, the language had been cultivated and improved to as high a pitch as that at which we have at any subsequent period found it. It appears to be then, exactly the same in its principles of compounding words, as we find it at this day. The following names & words fully evince this, such as

Cymmry – Essyllwg – Dyfed

Gwynedd – Gwent – Myrddin

Prydain – Armorig – Alban – Dyfnaint

Caswallawn – Cynfelyn, Afarwy, Caradoc, Buddug, Derwydd – Ofydd, &c

&c &c &c of subsequent ages, Gwrtheyrn, Aneurin, Llywarch, Hywel, Collfrewi – Morgan, Rhiwallon, Cadfan – Cadwaladr – &c &c &c &c and a great number of common, compounds given by Camden. **(224)**

The oldest Greek and Norman historians assert that the Cimmeri and Cimbri were one and the same people, whence it appears that the same rules of changing the letters n in *Cyn* and b in *bry* prevail then exactly as at present cym-mry, and the same rule of forming the plural of *bro* i.e. *bry*, as at present. (See Pinkerton, *Hist. Goths.*) So far back as those times it was obviously an established grammatical rule in the *Cimbric* to change the O into Y in forming the plurals of monosyllables &c &c as in the following: **(225)**

Sing	Plur	
Bro	Bry	
Bod	Byd	
Bollt	byllt	
Cort	cyrt	
Corph	cyrph	
Cosp	cysp	
Col	cyl	whence cylion?
Colp	cylp	
Colf	cylf	
Coll	cyll	
Corf	cyrf	
Corn	cyrn	
Cors	cyrs	
Cloch	clych	
Ffordd	ffyrdd	
Fforch	ffyrch	
Ffonn	ffynn	
Gordd	gyrch	
Mor	myr	
Por	pyr	
Pont	pynt	**(226)**
Porth	pyrth	
Post	pyst	
Mollt	myllt	
Torth	tyrth	
Torch	tyrth	
Troch	trych, Glam.	
Tôr & Tawr	Ys-tyr	

Cymmro, plural, Cymmry, may be from Cyn, *prius*, or from *cyd*. Both the one and the other change into *Cym* in composition. The first etymology makes the word signify, *aborigines*, or the first inhabitants. The other signifies civil communities, compatriots, a name assumed by the civilized Celtae in distinction from *Gwyddelod* [Irishmen], savages, wildmen, woodmen, barbarians &c. This to **(227)** me seems the best etymology of the name by which we call ourselves.

Cymmru. cyd-fru – the common womb or mother of the *nation* or *community* of *Cymmry*.
Cymmro – Civis & Gwyddel *Sylvaticus*.

Caesar says that Druidism originated in Britain, so say the Welsh triads and traditions, whence we may, with some plausibility, suppose that the appellative Cymry &c originated in Britain. And here also in that part of the Island called from the remotest times *Cymry* in distinction from Lloegr, Alban, &c, as the place where Celtic civilization began or commenced. In Caesar's time, this civilization had spread itself, not only as a far as Kent &c but even into (a part at least) of Gallia. Supposing **(228)** it to have been so, we must of course suppose that a colony of Cymmry, or perhaps their System of civilization, was transplanted into Germany, whence the name and system extended itself amongst the German Celtae over Germany &c, as far as the Euxine &c. Another hypothesis may be laid down which is that the civil community of Cymry was first formed and with it the Druidical System, on the Germanic part of the continent, or even in Thrace or in the neighbourhood; of civil communities near the Euxine, or even perhaps in Asia whence it travelled westward over Germany into Britain and thence into Gaul. Whence, with respect to that country, it would appear of British origin, it is natural for a people to consider most things as originating in that Country whence they derive them, especially that of the matter. There **(229)** are some British traditions preserved in the Triads which may be thought to favour this idea, as that the Cymry came into Britain under the conduct of Hu Gadarn from Gwlad yr Haf (the Land of Summer) i.e. a warm climate. Some of our poets as Iolo Goch &c suppose Hu Gadarn to have been born in the country (Thrace) where Constantinople now is. These traditions, whatever we may be either able or unable to make of them, are of infinitely greater authority than the absurd romance of Brutus of Troy &c. Yet even this seems to have originated from some old tradition that the Cymmry came from that part of the world, to which the Trojan fable was added by Geoffrey, or probably by some romancer before not many centuries before him, making the Thracian origin of the Cymry the foundation stone of his fiction. And there having been a little of truth blended with this fiction, **(230)** it is so far imposed on the Welsh as to induce them to receive the history of our Trojan origin as in the main true and authentic. Where the ingenuous researcher finds some appearance of truth, he as such is willing to embrace it and will be thence insensibly induced to admit more than can be authenticated, whilst one (as Pinkerton, who has been detectedly, and even confessedly himself an impostor measuring the consciences of others by his own) is not able to admit as truth hardly any thing of pretty remote antiquity.

The Gauls seemingly derived their knowledge of Druidism from Britain, and thence supposed it originated there. This is however no sufficient proof that it was so. It must, I confess, be acknowledged that our oldest triads **(231)** assert that Bardism originated in Britain. By Bardism they always intend peculiarly the Druidical theology & polity. That the last should have originated in Britain may not only be with ease allowed but it is sufficiently probable. As for the theology, it is in its principles and doctrines the same precisely as that of the ancient oriental nations: the Brachmans, Magi of Persia, Phoenicians, Egyptians &c &c &c. It is therefore highly probable that the Cimbri, whilst they remained in the neighbourhood of these nations, became acquainted with their theological doctrines, and adopting them, with other principles of civilization, carried them into Britain &c. According to some of the triads, the three **(232)** orders of *Bardd*, or *Prydydd*, *Derwydd* ac *Ofydd* were termed Bards according to the Rights and Institutes of the Bards of the Island of Britain. But the Primitive Bard (*Prifardd*) or Poet, and him only, was termed *Bardd wrth fraint a defawd yr Hen Gymry*, i.e. Bard according to the Rights and Institutions of the Ancient Cimbri or Cimmeri. This implies fairly enough that this order existed before the Cimbri came into Britain; at least before the other two orders had been instituted in Britain, and that these two orders of Druid and *Ofydd* originated in Britain, there [are] **(233)** sufficient reasons to believe, for on the continent we find no traces of Druidism but in Gallia, who it is confessed, received it from Britain. Indeed the Primitive Bard (*Prifardd*) or Poet could not have originated in Britain, he was known to all nations from the earliest ages, and tho' he is termed Bard according to the Rights and Institutes of the Bards of the Island of Britain, it is only as being one of the three orders whereof the Druidical hierarchy consisted. Thro' him and his commemorative songs the ancient theology and mythology were conveyed to the new institution of **(234)** British Bards and Druids which, as the triads assert, is of no older date than the time of Prydain ab Aedd Mawr. That the Druidical polity or institution was not formed before the Cimmeri had arrived in the utmost western parts of Europe is sufficiently clear from its never having been noticed in any other part of the world, which could not well have been had it ever prevailed in those parts, as it thus appears obviously to have originated in the western parts of Europe, and there known only in Britain (with its Isles perhaps) and Gaul. It remains to decide **(235)** which of these countries gave existence to this celebrated institution. The old Welsh Bardic triads say that it was in Britain. So Caesar says, doubtless from information given him by the most intelligent of his Gallic friends and acquaintances. This is fully sufficient to enable us to decide in favour of Britain, and to maintain it until authorities in favour of Gaul shall appear indisputably greater than Caesar; till written memorials shall be produced that expressly oppose when the Welsh manuscripts assert. As these are not found in any ancient language, no modern **(236)** tongue can pretend to any thing of this nature. The Welsh, soon after the Roman conquest of Britain became acquainted with learning of the conquerors. According to Tacitus &c, the Welsh language became a literary language and lived, as such, a cotemporary with the living Latin and Greek languages for many centuries, and much of what it during those long periods acquired of knowledge, it has to this day retained, having never experienced the strange alterations and corruptions that have heaped confusion on all other European languages; that buried in oblivion almost every thing, of the **(237)** little they were, of knowledge ever possessed. The Welsh in all ages used only their own unchanging language. They have seen it survive all the ancient learned languages of Europe; survive, and far beyond it, the Greek and Roman periods of learning and civilization some of the wrecks of which it has carried down to another (remote a full thousand years form the first) great learned period; has been intimately acquainted with the ancient learned world, has seen its death and burial, and has now for almost three centuries seen its resurrection arising in all its pristine beauty from the grave, bringing **(238)** again to the eye of redawning light testimonials to the authenticity of the Cimbric written traditions.

II: [The Gwyddoniaid] (NLW 13158A, pp. 190–4)

Iolo invented the Gwyddoniaid (wise men) as precursors of the Bards of the Island of Britain. They bolstered his argument that druidism originated in Britain and his insistence on the rational and divinely inspired nature of bardism allowed him to claim that it was of equal standing with the major religious and philosophical systems of the world.

Gwyddon, plural *Gwyddoniaid*, a wise man, wise men, poets, philosophers. Such, according [to] our oldest writers and tradition were the appellations by which the wise men or teachers of the ancient Cymry were designated. The institution of the Gwyddoniaid was most probably of spontaneous origin, self-produced, as it were, and such possibly were all or most of the civilizing institutions of mankind in all ages and countries. They originated in obscurity, the unconscious founder whose name died with him, or soon after, was (as we may fairly presume) a good moral man, a good and friendly neighbour, a man of distinguished prudence and wisdom; and thence became noticed and respected, his advice attended to, others approved of his conduct, and copied his character. From time to time others of similar characters appeared and being approved of increased in numbers, the varying events and occasions of the community called for their advice, and several things were trusted to their management. This would suggest the propriety of associations or conventions **(191)** of as many of such characters as might have been brought together of them. They became thus formed by tacit consent into a very useful association of wise men, were caressed, obeyed and honoured by the communities amongst whom they had thus spontaneously, like the spontaneous vegetations of nature in fields and woods, sprung up; no body well knew when or how, but like those herbs, fruits and seeds of the natural produce of plains and forests which were found to be of greatest use, were deemed worthy of cultivation and of proper care. Thus spontaneous institutions having appeared to be upon the whole of important use and benefit, but being in some respects defective in principle, in knowledge, in power or authority &c. The community at large conceived an idea that they might be able to improve the institution, collected ideas, cases in point, objects in view, &c &c and assembled publickly for the purpose of giving more regular and permanent formation to it, vest it with privilege and authority, define the proper qualifications of the members of such an embodied association, suggest and patronize modes of such instructions as would qualify for the officialities of the institutions; and thence, as the various peculiarities of occasions might require, to extend to and ramify through all the several orders of the national community. Amongst the great names amongst the Gwyddoniaid recorded **(192)** by ancient traditions and written memorials are those of Menyw ap y Teirgwaedd [Menyw son of the three shouts], Einigan Gawr [Einigan the Giant], Rhufawn Brydydd [Rhufawn the Poet], otherwise Rhufawn Fardd [Rhufawn the Bard], Melfin ferch [daughter of] Rhufawn Fardd. We are told by our oldest writers that when Prydain ap Aedd Mawr had conceived the plan of a regular government and sovereignty (*teyrnedd*) he convoked all the wise men of the British nation, that amongst the Gwyddoniaid three were found of very superior wisdom and knowledge. These were Plennydd, Alawn and Gwron, who were appointed by Prydain and his convention of Elders (*Pencenedloedd*) to form the plan of an institution of wise and good men for the purposes of teaching the principles of virtue, religion, laws of political rectitude, of peace and general good order; and for the purposes of recording national events of importance, the preservation of laws and common rights and privileges. These three wise men, it is said, plan'd, form'd and became the founders of the Bardic institution. Thus the self-produced institution of the Gwyddoniaid, having grown up into a comely form of considerable beauty, a generally approved, rather a self-conceived institution than by any man or body of men formally appointed, it became the worthy parent of the Bardic or Druidic institution, **(193)** which according to our own writers and traditions originated in Britain, and such was the tradition also in Gaul not much less than 200 years ago Julius Caesar informs us. Thus, possibly, were all the institutions of the world originally produced by the spontaneity of nature, their utilities observed, and admitted, their defects noticed and subsequently remedied by national conventions, and improvements proposed and adopted, their sphere of action or authority enlarged and ascertained, their principles elucidated and regularly systematized. Human reason became the writing and active adjuror of nature, arranged her dictates, and rendered them binding on human communities. This is the best account we have of the origin of Druidism in Britain, and it appears so analogous to the course of nature that we can see any reasons for objection to its truth. We may however venture to assert that such institutions have had their primary principles in a much higher origin, in principles that have been coeval with human nature, implanted in men, otherwise revealed to him by the great author of his being who knew that without them he could [not] exist or subsist in any tolerable state of happiness, and thence provided for his intellectuary as well as for his corporeal wants. What else but such a divine revelation, as I will venture to term it, could have been productive (as a common origin) **(194)** of the wonderful similarities or coincidencies which we find in the most ancient theologies in the world? The Chinese, the Buddhism, the Brahmin, the Persian, the Egyptian and Druidic theologies &c, not excepting the Abrahamic or Jewish system.

III: [Bardism or Druidism] (NLW 13144A, pp. 390, 399–400, 408–18)

This essay exemplifies the way in which Iolo conflated bardism and druidism and also provides an excellent example of how his system and its primitivist framework testified to the indigenous civilization of Wales.

(390) Bardism, or as commonly termed, Druidism, is purely monotheistical and theosophical. It is as pure a specimen of the Patriarchal, or primeval religion of the world, as any where can be found; more simply so than the Brahmin or the ancient Persic systems, and is on that account valuable, as it not only harmonizes with, but confirms the truth of the ancient Jewish and the regenerated Christian systems. It proves that God has in all ages and countries so ordered in his divine providence, that the evidence of his truths should never be lost. It is honourable to any nation and language to have retained it, and ought to afford pleasure and even consolation, to all the nations of the world.

(399-) *Bards – Druids*
It was their polity or discipline, rather than their religious creed, that constituted them Druids, Bards, &c. This is also the case with the Episcopalian, Presbyterian &c systems. The Episcopalian has, as such, no peculiar creed: he may be a Catholic, a Lutheran, an Arminian, a Calvinist, or a Unitarian, in his creed, one or the other, and never the less, or more, an Episcopalian for being so. So may also the Presbyterian be. The belief of the metempsychosis alone did not constitute a Bard or Druid, for this tenet was held by Pythagoreans, the magi of Chaldea, the Guebres of Persia, the Brahmins of Hindustan, the Talapoins of Siam, the Bonzes of China, by many of the ancient Jewish and Christian sects, but neither of these were, or are, Druids, from whose polity theirs are widely different. There are very strong reasons for believing that the first Christian ministers of religion in this island retained the Bardic polity, and I can see no reason why it should not be considered as proper and efficacious as any other system of priestcraft; for priestcraft prevails in all these human institutions, yet they are, I freely acknowledge, necessary evils that cannot in some cases be dispensed with. **(400)** Whilst the generality of mankind continue in their present lamentable ignorance, I am however happy in having it in my power to declare honestly that I know many Episcopalians, Presbyterians & others who are as free from the charge of priestcraft as any that can be found in this world. And I am convinced that a society of genuine Christians may be as well regulated and governed on the principles of a Druidic polity as on any other, if not better; for the Bardic liberality of considering every minister of a monotheistic religion as of the Druidic order without any additional qualification or ceremony of initiation is what has not been much, if any thing, acted up to by any other hierarchy that I know of.

(408) Religion, civil polity, and philosophy, almost as soon as they become known [?are] divided into sects and parties, each varying from all others, and having its own peculiar set of institutes, doctrines, dogmas &c. Hence it appears to be very absurd for us to think that Bardism should have been more uniform in Gaul, Britain, Ireland, and amongst all the various tribes in either of these countries, than any thing of the kind has ever been found any where else or at any time whatever. And tho' we should suppose that, on its original plan and first introduction into each of these countries, Bardism was alike or nearly uniform every where. Yet it is obvious that new ideas, discoveries, **(409)** inventions, and accidental circumstances and occasions would unavoidably superinduce many alterations and deviations from the original system; some of them improvements, others corruptions, and (what was neither this nor that) other material alterations. Hence we are unable to demonstrate whether the primeval Bardism was retained in its greatest purity by the southern Britons the northern Britons, or the Irish. Conjectures however may be formed.

That the profession of Bard, or what is termed the Primitive Bard, was known to the Cimbri and Celtae whilst yet in their nomadic state is highly probable and it remained after them in **(410)** all or most countries thro' which they passed into Gaul, Britain &c, after they became fixt. It is in the natural course of things that they should be often inclined and often necessitated to conceive [of] improvements, to make such alterations as occasions required, and to form original principles and great ideas that appeared to be of importance to society into regular compact, and comprehensive systems. And as nothing of this kind at its first formation ever possessed perfection, improvements would unavoidably take place, and that in various detached communities who had mutually adopted the first draught of an institution. The occasions would be different and those would unavoidably **(411)** render the system or institution different in one place from what it was in most or all others, and in remote futurity it would be almost, if not absolutely impossible, to determine where, if any where, the primeval institution remained.

Formed societies, civilizations &c must have originated in the necessities of things. We may suppose that after the first civil society was formed, all others would have copied after it, but I see no necessity for such a supposition, nor indeed any great plausibility in it, for we may with equal reason suppose that such occasions and inducements to social community occurred independent of, and unknown to, each other in various, even in all parts, of the world; **(412)** and that mankind would act from the motives that would naturally arise from such occasions. The first of such occasions and inducements would naturally occur in such places where from peculiarity of circumstance the inhabitants would become fixt to the spot. Security from wars and the depredations or encroachments of neighbouring nations is one of the first of these inducements. Another is the greater difficulty of removing or continuing in the nomadic state. Both these circumstances would sooner occur and operate in Britain from its insular situation, than in Gaul in Britain when it became sufficiently populous. There was no great room to wander and change habitations. It was not easily possible **(413)** for such a number of families or persons as would be powerful enough to establish themselves by conquest in another country to pass, with wives, children, horses, &c over the sea. Hence they were in the Island of Britain sooner reduced to the necessity of forming into civil societies than in Gaul, and these reasons account well for what Caesar and our own Bardic voice conventional says, that the Druidic institution originated in Britain, whereto the Gallic Druids resorted for a perfect knowledge of its principles. The Britons were in greater security from invaders to form, digest, and experimentize **(414)** on a civil institution than the Gauls were, who, as appears from depredations in Italy and Rome, continued longer in a state of savage warfare, having a large and fertile continent open to them. The recent instances of the new discovered islands in the South Sea, the Pelew islands &c prove the truth of my position that Islands become sooner civilized than large continents, and smaller islands sooner than the larger: compare Otaheitee, the Pelew &c with the continents of Africa, America, the large island of New Holland [Australia] &c. **(415)**

It may be with some reason suspected that the British Druidic institution never extended over all the island, and hence we perhaps form some kind of conjecture of its antiquity. If it had not filled the whole isle, it could not have been established many centuries before the Roman conquest. Bardic tradition says that Alawn, one of the three first institutional bards, lived in the time of Prydain ap Aedd Mawr, about . . . years before Christ. We must however suppose that the British institution of Bardism was an improvement in its polity and not the original idea with respect to its theology, **(416)** for that is, in all probability, as old as human nature in this world.

That it had not extended over Britain at the Roman conquest may be probable enough if we grant that the Erse tribes were aboriginally Britons and not from Ireland. And if we also grant that Mr Macpherson had in reality some genuine ancient fragments of Erse poetry, for in them no traces of the Druidical mythology or theology can be found, and Mr Macpherson has a very bungling way, as I hope to demonstrate in a proper place, of accounting for this; or rather of getting rid of the difficulty wherein his ignorance of the Druidic theology involved him. All the real ancient poetry of patriarchal nations (I **(417)** avoid the invidious term savage) is strongly tinctured with the religion of its own people and country. We know of no exception to this observation, supposing the ancient Scots had in reality (as Macpherson will have it) abolished the hierarchy of Druids, they could hardly have in so short a period have suppressed all their deities, and superstition. The history of man in all ages and countries shew this to be a thing impossible. Of course either the ancient Scots had neither Gods nor religion, or the poems of Ossian &c are not genuine. If they are not so, which I firmly believe, then there remains no argument or inference from them, but if they are and the Scots not in Ossian's time a recent tribe who settled in Britain subsequent to the Druidical institution, the fact will be tolerably obvious that the Bardic theology had not spread **(418)** itself over the island.

But as I have just observed that it was the polity and not the theology of Druidism that originated in Britain, it is thence clear enough that the primeval Bards which are supposed to have remained unabolished in Scotland, must have been well acquainted with their ancient religion tho' its priestcraft was no more. Indeed, we cannot think the contrary possible, so that to rid ourselves of this perplexity we must, and we fairly may infer, that no other Ossian but Mr Macpherson ever existed.

IV: [The Romans and the Druids] (NLW 13144A, pp. 242–4)

The following brief note is characteristic of the scribbled memoranda found in vacuo *in Iolo's manuscripts. Here he rehearses his thoughts on Roman influence on Wales and bardism, notably the decline of druidism and the introduction of Christianity. As well as emphasizing the indigenous nature of bardism, it also highlights the system's anti-Catholic strain.*

It was very much [in] the interest of the Roman government and its institutions to suppress the Druidical institution, which viewed in the light it now appears to us as preserved in the Bardic manuscripts, seems to have been founded and constructed on principles the most noble, excellent, rational, and at the same time simple, that can well be conceived; admitting most freely into its system all conceivable truths whether of revelation or philosophy without the least deviation from its genuine principles. It was intended, not to bulwark and propagate errors, falsehoods and priestcraft, but to collect truths from all its possible sources, to guard and preserve the knowledge of them, and on the most liberal and effectual principles to all mankind. Or, to use another mode of expression, its purpose was to feel about on all sides, in **(243)** every place, in every thing and in every direction for important truths and to communicate the knowledge of them to all, *hyd y cyrch haul a goleuni*, as far as the sun travels, as far as the light extends itself. It was suppressed in Britain in Gallia &c, not because it was in itself defective, but because its excellencies stood in the way of institutions of the rankest priestcraft that dared not meet Druidism on its openly and widely conspicuous ground in the face of the sun and the eye of light. Genuine Christianity would beyond a doubt fly into the arms of Druidism as into a fortress that would afford it as much protection as any merely human institutions could possibly do. But what has for the most part by far been imposed on the world under the name (most blasphemously) of Christianity, dares not venture to approach Druidism, before which it would vanish away like the mists of night before the **(244)** bright sun of a serene summer's morning. The first ministers of Christianity were according to the principles of the Druidical polity, but those were driven from their functions by the avaricious and, thence antichristian, episcopacy that Germaine and Lupus &c &c, backed by the Roman pontiffs pushed forcibly down the throats of the then greatly depraved Britains, whose eyes had been blinded by the dust of superstition thrown into them by those who wished to make a gain of godliness, if godliness we may call those systems of infernality that have been imposed on the credulity of mankind by designing knaves.

The History of the Bards

Iolo began to plan the volume as early as 1791 and started working on it in earnest in 1794, but he appears to have abandoned the project following the breakdown of his friendship with Owain Myfyr and William Owen Pughe. Disparate material is scattered throughout his manuscripts and a selection is provided here.

V: Rough Sketch Hist. Bards *(NLW 13112B, pp. 318–20)*

History of the Bards &c

Before I can otherwise proceed in this history, I think it expedient and even necessary to give the Bardic system, as I find it systematized by writers of the 16th century. The reader will hence better perceive the object of investigation.

The writer who has the most ably treated on this subject is Llywelyn Sion. He wrote about 1580, and says that he collected his materials from more ancient Bards as Edeyrn Dafod Aur &c &c &c. It appears by what he says that those old writers have left systematic treatises on Bardism, but I have not been so fortunate as to meet with [them]. I conceive that something of this nature is contained in a manuscript in the Hengwrt Library of which Mr E. Llwyd gives the following account &c. But whatever it contains, its possessor, with an illiberality of mind seldom before known in the world, is determined that no one shall see it. Nor, if he were equal to the task, will he make any use of it himself. This is a character that no country but Wales, and there no family but the Hengwrt Vaughans, has yet produced. The collector of this library seems to have had no object in view but that of depriving his country and nation of their most valuable writings by purchasing them from all quarters, and then hiding them for ever. What strange curses have befallen mankind.

It may appear strange to some that I produce written systems of Bardism of higher antiquity than the reign of Elizabeth, but let it be remembered that before the downfall of popish tyranny, nothing could have been written and published that was inimical to Romish infallibility, nothing that was averse to the Church-and-Kingism of those days as the poor Bards fatally experienced in the days of Edward the Bardicide. And if the priests and monks occasionally met with any thing of this nature, we may well suppose that it was properly for their interests disposed of. And they had during the 14 & 15 centuries good opportunities of getting these things into their hands, of course, and into the flames from those unbardic bards who were their retainers at monasteries &c, and who probably were no less loyal and orthodox than even high Parson Horsely or placeman Reeves. **(319)** However when a sufficient degree of religious liberty made its way into Wales, the ancient

British Bardism appeared, returning from the wilderness whereunto it had for 3 centuries at least been driven, but not without some opposition from the half-reformed priesthood, as we have some reason to conclude from what E. Prys says &c. We must rather pity than blame them for not having been able to clear all the dust of a very long and inveterate superstition from their eyes. This was probably the reason that Llywelyn Sion's book, which it seems he had prepared and intended for the press, was forced (necessitated) to remain still in manuscript. It is in 3 books. The first treats of Welsh poetry and poetical criticism which was then deemed the most important part of the Bardic science, perhaps because it was the initial branch of it, for a poetical genius and a knowledge of the poetic arts were indispensably necessary, as with good morals, [for] primary qualifications. The second part contains the Bardic institutes, and the third the Bardic theology. I conceive that I can, with sufficient propriety, abide by this arrangement of the Bardic sciences, premising that the first or poetical part has been, about 200 years after it was written by Llywelyn Sion, received some additions from that very respectable Bard, Edward Dafydd of Margam, who added a preface of his own, a great number of examples in versification, with some additional criticisms at the end of this treatise. These were sanctioned by a Gorsedd or Eisteddfod that was in the year 1680 held at Bewper [=Beaupre] Castle in Glamorgan under the patronage of Sir Richard Basset, where the following Bards with others unnamed were assembled:
Edward Dafydd of Margam
David Williams of Penlline. see *Archaelogia*.
This Gorsedd lasted three days, where the principles of poetry, versification and criticism were attested to be truly those of the ancient British Bards retained in purity by the Bards of the Glamorgan Gorsedd only, and were there ratified, according to the forms and requisitions of the ancient Bardic institutes. The institutes were also declared to be genuine and authentic as far as could be collected and known genuine and authentic. The theology was not taken into consideration, or in the least noticed. We may however conclude from hence that it was not **(320)** considered as authentic it would have met with some reprobation, but this could not have happened with any one who had a proper acquaintance with our old manuscripts, for its principles and doctrines are scattered thro' them all, and thro' all ages up to Taliesin &c who is, of all others, our most theological Bard. The title of the first Book of Bardism as amplified by Edward Dafydd is as follows.

Cyfrinach &c
i.e. The *Mysteries of the Bards of the Island of Britain
(*note on the word mystery)

VI: Preface to History of the Bards – hints (NLW 13121B, p. 445–8)

Reasons for undertaking the work: to give a true account of what the manuscripts and in memorial usages of Wales afforded of information.

At first intended what I had for Jones the harper's history, put some of my most valuable manuscripts into his hands, but after he had read the preface of Llywelyn Sion and of Edward Dafydd, said that they were illiberally severe on the north Wales Bards and would make no use of them. The truth was they contradicted his wild jumble of ignorance and inconsistence.

[In] his perversion of the account of the dresses I endeavoured to put him right, but poor Jones was proof against such attempts.

The triad of gov., *Bardd* [Bard], a llafurwr [labourer/husbandman], here I made another attempt to dissuade him from wil[ful] perversion, but on this occasion I felt myself a feeble pigmy warring with a giant – but Jones had an hypothesis of his own manufacture to support, and where authorities could not be found, he felt himself able to forget them, **(446)** and unluckily our laws have not yet consigned such fellows to the gallows, but it is, I believe, high time that they should. There is one happy circumstance however attending these kinds of forgeries. They are always inconsistent with themselves, with historical truth, and with the nature of things, even the superlatively great genius and abilities of Macpherson was not able to bear him out in this, especially in his stark blind (I was going to say stark mad) account of the Bards and Druids of Morven.

Some may think that I have been too severe on poor harper Jones, but truth is the object of history and this is the true history of Bard Jones's history.

It will be said of me also that I have been mistaken. I do not doubt it, and I shall esteem it a very great favour if any candid reader will favour me with their rectifications, but I can assure the world that I have not wilfully perverted any thing. I give my authorities, what they are, and where to be met with, and of these the reader is for my part allowed freely to think as he pleases.

I have not blended what I found in Welsh manuscripts with what Greek and Roman writers have said. I know very well **(447)** that many would have done so, and have thence formed a very curious system of what never existed – probably a pleasing novel, or romance. But such things, the hotbed or forcing-frame productions for which our age is either famous or infamous, let posterity judge, must not be called history. 'Tis rank blasphemy. The business of history is to give us honestly, matter of fact, rather than of speculation. At least then things should never be so jumbled together as not to be separated. I have myself indulged my conceptions of some things and have given them to any one that may think them worth reading, but separately from the purely historical part of the work. These, the best reflections that I could make, are either thrown into the notes, or into the two dissertations on the Bardic theology and philosophy, the other on the Bardic system of discipline and polity.

Popular superstitions that are in reality no part of the national religion, exist in every age and country. They doubtless existed in Britain in the Druidical ages, but why must all these be laid to the charge of Druidism? It is contradictory to the experience of all ages and countries. It is unphilosophical. The superstitions of every country originate in truths not well understood or that have been veiled in allegories. Those of the populace at large far outdo the clerical wicked and foolish as **(448)** parsons have always been. The clergy of the Church of Rome, bad as they are, have never been so piously credulous of nonsense and blasphemy as the laity of the lower classes, who will not any more than we the poor Swinish Multitude* of Britain suffer our teacher to tell us the truth. We will not be convinced that there are neither ghosts, goblins, or conjurers, and without a devil we could never well manage matters, especially such of us as are Methodists, for we honestly confess that we were moved by the devil, who, it seems is often more than a match for ++++ our three Gods. I am very willing for any one to saddle the old gentleman in black with as many of our rascalities as he may please, but who will not mourn to find these things heaped on the back or shoulders of Christianity?

* Of the British Swinish Multitude here are two classes of herds. One, the natural swine, consisting of those that are deprived of their due portion of grains by those of the lordly class, into whom the famous legions of infernals have long ago entered and who are now running headlong down the precipice of self-destruction, they consist of crowned, mitred, coroneted or cornuted heads, and amongst them an astonishing number of parsons.

VII: A Short Account of the Ancient British Bards (NLW 13097B, pp. 97–111)

'A Short Account of the British Bards' exists in numerous drafts, each in various degrees of completion. Since it includes musings on metempsychosis, this particular version bears comparison with the sketch of Bardism included by William Owen Pughe in his introduction to The Heroic Elegies of Llywarç Hen (1792)*, and may date from the same time. Another untidy draft may be found in the same manuscript, NLW 13097B, pp. 239–76.*

Beirdd Beli. Institution.

A SHORT ACCOUNT OF THE WELSH BARDS

The genuine succession of the Welsh Bards is not entirely extinct yet, tho' nearly so, and will be entirely so in a few years in all probability. They call themselves *Beirdd Ynys Prydain*, The Bards of Britain. There are five orders of them.

First. *Prifeirdd Ynys Prydain*, Chief Bards of Britain, or National Chief Bards. Their number must be no more than three.

Secondly. *Prifeirdd Gwlad a Chyfoeth*, Chief Provincial Bards. The number twenty four.

Thirdly. *Dryw* or *Derwydd*, plural *Drywiaid* or *Derwyddon*, Druids. The term signifies very wise or very learned. They were the highest order, properly speaking, for the national and Provincial Chief Bards were of this order, only elected from amongst them to offices. The number of Druids unlimited.

Fourthly. *Bardd Trwydded*, Bard of Discipline or Graduated Disciple. One that had passed the lowest stage of probation.

Fifthly. *Ofydd*. The word signifies man of genius. It is an honorary degree, bestowed without the delay of discipline on a man who was found to possess very extraordinary abilities and knowledge. He however could not be admitted a Druid without undergoing the probationary discipline, which was very long; sometimes ten or fifteen years, and possibly, more. It could not be shorter than three years. **(98)**

The qualifications necessary for the *Ofydd* were in some things beyond what was necessary in a Druid. It was all that was required of the Druid in metrical skill, if he knew the nine primary metres, but the *Ofydd* must be well skilled in the fifteen secondary or auxiliary metres also; and besides he should be acquainted with music and other sciences. This was by far the most learned order. In mere gradation he ranked with the *Bardd Trwydded*, Graduated Disciple, and was considered no more than a disciple.

There was another inferior order of disciples that were not allowed the appellation of Bard called *Trwyddedog nawdd*, which may be rendered the Probationary Disciple. They were the lowest order of disciples, and admitted by any of the other orders. He was to undergo a very severe discipline before he could be initiated into the lowest graduated order. He was taught the maxims of poetry and versification, enjoined to compose verses, and to learn a great many more, which he was called upon to expound. And, tho' most of them were mystical, he was never let into the meaning, but was obliged to find it out himself. Great numbers of those mystical verses are to be met with in old manuscripts.

The Druids elected the Chief Bards from amongst themselves. They also admitted into their own order such of the Graduated Disciples as had been properly qualified by necessary probation.

Three Druids could elect into the higher orders, into their own, and into that of Graduated Disciples. Two could not, as there could be no election by two. But one Druid, the law of necessity taking place, could elect two into his own order at discretion, to supply the deficiency, and no more, as after that they could proceed regular. One Druid, at all times, **(99)** could admit if necessary to the lowest degree, as many as he pleased. When no Druids remained, the Graduated Disciple could appoint, by election from amongst themselves, three Druids which supplied the deficiency. When no more than one Graduated Disciple remained, he could admit two into his own order. Then, being three, they could elect a Druid, and so regularity could be restored.

The term Bard includes all the five orders, all were Bards.

The Welsh Bards maintain that their institution originated in Britain, from whence other nations, as Gauls, Irish &c derived it, but not without blending their own superstitions with it. It is believed that it is still retained in its pristine purity by the Welsh Bards in Glamorganshire, where they are called in contempt *Gwyr Cwm y Felin*, i.e. the Mill Valley men, from the name of the place where of late times they usually met, and are supposed to be Deists, Atheists, and some deem them Turks, and I know not what, every thing that is bad. Fortunately they have always been noted for their strict morals, and they profess themselves Christians, and are so in reality, but are not believed.

The necessary qualifications of a Bard are unimpeached morality, a sound understanding, skill in the language, the constitutions of the Bards, principles of religion &c &c, a poetical genius, a knowledge of the laws of poetry, at least of the nine primary metres which was all that was necessary for a Druid, as observed before. Those are the most simple, and also the very best of all the twenty four metres. Where all other qualifications were possessed in an **(100)** eminent degree, a genius for poetry could be dispensed with, for the word Bard does not necessarily imply a poet. The most wicked man living might be a very good poet (*prydydd*), or at least a good versifier, tho' destitute of every thing that could qualify him to be a Bard.

The Bards entertain an absurd prejudice against the use of letters, but deem poetry the noblest of all sciences, as it is able to give such a peculiar arrangement and connexion to words and ideas; that a poem or song can be easily taught to the most illiterate; memorials of events, principles of science &c can be conveyed in a song to the most distant parts of the world, or to the remotest futurity. In song without the aid of any other art. Thro its medium the most illiterate may be instructed where no other method of instruction could take place.

So sacred was truth held amongst the Bards, that if any one admitted falsehood into his verse, he was to be degraded and could not possibly be readmitted.

It is very singular that the regular Bards in all ages affirm that they have a right to exercise the functions of priesthood. This claim is probably derived from the Druids, their higher order, who were formerly the priests of Britain. And the Bardic (if the term is allowable) tradition says that they continued in possession of this right till deprived of it by the Romish Clergy. It is not impossible but that the Druids, on assenting to Christianity, were left for a long while in full possession of the ministerial offices. The nature of their discipline seems to be unobjectionable. **(101)**

The discipline of the Bards was very singular. The particulars of it could not be committed to writing, or even to song, or oral information. It was kept as much a mystery as possible. It was their opinion that, if reduced to a regular system, its intention and effects would be totally frustrated. Theory, they said, was an acquisition of memory and self-interest, not of the heart and intellect; and only enabled a man to assume the specious appearances of wisdom and virtue, of all that was laudable and excellent, when, at the same time, he was, at bottom, the most detestable villain existing, deeply skilled in the art of imposing on the world. Instead of this, the Bard closely watched the conduct of his pupil, in his most unguarded moments; in the most minute and least suspected particulars. The disciple could not, upon the whole, possibly discover what experiments were made on his head, his heart, his very soul. Temptations were thrown in his way, the strength and bent of his genius was put to the proof: where, when, and in what, he could not possibly dream of. His only certain method of qualifying himself was to be, in good earnest, a good and wise man, to rectify his passions, and to cultivate his understanding. If he was ordered to produce a poem; or make an oration, the subject or theme was never, or very seldom, given him. An experiment was here to be made on his morals and intellects. And whether his productions were approved of, or otherwise, he was but very seldom told for what reason. After he had passed thro' a very long probation, and had, from long habit, experimentally acquired, rather than **(102)** been taught, wisdom and virtue, he was at last, after perhaps twenty years discipline, admitted a Bard of the Druid order. His soul was delivered up to his own care, as they termed it. He was made acquainted with all their mysteries, and enjoined never to commit them to theory, which would infallibly pervert them to the purposes of villainy. That his chief study was that of the human heart, that he should observe nature with the eye of the understanding as it presented itself to the senses, not as it is represented in systems drawn up by art. He was reminded that virtue and wisdom were the real acquisitions of his own head and heart, not what had been forced into them by others.

When a disciple was to be examined, it was not by his own tutor, but by one he hardly knew, or knew not at all. No two were examined in the same manner, that no one might avail himself of what passed at the examination of another, so as to be able to deduce a rule therefrom that might guide him thro' his own examination. The disciple had nothing to trust to but his own real self-acquired knowledge and unaffected wisdom.

The form of admission was to proclaim a congress of Bards in his name at a certain place and time; where he was to be attended by certain persons named, Graduated Disciples, (this was their initiation). Assisted by the named *Ofydd*, (who was thus admitted). It was common, but not necessary, to invest the newly admitted bards with their characteristic robes at their admission. **(103)**

The Robe of the Bard was always unicoloured, emblematic of truth, whose colour was said, emblematically, to be that of the brightest day light, white. The *Ofydd* wore green, an emblem of learning, the Graduate Disciple sky blue, the emblem of peace. But none of these were deem'd essentially necessary, but on certain occasion, as in proclaiming truces &c.

No Bard was allowed to bear arms. He was the messenger or minister of peace, and wherever he appeared in his unicoloured robe, it was not lawful to bear a naked weapon in his presence. His person was sacred. He was called *Trwyddedog Byd*, free or privileged thro' the world.

The Bard was not to side with any sect in religion, or with party in any thing whatever. He was to be independent of all, indifferent to all, but friendly towards all. His answer, when asked of what religion, profession or party &c, he was: "I am a Bard."

The Bards were entrusted with secrets of state, went on embassies, were arbitrators between contending parties and, appearing in their Bardic robes, were everywhere safe. To divulge secrets with which they were entrusted was certain death.

Their public meetings were always in open air, in conspicuous places, when the sun was up; in the eye of light, as they term'd it. The times: the solstices, equinoxes, new and full moons. Some say Sundays, and it might be so after they became Christians. **(104)**

The British Bards hold remarkable opinions, religious and philosophical. Even after their conversion to Christianity they were very much attached to their old mythology. The poems of Taliesin abound with those primitive doctrines of the Bards or Druids. So do the works of almost all succeeding Bards to very recent periods, and there are yet remaining some that believe them, at the same time professing themselves Christians, and think that the scriptures, when impartially examined, contain all or most of those doctrines, some of which are as follows:

1. The existence of every thing is as positive as that of nothing, absolute privation of evil, and an absolute privation of good. Perfect life is an absolute privation of evil; death of good. God is the absolute privation

of evil. Such a mode of existence cannot possibly be limited, as it admits of no privation but that of evil. It is impossible that such a being should not exist.

2. God created a certain limited number of beings out of evil, converting it to good, to his own nature; and all beings originate in the lowest point of existence, (*Annwn*, extreme depth; Hell in the vulgar acceptation). From whence they are gradually, in regular progression, moving on towards good, thro' gradually improving modes of existence, till they at last attain to the highest good that limited beings are susceptible of or bear. **(105)**
3. In all states of existence below the point of humanity, evil preponderates. Beings in such a state are prone to evil of necessity, which God only resists, but never punishes. As they have not the power to be otherwise, so punishment would be unjust.
4. In all modes of existence above the point of humanity, good preponderates, so cannot be rewarded, as it is not of choice but of necessity and must be left to its natural course which goes on progressively towards the utmost that it can attain to; and in that is its own reward.
5. Man is in that point of existence where good and evil are equally balanced, so becomes free, as he is neither good nor bad of necessity. Consequently in a state of probation, and an object of rewards or punishment. Love is natural and essential to all states of existence, but evil beings necessarily love evil, and good beings as necessarily love good. Man's love is free, consequently meritorious.
6. Free love is the only thing meritorious. Man's probation is to love or not to love. His love is evinced by suffering, which is the only test of love; that love which suffers not is not free, but self-interest and enjoyment, which all beings are naturally, and of necessity, prone to; so love attended with present enjoyment is not free. Love is great or little, in exact proportion to what is suffered for its object. Man, being free, may love evil and suffer for it, the just retribution for which is degradation to a lower mode of existence, suited to his accession of evil; from whence, as before, he is to proceed towards good in a regular progression. **(106)** Man by loving good, evinced by his sufferings for it, obtains an accession of good, so that it preponderates, he upon this attains to necessary communications with supernal beings, is assisted by them in his conflict with evil, and God bestows on him such rewards as are consistent with the regular course of creation.
7. Fortitude is the only criterion of free love, and a man that does not suffer with fortitude does not suffer freely, but necessarily; one that repines would not suffer if he could help it [and] consequently attains to no merit.

8. All finite beings must necessarily in their highest point of existence participate, tho' in the least degree possible, of evil. It is this that constitutes conscious individuality. It is in this they feel themselves individually separate from God and all other beings. It is this alone that produces a multiplicity of beings. It is in the least possible degree a principle of death, which will, at limited periods in an infinite series, to all eternity, produce a renovation of existence, which will interrupt the tedium of eternity, which finite beings could not, otherwise, possibly endure. None but God can possibly bear an uniform uninterrupted eternity.
9. In the state of humanity, being that of probation, a man may attain to supernal communications, which consists in a participation of the divine nature by having attained to a preponderating degree of good, or of life. Yet in this state, his love being free, he may recede or fall from this point to its opposite, which is the lowest point of existence (*Annwn*). Because he had attained to a participation of the highest good, from this low point, he is to return in a **(107)** regular progression as before, but retaining, woefully, the memory of what he fell from.
10. All knowledge is derived from men who in their probation had so much detached themselves from evil, and attained to such accessions of good, as to produce supernal communications.
11. All created beings must pass thro' all possible modes of existence, otherwise justice could never take place, or knowledge of all things obtained. And partiality to any being is unjust and inconsistent with the nature of God.
12. The lowest point of existence is that which has the least participation of life. The highest point of finite existence, that which has the least participation of death, positive life, is God. Positive Death is nothing, which is that degree of evil that consists in an absolute privation of life.
13. The life or soul quitting its body, at the termination of its present mode of existence, enters another body adapted to the state of exaltation or degradation to which it must in its nature pass.
14. God loves all beings, even those of the lowest orders of existence and, as much as possible, consistent with the regular course of existences, accelerates their progress towards the supernal mode of existence; for God does not admit of the least privation of love, or the least degree of malignity in his nature. **(108)**
15. The highest point of merit is for a good man to reject all enjoyments, to submit to all possible sufferings – even death – to obtain good, to promote the happiness of others, and to prevent evil.

16. The lowest point of depravity is that where we feel enjoyment from what is derived from evil, promotes evil, occasions misery to others, or deprives them of the good they would be possess'd of, if we abstained from such sensuality.
17. A man feeling himself so depraved that he cannot avoid doing evil, yielding himself up to such a kind of suffering as will effectually prevent his acting wickedly in future, or even to death, if necessary, does all that he can do towards promoting good and obviating evil, and thus attains to merit.
18. Abstinence from sensuality leaves our fellow creatures in possession of what they would otherwise be deprived of, and want; and is free [love] suffering in a good cause.
19. Man may not destroy any being that, by being permitted to exist, would not destroy man immediately or effectually.
20. Man's subsistence is from the fruits of the earth without which he cannot live. Any being or animal that would so destroy the fruits of the earth as to leave man destitute of subsistence, may be destroyed, and no other.
21. We can not judge of any thing but from what we know and feel. To know what God is we must endeavour to be perfectly good, by feeling what goodness is, we feel and know by experience what God is, and know what God does. Let us ask ourselves what we with his power would do **(109)** when we feel in ourselves a perfect love of good: and that will be what God actually does.
22. God being positive goodness and positive love, cannot possibly withhold from his creatures any thing that would, consistent with general good, conduce to their happiness. This would imply a privation of love and goodness, and it is impossible for a being to be a god; that admits the least privation to those attributes.
23. Supernal communications are highly conducive to man's happiness, and not obstructive to that of any other being. It would consequently be malignant to withhold this source of happiness from man, which God cannot possibly be. A good man putting the question to himself whether he would thus befriend man or not, would instantly answer yes. God is more benevolent than man.

These are the leading maxims and doctrines of Bardism (I think I may venture to say Druidism, tho' we do not use the term: Barddas is the Welsh term. Bardism, see Barddas in Richards' Dictionary). They are every where to be found in our oldest manuscripts. Taliesin says:

Wyf syw wyf Dryw – I am wise, I am a Druid.

His poems are a complete, and very clear system of Druidism. Cynddelw in the year 1160 was denied Christian burial by the monks of Ystrad Marchell for being a Druid. In all ages the Bards were, as it were, at war with the popish clergy, even down to the time of the Reformation. **(110)**

Their ancient mythology is still traditionally retained by a very few in Wales, tho' rather confusedly. The Welsh language is Druidism itself, we can not possibly express our Christian opinions but in terms and phrases highly Druidical. Yet Druidism has been sought for every where, but in the Welsh language; its pristine language, where it is still to be found, and there only to be found, and will never be lost as long as the language exists:

	Common acceptation	Literal sense
Annwn	Hell	lowest point, extreme depth
Einioes	Life	limited existence
Angau	Death	Liberation
Trengi – traengi Marw	to die	to advance higher
Aberth	Sacrifice	A present
Cythraul	the Devil	What is gradually falling to nothing, or into non-existence
Dihenyddu Dihenydd	to renovate renovator	
Cared	Sin	Object of pity or love
Aphan	Hell	a degree lower
Andras	The Devil	Inconsistency
Dyw	God	He is
Dwyf	another name of God	I am

Celi	another name	Incomprehensible **(111)**
Derydd	a name of God	creation, first cause
Dŷn	Man	Individual
Diwedd	end	self-appropriation, change of form
Nêf, plur. Nefoedd	Heaven	new place, or places
Cyrch	resort	Circus, resort
Damwain	Chance	concurrence on all sides
Huan	Sun	Supernal abode
Llan	Church	Circus. Circumvaluation like stonge henge

There are about thirty names of God in the Welsh language, but no traces to be met with of polytheism; but abundance of words that express, in a lively manner, patriarchal customs, manners, opinions &c. One, on becoming well acquainted with the Welsh tongue, proverbs, old manuscripts &c would be strongly inclined to think that the Patriarchal religion was retained in its original purity, or nearly so, down to the time of its renovation, in the introduction of Christianity. And if Druidism was really then, what it appears to be in the days of Taliesin (560) and what it now in its ruinated state seems to be, it is no wonder that the Christian religion soon penetrated farther in this Island than ever the Roman arms could, as both religions were so congenial in their main doctrines.

VIII: A Short Account of the Ancient British Bards (NLW 13097B, pp. 123–52)

This draft, which includes more detail on the practical aspects of Bardism and formulas for Gorsedd ceremonial, was probably written c.1791–2 during the excitement which accompanied Iolo's first Gorseddau in London.

Account of Bards
(123) The Ancient British Bards or, as they call themselves, *Beirdd Ynys Prydain*, assert that their institution originated in Britain, from whence it was

introduced into Gaul, Ireland &c, but with considerable deviations from its original simplicity and purity. The Bards have always considered themselves a priesthood, and still lay claim to that character. There are but few now remaining of the genuine succession, or of the regular continuation of the ancient order. The term Bard does not signify merely a Poet, it is more properly synonymous to the term priest, for such it certainly originally meant. A genius for, and a knowledge of, the laws and nature of poetry, was absolutely necessary (except on very extraordinary occasions, hereafter to be noted) towards qualifying any one to be a Bard. And the reason of this was that in the infancy of society before the use of letters was known, verse or song was the only means, or at least the best, of transmitting **(124)** to futurity, and to distant persons and places, what they then possessed of knowledge. The doctrines of religion, precepts of morality, laws and regulations of society, and other articles of useful knowledge, were in verse capable of being learned, remembered, and transmitted to posterity. Men will learn songs or poems of each other with ease, and with equal ease remember them, whereas prose discourses can not possibly be learned, or retained in the memory, with sufficient exactness and fidelity; or at least not by one in ten thousand. But all, even persons of very slender capacities, may learn a song, remember it, and transmit it with fidelity and accuracy to another. For this reason poetical genius and abilities were deemed indispensable requisites in the qualifications of a Bard, hence the word came at last to be used as synonymous to poet.

The primitive religious opinions of the Bards are purely Patriarchal. It is very possible that in ages of ignorance, some corruptions and superstitious practices might have crept into their system, but on the introduction of Christianity, these were exploded and Bardism, or, as it is called, Druidism, (perfectly congenial to the Gospel doctrines) was restored to its ancient purity. And the tradition, still retained, that the Bards were the first ministers of the Christian Religion in Britain, is probably true. And it is remarkable **(125)** that some of those places on the tops of hills, and in conspicuous places, which we call Druidical Temples, retain in their names and other circumstances evident marks of their having been places of Christian Worship: Carn Moesen [Moses's cairn] in Glamorganshire, Carn y Groes [the cairn of the cross] in the same county, where a very ancient cross stands (it is on the mountain of Gelli Onnen, and mentioned by Camden), Ty Illtud in Breconshire, and many others, seem to indicate this; as does also the word Llan (circus) a church. Why this word should be retained by Christians I know not, unless it was the term they used, as well as the ancient Bards or Druids, for a place of worship. *Golychwyd* [prayer], and many other terms are of the same cast.

It is worthy of remark, that thro' the long and dark ages of popish superstition, the Bards in general, retained the Christian religion, (which is only a brighter manifestation of ancient Bardism, or Patriarchal Religion) in its original purity and simplicity, violently opposing the depravity and absurdity of the Popish doctrines. Innumerable instances of this could be produced from the works of the Bards of all ages, from Taliesin in the sixth century down to the Reformation. A good history of the Welsh Bards, with proper extracts from their works, would be a very interesting work but when will it appear? All that has hitherto been imposed on the world, under pretensions of this kind, is only a crude jumble of absurdities, falsehoods, and misconceptions, and may as well be called the 'History of the Man in the Moon', as that of the Ancient British Bards. **(126)**

The Bardic Institutes were, in the first ages, only retained by tradition, in poems and adages of a peculiar cast, and it is on tradition that they still found their system of knowledge. They have indeed written memorials but their authority is not deemed equal to that of tradition. For this reason they never refer to written authorities. The first thing taught their disciples are the Bardic traditions, or mysteries as the word *cyfrinach* signifies: their institutes, maxims, the rudiments of language, laws of verse, and such kind of knowledge as constitutes the formal or external organization of the order.

The Bards were divided into four essential classes. The lowest are the *Awenyddion*, *Beirdd Nawdd*, or *Trwyddedogion Nawdd*, *Noddedigion*, and *Trofedigion*, which we may call in English the Discipled Bard. The first requisite towards admission into the class was unimpeachable morals; it was indispensably necessary that he should, above all things, be a good man. He was seldom initiated into any thing considerable till his understanding, affections, morals, and principles in general, had undergone severe trials. His passions and understanding were closely observed and exercised, when he was the least aware of it, and least on his guard; at all times, in all places possible, and on every occasion there was an eye, hid as much as possible from his observation, continually fixt on him; and from the knowledge thus obtained of his head and heart an estimate was made of his principles and mental abilities, and according to the approbation given, and in the manner and degree thought most proper, he was initiated into the mysteries, and instructed **(127)** in the doctrines of Bardism. He was during this probationary state of discipline, to learn such verse and adages as contained the maxims of the institution, to compose poems himself, and form adages. After having acquired a proper proficiency in these things, and when time had afforded opportunities of making all possible experiments on his mental faculties, the propensities of his heart and, in short, his very soul thoroughly scrutinized, he was, if deemed properly qualified and worthy, admitted to the graduated order of *Bardd Braint*, *Bardd Trwyddedog* or *Trwyddedog Braint*. This was the Corporeal Degree, for he was fully qualified and capable of exercising all the functions of Bardism, and could not be admitted to it without having undergone the regular discipline. It was as of this degree and character that the Chief Bard always presided. His order implied the full possession of all Bardic accomplishments and powers, for all the purposes of the institution. He could proclaim and hold a Gorsedd, admit disciples, and *Ofyddion*, was capable of being employed in embassies, in the office of Herald, to instruct youth and teach them the principles of morality with the mysteries of religion, he could publish his poems. The Bards of this, as well as of all other orders, were under certain restraints. They, as being the Heralds of Peace, were not allowed to bear a naked weapon, were to observe the profoundest and most inviolable secrecy on all occasions, between princes, and other parties that engaged them in confidential offices. **(128)**

They were to side with no particular party in religion or in politics, or to engage in any kind of contention whatever, as all this was inconsistent with their character as the Heralds of Peace. Their persons were held sacred. It was not lawful for any one to bear a naked weapon in their presence. They could pass, unmolested, from one hostile country to another, and whenever a Bard appeared in his unicoloured robe, by which he was known, if it was even between armies in the heat of action, both parties would instantly desist, and lay down their arms; so that the appearance of a Bard, on such occasions, operated as the modern flag of truce. His word was to be credited in preference to that of any other person whatever: *Gair ei air ef ar bawb* [his word is above that of all others].

The *Derwyddon* or *Derwyddfeirdd*, were such as the Bards of either of the orders, of *Bardd Braint* or of *Ofydd*, that were set apart to, or employed peculiarly in the exercise of religious functions, and the ministers of religion were even long after the conversion of the Britons to Christianity called by this term. They were for ages, not only the pagan priests (as it seems they must be called, tho' they worship'd the true God, as much as Abraham did), but even the Christian divines of the Ancient Britains. Tho' the *Derwydd* was more peculiarly, yet he was not exclusively, the minister of religion – for the *Bardd Braint*, and even the *Ofydd* might officiate as such, after being confirmed by reception into the order at a Gorsedd – there was nothing in the Bardic institution (for it enjoined nothing but a search after truth), that could possibly disqualify the Derwydd, or Bard from being the minister of the Christian or any other true religion. On the other hand, if severe discipline can be deemed a qualification, the Bards and Derwyddon were highly qualified for such functions. **(129)**

The order of Derwydd was not deemed superior to that of *Bardd Braint*, or *Trwyddedog Braint*. It was only a peculiar officiality, for which the other orders were deemed equally qualified, but which, for convenience, was allotted to an appropriate set of Bards who were to be distinguished by that name to give notoriety and discriminate visibility to their function. Each order was held in a peculiarity of estimation, tho' neither of them were entitled to a superiority. Thus *Bardd Braint* was peculiarly the ruling order, *Derwydd* the functioning religious functionary, and *Ofydd* was the learned literary or scientific order. The *Derwydd* was exempted from some offices that were incumbent on each of the other orders. Sanctity of life, and celebrity for wisdom were recommendatory qualifications for the order of *Derwydd.* He was, most immediately and peculiarly, the instructor of youth and was, from the necessary obligations of his office, the Residentiary Bard of his district; an obligation which other Bards lay not under, whose continual residence was neither necessary nor required.

It has already been observed that the Bards founded all their institutes, knowledge &c on tradition; and in order to fix those traditions permanently in the memory, they were required to learn a great number of verses and adages, and to be able to compose such, and in many other ways to exercise the memory, to which all their learning was committed. They preferred the traditions of persons set apart for the study, preservation and continuation of them, to letters, as being better guarded against imposition, by coming more immediately under the notice and cognizance of the public at large. As one **(130)** of their methods of preserving them, was the recital of them at the Gorsedd, by which all, the illiterate as well as the literate, became acquainted with them, till they were so rooted in the public memory as never to be capable of changing or undergoing any alteration. But writers have much more imposed on the world than it was possible for a well-guarded tradition to do. Oral tradition is more open to the world at large than written memorials. Consequently, more out of the reach of perversion and innovation. Men, by exercise of memory and mental retention, improve and strengthen their intellects, whereas those who trust to books never exert the faculties of memory, and in a short time, being in a state of mental indolence, so far forget their subject as not to be able to see when, and where imposition intrudes. And where a greater dependence is laid on writings than tradition, books of distant places or ages, will be admitted as authorities, when their authenticity and veracity has not been proved and it may be impossible to bring any kind of proof for or against them. But this can never be the case with a national tradition when, thro' all the territories of that nation, there are men set apart to study, guard, and continue it by public and frequent periodical recital. Those traditions, songs or poems are the most proper means of continuing those traditions and of transmitting them to distant times and places. The most illiterate, the most ignorant, and even those of very weak capacities, may learn and remember a song with ease in a short time; teach it to others, and so **(131)** transmit it to future ages and remote places with correctness, as the sentiments and words of it are fixt to such a peculiarity of arrangement, as not to admit, easily, of alteration, which is not the case with prose discourses. The harmony of verse also makes it delightful, and people become very desirous, and even anxiously eager, to learn a poem, which highly favours the continuation of it; and those being besides recited at proper and frequent times and places, become permanent in the memory of that nation for whom they are intended. For these reasons and considerations, it becomes absolutely necessary that a Bard should be also a good poet; that he may in his verses be able to transmit to posterity such instruction as he may, by such means, be able to communicate. But no poem of this didactic nature was allowed to be published, but at a Gorsedd after having been examined, judged, and approved of; when the *Dadceiniaid*, who were generally Disciples (*Awenyddion*), were to recite and publish it. But tho' the Bards were thus very tenacious of their traditions, and anxiously intent on guarding them from perversion, imposition, and oblivion, yet they were not, as some have ignorantly asserted, enemies to the use of letters. There is reason to believe that they were very readily admitted and practised the use of them as soon as they were brought fully acquainted with their nature and utility, for a third order amongst them termed *Ofydd*, was a literary one, and admitted on no other qualification but that of having the knowledge of letters, and the sciences dependent thereon. It was an honorary degree to which the candidate could be immediately admitted, without being obliged to pass thro' the **(132)** regular discipline. The requisite qualifications were, in general, an acquaintance with valuable and highly useful discoveries in science, the use of letters, medicine, languages &c. It was not an easy thing, even in this order, to dispense with the knowledge of, and a genius for, poetry; but this on some particular occasions might be done, as where the candidate was possessed in an eminent degree of all other qualifications. The *Ofydd* was however enjoined to acquaint himself with the Bardic institutes and traditions, for, from several contingencies, it was possible that the order or institution might be perpetuated only by *Ofyddion*, which in its original purity, it could not be done, unless they were acquainted with its true principles, nature, and intention; for which reason the decision of a Gorsedd would be sometimes [be] suspended, if great ignorance in the nature and external organization of the order appeared in the newly admitted *Ofydd*.

The *Ofydd* was elected at a Gorsedd, where he was proposed as a candidate on the recommendation of a graduated Bard of any one of the three orders, who might, from his own knowledge, declare that he was a proper candidate, and possessed of the requisite qualifications. If he was not known to a Bard, the recommendation of a judge or magistrate, or of twelve reputable and responsible men, could constitute him a candidate, on which he was immediately elected by *coelbren* (ballot). But if it ever happened that the number of Bards were not sufficient to elect, then a graduated Bard might arbitrarily admit three, who were thereupon deemed, finally graduated. He could admit no more than three in this manner, for that was a sufficient number to proceed by election, in the regular manner, and arbitrary proceedings could not **(133)** possibly be admitted but where the number was too small to act any other way, and consequently, a thing of necessity. Proclamation was another way of admission to the degree of *Ofydd.* That is, it was proclaimed at a Gorsedd that a person of a certain name, place, and qualifications was, on specified recommendation, proposed as a candidate, and that at a certain future time, not less than a whole year, he was to be admitted to that degree for which he was a candidate; and if no objection was during that time brought against him, he was deemed admitted and graduated. Let it here be noted that by proclamation a candidate could be admitted, in case of necessity, to supply deficiency of number, into any of the three orders or degrees, or into any two of them at once, having been before admitted to one. It was deemed more honourable to be admitted into the orders by having been first admitted an *Ofydd*, than by going thro' a long discipline at least such an idea now prevails. The *Ofydd* could exercise all the functions of Bardism, and by some particular acts he became entitled, by virtue of having performed them, to other degrees, after such acts had been acquiesced in by a Gorsedd. After an Ofydd had been admitted by a Bard, or proclamation had been made of any one being a candidate for this or any other order, such a candidate was called *Ofydd*, (or *Bardd*) *ym mraint hawl ag arddel* [Ovate, (or Bard) according to the title and claim], which may be rendered, presumptive Bard, or Bard claimant. He was entitled after such proclamation to all passive privileges of the order, but not to act officially, for such acts were not valid. After having been confirmed in his degrees by a Gorsedd, he could perform all the acts and functions of the order, and virtually became entitled to that particular degree incidental to the officialities which he executed. By officiating as *Derwydd*, after a certain time he became of that degree. By presiding at a Gorsedd he became, what presidency implies, a *Bardd Braint*, by admitting, and after confirmation of, an *Ofydd*, he became entitled to that degree if he was **(134)** not of it before. And this general rule holds, that any graduated Bard, executing any of the officialities of the institution, after the acquiescence of a Gorsedd, became entitled to the degrees incident to, and implied by, such officialities. This order of *Ofydd* was a provisionary one for the purpose of admitting into the Bardic system in a regular manner everything useful and laudable in science.

Three or more Bards could admit by election.

One Bard only remaining, could perform arbitrarily all officialities till three had been by him admitted. The deficiency then supplied, arbitrary power ceased, and all was to go on regularly.

Two only remaining Bards could only act by proclamation. Two can not elect, as there can be no majority or casting voice. One of them can not act arbitrarily because there is another opposing power of equal authority. Proclamation is an appeal, recurrence, or reference, to public opinion, and to that original authority from which the institution was first derived; the acquiescence of which, in bringing no objection to the proposals of such proclamation, constitutes the legality of any act done or performed in consequence of its having been proposed in the public notice. Some hold, and that with reason, that, unless in cases of urgent necessity, the most regular way for one remaining Bard to act is by proclamation, rather than arbitrarily, and that this ought also to be preferred, even to election, as coming more immediately under the cognizance of the public. In answer to this, it may be allowed for most reasons to be the best, but it is evident that, in some ages, the institution could never have been perpetuated by such proceedings, and would long ago have become extinct, from opposition of public prejudice, but for the elective mode of admission; and, on unavoidable occasions, the arbitrary authority, which, by **(135)** the original institutes, was vested in one only remaining Bard. It is certain however that all these modes have been practised, and each has its propriety on certain occasions, and under certain circumstances, but, when all things will admit of it, it is deemed best to recur to that authority which first established the institution: the consent of the public obtained by virtue of proclamation. The next is Bardic election at a Gorsedd and, when occasion calls for it, arbitrary admission is deemed valid, and purely consistent with a provisionary maxim of the institution, for creating a necessary and, for that reason, legal, power; to effect what is beneficial at a time when no other power or authority exists to recur to, on immediate emergencies.

All the orders were deemed of equal respectability. Each, it is true, had a peculiarity of estimation, but those were not deemed the one more intrinsically excellent than the other. If, with respect to qualification for certain officialities, one was deemed inferior to the other, it was in other particulars allowed to be superior. So that considered in the whole, each of the orders were considered equally honourable, and of equal general estimation in the institution.

In their Titles the Bards observed the order of their Graduation as,

Bardd Braint,
Bardd a Derwydd,
Bardd ag Ofydd,
Bardd, Ofydd, a Derwydd,
Bardd, Derwydd, ag Ofydd,
Ofydd, Bardd, a Derwydd,
Ofydd, Derwydd, a Bardd.

Their titles were, thus, a history of their manner of admission and graduation. To each of these titles was added *ym mraint* (or *wrth fraint a Defod*) *Beirdd Ynys Prydain* [in the (or according to the privilege and institute) of the Bards of the Island of Britain].

There are certain mottoes pertaining to the Bards, as for *Beirdd Ynys Prydain* or *Gorsedd Ynys Prydain*: *Y gwir yn erbyn y byd*. [truth against the world].

Cadair Gwynedd – Iesu. [The Chair of Gwynedd – Jesus]

Cadair Powys – a laddo a leddir. [The Chair of Powys – he who kills will be killed]

Cadair Morganwg – Duw a phob daioni. [The Chair of Glamorgan – God and all that is good]

Cadair Deheubarth. – Calon wrth galon. [The Chair of south Wales – Heart to heart]

These were used as declaratory of the *Cadair* or *Talaith* [region] whereof the Bard was, or of the *Cadair* that enacted any thing regarding the institution. **(136)**

The Bards always held their meetings or Gorseddau in the open air and a conspicuous place, whilst the sun was above the horizon: *yn wyneb haul a llygad goleuni* [in the face of the sun and eye of light], or *yn llygad haul, ag wyneb goleuni* [in the eye of the sun, and face of light]. The place was set apart by forming a circle of stones, with a large stone in the middle, beside which the presiding Bard stood. This circle was termed *cylch cyngrair* [the circle of convention], and the stones with which it was formed were called *meini gwynion* [white stones], *meini cyngrair* [stones of convention] or *meini crair* [relic stones]; and the middle stone, *maen gorsedd* [gorsedd stone], *maen llog* [rocking stone] (Qu? for what reason?) or *crair gorsedd* [gorsedd relic]. At these Gorseddau it was absolutely necessary to recite the Bardic traditions, and with this whatever came before the Gorsedd was considered and determined upon. The Bards at those places, and on all occasions where they acted officially, wore unicoloured robes. That of the *Bardd Braint* was sky blue, emblematic of Peace. The *Derwydd* wore white, the symbol of sanctity or holiness. That of the *Ofydd* was green for learning, and all those by being each unicoloured were, in that, symbols of truth. But the white peculiarly so, being the colour of light or of the sun. Of late ages, a wand or *ffon gynghrair* [wand of convention], with a ribband tied about the right arm, called *breichrwy* [armband] or *creirwy* [?reliquary], of the colour of that order to which the Bard belonged, has been substituted for the unicoloured robe. The *Awenyddion* or Disciples before Graduating, were distinguished by a parti-coloured robe of the Bardic colours, or, in modern ages, a parti-coloured wand and ribband. **(137)**

It is received opinion that the Bards, in the character and being of the order of *Ofydd*, may hold a *Cadair* under cover within doors. As of any subordinate *Cadair* or *Talaith*, provincial meetings are most properly called *Cadair*, as *Cadair Gwynedd* &c &c, but it is *Gorsedd Ynys Prydain*. The degree or order of *Ofydd*, in every circumstance of its peculiar institution, appears to be intended to create a power that was capable of acting, in emergencies, on a plan different from the regular mode of proceeding, as well as of bringing within the system such kind of knowledge as was unknown or foreign to the original institution.

The office of *Datgeiniad* (Reciter) was to recite the traditions, poems, to make proclamations, open and close the Gorsedd, announce candidates &c. He was generally a Bard, but this might be done by one, or as many as were necessary, of the *Awenyddion*. After a Bard had presided at three Gorseddau, he was one of the *Gorseddogion* or *Beirdd Gorseddog*, or simply *Beirdd Ynys Prydain*. All the *Beirdd Ynys Prydain* are representatively and virtually present at a Gorsedd. Those named are presiding Bards. If any named in a proclamation, and are at a Gorsedd called, after being named, *Beirdd wrth hawl ag arddel* [Bards of title and claim], it implies suspension of the decision of the Gorsedd concerning them till a future opportunity, for good reasons. **(138)**

Those named in a proclamation (*Rhybudd wrth Osteg undydd a blwyddyn*) [a warning by proclamation of a year and a day] and passed over in silence at a Gorsedd are rejected, and can never afterwards be admitted.

The Bards always stand bareheaded and barefooted at the Gorsedd within the *cylch cyngrair*. The Gorsedd is opened by sheathing a sword on the *maen Gorsedd* with a very short discourse on the occasion, and is closed by taking up, but not unsheathing, the sword, with a few words on the occasion, when all cover their heads and feet.

It may not be amiss here to give some account of various sets of people of several descriptions or denominations who have been confounded with the Bards by many; who either knew nothing of the ancient Bardic Institution, or having romantic notions of their own to palm on the world for true history, have so distorted and misrepresented every thing that has been said of the British Bards, that this once celebrated institution seems such an absurd, unmeaning thing as would be a disgrace to the rudest nation upon Earth.

The *Prydydd* signifies, is, and always has been, precisely the same thing with the English 'poet', a highly respectable literary character. He is not a Bard in the proper and original acceptation of the word, for, as before observed, the term Bard **(139)** properly signifies priest. It came to be used as synonymous to poet, because, for reasons already given, it was absolutely necessary that the Bard should be a poet; except (and it is almost a single exception) that one could be, by being acquainted with letters – which was a good substitute for verse, and with this possessing very excellent qualifications – admitted to the Bardic degree of *Ofydd*. But even in this order, it was, but one degree short of indispensability, necessary that the candidate should be a poet.

The *Clerwr* was a character very much like that of the provincial jongleur: he was a poet, a genealogist, an historian, or tale-teller, was well-skilled in the twenty four games, could sometimes blazon arms, was often an excellent juggler, something, now and then, of a crowder; was sometimes constituted master of the ceremonies at the house and tables of Welsh barons bold. He knew, generally, more fine things than becomes any man to know. He was an excellent buffoon, could lampoon a good man (to use his own phrase) devilish well. In short, he was a most consummate coxcomb, or (in the Cockney dialect) a d[amne]d clever fellow.

To fill up the jumble, musicians have been added, They have been said to be of the Bardic orders. This is to say that in order to be a parson it was necessary to be a fiddler. A parson, certainly, the Bard originally was, but there are laws, still extant in many of our old manuscripts, and oldest printed books, that expressly forbid the Bard to thrum the harp or scrape the fiddle. **(140)** In short, there was a strict injunction that a Bard should not practice or profess music; and, by the same law, it was impossible for a musician to be a Bard. The musicians however were always esteemed a very respectable class of people. They possessed many immunities, and were under regulations that in some degree (I say in some degree) were similar to those of the Bards. There were several very honourable degrees to which, according to what skill they had in music, they were admitted; and they were held in good estimation, equal to that of the musicians of our present age, at least.

Those heterogeneous characters, properly coddled together, make up, in many modern writers their imaginary character of the Ancient British Bard. It seems to me that Geoffrey of Monmouth will never die as long as the pregnant pen of Welsh History, boldly brandished in defiance of truth, is secured in its assumed privileges, by the general ignorance of the Welsh language that prevails amongst English, and all European, writers. Our oldest Welsh manuscripts that contain a rich fund of very interesting historical truths, are neglected and suffered, even by Welsh readers, to moulder into dust. **(141)**

ADDENDA

The regular times of holding a Gorsedd, were the two different solstices and the two equinoxes. Subordinate meetings might also be held every new and full moon, and also at the quarter days. Those were chiefly for instructing disciples. Regular meetings were supposed to be well known with respect to time and place, for there were appointed places as well as times, but irregular meetings with respect to time and place could only be done by proclamation or, if arbitrarily held on urgent occasions, the acts of such meetings required the confirmation of a Gorsedd, or public assent by subsequent proclamation.

The arbitrary acts of a Bard, such as admission of an *Ofydd*, or any thing else, were done in consequence of a supposed, or implied, decision or order of Bards at a Gorsedd, who, existing in a necessary fiction, to sanction an arbitrary act not otherwise allowed, were the supposed actors in all officialities. In this fiction they always exist. They may be visibly, but can not be virtually or essentially extinct; the utility and principles of their institution exist in nature. That being the case, the officiating agents of those principles are rather dormant than extinct, and are to be called into action by public proclamation, thus announcing to the public what before existed, but was not till then known. The regular manner of qualifying ultimately, or graduating a Bard is by giving him a Gorsedd or *Cadair*; that is by including him in the number, which must be three at least, of Presiding **(142)** Bards at a Gorsedd or *Cadair*. Amongst the number mentioned in the proclamation, it is impossible to know from any thing in the words, or form of it, which are the old Bards and which the newly admitted ones. There is nothing in the Bardic regulations that can entitle any one to take precedency of another, and to preside at a Gorsedd is only doing the necessary officiality of the day and occasion, which may be done by any other Bard present with equal propriety, without considering this as any thing in the least incompatible with the established regulation. And it is not necessary that the presiding Bards should punctually be those that had been mentioned in the proclamation, or that they should be visibly present, for they are virtually or representatively so, and so are all the *Beirdd Ynys Prydain*; though no more than three are actually and visibly so. Thus, to obtain the degree to which he was admitted by giving him presidency, it was not necessary that he should be present, for there was nothing implied as an act of his own in his being or not being present in person. The sole intention of giving him the presidency, was to announce him to the Bards, all virtually present, and to the public as of the particular order to which he was admitted.

With respect to the Gorseddau or *Cadeiriau*, as *Gorsedd Ynys Prydain*, *Cadair Morganwg*, *Cadair Powys* &c &c, they always virtually exist, and if they do not visibly appear, they are to be called on to make their appearance by the proclamation of a *Gorsedd Ynys Prydain*; where three *Beirdd Gorseddog* must preside, and, as in individuals, so in collective bodies, those *Cadeiriau* or provincial Gorseddau, took no precedency one of the other on any occasion, but all were equal in estimation and dignity. It was necessary that every one should be known as of some provincial *Cadair*. It was not necessary that a provincial *Cadair* should be actually held within its peculiar territory, for it might be held any where in Britain, or even in a foreign country; as might also a Gorsedd **(143)** Ynys Prydain, retaining on such occasions the appropriate Titles. It is *Beirdd Ynys Prydain* thro' the World, and they are termed *Trwyddedogion Byd*.

When it had been proved before a Gorsedd or *Cadair* that a Bard had been guilty of any criminal, or highly vicious enormity, he was suspended or degraded as occasion required. The first was by proclamation in which he was called *Bardd wrth hawl ag Arddel* [Bard of title and claim], which expression, according to its established acceptation, implied suspension. Degradation was by what was deemed *dwyn Cyrch Cyflafan yn ei erbyn* [to bring an assault of outrage against him]. After the Gorsedd had decided on him, all the Bards, covered their heads, and one of them unsheathing the sword named the person aloud three times with the naked sword lifted in his hand, adding when he was last named, *Noeth yw Cledd yn ei erbyn* [a sword is naked before him]. This was the whole of the ceremony, and he could never after be readmitted. He was ever after called *Gwr wrth ddifrod ag anraith* [a man lawless and depredatory].

Short speeches were used in opening and closing a Gorsedd; formal with respect to the matter, but they need not be so in the words, such as the following:

> '*Y Gwir yn erbyn y Byd.* Ag yn nawdd Beirdd Ynys Prydain pawb a gyrchant hyn o le, lle nid noeth arf yn eu herbyn, a phawb a geisiant Urddas a Thrwyddedogaeth wrth Gerdd a Barddoniaeth, Ceisiant gan Wallter Mechain, a Gwilym Owain, a Dafydd Ddu Eryri, a Sion Penllyn, a hwynt oll a yn *Feirdd Trwyddedog ymraint* Beirdd Ynys Prydain. *Y Gwir yn erbyn y Bŷd.*'

> [The Truth against the World. Everyone, under the aegis of the Bards of the Island of Britain, will approach this place, where no weapon will be unsheathed before them, and everyone who seeks the Grade and Bardic Licence, should ask Gwallter Mechain, and Gwilym Owain, and Dafydd Ddu Eryri, and Sion Penllyn, all of whom are Licensed Bards according to the privilege of the Bards of the Island of Britain. The Truth against the World.] **(144)**

If any Bards are to be graduated, the conclusion of the above form must be to the following purpose:

> 'Ceisiant gan Wallter Mechain, a Gwilym Owain, a Dafydd Ddu o'r Eryri, a Sion Penllyn, a Iolo Morganwg, a Ieuan Tir Iarll, a hwynt oll yn Feirdd Trwyddedog ymraint Cadair (or hyn ymraint Beirdd) Cyfoeth *Morganwg a Gwent ag Euas ag Ergyng, ag Ystrad Yw. Yn enw Duw a phob daioni.*'

> [They should ask Gwallter Mechain, and Gwilym Owain, and Dafydd Ddu of Eryri, and Sion Penllyn, and Iolo Morganwg, and Ieuan Tir Iarll, all of whom are

> Licensed Bards according to the privilege of the Chair (or according to the privilege of the Bards) of the region of Glamorgan and Gwent and Euas, Ergyng and Ystrad Yw. In the name of God and all that is good.]

This constitutes it a provincial *Cadair* or Gorsedd, from which it would be denominated *Cadair Morganwg* or *Cadair Beirdd Morganwg* [The Chair of Glamorgan Bards] &c, but as all the *Beirdd* [Bards] and *Cadeiriau* [Chairs], are *ymraint Beirdd Ynys Prydain* [according to the privilege of the Bards of the Island of Britain], the first part of the form, or words to the same purpose must remain.

To close the Gorsedd, the Bard President took up the sword and naming the Bards, thus, as we may say calling them over:

> 'Gwallter Mechain, Gwilym Owain, Ieuan Tir Iarll, Beirdd Trwyddedogion ym mraint Beirdd Ynys Prydain, a *Dafydd Ddu o'r Eryri*, a Sion Penllyn, Beirdd wrth Hawl ag Arddel ymraint *Cadair Deheubarth. Calon wrth Galon.*'

> [Gwallter Mechain, Gwilym Owain, Ieuan Tir Iarll, Licensed Bards according to the privilege of the Bards of the Island of Britain, and Dafydd Ddu of Eryri, and Sion Penllyn, Bards of title and claim according to the privilege of the Chair of south Wales. Heart against heart.]

This alteration in the manner of naming the Bards, from what was done in opening the Gorsedd, implies that Dafydd Ddu o'r Eryri and Sion Penllyn are suspended, and Iolo Morganwg and Ieuan Tir Iarll rejected or excepted against; and for that reason not admitted to their degrees for which **(145)** they were candidates. Degradation was a particular act of the Gorsedd before the close of it. If none were to be suspended or rejected, then in closing the Gorsedd their names were repeated as at the opening of it. Some say that for the purpose of degrading a Bard, it is the most proper way to hold a particular Gorsedd for that purpose, by proclamation, in which the occasion is to be specified, with this peculiar form of words,

> '*Lle ni bydd noeth arf yn erbyn neb ond Iolo Morganwg, Gwr wrth ddifrod ag Anraith.*' [Where no weapon will be unsheathed against none but Iolo Morganwg, a man lawless and depredatory].

All besides in the proclamation to be in the usual manner. After such proclamation it is said that it is not necessary that such a Gorsedd, so proclaimed, should be actually held, for it has a virtual existence, and all that is necessary on this occasion is to announce to the public the degradation of such a Bard; a purpose fully answered by the mere proclamation. Some say that even for graduation it is not necessary that the Bards so proclaimed should actually meet at a Gorsedd. But confusion in the knowledge of this, and many other things, is gaining ground every day.

A proclamation should be to the following purpose:

'Pan oedd oed Crist yn unmil saithgant nawdeg a dwy, a'r haul ynghyfnod Cyhydedd dydd a nos yn y Gwanwyn, y rhodded gwys a gwahawdd, ynghlyw Gwlad ac Arlwydd dan Osteg undydd a blwyddyn, a nawdd i bawb a geisiont urddas a Thrwyddedogaeth wrth Gerdd a Barddoniaeth, gyrchu pen Mynydd Berwyn ymhywys ymhen undydd a blwyddyn yn oriau'r echwydd, lle ni bydd noeth cleddyf yn eu herbyn, ag yno'n erwynebol *Gwallter Mechain* Bardd ym mraint Beirdd Ynys Prydain, a chydag ef **(146)** Gwilym Owain, a Hywel o'r Eryri, a Iolo Morganwg a hwynt oll yn Drwyddedogion wrth fraint a Defod Beirdd Ynys Prydain, er cynnal Barn Gorsedd, yn Llygad Haul ag wyneb Goleuni, ar bawb o barth Awen a buchedd a geisiont Fraint ag urddas, herwydd Braint a Defod Beirdd Ynys Prydain.' (Yng nghadair orseddawg Gwlad Bowys). *Y Gwir yn erbyn y Byd.*'

[In the year of our Lord 1792, while the sun is at the Spring equinox, a summons and invitation was given, in the hearing of lord and country, under proclamation of a year and a day, and patronage for all who seek rank and bardic licence, to go to the top of the Berwyn mountain in Powys in a year and a day at noon, where no weapon will be drawn against them, and there present will be Gwallter Mechain Bard according to the privileges of the Bards of the Island of Britain, and with him Gwilym Owain, and Hywel of Eryri, and Iolo Morganwg and all of them licensed bards according to the privilege and institution of the Bards of the Island of Britain, in order to hold a Gorsedd, in the eye of the sun and in the face of light, on everyone of poetic inclination and of good morals to seek the privilege and rank, according to the privilege and institution of the Bards of the Island of Britain. (In the Gorsedd Chair of Powys). The Truth against the World.]

The above is a Gorsedd Beirdd Ynys Prydain, to constitute it *Cadair, or Gorsedd Pywys*, conclude thus: '*Herwydd Braint a Defod Beirdd* (or *Cadair*) *Pywys. A laddo a leddir*' [according to the privilege and institute of the Bards (or Chair) of Powys. He who kills must be killed]. It is always deemed the best way to hold the Gorsedd as of Ynys Prydain, except the occasion is local. Then it ought to be of that particular province.

The following form is that of admission to different degrees, when the Bards are named say:

'Ag yno'n erwynebol Dafydd Ddu o'r Eryri, a chydag ef Iolo Morganwg, a Gwilym Owain, Beirdd Trwyddedog, a Sion Penllyn, a Daniel Dafydd, Beirdd ag Ofyddion, a Gwallter Mechain a Ieuan Tir Iarll. Beirdd a Derwyddon wrth Fraint a Defod (or Ym mraint) *Beirdd Ynys Prydain* &c &c, or Wrth Fraint a Defod Beirdd (*or* Cadair) Gwynedd, &c *Yn Enw Iesu.*'

[And there present Dafydd Ddu of Eryri, and with him Iolo Morganwg, and Gwilym Owain, Licensed Bards, and Sion Penllyn, and Daniel Dafydd, Bards and Ovates, and Gwallter Mechain and Ieuan Tir Iarll. Bards and Druids according to the privilege (or according to) the Bards of the Island of Britain &c &c, or according to the privilege and institute of the Bards (or Chair) of Gwynedd, &c in the name of Jesus.] **(147)**

The following, or words to the same purpose, is the form of admitting to the order of *Ofydd*; the only Order to which any one may be immediately admitted, or admitted by the arbitrary act of one Bard. Yet tho' it is an arbitrary act, it is always done on the fiction or supposition of a prior decision, in favour of a candidate, of the Bards at a Gorsedd. Arbitrary admission was only allowed on emergent occasions, such as the want of a sufficient number of Bards to constitute a visible Gorsedd. Or (as some say) when the Bard wanted an immediate assistant; and this last could be done, on urgent occasions, when even a sufficient number of Bards existed. But the Bard so admitted must be confirmed in his admission by a subsequent Gorsedd:

'Y Gwir yn erbyn y Byd, Yn nawdd Beirdd Ynys Prydain bawb a gyrchant hyn o le, ag nis dygir arf noeth yn eu herbyn, a phwy bynnag a chwenychont Urddas a Thrwyddedogaeth ym Mraint Beirdd Ynys Prydain, ymgeisiont a Gwallter Mechain, a Iolo Morgawng, ag Iorwerth Wyllt, a elwir yn gyffredin yr *Hen daro Tant*, Beirdd ag Ofyddion ym Mraint Beirdd Ynys Prydain, sef y dywed Dafydd Ddu o'r Eryri, ar air a chydwybod y gellid Beirdd o honynt, ag yna barnasant y Beirdd yngorsedd y dylid Beirdd o honynt yngradd Ofyddion ymraint Beirdd a Chadair Gwynedd. – yn Enw Iesu.'

[The Truth against the World, all who come to this place are under the aegis of the Bards of the Island of Britain, and no weapon will be drawn against them, and whoever seeks rank and license according to the privilege of the Bards of the Island of Britain, should apply to Gwallter Mechain, and Iolo Morganwg, and Wild Iorwerth [Edward Jones], commonly called Old String Strummer, Bards and Ovates according to the Bards of the Island of Britain, and as Dafydd Ddu of Eryri said, they can become bards on the the strength of their word and conscience, and then they will judge the Bards. At a Gorsedd they should be made Bards in the degree of Ovate according to the privilege of the Bards and Chair of Gwynedd. – in the name of Jesus.]

Closing the Gorsedd, say:

'Gwallter Mechain, Iolo Morganwg, a'r *Hen daro Tant*, Beirdd ag Ofyddion, wrth Fraint a defod Beirdd Gwynedd, yn ymddal wrth Brif Ddefod Ynys Prydain. Ni noethant arf yn erbyn neb, ag ni bydd noeth arf yn eu herbyn. Yn enw &c.'

> [Gwallter Mechain, Iolo Morganwg, and the Old String Strummer, Bards and Ovates, according to the privilege and institute of the Bards of Gwynedd, adhering to the main institute of the Bards of the Island of Britain. They will not bear a weapon against anyone, and no weapon will be drawn against them. In the name of &c.] **(148)**

N.B. The foregoing forms have often been, and may be, adhering to the substance and true meaning of them, lengthened out into long discourses, which, well managed, have a pleasing effect.

The Bardic tradition should always be recited at a Gorsedd, and on this occasion several of the Bards assist, and it is often allotted, as an exercise, to the *Awenyddion*.

The *Gorseddogion Ynys Prydain*, or *Beirdd Ynys Prydain*, are of every *Cadair* or Gorsedd, as of *Powys*, *Gwynedd*, *Deheubarth*, *Morganwg*, &c; for all those exist in them, as the fountain from whence all are derived, and when any of those disappear, the *Beirdd* or *Gorsedd Ynys Prydain*, may call them out by proclamation, or, by actually appearing as such, give them immediate visibility or, by the same means, constitute new ones, as Cadair Caerludd [the Chair of London] &c.

A Gorsedd may be held *wrth Fraint a Defod Beirdd Ynys Prydain ag ymraint Beirdd (or Cadair) Powys* [according to the privilege and institute of the Bards of the Island of Britain] &c. It was thus a national or general, and also a provincial Gorsedd.

It is now customary to term the Presiding Bards or *Gorseddogion*, *Pencerdd* plural, *Penceirddiaid*, the literal sense which is *Chief Songsters* or Versifiers; a term that strongly marks the original character of the Bards. And that a genius for, and skill in, poetry was a qualification indispensably necessary, *Cerddor* for the same **(149)** reason, is considered and used as synonymous with Bard, tho' according to its etymology, the original sense is considerably different. *Cerdd* is the same as the Latin *carmen*, and signifies an artificial or scientific arrangement of words, for as we trace the word up towards its source it seems to signify science, and is explained in old vocabularies by the word *crefft* [craft]. *Prydydd*, literally, beautifier, embellisher, regulator, &c &c, is also used as synonymous with Bard, but the most approved acceptation of this term is the same as the English 'poet', Latin 'poeta'.

The Regular Bards call those that are not so, *Oferfeirdd*, pseudo Bards, and Beirdd Beli. This word or term, will bear a variety of explanations, as The Bards of Beli, The Warring Bards, The Belgic Bards. *Bel* signifies war, whence *rhyfel*, *bela bele*, and it was, perhaps, from this word that the Belgae derived their name, i.e. warriors. *Brython*, the name of another Cimbric tribe is of the same import. *Bel* or *Beli*, seems to have been a Deity, seemingly of the Belgic Tribes, and is called by the Romans **(150)** *Belateucadrus Bel-dduw cadr*, *Bel y Duw cadr*, or *Beli Dduw cadr*, i.e. *Bel* or *Beli* the puissant God.

There is one reason for thinking that *Beirdd Beli* were so called from some Prince called Beli (a very common name amongst the old Britons) rather than from any thing else, because it appears from the laws of King Arthur, given by Llywelyn Sion o Langewydd, that like the regular, original, or primitive Bards, they were deemed the ministers of peace. The term will admit of farther etymological conjectures, but what ever the original meaning may be, this class or order of Bards, seem to be a kind of schismatics, seceders, or such as had introduced some innovations into the institution. And perhaps we may amongst other things, conjecture that Beli ab Benlli Gawr or some other Prince of his name, about the time that the Bards ceased to be the ministers of religion, made some new regulations in their institutes, adapted to the circumstances of the times. The laws of **(151)** Arthur, Gruffudd ab Cynan, and others are given by Llywelyn Sion as the laws of *Beirdd Beli*, who, in his opinion, had been for some ages held in greater estimation than the *Prifeirdd* (Primitive Bards). Possibly they were not so inimical to the clergy. I have not been able to find how long the *Primitive* or regular Bards have bore the nick name of *Gwyr Cwm y Felin*, which has a stigma pin'd to its tail. They are generally considered as Deists, atheists and conjurers by those who, we may venture to say, are no conjurers themselves. The late Mr John Bradford of Bettws near Bridgend, in Glamorganshire was so well acquainted the Bardic traditions or institutes, rules of versification, criticism, &c, that, probably, there has not been for some centuries his equal, and he certainly left not behind him any one to be compared to him for this kind of knowledge. Sion Bradford! Ieuan Tir Iarll! Thy name must be remembered.

Perhaps that *Beirdd Beli* were no more than those who were regulated by a new institution founded by some Beli, who was probably a Prince about the time the Bards ceased to be the ministers of religion, but were retained in a character, and official avocations something different from the ancients. **(152)**

Mottoes of the Island of Britain and the several provinces:

Island of Britain – *Truth against the World,*
Siluria – (east south Wales) *God, and all that is good.*
Venedotia, (north Wales, west) *Jesus,*
Powys (north Wales, east) *The killer must be killed*
Dimetia (south Wales, west) *Heart in union with heart,*
Trinobant (London or Primrose Hill) *Peace and Liberty*
Dosparth Llawdden. *Nid da lle gellir gwell.* Nothing good, where better can be obtained.

Rhai a fynnant mai ar Gadair Tir Iarll ai doded gyntaf. [Some insist that it was placed on the Chair of Tir Iarll first.]

IX: [The Carmarthen Eisteddfod] (NLW 13144A, pp. 246–51)

The Carmarthen Eisteddfod c.1453, *at which Dafydd ab Edmwnd's classification of Welsh metrics was endorsed, was a decisive locus in bardism. For Iolo, it denoted the beginning of the bifurcation of the druidic and civilized tradition of south Wales and the undruidic and barbarous tradition of north Wales.*

The great Eisteddfod at Carmarthen produced effects that are strongly obvious, that are very remarkable and interesting in the views of the critic as well as the historian of Welsh literature,

The falsely, tho' highly refined, system of versification that received the sanction of that Eisteddfod was eagerly adopted by the Northwalians, for apparently no better reason than that a bard of theirs, Dafydd ap Edmund, bore away the chair from the Southwalian Bards. A huge degree of assurance will very often succeed in its attempts, and an unexpected flash of false science has often, like a glaring meteor, so dazzled the eyes of its beholders as to strike them with a temporary blindness. The palm of victory was awarded by Gruffudd ap Nicolas to this Northwalian. His countrymen exulted very highly in his success, if they had any better motive or better reason than this prepossession in favour of their own country, and their prejudices against the Southwalians, for adopting the system thus unaccountably established by Dafydd ap Edmund they do not now appear, nor can any such be discovered and to impute it to that great degree of ignorance that is always wonderfully taken with baubles, would be considered **(247)** as highly invidious. The disciplinary institutes that were there adopted were rather defective than false, so far as they went they appear to have been compiled from the genuine institutes of the Ancient Bards, but the excessively false principles and refinements in versification were adopted in north Wales by all, and in south Wales by many. Many however of the Southwalian Bards rejected this system. Those of Glamorgan publickly entered their protest against it, and in the Carmarthen institutes of either poetical criticism or of discipline they found nothing equal to what they had previously and from time immemorial amongst themselves. This Eisteddfod of Carmarthen produced one good effect: it engaged the nobles and gentry to notice and patronize the Bards and this patronage would probably have not been exited but for this cause.

The protesting Bards of Glamorgan with some of other parts of south Wales succeeded in conciliating the patronage of the Lords Marchers of Glamorgan &c, and under their sanction held conventions on their ancient principles, and their most actuating motive was perhaps no better than that of wresting from the Northwalian Bards their lately acquired honours. This, or whatever the motive was, ended in all the success that could be wished for. They set about exploring their ancient literary remains, and from their old manuscript books compiled such a system of discipline, **(248)** of poetical criticism, of versification, and of whatever appertained to their science, that were it not for the oppositions and contests that on these occasions took place between the North- and Southwalian Bards we should, most probably, have lost long ago what remained of our ancient Bardic literature and its hierarchical system.

The Northwalian Bards, with some of the less discerning and least informed Bards of south Wales, had in the meantime adopted and established the Carmarthen system in all its particulars, and they continued to harp upon it for a century and a half. But all overstrained things are of no long duration, they frustrate their own intentions. Instead of being able to establish themselves permanently they at length cloy, and soon afterwards disgust, they are then rejected. The Carmarthen System died at about the same time that King James the first did both equally pedantic and the dupes of false refinement. It died in spite of all the medical assistance that it received, in spite of the books that were written for the express purpose of propping it up, with the most anxious wish to perpetuate it, by Dr Griffith Roberts, Dr John David Rhys, Captain Middleton &c. Besides those in print, there are many more to be seen in manuscripts. The ghost of this system has indeed made its appearance now and then since it departed this life, has haunted a few, and indeed has been conjured up lately by those who are very defective in the knowledge of the ancient Welsh poetry. But the shadowy **(249)** appearances this produced, as it were by the means of a magic lanthorn will soon vanish, and common sense will most weightily press down the earth that covers the worthless carcase.

Some, as already mentioned, of the Southwalian Bards taken with the tinsel glare of this false system, adopted it, but in the use of it were, excepting a very few instances, inferior to, or less successful than, the Northwalians. But the most learned and discerning of the Southwalian Bards treated this flimsy sing-song system with contempt, and holding as already observed, several sessions amongst themselves and those frequently under the patronage of the Lords Marchers of Glamorgan, they instituted such enquiries and researches into the ancient institutes, discipline, criticisms, versifications &c of the original or Primitive Bards that enabled them to ascertain their principles. In this they were successful. These researches were carried on for a long period, from the middle of the 15th to that of the 17th century. This compilation was regularly drawn up, under the sanction of such sessions, by Llywelyn Sion o Langewydd about the year 1580, under the patronage of Sir William Herbert Earl of Pembroke, from the most ancient and authentic manuscripts, many of which are still extant. And afterwards about the year 1670, a session of Bards was held at Beaupre Castle under the patronage of Sir Richard Basset where this system was reconsidered and improved by the addition of whatever had not hitherto been found of it unrecovered from ancient writings. **(250)** On a fair comparison of the system thus regenerated, with the numerous passages and allusions that we find in our old manuscripts, we find no reasons to be dissatisfied with it, we find nothing to contradict it or materially differing from it and in all its parts we find a sufficiency of authority to establish its authenticity and the fidelity of those who laboured for so long a time at the recovery of it. We are able to confide in its being of old our Primitive Bardic system in all its various branches, its institutes, discipline, theology, mythology, ethics, poetry, poetical criticism and versification &c &c &c.

This ancient system, thus recovered, became at last a Southwalian bardic hobby-horse for in the numerous meetings of Bards that have since that time been held, particularly in Glamorgan, much more of the externals than of the essentials of Bardism, especially if in the modern acceptation of the term we mean poetry, has been exhibited. Not many truly good pieces of poetry have been produced. Our Glamorgan Bards, properly speaking, are rather Bardic antiquaries, than poets; well versed in theories, on which they act but very little, they talk much but practice very sluggishly.

The late Revd Gronwy Owen of Anglesey, in attempting without understanding the system of Dafydd ap Edmund in his versification stumbled unawares on a manner that is far from being bad, tho' equally far from being what it ought to have been. Yet it may be **(251)** considered as a very long and happy stride towards the true old and excellent system of versification, the superlative excellence of his poetry will powerfully sanction his breach of the fetters with which Dafydd ap Edmund had hampered our poetry, so that it is not very likely that any one of tolerable understanding will bind himself again with them. Edward Jones of Bodfari indeed did this, but who now knows any thing of Edward Jones? And who able to read Welsh is there that is not well acquainted with Gronwy Owain?

The Gwyneddigion (Venedotian) Society in London have for many years given medals for the best piece of poetry on a given subject, it is to be lamented that they sanction and endeavour to restore the system of the Carmarthen Eisteddfod. It were to be wished that they would examine the works of their own Northwalian Bards, where they would infallibly discover principles of versification greatly superior to those of their idolized system imposed on them by Dafydd ap Edmund, and such as coincide in most, if not in all, things with those of the Southwalian recovered system. But unaccountable as it may appear, their prejudice against whatever may be approved of in south Wales, and prepossessions in favour of whatever they think Northwalian, is even at this day so very great, that no ear can be found open to a single syllable that may be thought adverse to their own nationality, to those things which they imagine to be peculiarly their own, and of course superior to every thing of the kind known elsewhere.

X: Schools of Welsh Poetry (NLW 13108B, pp. 104–5, 2–103, 112–136)

This essay provides an insight into Iolo's pseudo-druidical framework of the whole history of Welsh poetry. It ostensibly outlines his innovative classification of Welsh poetry into schools and periods and, as well as demonstrating the innate civilization of bardism and its national pedigree, reveals how he used primitivist arguments to highlight the north-south tension of his vision. See also a draft in NLW 13130A, pp. 188–91, 258–9.

(104) *Preface to the History of the Bards*
In this history I have availed myself of every easy opportunity of correcting the almost innumerable mistakes that have long distinguished the history of Wales for its absurdities, to detect the glaring and, I am certain, wilful falsehoods that disgrace it. Let it not be supposed that I utter this either ignorantly or inconsiderately.

I have endeavoured to introduce in it as much poetical, and otherwise literary criticism, respecting the Welsh literature as I possibly could without leaping over the bounds of history.

And above all, I have strained every nerve to render it a vehicle of sound and impressive morality.

My account of the first settlement of the Saxons in Britain is from our most ancient and most authentic Welsh manuscripts. It differs widely from those accounts with which all our printed histories whether Welsh or English have hitherto furnished us. I however believe it to be the truth, and believe that this truth has a tendency to extinguish that animosity towards the Saxons (Saeson), for so in Welsh we call the English still, which many of my ignorant countrymen in the interior of Wales, where but very little English is spoken, still entertain.

I have on all occasions strenuously endeavoured to keep clear of such political sentiments as apply to the present times, but in a few instances I could not avoid giving something of my opinions. Others may think as they please of them, but they are the convictions of my understanding after the most mature consideration; they are the dictates of my own conscience. Let those who animadvert upon [it] keep their consciences awake, but the sentiments of one who like me cannot on any pretence admit of war, of lifting the sword against an human being whatever, can never be very dangerous. **(105)**

As a mere narration of events and facts this history will not be found exuberant of our old Bards, we have but very little knowledge of the occurrences of their lives. They appear now amongst us only in an intellectual mode of existence. It is of course the Bardic intellect that is properly the object of this work. This intellect I have endeavoured to trace up to its origin, and thro' its medium have endeavoured to take a view of that state of society, I may say of the world, wherein it commenced, and thence to retrace it down through all its subsequencies of age and circumstance to the present time to view it in all its exaltations and depressions, through all its changing appearances, as acted, or acting upon, in all times and under all the accidents that befell it; to exhibit all the peculiarities of its character, and the various effects it had, from time to time on the nations amongst whom it has subsisted for more than three thousand years.

Parties will feel some alarm as they ramble over my book, but they will find, if they suspend their prejudices for a while, that I am of no particular party, yet I have endeavoured to furnish my sentiments with a lash that will fall, I hope, with some effect on the brawny shoulders of some of all parties who are not so far hardened in wickedness as to become absolutely callous. Hear ye Kings, and give ear o ye Rulers of the Earth!!!

It has been usual, when speaking of the fine arts, as paintings, sculpture, music &c, to define them, and what has been exhibited in them, as a certain school. Thus in painting we have the Italian School, the Flemish School, the English School &c and so, or similarly, of the other arts.

In poetry too we have our several schools: the schools of Spencer and Milton, Dryden and Pope, of Thomson, &c. I cannot think of a better manner of treating of the poetry of the Ancient Welsh Bards than by using this kind of language. And in the first place:

I: The Ancient or Primitive School or that of the Druids.

The great object of this school was to propagate useful knowledge and to convey effectually from one person, place, or age to another, such principles of theology, morality, jurisprudence and whatever had a tendency to forward the progress of civilization, and to ameliorate the condition of society.

We have good reasons for believing that the Cymry were acquainted with the use of letters from a very early period, before the arrival of the Romans in Britain and indeed the probability is considerable that they were, on their first coming into this island, acquainted with letters. But then the manner of using them, which was by cutting them on wood, required so much time and labour, that to convey useful knowledge to the great body of the nation by means of letters was a thing of very great difficulty and almost impossible. **(3)** Paper and parchment, and probably the use of ink, were yet unknown, and it was of the utmost importance to teach the people those indispensable principles of civilizing arts and sciences with which no nation or political society can comfortably and securely subsist.

Poetry was adopted as the most feasible mode of effecting this great end, the artificial arrangements of language on well known principles in verse, that could not be but with great difficulty, altered; connections of words phrases and of course ideas that closely adhered together and could not be broken without the consequent defects, becoming obvious, rendered verse very feasible as well as very effectual for this important purpose. Well constructed verse is easily remembered, easily learned, and that by those who have not the least idea of letters, such persons as these can very correctly and with speed learn verse from others as illiterate as themselves, can teach it [to] those of the same description. In verse knowledge may be conveyed along an unlettered path (if I may use such expressions) from one person to another and to very great numbers, from one place to another however distant, from one age to another, even to very remote futurity. To this great principle of oral and traditionary instruction by means of verse, letters were only used as auxiliaries: poetry was the principal. Hence we find it an historical fact that the poetical fragments that remain of the Primitive School are exactly of such a description as I have instanced. They contain religious doctrines, strongly and clearly expressed: aphorisms of morality in very concise, strong, and luminous language; maxims of legislation and jurisprudence are **(4)** frequently to be met with in those ancient poetical remains. Of these the versification is generally very regular in every thing, the lines are always or with very rare exceptions, severely restricted to a fix'd or established number of syllables, and formed into stanzas, most frequently in triplets. Sometimes the stanzas are longer, of 4, 6, 8 and more lines, and generally all unirhyme, or ending in the same rhyme. There are however some exceptions but they are rare. Some of these ancient fragments are in short rhymed couplets, but the rhymes changing with the couplets. These however are rare: but it appears to have been an established rule that where the lines exceeded the length of five syllables, or at furthest of six, they should be cast into unirhyme stanzas of from three to any greater number of lines.

This most ancient kind of poetry is the most simple in the structure of the verse of any. It has a stated number of syllables in each line and from this rule there are but seldom any deviations to be seen. They have a simple kind of *rythmus* that is pleasing to the ear and which admits of great variety, are always in rhyme, but have none of those artificial embellishments that we find in the poetry of the later schools.

It must be well observed that truth was on every occasion an indispensable requisite. No falsehood or fiction in history, no conjectural theology or morality were admitted, and it is remarkable that nothing of that ferocious or savage cast of sentiment that we find in the primeval poetry of most **(5)** other nations, and indeed in that some of our own later schools have yet been observed in what we may call our Patriarchal Poetry, of which we have no inconsiderable remains, and which clearly indicates a very early and genuine civilization. We the Cymry seem clearly to have been barbarized rather than more highly civilized by the Romans &c. Such had been the happy effects of that simple poetry in which our ancient Bards communicated their doctrines of pure theology and principles of genuine morality.

This school never became extinct. In all ages some of our Bards have been students of it, and have attained to a high proficiency in its principles. Of this we have fine instances in many pieces of Taliesin, in what appears under the names of Cattwg Ddoeth, Bardd Glas o'r Gadair, Sippyn Cyfeiliog, Macclaf ab Llywarch, and many others, down to the time of that fine moralist, Thomas Dafydd ap Ieuan ap Rhys of Pwll y Crochan, Arllechwedd in Caernarvonshire, who flourished about the year 1660. Since his time however this school has been very much on the decline, but has not become extinct.

The triplet, consisting most commonly of three seven-syllabic lines in unirhyme, was the most favourite metre of this school in all ages. The last line always turned on some very important moral sentiment, some theological truth, or some prudential maxim. The two first were illustrative of the last, and sometimes highly and often beautifully metaphorically so. Unirhyme stanzas of six or eight lines were also used frequently as in 'Dyhuddiant Elphin' [Propitiating Elphin], 'Englynion y Misoedd' [Stanzas of the Month], some of 'Englynion Eiry Mynydd' [Stanzas of the Mountain Snow] &c. (6) The very beautiful stanzas of 'Coronog Faban' [Crowned Baby], each of four unirhyme lines are purely of this school. Of these we have several sets, one of them attributed to the celebrated *Gildas Sapiens*, and certainly of great antiquity. Others are of later ages.

The poem entitled 'Gosymdeith Llefoed Wynebglawr' [The Spiritual Guidance of Flat-faced Llefoed] belongs to this school, and is one of its finest productions. It abounds with the most beautiful moral sentiments that are any where to be found, impressively just, and many of them surprisingly philosophical.

'Englynion Dyad' [stanzas of nature], 'Englynion y clywed' [stanzas of hearing], 'Englynion y Gorwynion' [stanzas of the delightful things], 'Y gnodiau' [the customary things], 'Cain cynwyre' [It is fine to set out], 'Marchwiail' [Saplings] and many others, of equally fine morality, are of this school.

The excellence of the poetry of this school consists in the justness of its sentiments expressed in a rich simplicity of language: very copious but very natural. It thinks deeply but never deals in the bold tropes and figures of the Middle Aged schools nor in their often overstrained compounds. Yet it uses compounds with moderation and a propriety, I will say an elegance, that to find in such a remote age appears a little wonderful. It deals much in a theology that is pure. Its morality is rich in the perspicuity of its truths, in the powers of language that express them, and in the sublimity of its conceptions. In these things the Druid poetry submits to a comparison with no other yet known but that of David, of Isaiah, of Job, &c. This morality is generally connected, and that very naturally and we may say neatly, with the most rational piety. Instances of this are numerous, I would particularly instance 'Dihuddiant Elphin', 'Eiry Mynydd' verses, 'Cain Cynwyre', 'Arthur ac [and] Eliwlod', &c.

In this school we find the knowledge of the human heart attained to in such a high degree. The human affections were closely studied and lovingly described, their effects minutely observed, and exhibited in the clearest and strongest lights. **(7)** A singularity appears in the Welsh poetry which originated in this school. This is the practice of beginning every poem on important subjects with an address to the Deity. Thus in Taliesin:

Golychaf fy Nhad,
Fy Nuw fy Neirthiad,
A ddoded trwy'm iad
Enaid ymbwyllad,
am gorug ymgwylad,
Dy saith llafariad,

I adore my Father, my God, my helper, who infused into my brain a soul of reason, who created in me the perceptions of my seven faculties (or powers).

He adds,

Seith synwyr pwyllad ym pwyllwys fy Nhâd,

With these seven powers of reason did my father rationalize me.

These seven faculties were 1st mental perception, 2nd corporeal vision, 3rd feeling including taste, 4th language or vocality, 5th hearing susceptibility, 6th bodily exertion, 7th mental exertion. These things sufficiently prove that the Bardic philosophy was not derived from Greece or Rome.

To this school belong the triads, in this they originated. They were however retained by all the subsequent schools, so were some of the other peculiarities of this school. The addresses to the Deity introductory were more generally retained by the School of Gruffudd ap Cynan than by any other.

Every thing within the circle of finite existence points at its origin, at the cause that produced it, a state of nature, of intellect, of society, or of something, whence it sprung. Our Primitive School is most obviously derived from a state of society wherein the noblest and most benign of the human affections had obtained the ascendancy over all others, but wherein intellect rather than anything else had been the object of science; where mind rather than matter had been that on which ingenuity had bestowed its labours. That the Cymric nation had for the founder of its polity a patriarch whose principles were those of justice, peace and benevolence, and such we are told was our Hu Gadarn, had the name of our Great Patriarch never been named, had his existence never have been recorded, yet our ancient institutions, our ancient moral principles, and our ancient conduct towards other nations, excepting two or three instances, and those by the universal consent of our own nation in after ages highly reprobated, would have clearly indicated the infallible existence in some early period of such a man, of such a state of society. **(8)**

Aphoristical Poetry, Druidical

Edward Llwyd and others after him, have attributed the 'Englynion Eiry Mynydd' to the ancient Druids. It is very probable that they are in the manner of our ancient Bards and Druids. This manner has been retained thro' all ages down to nearly the present time, but those who think that the aphoristically moral stanzas of 'Eiry Mynydd' &c are of very ancient date are greatly mistaken beyond the least doubt, and shew clearly that they are very ignorant of the state of the language and of the principles of versification that prevailed in different ages.

'Englynion y Misoedd' attributed to Aneurin Gwawdrydd are certainly none of this, but were written by some Bard of the 14th century. They have neither the language nor the versification of Aneurin, his internal rhymes that every where occur and his assonances terminating the lines, instead of perfect rhymes which very frequently occur with many other peculiarities, never occur in 'Englynion y Misoedd'.

'Englynion Eiry Mynydd' were written about the beginning or middle of the 14th century at farthest. Most of them are indeed attributed to Mabclaf ab Llywarch a Southwalian Bard about the year 1360. I have seen some of them attributed to Rhys Goch Eryri, perhaps the idea of 'Eiry mynydd' in the beginning of each stanza originated with him? It appears from some passages in his *cywyddau* that he had a *Cadair* or Gorsedd on Snowdon which is a literal translation of 'Eiry mynydd'. He says,

Mae main mawrwyrthiog i mi
yr awrhon yn yr Yri.

[There are precious stones for me/Now in Snowdonia]

(9) There are 'Englynion Eiry Mynydd' attributed to Ystaffan Bardd Teilaw. I hardly believe that this Ystyffan (Stephen) Bard of Teilaw, lived in the time of Teilaw Bishop of Landaff, but that he was one of his devotees in a much later age. Teilaw was greatly venerated and worshiped in the diocese of Landaff of which he was the tutelary saint.

'Englynion Marchwiail' were most probably written by one, or partly by each of those three brothers who lived at Marchwiail at about the year 1360, or a little later perhaps. Their names were Ednyfed ap Gruffudd, Madawc Benfras, and Llywelyn Llogell. They were amongst the most celebrated Bards of that age. The sentiment on which these *englynion* turn is a caution not to reveal a secret to any one whatever, not even to utter it, or trust it to the voice; a sentiment very well adapted to the tumultuous and dangerous time of Owen Glyn Dwr's insurrection.

Sippyn Cyfeiliog lived about the same period, he wrote many pieces of aphoristical poetry, amongst others a poem in triplets descriptive of every part of Wales, the character of the inhabitants, &c. This poem has been with extreme ignorance attributed to Aneurin Gwawdrydd, but copies of better authority attribute this piece to Sippyn Cyfeiliog. Robert Vaughan of Hengwrt, and Dr Davies of Mallwyd give 'Englynion y Misoedd' to Sippyn Cyfeiliog, and I think very justly.

The three Bards of Marchwiail were the sons of Marchwiail; were the sons of Gruffudd ap Iorwerth ap Einion Goch o Farchwiail ym Maelor.

The real name of Sippyn Cyfeiliog was Dafydd Bach ap Madoc Wladaidd, called also Dafydd Maelienydd. He **(10)** also assumed the fictitious name of Cneppyn Gwerthrynion.

I have somewhere read that Mabclaf ab Llywarch otherwise called Mab Clochyddyn was the same as Casnodyn, a Southwalian Bard, but I am not clear that it was so.

The Bards of the age of Owen Glyn Dwr gave out their pieces under fictitious names, for reasons that are sufficiently obvious, amongst those are Casnodyn, Cneppyn Gwerthrynion, Sippyn Cyfeiliog, y Crach, y Cyw, Mab Clochyddyn, Mabclaf ab Llywarch, y Posned, and many others. The real names of those are for the most part unknown now.

Many pieces of that period were fictitiously attributed to Taliesin, Merlin &c, most of them prophecies, some of them mythological and druidically theological, a great number of pieces, such as those of 'Eiry Mynydd' &c consist of fine moral aphorisms in verse. All of those pieces under the names of Taliesin, Cattwg, &c are such attempts as the bards of that period were able to make, to imitate the manner of the ancient Bards of whose works we have many pieces remaining.

I admit the probability that a Bard of the name of Ystyffan lived in the time of Teilaw whose Bard he might have been, but I greatly question whether the pieces that are now to be met with under his name are genuine. They are so much in the manner of pieces that are well ascertained to be of the 14th century and differ so widely in language style and versification from our genuine ancient poems, that no doubt can remain as to their being of a comparatively recent period. Edward Llwyd, whatever some may think was extremely ignorant of the Welsh language, of Welsh versification and of the ancient Welsh mythology, and so are all those who adopt his sentiments. **(11)**

Let any judicious and unprejudiced critic compare the language of the poems under present consideration with the authentic pieces of Aneirin, Taliesin, Llywarch Hen, the ancient Charter of Landaff, which is the oldest specimen of Welsh prose extant, and he will be, I think, clearly convinced of the justice of my observations. **(32)**

Schools of Welsh poetry, school of Taliesin

II. The School of Taliesin derives many of its peculiarities from the Roman literature which had in his time established itself in Britain. Hence it is that some of our most favourite metres have their origin, as the *toddaid*, hexameter, *ynglyn unodl union*, distych, hexameter and pentameter &c. Those who in all ages have written on the principles or rules of our versification attribute these and others that are obviously of Roman origin to Taliesin, i.e. the introduction of them into our language. This has been so generally and so uniformly asserted that we have no reason to doubt the fact. Of these metres however we find, and but barely find, samples in what now remain of what are acknowledged to be the genuine poems of Taliesin. His cotemporary Aneurin Gwawdrydd affords a more ample supply of specimens in his 'Gododdin'. Taliesin retains a greater variety of the metres of the Primitive School than any other Bard of his period, and (tho' their introduction has been attributed to him) has fewer than any one of his age of those metres derived form the Latin modes of versifying.

An embellishment was introduced into the versification of this that was unknown to the Primitive. This consisted in a species of rhythm in lines of eight syllables or upwards that required two internal pauses, and each pause to rhyme to the other, as

Golychaf i Gul*wydd* argl*wydd* pob echen
Arbennig torf*oedd* ynghŷ*oedd* am Ardden,
Ceint yn yspydd*awd* uch gwir*awd* aflawen,
Ceint rhag meibion Ll*yr* yn eb*yr* Henfelen,

Taliesin

[I ask God, lord of every kin,/Leader of hosts, famous for consolation/I sang at the ?feast above unhappy drink/I sang before the sons of Llŷr in the estuaries of Henfelen]

(33) . . . Alliteration was not known to this school; it had not till some centuries later been introduced. It had however one peculiarity (if not rather a continuation of a primitive usage): this was a method of connecting the several stanzas in a poem so that they could not be misplaced, or otherwise arranged, than as the poet intended them. This has been, by the continuators of this school, termed *cyrch gymmeriad*. The English word *precapture* gives a tolerable idea of this term. It consists in beginning the second stanza with a word that rhymes to the last word of the first; the third with a word rhyming to the last word of the second stanza, and so on through the poem, as follows:

1.
Ceingeneis canaf
Byd undydd mwyaf
Lliaws a bwyllaf,
Ac a bryderaf,
2.
Cyfarch*af* i feirdd bŷd
Nam dyweid Pryd,
Py gynneil y bŷd
Na syrth yn eissywyd,
3.
Neu'r *byd* pei syrthiei
Py ar yd gwyddei,
Pwy ai gogynhaliai, &c
Taliesin

[I have sung skilfully, I shall sing/ Until the greatest day/There are many matters which I consider/ And about which I am concerned./I challenge poets of the world/– since you do not tell me –/What sustains the world/ So that it does not fall into need?/Or the world, if it were to fall,/Onto what would it drop?/Who would hold it up?][1]

(34) Another mode of linking the stanzas or couplets was to begin the second with the last word of the first, the third with the last word of the second &c, thus:

1. Yngorphowys
Can rychedwys
Parch a chymrwys
A medd *meueddwys*

[1] Translated by Marged Haycock in eadem, 'Taliesin's "Lesser Song to the World"' in Tegwyn Jones and E. B. Fryde (eds.), *Essays and Poems Presented to Daniel Huws* (Aberystwyth, 1994), p. 246.

2.
Meueddwys medd,
Ei orfoledd,
A chain diredd
Imi yn rhyfedd . . .
Taliesin
I Urien Reged

[1. My place of ease/With Rheged's men/Respect and welcome/And mead in plenty
2. Plenty of mead/For celebration/And splendid lands/For me in abundance.][2]

The first stanza is on this second principle linked to the second, and this on the former principle concatenated with the third, and what follows will be obvious from what has been observed.

The poem by Taliesin beginning p. 76 and ending p. 77 has its long stanzas as connected by beginning **(35)** every stanza with the last word of the foregoing.

The first stanza ends and the second begins thus:

Gwaranrwy Reged
Rann gann *ogoned*
2.
Gogoned am rann
Am roddes rwy fuan
&c
Eu clod cleu *rhagod*,
3.
Rhagof rinweddau
Ran gan gyn anghau, &c
Taliesin

[Rheged's surety/Glory in a bright share/he deals out glory to me/who gave it very swiftly to me/Their fame clear before you,/Virtues before me,/A bright share before death.]

Taliesin has a greater variety of metres than any of the other ancient Bards, and versifies on a greater variety of principles, sometimes retaining the same rhyme for 12, 20, or 30 and even 30 lines together. This most commonly in his long-lined metres, and often also on those of short lines; but his short line verses often rhyme in couplets, the rhyme changing with every couplet, as in the following instances:

[2] Translated in Thomas Owen Clancy (ed.), *The Triumph Tree: Scotland's Earlist Poetry AD 550–1350* (Edinburgh, 1998), p. 82.

Gwae a roes ei fryd
Ar lawr creufyd,
Fal y traetha Ieuan
Yn yr ysgrythur lân,
Gwae a ymddirietto
Yn yr hwnn nid eiddo . . .
Taliesin

[Woe to him who has set his mind/upon the floor of the bloody world./As St John says/In the Holy Scripture/Woe to him who trusts/In what is not his . . .]

(36) and many more instances might be produced. Four lined unirhyme stanzas of 5 or 6 syllables in the line are very common in Taliesin.

Llywarch Hen, another famous Bard of this school, was a prince who had been despoiled of his territories in the defence of which he had been thro' a long life engaged. His favourite metre was the warrior triplet, which in his poems is in general very regular, and the number of syllables in the line is, as the legitimate rules of the verse require, always seven. He sometimes uses the *triban toddaid*, i.e. an hexameter, or *toddaid* with a seven syllable line concluding it: he in a few instances uses other metres also. His subjects are mostly martial: heroic odes, heroic elegies, but numerously interspersed thro' all his pieces we find some of the finest moral and prudential sentiments, clearly indicating that his taste and manner was formed on the principles of the Bards of the Island of Britain.

Taliesin writes frequently on heroic subjects, but he seems to delight mostly in the mysteries of Druidical theology and philosophy, and in these things is of all our ancient Bards the most learned.

Another peculiarity of this school is the use of vowel assonances instead of perfect rhymes. Frequently this was the practice also of the ancient Irish Bards, and is, I believe, also that of the modern poets of Ireland; was in use also, I am informed, by the ancient Germans, by the **(37)** old Spanish poets (see Percy's *Reliques*). These assonances consist of words that instead of perfect rhymes have only the same vowel in the ultimate syllable of the line or verse. The ultimate consonants, if any, after the vowels may differ. The following are instances of this:

From Aneurin's Gododdin
Gwyr a aeth Gattraeth buant enwawc
Gwin a medd o aur fu eu gwirawt,
. . .
Nyt ef eisteddei yn tat lleithic,
Y neb a wanei nyt adweinit.

[Warriors went to Catraeth, they were renowned/Wine and mead from gold vessels was their drink . . . Truly he would sit at the end of the bench/Whomsoever he struck would not be struck again.][3]

(51) An additional number, equally great were it necessary, might be collected from the ancient Bards of this school. These assonances and the rhyming pauses or rests, are amongst the most remarkable characteristics of the versification of this period. There **(52)** are other peculiarites of rhyme, and what may be called consonant assonances. These were when two or more semivowel consonants came together at the end of a word. (The semivowel is singly called *llythyren dawdd*, two together are called *crechlythyr*.) In this case the final consonantal sounds were considered as sufficient rhymes, the preceding vowels might be either one or the other of them, it matter'd not which, I shall only give one instance of this from this the 'Afallenau' of Myrddin:

Afallen beren a dyf yn llannerch
Angerdd ei hargel rhag rhieu Rhydderch
Amsathr yn ei bôn Maon yn ei chylch,
Oedd aeleu uddudd dulloedd dihefeirch.
Mi nim câr Gwenddydd ac nim hennyrch,
Wyf gas gan wasawg gwaesaf ryddyrch . . .
Myrddin

[O sweet apple tree which grows in the glade,/[Its] special quality conceals it from Rhydderch's lords;/A concourse about its trunk, people around it,/Numerous for them were bold ranks./Gwenddydd does not love me and does not greet me,/I am hated by Gwasawg, Rhydderch's protector . . .]

It will be observed that in this long unirhyme stanza the stress of the rhyme depends on the crispitude (*crechlafar*) of the sound produced by the crispitude of the two semivowels *R* & *Ch* with *L* & *Ch* in one line wherein there is only an imperfect assonance either of the consonants or of the vowel. Similar to those consonantal assonances are those rhymes, admitted as legitimate by the best English poets, produced by the words *birth*, *worth*, *earth*, *sworth*, any two of which are allowed **(53)** to be rhymed sufficiently legitimate, but the Welsh poets of our later schools have entirely exploded them.

Many pieces have for some centuries passed under the names of Taliesin and other Bards of his age and school, but from a great number of circumstances the most judicious critics believe them to be spurious, their not being found in our most ancient manuscripts is not of itself sufficient reason for

[3] Translated in A. O. H. Jarman, *Aneirin: Y Gododdin* (Llandysul, 1990), pp. 16, 26.

rejecting them as the productions of Taliesin &c, for a transcript of later ages may remain tho' the more ancient one whence it was copied might be lost. We believe this to be really the fact in some instances where the pieces possess all the required internal evidences of authenticity. But in most of the pieces we think spurious the language, in its words, idioms, and construction, is comparatively very modern. Those pieces have none of either the vowel or consonantal assonances of the ancient Bards which with was often substituted for regular rhyme, none of the rhyming pauses and other little embellishments that so generally appear in the verse of Taliesin's age. They have only the externals of the ancient versification but none of its internals, on the other hand some of those forgeries as we may call them are full of those little ornaments of alliteration, of that complex embellishment first introduced by the bards of the School of Gruffudd ap Cynan, called in Welsh *cynghanedd sain*. This had two rhyming pauses, the last of which alliterated with a third pause or correspondent foot. Of this description is a piece very mistakenly attributed to Taliesin, the first line of which is the following:

Ar ddwr mae cyflwr can fendigaw

[water has the capacity to bless a multitude] **(54)**

This, with several others have been taken from a romance, entitled 'Hanes Taliesin', i.e. the history of Taliesin, written so late at least as the fourteenth or rather fifteenth century, wherein Elphin (the patron of Taliesin), his Lady, Rhun son of Maelgwn Gwynedd &c are principal characters. This romance has been mistaken by many for true history but that it was not might have been easily discovered by proper attention to the language and its structure, to the structure of the verse in the poems attributed to this fiction to Taliesin, having nothing but the externals, as I have before observed, of the verse of the genuine Taliesin, and nothing of its internal rhythm, and other peculiarities.

The Druidical mysticism of many of Taliesin's pieces render them very obscure; not that there is any thing very difficulty in the etymological acceptation of his language, but his allusions are very frequently to things and ideas of which we, at this day know but very little, and the wild conjectures of some, and the extravagant systems built thereon, are truly curious. It is to be hoped however, that in future nothing but the truth will be sought for in the poems of Taliesin, whatever that may be found to be. But some persons seem to possess eyes that see every thing, or any thing but the truth, not only in the poetry of Taliesin, but in writings of far greater importance, and some have found out the knack of turning this to a very good account. **(55)**

In one part of Wales there have been Bards that may be considered as of the School of Taliesin till very recent times. I have before me a pretty large volume of manuscript Poetry written in the time of Elizabeth and by Bards of that age from this manuscript I compare the following extracts with the versification of Taliesin, in parallel passages from him.

One of the metres of Taliesin is that called by the Bards of his school *cyhydedd gyrch* but by those of the school of Edeyrn Dafawd Aur, *owdl gywydd*, and by the New Northwalian School, *owdl gywydd o'r hen ganiad*. Taliesin's elegy on Owain ap Urien is in this metre, which is unirhyme throughout, as follows:

Enaid Owain ap Urien gobwyllid ei Ren oi raid
Rheged udd ai cudd tromlas nid oedd fas ei gywyddaid,
Ysgell cerddglyd clodfawr Esgyll gwaywawr llifaid,
Can ni cheffir cystedlydd I udd llewenydd llathraid,
Medel calon gyfeiliad Eissillydd y Tad ai Taid,
Pan laddawdd Owain Fflamddwyn nid oedd fwyn og ef cysgaid . . .

[May his Lord attend to the needs of the soul of Owain ab Urien/Rheged's lord, a green burden hides him, it was no light thing to praise him/Locked below, a famed song-praised man, dawn's wing-tips his whetted spears,/For there is no equal to splendid Llwyfenydd's lord/Reaper of foes, grasper, of father and grandfather's make/When Owain cut down Fflamddwyn, there was no more to it than sleeping.][4]

The following on the same principle of versification and in the same unirhyme metre is from Hopcin Thomas Philip who flourished about 1560:

Trugaroccaf Dad a Duw a wyr pob rhyw feddylon
Trwy ras a seiliawdd y nef lle preswyl ef ei engylion,
Tri undod sy orau gyd a wnaeth y byd mor gysson,
Tonnau, tiroedd, trystau, mellt, a gwydd a gwellt yn leision.
Tes ag oerfel crwybr a gwlith, Haidd, Ceirch a gwenith ffrwythlon . . .
Hopcyn Thomas Philip o'r Gelli Fid ym Morganwg ai cant. **(56)**

[Most merciful God and Father who knows all thoughts/Who founded heaven through grace, where he dwells and his angels,/Three in one who are the best, who together made the world so coherently/waves, lands, thunder, lightning and trees and grass to be green/Warm wather and cold, honeycomb and dew, barley, oats and fruitful wheat . . .]

[Hopcyn Thomas Philip of Gelli'r-fid in Glamorgan sang it.] **(57)**

4 Translated in Clancy (ed), *The Triumph Tree*, p. 88; Tony Conran, *Welsh Verse* (Bridgend, 1992), p. 112.

The specimens of versification with rhyming pauses by Taliesin and others are exactly parallel'd by the following by Thomas ab Ifan ab Rhys in the time of Queen Elizabeth. Compare this specimen with the samples from the ancients already given:

Tri Chyfaillt *sydd* nos a *dydd* yn daeron,

Gwrthwynebwyr *Duw ydyw*'r cyfeillion,
Y Cnawd y *byd* ar *yspryd* creulon,
Drwg yn *troi*'n *ymloi*'n y meddylon . . .

[Three friends are insistent night and day/The friends are God's opponents/The flesh, the world and the cruel wicked spirit/Turning . . . in the mind . . .]

And so on, all unirhyme to the end of the poem. The following are in exactly the same kind of verse.

Rhagwedd rhoddyd
I Feirdd y Byd,
Byd yn geugant
Itti yd weddant,
Wrth dy wyllys
Duw ny'th beris
Taliesin

[He gives great honour/to the world's poets/the world for certain/submits to you/to your will/God, for your sake.][5]

Gair Duw in mysg
Drwy gywirddysg
Sy'n rhoi cariad
Perffaith difrad,
A phob rhinwedd
mewn anrhydedd.

[God's word amongst us/Through true knowledge/Brings perfect innocent love/And every virtue/in honour]

Thomas Llywelyn Deio Pywel, o Regoes.

(58) In these kinds of ancient verse a great number of Bards wrote in Glamorgan from about 1500 to 1600, and even since that time we have many specimens of such poetry, and in all the intermediate centuries (or nearly so from the above periods up to the time of Taliesin) we have specimens of this kind of versification. A noted Bard of this school about the year 1130, or

[5] Translated in Clancy (ed.), *The Triumph Tree*, p. 82.

thence to 1150, was Rhys Goch, ap Rhys, ap Rhiccert, ap Einion ap Collwyn, or Rhys Goch o Dir Iarll, as he was often called. Of his pieces there are extant more than 20, more perhaps than 30.

The Bards of this school have thro all ages also retained the triplet (*englyn milwr*), whilst it had been rejected by those of nearly all subsequent schools.

Cotemporary with Taliesin lived Dygynnelw Bard of Urien Reged (as most writers call him) or of Owain ap Urien Rheged. He was probably Bard to both father and son, He introduced blank, or rhymeless, verse, and those who have written on the Welsh art of versification always when treating of blank verse call it *dull Dygynnelw* [Dygynnelw's manner]. Edward Dafydd in his 'Cyfrinach y Beirdd' [Mysteries of the Bards] gives a specimen of it by Dygynnelw himself. The Northwalian writers also mention it under the appellations, but generally exemplify it in the following *englyn* which has no rhyme:

> Llafuria gweithia ym mysg gweithwyr byd
> Bid d'enaid yn deilwng,
> Rhag ofn o fewn rhyw gyfnod
> I'd farw yn dy oferedd.
>
> Hywel Bangor ai cant i fab Dafydd ab Edmwnd oferwr mawr a diogyn hynod.

> [Labour, work among the workers of the world/Let your soul be deserving/For fear within a time/That you might die in your folly]
>
> [Hywel Bangor sang it to the son of Dafydd ab Edmund, a great waster and remarkable idler.] **(59)**

This kind of verse however has never been much used by the Welsh Bards, some Bards of the School of Gruffudd ap Cynan, or the Ancient Northwalian School, such as Llywarch Brydydd Moch, Mab Cryg, Ustus Llwyd, and one or two more have written in blanck verse, it will be more fully noticed in the account of that school.

It should seem that the Bards of all other schools have retained the manner of Taliesin and his cotemporaries, both as to subject matter and the simple structure of the verse. Under the terms of *cerdd deuluaidd* and *teuluwr-iaeth*, Edward Dafydd and others say that what in former ages was called *Derwydd* (Druid) has in later times been called *Bardd Teulu* and *Teuluwr*: he was the family or domestic Bard. His vocation was to teach in the family that retained him, the doctrines of religion, the principles of morality, the maxims of domestic and social decency and good manners. It was his duty also to educate the young person of the family in these things and in the knowledge of the most important points of the national laws. He was the recorder of the family, kept written pedigrees, registered marriages, births &c, kept memorials of the boundaries of lands, taught to read and write the Welsh language &c. His poetry was always in easy and simple verse without the trammels of alliteration, as best adapted to the purposes of conveying useful instruction in clear and appropriate language. This practice was continued thro' all ages in every part of Wales, I believe, till that huge mushroom of a very foggy night, the New Northwalian School, or rather the School of Caerwys, whose founder was Dafydd ab Edmwnd, obliterated every trace of antiquity in North Wales. New versification, new Bardic regulations, new orders of Bards, new of every thing that was absurd and irrational took place, and was established to the utter damnation, as I may **(60)** justly say, of all our ancient and magnificently rational principles of Bardism, poetry, moral discipline and regulations of the Bards in their several orders &c. But more of this new-fangled school when I come [to] treat more particularly of it, or to take it in hand, as we often say of things and persons that merit castigation.

The revival of the School of Taliesin which, properly speaking, is only a continuation of the Primitive School would be a very desirable thing. Rational improvements and embellishments of later ages should be admitted, and I would be a little indulgent, but for the sake of good sense, of good taste, of every thing that is purely natural and consequently purely beautiful and just. Let us absolutely dismiss, and that for ever, the extravagantly ridiculous School of Caerwys. It has thrown into the lowest degradation principles of versification, of poetical composition and criticism, that are infinitely superior to its own, and in the room of them has substituted absurdities that baffle all the powers of conception in any mind that has never been acquainted with the Welsh poetry especially the Northwalian poetry of the 16th and 17th centuries. In the 18th century indeed it had one foot in the grave and the other on the point of slipping in, but there have been such as have endeavoured by efforts of some strength to crutch it up, in doing this they only consign to future ages names that will be uttered with contempt . . . **(70)**

Schools of Welsh Poetry: School of Gruffydd ap Cynan Alias of Glynn Achlach

At the commencement of the 11th century, the state of poetry and of the Bardic literature in general, appears to have been at a very low ebb. We have hardly a Bard that can be ascertained to have lived in that age. Whatever the rude poetry of that age might have been, it was not such as made a lasting impression on the public mind, it was to such as was thought worthy of being preserved.

Soon after however, or towards the close of this century, and more obviously in the beginning of the next, an extraordinary revival took place. This was chiefly in north Wales. In Anglesey appeared one of our noblest poets of any age whatever: Meilir Brydydd about 1120, and soon after him, or about 1150 Gwalchmai his son cotemporary with whom were in north Wales,

Cynddelw, Bard to the princely house of Powys, a great number of whose poems are still extant. Daniel ap Llosgwrn Mew, Gwilym Rhyfel, Llywarch ap Llywelyn, Seissyllt and the two princes Howel ap Owain Gwynedd and Owain Cyfeiliog appeared all about the same time in north Wales and Powys; and in south Wales only Gwynfardd Brycheiniog, at least no other that can be considered as of this school, which I will call the School of Gruffudd ap Cynan, or the School of north Wales for reasons which I imagine will appear sufficient. **(71)** Some Bards indeed appeared about the same period in south Wales, but we must class them as of the School of Taliesin, or rather, perhaps of the Primitive School. Such were Gwrgan ap Rhys of whom we have a few short pieces, Caradoc of Lancarvan who distinguished himself more as an historian than as a poet, Rhys Goch ap Rhys ap Rhiccert o Dir Iarll, with others of these an account will be found in a more proper place.

The rising of an unclouded sun at the deep moon of the darkest winter's night is the only simile that can be used in speaking of the wonderful revival of poetry (I say poetry rather than Bardism) that blazed out as if it were instantaneously at this time, that it can not be referred to any earlier period, nor has it the least appearance of having been the effect of any kind of gradationary improvement. It is not greatly short of a miracle. Still, it started up out of deep obscurity. We find ourselves entangled in very considerable difficulties in endeavouring to trace it up to its origin, to the time and place of its commencement, yet we have some clues, but they are in some places perplexingly tangled, and to untangle them requires a careful hand.

We have a little code of Laws for the regulation of bards and musicians ascribed to Gruffudd ap Cynan Prince of north Wales, Bleddyn ap Cynfyn Prince of Powys, and (as some copies say) Rhys ap Tewdwr, Prince of south Wales, but the name of this Prince is not found in the greatest number of copies. We shall in time see whether there may **(72)** or may not, be sufficient reasons for admitting or rejecting him.

The title of this little code is, in general The Statute of Gruffudd ap Cynan, the preamble to which runs nearly in these words. [marginal note: I find no mention of the Statute of Gruff ap Cynan before the Time of Gruff Hiraethog]

'This is the Statute of Gruffudd ap Cynan Prince of north Wales and of Bleddyn ap Cynfyn Prince of Powys, respecting the Men of Vocal Song' &c. (Here introduce the whole of the Statute). Thus it begins in the greater number of copies, then follow the regulations, or laws, the purport of which is to enforce good order, moral conduct and decent behaviour, under pretty severe restrictions, after which ensues the following:

'After Gruffudd ap Cynan, these laws and privileges were confirmed, or ratified by Bleddyn ap Cynfyn Prince of Powys.

'And in like manner, Prince Rhys ap Tewdwr, of south Wales, enacted similar laws (or the same laws) after he had built his new castle in Cardigan. Inviting all who might wish to profit by the science of song in England, Ireland and Scotland, to resort to the **(73)** New Tower in Cardigan, notice of a year and a day having been given thereof.'

Thus, or nearly so, it is expressed in the greatest number by far of old copies that I have yet seen, and I have by me correct transcripts of more than twenty copies of considerable antiquity, some not less than 300 years old and none of later date than the time of Elizabeth.

The historian who attends to what has thus been said in the statute, as it is usually termed, will immediately perceive that it can not possibly be true that Gruffudd ap Cynan as a Prince of Wales could have ever made any such laws, for Bleddyn ap Cynfyn died in 1072, and Gruffydd ap Cynan came not into possession of the principality of north Wales till the year 1080, and he died in 1136.

Rhys ap Tewdwr recovered south Wales in 1077. He might have made such laws but not before Bleddyn ap Cynfyn, who was dead before he began to rule five years. It is true that he built the Castle or Tower of Cardigan first, and might have invited bards and musicians there and have enacted laws for their regulation, but it must have been before Gruffydd ap Cynan.

Caradoc of Lancarvan our historian was cotemporary with Gruffudd ap Cynan, and himself a Bard, but he makes no mention of any such laws by either Gruffudd ap Cynan, Rhys ap Tewdwr or Bleddyn ap Cynfyn, but he relates something like this of other princes, successors of Bleddyn and Rhys ap Tewdwr. **(74)**

The castle of Cardigan was in the possession of Cadwgan the son of Bleddyn ap Cynfyn in 1107. He in that year proclaimed a grand feast to be held at this castle to which he invited the princes and nobles of all Wales, and also the bards and musicians, or, as the historian expresses it 'The men of vocal and of instrumental song, were invited, for whom he prepared chairs and instituted contests of skill between them, according to the usages of the Court of Arthur, and also instituted laws (or regulations) and privileges to them, with honourable rewards or perquisites, and then he dismissed with honour and rich presents every one to the place whence he came.'

Gruffudd ap Cynan at the time of this splendid feast, or assembly, was living and governed north Wales. Whether he was amongst other princes and nobles at this meeting, which appears to have been partly legislative, is not particularly mentioned, but it is probable that he was, and it should seem that whatever laws and institutes were enacted for the regulating of men of vocal song and men of instrumental music (for it is thus they are termed in the statute) at this assembly, they were done by the general consent or united powers of all the princes and nobles of Wales, each of whom returning to his own dominions there enforced them. Hence in north Wales they would with strict propriety be called the laws of Gruffudd ap Cynan. In other sovereignties **(75)** they might with equal propriety have been termed the laws of their several princes, and, if the sovereign houses bore the names of their founders, which they seem to have done, for which opinion reasons will in a proper place appear, then in north Wales they would bear the title of laws or statutes of Gruffudd ap Cynan, in Powys of Bleddyn ap Cynfyn, in the province of Dinevor of Rhys ap Tewdwr. For those princes were the actual founders of these three sovereign houses, or perhaps more properly the refounders of them, for their dominions in all parts of Wales had been for several successions in the possession of such as they might have justly termed usurpers.

In the year 1135, Gruffudd ap Rhys ap Tewdwr (as Caradoc says) having recovered his principality in south Wales, prepared a princely feast in Ystrad Tywi to which he invited all the princes of Wales and of the Marches. To this feast it is said Gruffudd ap Cynan and his sons came, and a great number of the nobles of every part of Wales. This grand feast was held for forty days. To this feast were invited the poets and musicians; contests of wisdom and skill were instituted, amusements of representation (probably dramatics) and all the manly games; after which these were all dismissed to their homes, with honourable gifts or presents to such of the Bards, wise men, and musicians, as were deemed worthy of rewards, and also to all who excelled in the manly accomplishments. **(76)** When this feast was over, Gruffudd ap Rhys set himself about revising the laws of his country, for this purpose he summoned (or called as the historian expresses it) to him all the wise men and scholars of his dominions, and entering into council with them he enacted laws and regulations for his dominions, instituting courts of justice in every cantref with subordinate courts in every commote. Gruffudd ap Cynan did the same in north Wales. This (says Caradoc) gave offence to the Normans and Saxons, who dreaded the establishment of good order amongst the Welsh, and they brought complaints against the two princes to King Stephen, to which, not knowing what was best to be done he returned no answer.

These I believe are the only legislative proceedings of this period that our historians mention and it was, most probably, in one or the other of them, that the Bardic regulations under present consideration were enacted. There were most certainly some ordinances of that nature made at the grand feast of Cadwgan at Cardigan Castle, for they expressly mentioned, and in the legislative assembly of Ystrad Tywi under Gruffudd ap Rhys as well as in the immediately subsequent one in north Wales under Gruffudd ap Cynan, the whole body of the laws appears to have been revised and such new ones as were deemed necessary exacted, and doubtless amongst other things the Laws of the Bards were brought under consideration.

Another view may be taken of this clouded object of history, if it might be deemed necessary to vindicate **(77)** in a literal sense what the preamble of the Statute positively declares, that they are the 'Laws of Gruffudd ap Cynan, Bleddyn ap Cynfyn and Rhys ap Tewdwr conjunctively, or rather of Gruffudd ap Cynan, previously, and by subsequent ratification of Bleddyn ap Cynfyn and Rhys ap Tewdwr. If this must as a fact be established I know of but one way to do it, with any degree of probability which the following facts and observations will exhibit.

It has been already observed that in Wales, as sovereigns in possession of their dominions, these three princes never lived together. Bleddyn was dead eight years before Gruffudd ap Cynan recovered north Wales, and five years before Rhys ap Tewdwr recovered south Wales.

I have already observed that there are various copies of the statute of Gruffudd ap Cynan extant, the greater number of which have been in subsequent ages so interpolated as to accommodate them to the times as circumstances required. Whether the existing circumstances of those ages were any more than the supposed ones of our own day's realities, I shall not enquire. Governments of all ages have known very well how to form a huge or mountained mass of monstrous lies and to turn them to, what was to them, a good account.

In one of the interpolated copies (I mention'd the fact of its being interpolated that the reader may be the more able to appreciate its authority), observing at the same time that historical interpolations are of all others the most admissible, **(78)** for the subsequent interpolator may from the best authorities become acquainted with an event that was unknown to his original writer, and the passage from the interpolated copy that I am now going to produce is of a purely historical nature it is as follows, or in the preamble.

'These are the regulations made by Gruffudd ap Cynan, prince of north Wales respecting men of vocal song and of stringed music, in the Vale of Achlach in Ireland to which place came from Wales Alon son of Ceneu a man of south Wales, and Rhydderch Voel of Arvon (in north Wales). These were poets and men of vocal song. The men of stringed music were Olof the musician, Matholwch the Irishman, and these formed regulations for vocal song and stringed music. This was in the time of Gruffudd ap Cynan and of King Stephen, where it was enacted that none should become men of vocal song or string music subsequently, but according to what was required by the regulations of those laws (regulations).'

We have in manuscript in the Welsh language a great number of copies of a little tract on instrumental music entitled

'The preservation (or preservatory) of the science of string music, that is of the harp, and *crwth* (viol) within the three sovereign states (or principalities) of Wales. This was deduced from the **(79)** scientific principles of music at the desire of four chief musicians, performers on the harp and the viol, and from the ideas and ingenuity of each of them conjunctively, for the purposes of teaching the art of composing music, and of preserving the memory of knowledge thereof, to perform correctly, and to class properly (or systematically). The names of these four chief musicians were Alon ap Ceneu, Rhydderch Foel, Matholwch the Irishman, and Olaf the musician, and listening to them were Henry Gevnrudd and Carsi the harper, and many more of their council and of their science with them, and with the advice of those teachers (or doctors) and according to the doctorial science of music, and the four chief musicians, and their science, conjunctively in council, each assenting to the other the twenty four elementary principles of music were conceived and instituted, and to secure or establish these, were formed the twenty four musical metricities, and for three reasons were these things done. First, to teach the principles of musical composition – secondly, to distinguish properly and recognize, and, thirdly to retain in memory musical compositions, (or musical metricities) the names (or titles of which) follow in the Irish language. Mwrchan the Irishman was at that time sovereign of Ireland, and he confirmed these things by virtue of all his sovereign powers and authorities in the Place called the Vale of Achlach.' **(80)**

All the Copies of this little manuscript treatise that I have hitherto seen, and I have seen many, are remarkably uniform. Their readings vary but little or nothing; in none of them does the name of Gruffudd ap Cynan occur; and yet the regulations and musical principles agreed upon and confirmed by an Irish Sovereign, and in Ireland at a place called Glynn Achlach, are said to have been intended for the three sovereign provinces of Wales. There is something very singular in this, but before we proceed some account of the first part of the life of Gruffudd ap Cynan must be given.

The Northwalian princes of the house of Anarawd had been for a hundred years disposed of their sovereignties by Aeddan ap Blegywryd, Llywelyn ap Seisyllt, Gruffudd ap Llywelyn and Trehaearn ap Caradoc; most of whom however, singularly enough, do not seem to have been considered as usurpers by the Welsh. On the contrary, Caradoc says that the princes (claimants) of this house were not beloved by the Welsh on account of their cruelties and violations of the laws, murdering or pulling out the eyes of all that opposed them in their tyrannies. The Welsh seem to have been a sensible people about this time, would to God they had continued so. They justly thought that loyalty and obedience due only to those who governed them with justice and equity, and protected them and their country. Let all the abettors of tyrants read the character given, by the candid and impartial Caradoc, to Llywelyn ap Seisyllt whom they will call an usurper, and tremble for the respectability of their Principles. **(81)**

In the year 993, Idwal ap Meuryg ap Idwal foel ap Anarawd, recovered north Wales of which he had been dispossessed, at a time when that part of Wales had no sovereign, (heb na phen na pherchen) [without a leader or owner] but in 1000 Aeddan ab Blegywryd subjugated north Wales, Iago the son of Idwal who was the hereditary claimant of north Wales, fled into Ireland where he died leaving his son Cynan to claim the principality of north Wales. Cynan made several attempts assisted by the Irish, or rather by the Irish Danes, to recover his dominions but could not succeed. His wife [was] Rhacwel, daughter of Aulaff the Danish King of Ireland, or of Dublin as some of our manuscripts call him. This Aulaff was a celebrated scald and harper as well as a sovereign prince. Gruffudd ap Cynan was born and educated in Aulaff's court. Aulaff assisted him at various times, and in 1080 with success to recover north Wales. Gruffudd ap Cynan may be fairly supposed to have been taught the Welsh language by such of the North-walian nobles who were sharers of his misfortunes and with him into exile. Be that as it may, he doubtless had been educated in the language of his mother and royal grandfather Aulaff, who lived to see his grandson on the throne of Aberffraw. This Aulaff, according to the Irish historians, greatly patronized poetry and music, whence it may be reasonably inferred that Gruffudd ap Cynan had conceived a powerful predilection for these elegant arts, in all nations and ages the precursors of civilization and literature. Admitting this we may well suppose that he interested himself greatly in **(82)** their cultivation, and in the revival of them in his own sovereign dominions, where they had once flourished in a high degree. It was as natural for his grandfather Aulaff to assist him in this, as well as in the recovery of north Wales, thence we may consider it, not only as possible, but as highly probable that the poetical and musical proceedings in Glynn Achlach were chiefly for this very purpose, especially as two or three Welshmen skilled in those arts attended the meeting.

The copy, quoted page 78, says that Gruffudd ap Cynan attended the meeting of Glynn Achlach expressly for this purpose, that two bards, poets, or men of vocal song from Wales attended: Alon ap Ceneu, and Rhydderch Foel, and the musician, or man of song. Olaf is very probably the same as Aulaff, who, as before observed, was a celebrated scald and harper, and what was more on this occasion to the purpose he was a man of powerful authority and deeply interested in such regulations as might be intended for Wales, the sovereignty of which was claimed by his own grandson. This admitted, it will become very probable that all this took place some time before Gruffudd ap Cynan recovered north Wales, as preparatory to such an event. Rhys ap Tewdwr, Prince of south Wales was at the same time an exile in Ireland, he might have interested himself in such things as these, and this idea is in some degree countenanced by the circumstance of Alon ap Ceneu, one of the men of vocal song being a Southwalian. If all this took place **(83)** before the death of Bleddyn ap Cynfyn, he might have acted a part in this affair by being the introducer of those laws into Wales where they were, of course, in a very proper sense confirmed or ratified by him, and thus will the preamble of the statute be literally true, that Gruffudd ap Cynan (tho' not then in Wales) first enacted these laws, and that subsequently Bleddyn ap Cynfyn ratified them (for he was not the enactor of them) in Powys. Rhys ap Tewdwr might have done something similar in south Wales.

That amongst the numbers of copies that I have seen of this code of laws for the Bards, or poets, only one copy should contain the account of the time and place where it was formed may be thus very fairly accounted for.

By one clause in it, the teacher or doctor, in each of the sciences of poetry and music was enjoined to furnish each of his disciples with a copy of the whole statute that he might know how to regulate his conduct on all occasions. It was for such regulation that this law was originally intended, and to secure good morals and decency of manners. For it seems that amongst the professors of these, at that time, highly respectable sciences, a great laxity of morals had prevailed for some time. It was a work of some labour for the teacher to make such copies for his disciples, and as nothing **(84)** but the absolute laws were of absolute importance to be known, nothing of the preamble would be retained by the abridged account of their having been enacted by the Gruffudd ap Cynan and Bleddyn ap Cynfyn, without any mention of Glynn Achlach and the persons who there attended on the occasion. Hence the oblivion into which those particulars had sunk. Thus have I given all the accounts of those transactions that I have hitherto found, and the best conjectures that I have been able to make from. How just the results may be deemed must be left to the reader's judgement, as also whether what follows may, or may not, in some degree, corroborate them.

It was the School of Gruffudd ap Cynan that introduced, properly speaking, at least systematically, alliteration into the Welsh Poetry. It must indeed be confessed that some time before a few faint traces of it had appeared, but so few do we find them that we are at a loss to say whether they were intentional or things of mere accident. Some of our modern would-be poets and critics have considered this fantastical and I will boldly say, false ornament, as the great excellency and indeed the glory of our versification, but rationality, sound criticism, and good taste are things that have not for too many centuries to be well remembered appeared amongst our self-boasting Welsh. If I offend some of them I cannot help it, for I have, unfortunately for them, some predilection for truth, and also some fondness for pure nature. Had our poetry for the last five centuries been what might have been expected from the genuine character and energetic powers of our copious and luminous language, what a high rank would it have held **(85)** amongst the poetical compositions of the world. We have, it is true, some pieces that appear tolerably decent, but why am I not able to speak more highly of them? Why? Because false principles of ornamental verse have so graspingly laid hold of our versemongers, that they have not been able to disengage themselves from the clutches of those illegitimate refinements, that have heavily hampered us for ages. But to proceed.

Alliteration was in the School of Gruffudd ap Cynan considered as an indispensable requisite of versification, at least what was not greatly to be dispensed with. Meilir appears to be the first of this school. He used alliteration in by far the greater number of his lines; I say the greater number, for he sometimes contented himself with the rhymed pauses of the School of Taliesin, such as the following lines:

Pan ddyfo Dof*ydd* yn n*ydd* pennawd
Peryf par wrthf*ynn* yn er*bynn* brawd . . .

[When the Lord shall come on the appointed day/Lord, make a welcome [for me] before judgement]

Such lines are very frequent in Meilir, but alliterative lines are much more at least three to one. His son Gwalchmai improved on this new embellishment of verse, at least was much more sparing of the internally rhyming verses with alliteration, but it was contrived to combine both principles together. The following lines are instances:

Ergyrwayw brwyd*rin* cyn rhew*ir* rhawd, –
Pedryddawc de*yrn* uch c*yrn* coned . . .

[Thrusting spear before the destruction of a host/Mighty lord above drinking horns of splendour]

(86) Of this combination there are numerous varieties.

Though alliteration had been adopted by the School of Gruffudd ap Cynan, it was pretty long before it was brought under any fixed rules, and did not arrive at its ultimate perfection till a more recent school, that of Edeyrn Dafawd Aur, superseded it about the commencement of the 14th century.

Here we must deviate a little to search out the origin of alliteration, and the source whence the Welsh poetry derived it. It appears to have been known to the runic scald many centuries before the Welsh Bards adopted it. The dying ode of Regner Lodbrog was composed about the year 550, cotemporary with Taliesin, it not only had alliteration but this appears to [have] been completely systematized, brought under well defined rules; a sufficient proof that it had been very long in use, for every principle, in art and science has its incipiency and progressive state and it is a long time before it reaches its ultimate point or such a degree of perfection as to be deemed sufficient so as to render it stationary, to arrest it in its career and to say "hither to shalt thou come and no farther." The Welsh alliteration did not arrive at such a point till a thousand years after the ode of Regner was written. I am not to be understood as if I meant to say that Welsh verse was, prior to this event, in a state of imperfection. On the contrary, I assert with confidence that it only arrived at its ultimate deviation from its original perfection then, when we read the energetic verse of the 'Gododdin' where it remains unmutilated, of Llywarch Hen, of Myrddin in his Afallenau, of Meugant, of Llefoed Wynebglawr, of 'Englynion y Misoedd' &c that have no alliteration. We are astonished how the Welsh Bards ever suffered this false embellishment to **(87)** [have] arrived at the extravagantly high pitch which it attained.

The late Lewis Morris boldly asserted in some of his letters that are now printed, that alliteration had been in all ages in use amongst the Welsh Bards. Lewys Morris was a man of extreme ignorance in ancient Welsh literature, much as he pretended to the contrary. Much [of] the ignorant at present think otherwise of him. A man of unconquerable prejudice: witness the hard and long labour of his whole life to establish that romance of Geoffrey of Monmouth, and a number of other instances. Much as he affected the characters of poet and critic, he never had any skill in the Welsh versification of any period whatever. A raw schoolboy portion of knowledge in its more modern principles was all that he ever possessed, but in favour of his own systems; what audacious falsehood has he uttered in his letters to learned and candid English historians and antiquaries who applied to him for such information from the Welsh manuscripts as they wished to obtain, and which a man of any conscience would have honestly given. But to proceed in our research.

Gruffudd ap Cynan was undoubtedly acquainted with the scalds, spoke their language from his infancy, was versed in all their learning, in their principles of versification, and had acquired a taste for their poetry and its peculiarities of verse, turn of sentiment &c &c. Hence he might wish to transfer those (imagined) graces into the poetry of his own or the Welsh language. He had probably some experience of the animating effects of the scaldic heroic odes, and might wish to patronize an order of Bards or poets similar to the scalds in his own dominions to effect the same ends as were known to be effected by the runic poetry. This could not be effectually accomplished but by establishing a school of such poetry and an order of Bards similar to the scalds. This he did, and with complete success. That the poetry of the School of Gruffudd ap Cynan has a great number of characteristics derived from the scaldic poetry must be in the highest degree obvious to any unprejudiced critic, but there are persons of strong prejudices who are

(88) such hot-brained, self-dubbed critics, that will not admit that the Welsh poetry is in any particular instance derived from any other source than their own ancient (supposed to be divinely inspired) *Awen* (poetic genius) give every such person his own way. Indeed he will have it, whether we will or not.

Alliteration is not the only peculiarity of metre derived from the runic poetry. To begin, two or more lines together with the same letter is by the Welsh poets called *cydsaingymmeriad*, this was used by the scalds long before it appeared in the Welsh, three or four centuries at least.

The poetry of the scalds has a species of ferocious grandeur in its sentiments that is very remarkable. So has the poetry of the School of Gruffudd ap Cynan.

1. Arddwyrcaf hael o hil Iago –
A borthes branhes Brynaich gyffro
Gwalchmai 198

2 Dysgwedwn gwelsant ar gant celain
Am draeth Edrywy adryweded brain. – ib 200

3 Ar edrywedd gwaed gwaeddai gigfrain.
Marchogynt ar feirw fil frain
Marchogion Brynaich branhes Owain,
Calenig uddudd coludd celain. –
Y dan draed adar gwyr gwanar gwain,
Gweleis eu trychni trichant celain
Gweleis wedi cad coludd ar ddrain
Cynddelw, 204

(89)

Thus Englished:

1 I extol the liber descendant of Iago
Who fed the ravens with the carcases of his enemies.

2 I assert it, along the strands of Edrywy were seen,
On hundreds of the slain, the scenting ravens.

3 Loudly screamed the ravens in the scent of blood,
Thousands of Crows rode on the dead,
A feast to them were the entrails of carcases, –
Under the claws of birds of prey were seen men in whose bodies our sovereign sheathed his sword,
I have seen mangled three hundred carcases,
I have seen after the battle entrails hanging on the thorns

. . . **(91)** These are coincidences of such numerous particulars, of verse, of sentiment – in short, of the whole, of every idea in the poetry of the two nations – and nothing can be more clearly proved than that this species of heroic poetry existed amongst the Scandinavians several centuries before it appeared in the Welsh language, whence could we derive this kind of infernal sublimity; for sublimity we find the barbarian bards of our own age, and of (I am ashamed of my being a Briton) our own country have generally agreed to term it.

It is said by many of our writers, and I believe that what they say is true, that such heroic odes as these were sung to the harp in the hall of our princes when they met to rejoice and celebrate the victories they had won. But surely it will be allowed, by every one whose heart approaches in some degree to what should be found in a human breast, that Pandaemonium is the only place where such triumphs can be with propriety and full effect exhibited.

Passages indeed of less ferocious aspect might be selected from the Bards of this school, and lines that truly and uncommonly sublime in sense sufficiently good, others that are charmingly beautiful. And a beauty that would charm a ferocious barbarian runs through (we may generally say) the whole of the poetry of this school.

Whencesoever any thing in literature or science may be derived, it will bring along with it its concomitants. Hence most probably the Irish idioms, especially those of using auxiliaries instead of inflections in forming verbs, what **(92)** prevails considerably in, and is peculiar to north Wales. The Irish do the same. Hence, Irish words as *moch* (for mwth) *rhechdyr*, and others. Hence the Irish manner of forming compounds as *hindda*, *Gwrda*, *Pentir*, *y Borthwen*, *Treborth*, *minmor*, *minffordd*, *Llanfor*, *Coetmor*, *Llanycil*, *Penytir*, *Penyci*, *Cilgwyn*, *Mynyddfawr*, and many hundreds besides, unless we suppose that we derive them from the Irish invaders who settled in north Wales in the 5th century and continued there for almost 30 years, or 130 as other manuscripts say, till they were driven away by the sons of Cunedda Wledig, and afterwards by Caswallawn Lawhir. Great numbers however having been properly subjugated remained for ever in some parts of north Wales, particularly in Anglesey, where for a long time they kept themselves a separate people, often very troublesome to the Welsh natives and, as a nation, lost, but with a portion of their blood some traces or effects of their language permanently remain. If the accounts that many of our manuscripts contain of the achievements of the sons of Cunedda Wledig are pretty correct, it should seem that the Irish were at one time very generally spread over most parts of north Wales. We find also from history that a very considerable intercourse, and for the most part friendly, subsisted between north Wales and Ireland. This however is playing the truant and gadding out of Gruffudd ap Cynan's

School, wherein we must remain a little longer for what of further knowledge we want.

This school, as before observed, was the means of powerfully reviving the poetry of Wales that had been, as it were, dying away for almost two centuries. It selected the best and most grandly sounding of the metres and stanzas as the ancient schools, rejecting the less **(93)** dignified, and perhaps mistakenly in one instance, that of the ancient triplet (*englyn milwr*). This, tho' but simple in its form and the principles of its structure, possesses as it appears from the hands of Llywarch Hên, a dignity that is not common, and is susceptible of a rhythm that is at once easy, harmonious, and simply majestic. However in this school were a sufficient variety of our kinds of verse, and if adding to this variety had never been thought of, it would have been attended with advantages that may be said [to] be incalculable, when we lamentingly view the depredations which subsequent attempts at improvement have made on the Welsh poetical genius.

Tho' this school did not immediately extend itself into south Wales, yet it operated as a stimulus that produced a revival in the ancient school there, which probably would not have otherwise taken place.

The dialect of this school is much nearer the Silurian than any other Welsh dialect, and has absolutely nothing of what constitute the peculiarities of the modern Northwalian dialect. It obviously retains the dialect of the ancient schools, or the ancient literary dialect. How this happened to be the Silurian may thus [be] accounted for.

Caerleon in Siluria became the seat of government for many regal successions after the Romans had left Britain and the Britons had established an independent government. The dialect of that part of any country where government seats itself will infallibly become the court dialect, the fashionable dialect and thence the literary dialect. Thus being regularly formed, a number of literary works will in time appear in it, its words and its idioms will thus pass thro' a mint that will leave a permanent impression upon them and render them the only currencies of the language. Hence all the writings of the sixth century are in this dialect. This secured the same to works of succeeding times. A literary dialect being thus formed and permanently established, will not easily alter. It will not escape away; it is firmly bound up in the chains imposed upon it by literature. This having taken place, **(94)** let the sovereign courts and residencies remove to wherever choice or necessity may drive them; they will carry with them their own dialect of the national language; they will be attended by the literature of their country. Thus, tho' removed to a part of their dominions where a different dialect may be the popular one, or the *vernaculum*, they are under a necessity of retaining the more polished dialect, and they will also be strongly inclined to do so.

Owing to the incursions of the Saxons, or perhaps to other reasons elsewhere noticed, the supreme courts of the sovereignty retired into north Wales. They took along with them their own dialect and ever after retained it. Hence perceive why the Silurian dialect prevailed, at least in a greater degree than any other at the courts of all Welsh Princes both north and south Wales, and it is also very possible that being the court dialect of Caerleon, it might have been adopted by all the inferior princely courts of Wales and of every part of the island, before the seat of supreme government ceased to be at Caerleon. The English court may remove to any part of Scotland, of Wales, of Ireland, or even to where it will be more dangerous to Exmore or Zumuzetzhire, but it will carry with it its firmly established cultivated dialect of London and for ever retain it, in whatever dialect the surrounding rustics may converse.

The Northwalian dialect was never, at least but very sparingly, admitted into the national literature till the native princes and their royal courts were no more. It however began to appear conspicuously in poetry about the middle of the 13th century and not much before, but even so late as this Dafydd Ddu o Hiraddug wrote entirely in the Silurian dialect, tho' if not a native, he had long resided in north Wales on his benefice of Dinmeirchion. **(95)**

This school may be peculiarly termed the Ancient School of north Wales, because it never extended itself much into south Wales. There was indeed at the time of its commencement, or soon after, one of its pupils in south Wales, Gwynfardd Brycheiniog. In its second century we find Philip Brydydd and Prydydd Bychan, and besides these it does not at present occur to me that south Wales had any Bards of this school. Prose writing was however cultivated in south Wales and, it should seem, exclusively. Geoffrey of Monmouth, Caradoc of Lancarvan, Walter de Mapes, author of an ingenious little tract (for the age) on husbandry were Southwalians, so to all appearance were the writers of our old romances, at least as far as can be infer'd from dialects, the heroes and scenes of their tales &c, for no names of authors appear to them. The medical writers of Myddfai were also about the year 1200, so that the literary school of south Wales was a prose-writing school, not a poetical one. It is true south Wales had some poets thro' the whole of this period but they never greatly distinguished themselves as such, and the few that were must be considered as of the ancient School of Taliesin and the continuators of it. One Southwalian poet indeed, Rhys Goch ap Rhiccert, seems to have so much originality in his poems and manner, that I have ventured to put him at the head of a Southwalian School, having objects of indeed a more humble nature and much less sublimity in almost every respect than the School of north Wales, but more congenial to civilized humanity. These objects were rural description, rural and domestic manners, gallantry &c, and I have given some reason for supposing it, in some degree, a **(96)** branch of the school of the Provençal troubadours.

To the ancient schools no locality can be attached. They [were] peculiarly, neither of north or of south Wales, but equally common to each.

During the 12th, 13th and 14th centuries every thing was poetry in north Wales, and south Wales all prose. These are singular appearances, but I believe that facts will warrant my assertion. Not a single prose writer can I find during those centuries that can be ascertained to have been of north Wales, but the Northwalian Bards were numerous. In addition to those already mentioned, must be added Dafydd Benfras, Einiawn ap Gwgawn, Einiawn Wann, Einiawn ap Gwlachmai, Meilir ap Gwlachmai, Gwgawn, Gruffudd Llygad Gwr, Llywelyn Fardd, Bleddyn Fardd, Gruffudd ap Gwrgeneu, Einiawn ap Madawc Rhahawd, Hywel Voel ap Griffri, Gwilym Ddu Arfon, Llywarch Llaetty, and I believe many more.

Of the productions of these poets we have about 200 pieces most of them of considerable length, and in general, well preserved. Time has injured a few of them. Perhaps a few poets of this period may be found in north Wales that belong more properly to the Ancient School of Taliesin than to that of Gruffudd ap Cynan. In south Wales also a few Taliesinian Bards may also be found, amongst [them] Madawc ap Gwallter the Friar, for by his language I conceive him to have been a Southwalian; not indeed from the general cast of it for I have before observed that all the Northwalian Bards till a late period wrote in a Southwalian dialect; but from many local or provincial words of a comparatively recent age that are still common in south Wales, and never were so in north Wales. **(97)**

These not being derived from either the popular dialect of north Wales, or the ancient, are that period generally retained, literary dialect, must have been taken up from the popular language of his native place, or, at least of his place of residence.

The school of Gruffudd ap Cynan was very bold, metaphorical, strongly figurative, and rich in its language. Its compounds and abstracts are energetic, concise, and very beautifully and luminously express their intended ideas, and in this respect it has preserved uninjured and unrelaxed the gigantic nerves of the Welsh language, nothing inferior in this respect to the school of Taliesin at its most flourishing period. It exhibited a nice judgement in selecting the best of our ancient metres for its use, but otherwise added nothing to our versification. This was not amongst its objects, which were to inspire the Welsh of that age with a ferocity of character that was thought necessary to enable them to make a tolerable stand against their enemies, to excite in them a mortal hatred of the Saxons, and the Franks, as the Normans were termed by them. Hence it is that we meet with but very few instances of gallantry in this school. All the gentler and more genial affections of human nature were made to give way to [a] ferociously martial ardour, to the higher delight of plentifully feeding thousands of wolves, dogs, eagles, ravens, cormorants &c with the flesh and blood of their enemies, of their detested Saxons. Next to these enjoyments those of the mead horn engaged them, over which in frantically energetic song they triumphed over the sons of Alis, over the spawn of Rowena, for it was such epithets that those bards bestowed on the Kings of England.

The benign effects of the Roman civilization, thro' four centuries of the most luminous period of which our language and literature had passed, and which were strongly impressed on the School of Taliesin, made not the least **(98)** appearance in the School of Gruffudd ap Cynan. The literature of this school was that of barbarians, a perfect counterpart of the learning of those lettered savages, the runic scalds. A thought, yes a truth, occurs to me, and how sorry am I to utter it. Many of our modern literary savages, of our English bards and of their readers – what a shame! – have a wonderful penchant, a strong predilection, for such poetry as we have had under consideration. We see this in their fondness for the diabolical runic poetry, for what is equally diabolical in many parts of Homer, let them study the Welsh language and read the poetry of Gruffudd ap Cynan's School, and they will be gratified to [the] utmost extent of their infernalized wishes.

Such was the poetry of north Wales and Powys in those ages, the effects of it on the manners and morals of the peoples and of their governors were such as might be naturally expected: what castrating of brothers, uncles, cousins! What putting out of their eyes! What murdering of such relatives, giving their bodies to the dogs! were practiced perpetually by the house of Mathrafal and Aberffraw? What numberless things besides, horrid to relate. What a villain was Gruffudd ap Cynan himself? Let us turn our eyes for a moment to the poetry of our Primitive or Druidical School of which we have very considerable remains. In this we see expressed in language, almost to a miracle impressive, the most benign principles of morality, sentiments the most friendly to human nature; maxims the most friendly to the well-being of society, the most powerfully inculcative of justice, benevolence, peace, truth, and general good order.

From a huge aggregate of evil a little good will sometimes proceed. The school of Gruffudd ap Cynan kept **(99)** literature alive in north Wales when to all appearances nothing else could have effected such an end. It has given such specimens of poetical description, in its own sceneries, as cannot be surpassed, I believe, by any thing in the whole poetical world. Such animation, such strength and, at the same time, such justness of language and expression, such truth of colouring, as can not be well conceived by such [as] are not able to read those poems in their original language.

In the first century of its existence it was temperate in the use of alliteration and other embellishments that border on the false; in the last years of its life it ran into unpolished extravagancies that has communicated a taint of unnatural refinement to all subsequent schools.

It has left nothing peculiarly of being copied in its principles, unless we mention its boldly figurative and elliptical language, its elliptical metaphors, almost unknown to any language (perhaps) besides the Welsh. But these, I think, would at this day [be] of softer and more natural elegance. It is a recommendable thing, I believe, to make use always of such words, expressions, figures, &c as may with sufficient ease, be translated into other languages, without recurring to the unfortunate expedient of an awkward and nerveless periphrasis. Every language should be friendly to its neighbours, keep in idiom and construction as neat to them as purity can admit. Languages should so accommodate each other that what appears in one may be with [?ease] transfer'd into the other. What practicability may attach to such ideas, I know not, it must be decided by those of whose number I am not: the learned in languages.

For my own part, I know of nothing so far beyond the verge of possibility, as the translating of the Welsh of the poetry of Gruffudd ap Cynan's School into any kind of English that would have its strength exhausted before it arrived at the very distant end of periphrasis: dreadfully long, and yet this Welsh is, in itself, very luminous, and very minute and discriminative in every particular circumstance. **(100)**

In the poetry of this school there are some, tho' not many, traces of the Druidical mythology.

The theology of it is, with respect to the object of worship, monotheistical in a tolerable degree of purity as the Druidical as well as the Primitive Christian was. This is elsewhere more amply treated of and exemplified; but in other respects its god was the god of war, of blood, of carnage, and his favourites those who were the most successful in destroying their brethren who had the same god as themselves for a father, or in other words they believed in and prayed to a God who delighted in such of his children who the most remorselessly murdered the others. How strikingly similar to the practice of our modern, equally savage theologists, whose temples are decorated with the trophies of human carnage, whose Kings repair to those temples to worship their God of rapine and murder.

The most ancient Bards of whose works we have any remains, opened their poems most commonly, with an adorative address to the deity! Examples of this are numerous, and this practice was retained in the School of Gruffudd ap Cynan. Some of the passages that exhibit this are highly poetical. See elsewhere.

It should be observed that the popish theology was not admitted into the bardic schools, at least systematically, till the 15th century, wherein, and even in the preceding century, we find that many of our most celebrated Bards were professed Lollards, as Dafydd ap Gwilym, Sion Cent, &c even in the darkest ages the craft-pillar'd Church of Rome considered our Bards as heretics, and sometimes excommunicated them, as in the instance of Cynddelw, to whom the Monks of Ystrad Marchell denied what in the lying language of their religion, was called a Christian burial. **(101)**

As more immediately connected with the history of this school, I must here expose a wilful mistake of Mr Walker the historian of the Irish Bards. I say wilful, because I cannot think so meanly of that gentleman's understanding as to believe otherwise of it, and when the alternative is unavoidable, there are but few who would rather be called knave than fool. His words, p. 103, are thus:

Caradoc (of Lancarvan) The Welsh Historian, says that 'Gruffudd ap Conan when he determined to regulate and reform the Welsh Bards, brought over with him from Ireland many Irish Bards for this purpose' – What an Irish Blunder!! But I fear that is something worse. – One of Dr Powel's notes to his translation of Caradoc is as follows, pp. 191–192, speaking of Gruffudd ap Cynan:

> He reformed the disordered behaviour of the Welsh Minstrels, by a very good statute which is extant to this daye.
>
> There are three sorts of Minstrels in Wales,
>
> I. The first sort named *Beirdh*, which are makers of songs and odes of sundrie measures, wherein not only Great skill and cunning is required; but also a certaine natural inclination and gift, which in Latin is termed *Juror poeticus*, These do also keep records of Gentlemens arms and pedigrees, and are best esteemed and accounted of among them.
>
> II. The second sort of them are plaiers upon instruments, chiefly the Harp and the Crowth, whose musicke, for the most part came to Wales with the said *Gruffudd ap Cynan*, who being on the one side an *Irishman* by his mother and Grandmother, and also borne in Ireland, brought over with him out of that Countrie divers **(102)** cunning musicians into *Wales* who devised in a manner all the instrumental music that is now there used, as appeareth as well by the bookes writte of the same as also by the names of the Tunes and measures used among them to this daie.
>
> III. The third sort called *Atcaniad*, are those which do sing to the Instrument plaied by another, and these be in use in the Countrie of Wales to this daie.

Wonderful indeed must be the sagacity of that man who can discover from anything that has been here said that Irish Bards came over from Ireland [to] teach or reform the Welsh Bards. According to Mr Walker's account, the Irish Bards played also on musical instruments, or were musicians as well as poets. I hope for his own credit that he will admit it to have been so. Now we shall see the consequence.

It appears from what Dr Powel's note says that the first order of Welsh minstrels called mere poets, or as he says, makers of songs and odes, and also genealogists, and of all the three distinct, not blended professions, were the best esteemed and accounted of.

Of the second order who were performers on musical instruments, and not Bards, Dr Powel says that their music, and that only, as appeareth by the names of the tunes and measures, came from Ireland, but not the instruments, for these had for ages been previously known to the Welsh.

The Bard was not a humstrum as well as a poet in Wales, but a very different and very superior character. In short, he was strictly forbidden the practice of instrumental music, as the harper and crowder were also forbidden to exercise the functions of the Bard.

But some of the Welsh writers, tho' not Caradoc, admit that Gruffudd ap Cynan introduced something into Wales from Ireland. It is from these writers that Dr Powel compiled his **(103)** very correct note.

In the Llandegai copy of the Statute of Gruffudd ap Cynan we have the following passage. It would be well for Mr Walker's system if he could contrive to suppress it.

'The *Poets*, otherwise termed Bards, and Men of vocal Song, and of Information, were from the Country of Wales aborigine, and it was from them that the *Hibernians* derived their vocal song and its scientific principles of Song. The Men of instrumental, or of string music came from Ireland in the time of Gruffudd ap Cynan and of King Stephen and the regulations that were made respecting these were subjected to those of the Bards or men of Vocal Song, and for this reason, No degrees in Music can be confer'd but in the meetings or sittings of the Men of Vocal Song, for it is not incumbent on the men of string music to read the Welsh Language and to write it correctly, for which reason, they do not possess the essential and requisite qualifications for preserving the Memorials and knowledge of the Laws and regulations to which they ought to be subjected.'

There is excellent sense and very sound reasons, in this passage, and we are informed who, and for what reasons, the men of string song are considered as of inferior respectability, and rendered subordinate to the Bards or men of vocal song, because it is to be supposed from the nature of their professions that they cannot read the Welsh language and write it correctly, but without this indispensable qualification none could be admitted a Bard. It was necessary that a Bard's wit should be in his brain, but if the man of string-song had wit at his fingers' ends it would do very well . . . **(112)**

In the foregoing passage, and the note preceding it of Dr Powel, nothing appears more clear than that the Bard and the musician were different characters and of distinct professions. The following passages from the same statute make it more clearly so:

'It is secured that none shall engage in two professions, or practice two arts, such as poetry and music or playing upon the harp, or employ themselves in any trade or science but that which is their own, on pain of being deprived of their immunities, and of losing all the benefits of their professions, until they became conformable to the Laws.'

If, as Mr Walker says, the professions of poetry and music were inseparably united in his Bards, it will follow that the Irish and the Welsh Bards were very different characters, things of very different institutions. Had Irish Bards (if Ireland had any Bards at that time) been brought over by Gruffudd ap Cynan to act in part with him relating to what he was about to establish in Wales, they would have proposed something like their own institution, but the little Bardic code of Gruffudd ap Cynan was a very different thing, and whoever were the agents of its establishment the Irish Bards were not, had nothing to do with it. The truths in the statute of Gruffudd ap Cynan profess itself to be only a revival of the ancient laws and institutes for regulating the Bards, not a new thing – much less an Irish-sprung thing – as we see clearly evinced by its not being a code of blunderism. The Welsh Bard was not permitted to practice music professionally. He most probably **(113)** might for his private amusement, but this will prove (in the language of Paddy) nothing at all, at all. If a Bard in violation of this law practiced music, he was degraded, deprived of the power of exercising his functions of Bard and memorialist, for these were two professions inseparably united. The statute adds:

'The Bard must be able to read the Welsh language and to write it correctly, he must also be well acquainted with the laws that regulate men of vocal song, and the men of string music. He should be of good learning, of good memory, and of good morals.'

Another clause of the statute says that when a Bard composed a song or ode in honour of any distinguished person, he should not send it by a man of string music. This was esteemed degrading to the Bard, and disrespectful to the personage to whom it was sent, or addressed. Walker again has something curious:

'The Irish Bards had not been long in Wales, when there occurred an opportunity of displaying their skill, – in the year 1176 a great feast was made in the Castle of Cardigan by Rhys ap Gruffudd, to which all the Poets or Bards of Wales, were invited. Here poetical contests were held, in which the Bards of North Wales (amongst whom it is natural to suppose our Countrymen were predominant) won the Prizes.'

'It natural to suppose'! It is fact, but not very natural, that some suppose what is glaringly untrue. Where facts are not positively declared, it is natural enough for national prepossession to suppose in its own favour! The clearly recorded fact is that only the Bards and musicians of Wales had been invited to the feast at Cardigan Castle in 1176, where the Bards of north Wales won the mastery, or the men of vocal song of north Wales, as Caradoc terms them, but the men of music of Prince Rhys' own household excelled all others. If there were any from Ireland at these contests they must have **(114)** been men of music, who are expressly called harpers, fiddlers or crowders, and pipers by the historian, who in contradistinction terms the men of vocal song, poets. But harpers and crowders were not received and respected as Bards by Prince Rhys. If there were any poets from Ireland there they must have been skilled in the Welsh language and Bardic literature, must have been admitted as Bards of the Welsh institution. Of course tho' Irish men, they were not Irish Bards, for such Bards Ireland never had; at least we hope so for the credit of Mr Walker, for he would feel very awkwardly if on proof of the existence of such Bards, his book should turn out to be a mere humbug.

That the Irish had poets and musicians is certainly true; that they had some ancient regulations and institutions for the cultivation of those arts is admitted, at least for arguments sake, but that such institutions were in any thing similar to the Druidic or Bardic institutions of Britain does not in the least appear. They are obviously of a very different origin, founded on very different principles. Even the words Druid, Bard &c as Irish terms occur not in Mr Walker's book or any terms that are in any degree similar or that can be supposed to have any etymological affinity with our British terms. Thus for the technology, we may also say of our British Bardic theology, mythology, Bardic discipline, and of the Bardic literature in general, that nothing of these things have the least affinity in terms or principle with any thing of Ireland. Music, as I have already shown, is with us a very different thing from Bardism; but of our music it is not clear to me that we derive any thing except a few tunes from Ireland, (compare both institutions, in term, principles, and polity.)

One Jones, who most curiously nicknames himself Bard and harpist to the Prince of Wales, Poor Prince, how many coxcombs are there of this, that, and t'other thing, to the Prince of Wales, to the King &c – what impudence!

This Jones however has heaped a mixon in the guise of a pretty large book, a jumble of inconsistencies and falsehoods, beg'd, borrow'd and stolen, from every quarter whence he was able so to collect them. He, like Mr Walker, has made his Bards humstrums as well as rhymers, and this in **(115)** direct and intentional violation of the most obvious truths that stared him in the face in hundreds of authentic Welsh manuscripts that were before his eyes.

We have some hundreds of elegies on bards of every age from the 10th to the 16th centuries. The writers of those elegies are very particular and minutely so in their mention of the learning and abilities of the deceased Bard, but I have never met with any mention of his being a performer on any kind of musical instrument, or any thing in the most distant manner alluding to any such practice but his great skill in the Welsh language, in the principles of its poetry, versification, &c. His knowledge of the Bardic institutes, the Bardic traditions or memorialities, of history in general, of genealogies, of theology, of morality, of the arts of pacification, are very amply detailed. We have also elegies on harpers, crowders &c. They mention their musical skill, their performances on the harp, the crowd &c, but not a syllable of their being Bards, poets, or men of vocal song.

It is one of the Grand Blunders of the age to believe and assert that the British Bards were, as well as poets, performers on the harp. This mistake originates probably in the account which in Homer appears of Demodocus, who is represented as a poet and musician, and many a good Grecian, many a one learned in Homer, will frequently be found to be in every thing else, one of the most ignorant fellows under heaven. The ancient English minstrels are also said to have united in themselves the professions of poetry and music, but the learned Bishop of Dromore in his ingenious essay on the ancient minstrels pp. XXIII–IX informs us that the poet and musician were different persons, of two different professions.

The troubadours of Provençe were poets and otherwise literary characters, not musicians. The jongleurs on the contrary were minstrels, or performers on musical instruments and if in a very few instances both professions appear to have been united in the same person, it was considered as very **(116)** irregular, not an institutional practice. For these two different professions seem clearly to have subjected themselves to a system that had tacitly formed itself into a regular institution, and such perhaps is the origin of every institution. It had by a series of natural occurrences and concurrencies fallen together one part as it were attracting the other to it, before it had been premeditatedly noticed. Laws might subsequently establish formally what had been found by experience beneficial or interesting.

It may however be correct that, in some institutions, whether premeditatedly or, as it were, fortuitously formed, the poet and musician were united in the same character or profession. This appears to have been the case with the northern scalds who were at once the theologues and moralists of their countrymen, in whom the characters of historian genealogist, poet, and musician were all united, and perhaps it was the same in Ireland. Let it however be enquired whether Ireland in these things derives not more than has been hitherto acknowledged from the Danes and their scalds who settled therein.

In the poetry of our more ancient schools we find theological and moral sentiments that are extremely beautiful, and expressed in neat and, at the same time nervous language; but with a chasteness of figure and trope that induces us to think that our Bards had taken lessons of elegance and good taste from the Roman writers, with whose works they must have been well acquainted during the four centuries at least that their country had been a province of the Roman Empire, and one of the principal Roman colonies was in Wales, Caerleon. But the glaringly bold metaphors, **(117)** similes, and general imagery of the School of Gruffudd ap Cynan are so strikingly of the same character as what we find in the scaldic poetry, that no doubt can remain of its being thence derived. Nothing of the kind had ever before appeared in the Welsh poetry. The scalds call the tongue,

> 'The sword of words'
> – (Mallets *Northern Antiquities*. Vol I, 395.)

Dafydd ap Gwilym calls the tongue,

> *cleddau cerdd, celwyddawg* coch, and
> *llafn milain*, i.e.
> the sword of song, lying red thing,
> blade of brutality

The scalds term a ship,

> 'The horse of the waves' (Mallett Vol I, 395).

Cynddelw says,

> Gwyddfeirdd tonn torrynt yn ertai.
> The wooden steeds of the waves were broken at low ebb.

and Llywarch ap Llywelyn has,

> *Meirch Mordwy uwch mawrdwrf tonniar*
> The steeds of the sea on the loud roar of waves

And numberless instances of this nature might be given. These modes of expression were most certainly introduced into the Welsh poetry by the School of Gruffudd ap Cynan. **(118)**

The scaldic principles of versification were also introduced into Wales by this school. It established alliteration as a requisite of verse, and also another peculiarity of verse called in Welsh *cynghanedd lusc*, which consists in having a correspondent sound of vowels or consonants between the syllable of a preceding pause and the last syllable but one in the verse in Welsh thus:

Ac gwellygiaw PWYLL rytWYLLo
Gogynf. 299
CAR yn cyhuddaw ARall. Tudur Aled
Y fERCH ni chwsg ai GwERCHyd,
D.G[m].

And in Icelandic thus

Austur LONDum for UNDum
AVALDur sa er gof SKALDum
SLydyr TUNGur let SLINGra,
SVEKD leiks reigen FERDar
Ex Von Troil's Iceland

And Oläus Womrius gives the following specimen of it in Latin,

ChrISTus Caput nOSTrum
CorONet te BONis.

(119) It will, I am pretty confident, be a difficult thing to find any instances of similar characteristics of verse in any Welsh poetry before the time of Gruffudd ap Cynan. Or if something of such a nature may be found, it will, I trust, appear always to be a thing of chance rather than of intention.

The learned Bishop of Dromore, one of the most candid writers that ever existed, has in his remarks on a passage in the Edda of Snorro the following observation (pp.197, 198 &c):

'I am led to think that the latter Welsh Bards might possibly have been excited to cultivate the alliterative versification more strictly, from the example of the scalds, and their imitators the Anglo-Saxon poets, because the more ancient British Bards were nothing near so exact and strict in their alliteration, as those in the middle and later ages; particularly after the Norman conquest of England, and even after Edward the firsts conquest of Wales; ⋆ whereas some centuries before this the Icelandic metre had been brought to the highest pitch of alliterative exactness. This conjecture, however, that the Welsh Bards borrowed any thing from the poets of any other country, will hardly be allowed me by the British antiquaries, who, from a laudable partiality, are jealous of the honour of their countrymen; **(120)** nor is it worth contending for. It is sufficient to observe that a spirited emulation between the Bards and the scalds, might excite each of them to improve their own native poetry and to give it all that artificial polish, which they saw admired in the other language.'

On this passage his Lordship has the following note,

⋆ 'A very learned and ingenious British antiquary thus informs me.'

'Our prosody depends entirely on what you call alliteration, and which our Grammarians term *cynghanedd*, i.e. *concentus, vel symphonia consonantica.* This at first was not very strict; for the Bards of the sixth century used it very sparingly, and were not circumscribed by any rules. The Bards from the Norman conquest to the death of Llewelyn our last Prince were more strict. But from thence to Queen Elizabeth's time, the rules of alliteration were used with great nicety, so that a line not perfectly alliterative, is condemned as much by our Grammarians as a false quantity by the Greeks and Romans.'

'I can by no means think that our Bards have borrowed their alliteration from the scalds of the North, for there are traces of it in some very old pieces of the Druids, still extant, which I am persuaded are older than the introduction of Christianity, and were composed long before we had any Commerce or intercourse with the **(121)** inhabitants of Scandinavia, or of any branch of the Gothic Race whatever, and I believe before the Roman Conquest.'

I wish for the honour of my country that there were a little more truth in what this Welsh correspondent of Dr Percy says, for I feel a little of the partiality to my native land and language which his Lordship's politely honours with the epithet of laudable, but I have also some partiality for truth. 'A Scotsman', says Dr Johnson, 'must be a sturdy moralist indeed, if he loves not Scotland better than truth.' How justly might he have said the same thing of every Welsh antiquary that has hitherto appeared in the world. (Edward Williams)

'The Bards of the sixth century used it very sparingly,' says Mr Evans, for I think it was he tho' his name is not given. All these assertions are in his manner, but let me ask in what piece of any bard of the 6th century was alliteration ever used otherwise than in a line of mere chance? 'There are traces of it in some very old pieces of the Druids, which are older than the introduction of Christianity – before the Roman conquest.'

I have seen, I believe, as much of the ancient Welsh poetry as any man living, and I believe much more than ever Mr Evans saw, and I never met with any thing that appeared older to me than the fifth century. But of whatever age they may be, they most certainly are not alliterative, otherwise than in a line by accident. **(122)**

But admitting that some of our oldest ethical triplets might be of a date anterior to Christianity and even the Roman conquest, yet to allow them to be in any degree alliterative, is so glaringly an untruth that any child that could, not indeed read, but only look at the Welsh triplets written on paper, must have seen the contrary. These old things are in a very simple and very rude kind of verse ending generally every line in polysyllabic words with single rhymes, and the language is also much more rude, or at least more simple, than any thing in the poems of the sixth century, having no rhyming pauses, such as we find in the works of Aneurin, Taliesin, Merlin, &c, and it is those pauses and not consonantal alliteration, that were the embellishments of verse in the sixth century and down to the eleventh.

The learned Bishop is perfectly correct when he says that the scaldic alliteration had arrived at its height of perfection long before any thing of the kind appeared in the Welsh poetry. How unfortunately did he apply the epithets 'very learned and ingenious' to the man who could assert the contrary! On one who well knew that he was giving such information as was not true. How many truly learned and ingenious literary gentlemen applied to Mr Evans and also to his fibmonger Lewis Morris, for information relating to Welsh literature and Welsh antiquities, and how many of the most glaring falsehoods have they had in return from those fellows, who never turned their thoughts to anything relating to the ancient Welsh manuscripts but to that fruitless endeavour of vindicating Geoffrey of Monmouth's romance? This was the labour of their whole **(123)** lives. Of the more ancient principles of our versification they appear to have known nothing at all, otherwise they would never have refer'd ethical Triplets that were beyond a doubt written in the 14th century to a period anterior to Christianity or the Roman conquest. For this, with Mr Edward Llwyd, who also knew nothing of the Welsh versification, they did. Evans and Morris had some, but indeed very slender, knowledge of the versification of later ages, even not enough to enable them thence to judge of the authenticity of a poem only two hundred years old. This may be deemed bold in me. It is so. It is high time for somebody to be so, and on the assertions that I here make, I risk my character as a man of veracity, in opposition to all the puny brood of Welsh critics, who, for their own credit, I hope know something more of their Greek and Latin than they do of any thing that is Welsh.

Mr Evans adds, speaking of our old triplets, 'they mention the oak, high mountains, and snow, with honour, those are certainly remains of the pagan Creed.' My observations must be that there is not a word of truth in all this. The snowy mountains it is true are mentioned, not with any view to honour them, not with any reference to a religious creed, but on a very different idea, on which I have offered my conjectures elsewhere. But where is the oak mentioned otherwise than as the largest most useful of our forest trees, the noblest object in our woods and fields, just as English Poets mention it?

The field of Welsh antiquities has been, by those who in a more proper sense [rather] hognosed it up than cultivated it, sown, thickly sown, and planted with the rankest and most pernicious weeds. To eradicate these I find will be a hard labour, but I must endeavour to ring their noses, and, if possible, to check their depredations. I am ready for the obloquy that awaits me. **(124)**

Lewis Morris in his *Celtic Remains* (under Achlach) gives the following account:

'Achlach – Glynn Achlach, in Ireland, where in 1096, under Mwrchan and Gruffudd ap Cynan, the Irish and Welsh Musicians! met, and settled the Rules of Composition.'

In this short account we have no mention of bards or poets being there. And in the old manuscript tracts on instrumental music, all of them without a single exception that I have hitherto met with, represent the meeting in Glynn Achlach as one of musicians only. And in all the copies that I have yet seen of the Statute of Gruffudd ap Cynan (excepting the very modern and interpolated copy of Llan de Gai), there is no intimation given of its having originated in Glynn Achlach. There is no mention of such a place in it, or of any other place in Ireland.

After all, the copies of this statute now in existence are obviously of a much later period; the language, idiom, and words, of English etymology clearly evince this. What ancient copies may be hitherto undiscovered in ancient unexplored libraries I know not. In many Southwalian copies it is asserted that this little system (and it is a very good one) was drawn up by Llawdden at the desire of Gruffudd ap Nicolas for the use of his Bardic establishment at Carmarthen in 1452. The language is obviously of that age. It is peculiarly adapted to the manners and political circumstances of that period, to the state of the Welsh poetry and its principles of versification **(125)** in that age, and notwithstanding the minute and long continued enquiries that I have made, I have never heard of a single copy that appears to have been written before that period. That Llawdden might have some broken fragments of either written documents or oral traditions, may be very possible, is indeed highly probable, and those attributed to Gruffudd ap Cynan. But if he had ever instituted any regulations for the Bards, it must appear very strange to all that neither the historians of that age, or either of the numerous Northwalian Bards of the court of Gruffudd ap Cynan, allude in the least to any such thing, but the instrumental musicians have always uniformly mentioned the musical meeting in Glynn Achlach, and of the regulations therein made. But this is always exclusively of every thing relating to bards or poets. That these regulations originated in Ireland is evident from the technology of the system there adopted and established, almost every term is purely Irish, and not understood etymologically by Welsh, but nothing of such a cast appears in the Bardic regulations. The professed and copious biographer of Gruffudd ap Cynan is absolutely silent on this point. We admit that Gruffudd ap Cynan appointed good regulations for musicians. Bleddyn ap Cynfyn before him made laws for the regulations of genealogies. Genealogy was a part of the Bardic profession. A manuscript tract attributed to Caradoc of Lancarvan (not his more generally known history) says that Rhys ap Tewdwr made laws for regulating the Bards and that they were inscribed on stone tablets in front of his palace. I admit that the authority of this manuscript is doubtful, but it is certainly more admissible in history than the absolute silence of all writers, whether in prose or verse, respecting Gruffudd ap Cynan. A junction possibly of what those three princes did might have been the rude materials with which Llawdden formed his little neat code of Bardic laws . . . **(132)**

School of Welsh Poetry: Primitive School

To the Primitive School belongs the method in its origin of inscribing upon wood, at least so far as we may depend [on] the testimonies of our ancient writers. The etymologies of a great number of words in our language also evince this very clearly. *Celwydd, gwyddor, dedwydd, celwydd,* or *egwyddor, hywydd, arwydd, coelbren, gwŷdd, dedwydd, derwydd, gwyddon, gwyddor, allwyddau cerdd,* and a great many others, are words derived, either from, or in allusion to, this custom or practice; or from nothing at all that has the least appearance of good sense; from nothing but the most silly and unmeaning caprice, and yet these words are found in our most ancient writers. Indeed the very nature of the thing itself bespeaks a very high antiquity. It is highly probable that any, after the more convenient method of writing upon parchment, and the papyrus had been introduced by the Romans so early as the first century, would have racked his brains to no useful purpose in the invention of such a method of using letters. Or if he had that a whole nation should agree to adopt it in preference to the Roman method; a hundred times more expeditious in the writing, as well as in the preparation, of the materials whereon to write, for skins of sheep of lambs of kids, &c could be prepared and manufactured into parchment with much greater facility than wood in their manner of using it, or in any other manner. But having been invented and brought into pretty general practice before the use of the **(133)** other method before parchment and ink were known it would maintain its ground afterwards for a long while, even for ages. For all nations feel a strong prepossession in favour of their own peculiar arts and sciences, are stubbornly retentive of them, and when after a great length of time they are prevailed upon to adopt better principles, their antiquaries will still retain a predilection for these things, will study and preserve the knowledge of them; and that curiosity which excites every man to enquire into the antiquities of his own nation of whatever kind they may be, is very natural, is found amongst all the nations of the world, and is also very commendable. He that never turned his thoughts to the operations and progressive improvements of the human mind in different ages and places, of the origin and gradual progress towards perfection of the arts and sciences, has no mind of his own that will ever be susceptible of any improvement, beyond what may be exited by the mere animal sensualities that call for their gratifications, beyond the brutalities of the worst kinds of haughty ambition and of purse-proud wealth.

The Primitive School was completely superseded in north Wales by that of Gruffudd ap Cynan, so it was in Dimetia. Indeed this school might with equal propriety be termed the School of Rhys ap Tewdwr, for it is according to some ancient manuscript copies confessedly the joint establishment of Rhys ap Tewdwr and Gruffudd ap Cynan. And whatever may be thought of the Glynn Achlach School, **(134)** which was the only one of Gruffudd ap Cynan, it was rather a thing of Ireland than of Wales, and it is very clear from History that Rhys ap Tewdwr, and his son Gruffudd ap Rhys were the first that established this school in north Wales and Dimetia, or perhaps only in Dimetia. The name of Bleddyn ap Cynfyn is a mere humbug. This school however prevailed over all north Wales and the Dimetian part of south Wales or principality of Dinevor, so that what remained of the Primitive School, and of that of Taliesin are henceforth only to be found in Glamorgan and its dependencies. Gwrgant ap Rhŷs Caradoc Llancarvan, and a few others, of whose works we have a few pieces and fragments remaining, are the continuators of this ancient school. About 1130 flourished Rhŷs Goch ap Rhiccert, ap Einion ap Collwyn in Glamorgan. He, for the most part, if not wholly, retained the metres and manner of the older schools, but in his poems we find a cast of gallantry which had not before been to any considerable degree admitted into the Welsh poetry, at least as far as can be judged now from what remains of our old poetry. In this poet's sentiments and manner we find something of the manner of the Provençal troubadours. The Norman barons who had settled in Glamorgan were those who opened the way for this new cast in poetry. Their castles or courts were the gates thro' which it entered into Wales. Be this as it may, we about this period observe **(135)** a remarkable change in subjects and turns of sentiments, in our poetry, in the works of Rhŷs Goch ap Riccert the clear dawn of this new manner appears, which in a century and a half afterwards brightened into the bright summer's noon of Dafydd ap Gwilym. Thus founded by Rhŷs Goch ap Rhiccert, and beautifully superstructed by Dafydd ap Gwilym, we see a new school established in the Silurian district of Wales, differing greatly from such as preceded it but much more congenial to human nature in its civilized state. This school must now be considered as distinct from all others, and treated of as such.

The Primitive School however maintained its ground in Glamorgan in some degree till the close of the sixteenth century, and indeed till the seventeenth had advanced one third at least. Its metres, its manner, its subjects &c appear conspicuously in the poems of Thomas ab Ifan ap Rhys who died about 1612, if not later. Wiliam Cap Du and five or six more were his cotemporaries and his survivors in this school. Edward ab Evan o Ben y Fai, the last pupil of it, lived so late as 1650, or later. The subsequent traces that remain are very faint, but there are a few of them, to this day they are not entirely obliterated.

Morality and religion have been chiefly the objects of this school in all ages. It also recorded the historical events of the nation, but it did this in a manner widely different from the practice of most other nations. It adhered severely to simple truth, admitted nothing that can be compared to the fictions and machineries that are deemed by most other nations so essential to narrative poetry and indispensably requisite. If it were said that truth on all occasions, was its grand object, its only object and inviolably so, we should, I believe, find this to be the true and definite character of our Primitive School of poetry. **(136)** It is as curious a circumstance as any one that occurs in the history of our ancient Bards that Robert Duke of Normandy should appear as a pupil of this school, but we have it on respectable authority. The anecdote is related in a manuscript account of the Lords Marchers of Glamorgan from Robert Fitzhamon to Jasper Duke of Bedford, and as the writer of this account could not be excited by either personal interest or national vanity to invent any thing of this nature, we see no good reason for suspecting the truth of this account. It is to be found in a genealogical manuscript in the possession of the late Mr Truman of Pantlliwydd near Cowbridge in Glamorgan. It contains an account (amongst a great many other things) of the successions, genealogies &c, with some historical anecdotes of the Lords of Glamorgan.

XI: Schools of Welsh poetry, a sketch (NLW 13098B, 87–90)

This essay concentrates mainly on the medieval schools and highlights the north-south tension at bardism's heart, and the skaldic influence on the 'barbarians' of north Wales.

It is not improbable but that what remained in manuscript or retained by oral tradition, or rather Bardic tradition, of the most ancient of our Bards, as Taliesin &c, with the various triads, and such fragments as remained of history, might have been collected about the 10th and thence to the 12th century, when a dawn of revival of literature appeared in most countries in Europe, and amongst others, very remarkably in Wales. This may be fairly infer'd from the dissimilarities that appear in the language, versification, style, idiom, modes of thinking &c in the manuscript collections of those ages. In the 'Llyfr Du Caerfyrddin', where pieces of the 6th as well as of the 11th & 12th centuries appear, injudicious collectors, antiquaries, critics &c have not been able to make the proper and necessary distinctions when handling these subjects, amongst other very prominent characteristics of Taliesin are the Druidical mythology & philosophy, frequently blended with the Primitive Christianity. Spurious pieces attributed to Taliesin of the 12th century (obviously so from their language & versification) are stuffed with the depraved popish Christianity of the times, with attempts (doubtless to impose) to interlard them with something of the philosophy & mythology of Taliesin by such as appear to be totally ignorant of the character & true principles of these things. **(88)**

The 3 schools of Welsh poetry may be termed and described as follows:

1. The Ancient or School of Taliesin, for of what is still more ancient we have very little remaining, and nothing but what may be included under the head, or in the system of the School of Taliesin.
2. The Northwalian, or School of Gruffudd ap Cynan. This seems to have derived most of its distinguishing characteristics from the Scandinavian scalds, owing to the circumstance of Gruffudd ap Cynan having been brought up in the court of a Scandinavian Prince. Compare many of the odes of Gwalchmai &c with that of Regner Lodbrog: the same savage sublimity, the same ferocious grandure, in both. The versifications of this school are chiefly of the heroic kinds, very little of the lyric, if any, properly speaking, and the variety not great. It commenced under Gruffudd ab Cynan in the beginning of the 11th century.
3. The Southwalian. This is in a great measure, (and much more so than that of north Wales, the offspring, and in many things, a continuation of the Ancient or Taliesinian School. The variety of its versification and metres are very great. It seems to delight more in lyrical than in heroical subjects and metres, and all the pastoral, rural or domestic (teuluaidd) poetry appears as of this school, less heroical than the Northwalian, less grand, but more natural. Its subjects are chiefly rural description, love, conviviality, domestic manners, &c, and its deviations from the Ancient School appear to have been derived from the southern parts of Europe thro' the medium of the Norman conquest. (compare *Soniais feinwar am garu* of D. Gwilym with a scene in Romeo and Juliet.) Dafydd ap Gwilym &c are Bards of this school. In this the *cynghanedd* received its ultimate polish. After the subjugation of N.W. by Edward the 2nd the North Walian school declined and after Iolo Goch it became nearly extinct, whilst the more civilized School of south Wales extended itself into north Wales. Amongst the characteristics of the S. Walian School we observe the metres, rhythm and manner of the Taliesinian retained and familiarly known as late as the end of the 16th century. All the light lyric or song metres seem to have originated (at least for the most part) in south Wales, and very few are the instances of any such metres, or any such kind of poetry, to be met with in N. Wales previous to the commencement of the

17th century. Even some of the N. Walian writers affirm that the lyric or song metres now so much esteemed amongst then were derived **(89)** from S. Wales, and first introduced by Hwmffre Dafydd ab Evan about the year 1600. (Sion Philip o Hendre Waelod – Daf. Elis, &c). The *cywydd*, tho' in some use before D.G., seems to have first acquired its celebrity from his poetry which, excepting a very few pieces, he always wrote in. After him it came into so much esteem, that it was very seldom for nearly two centuries that any other metre was used.

About the year 1500 a school which may be termed new appeared in Wales. Not peculiar to either N. or S.W., its foundation was laid in S.W. by the two Bardic sessions of Carmarthen: the 1st in 1457, the other in 1461. It extended itself all over Wales rapidly, but more conspicuously so in N.W. where it was greatly supported by the bardic congresses that were held at Caerwys. But in this school false refinements were carried to such an extravagant pitch as to overwhelm it, and under them it was crushed to death. About the same time the Bards of Glamorgan in S.W. patronized by the Nevils, Herbets &c, Lords of that district, attempted the revival of the Ancient School, or rather a new school which was to retain all the characteristics and fundamentals of the Ancient or Taliesinian with, in addition to it, the discoveries and improvements of the later schools of north & south Wales. Its principles were undoubtedly good and superior to any thing that had ever previously appeared. But the revolution in Welsh literature that took place in consequence of the Reformation from popery &c, has left this unfostered school in a state of pigmy dwarfishness that is lamentable, for its efforts were certainly very great and highly laudable; judicious, founded on the true reasons and nature of things. Its principles were philosophically just and truly scientific, faithful to the language and its mythologies. It exhibits so complete a system of versification, that the like has never yet been noticed in any other age or language what ever. If it has errors these are the retention of some of the overstrained refinements of the new school that immediately preceded it, of these things it retains a few, not indeed as principles indispensably necessary, but as what may be occasionally allowed the sportings of a fanciful genius, and particularly as exercises of adolescent genius in its state of pupilage & discipline, that superinduce a dexterity that cannot perhaps be otherwise as well and effectually acquired and for this purpose such things may be of some use. **(90)**

About the 11th century a pretty familiar intercourse took place between the princes of north Wales and the kings of Norway, Denmark &c, especially the Danish Kings of Ireland, of the Isles &c,

intermarriages &c. Hence the similarity of manners in north Wales (in some degree) to those of the Scandinavians, castrating &c, putting out of eyes &c. Hence the similarity of images & sentiments in the Northwalian and Scandinavian poetry (see Cynddelw, &c). The barbarous custom of putting out of eyes &c appears first in history (I believe) amongst the Scandinavians, and soon afterwards in north Wales & Powys.

About the same time or soon after the Normans settled in Glamorgan, Pembroke, Cardigan &c, and into these countries they introduced their manners and usages. Amongst other things we observe a similarity of sentiment and imagery between the poetry of that period in Glamorgan and that of the southern parts of Europe, (the Troubadours &c). Gallantry, levity in general, &c and a taste [for] romance. About this time the Mabinogion, a Southwalian production, seems to have been written. This taste continued down to the time of Dafydd ab Gwilym and perhaps till so late as the time of Elizabeth. It also appears to have extended itself into Northwales in something more than a century after the subjugation of that part of Wales to the Crown of England, about the year 1400, or rather 1350. Iolo Goch in north Wales exhibited in his poetry the Scandinavian ferocity, and in south Wales we find in Dafydd ap Gwilym of the same period the gallantry & levity of the troubadours. We find traces of these two very different characters still remaining. The Christmas carols & May songs of north Wales are solemn and religious, those of south Wales convivial. In short, till of late the poetry of north Wales was barbarously grand, that of south Wales gay and light. Devotional Christmas carols &c songs on religious subjects are to this day the very common amusements of pothouse companions. In south Wales the convivial songs are of the same character as those of England – light songwriting appears as a very ancient thing in south Wales, and a very recent things in north Wales.

(Pursue this idea as far as possible, &c,)

Bardism's Legacy for Contemporary Wales

XII: Schools of Welsh poetry (NLW 13138A, 45–96)

This essay focuses predominantly on the modern and contemporary schools, and thus highlights the influence of bardism on the poetry of his day. A highly subjective piece, probably written c.1815, it demonstrates Iolo's partiality towards Glamorgan and his profound contempt for the poetic traditions of north Wales.

Bards of the 11th &c to the 13th centuries

That the Northwalian bards of the 12th, 13th &c centuries copied from the Scandinavian scalds has been already proved, I presume, beyond a doubt. The striking coincidences of their manner, style, and very bold and far-fetched metaphors, their violent figures, their inverted constructions their ferocious sentiments, their singular versification &c &c, could hardly be otherwise accounted for.

These circumstances afford convincing internal evidences of the authenticity of those poems. The Welsh Bards could not have borrowed such a manner &c from any other people under the sun, and it was not theirs *ab origine*, and that two different nations unknown to each other, or between whom there had never been any literary intercourse, should invent each of them a system of poetry so exactly similar to each other in all its principles, being at the same time highly artificial and very remote from nature in every particular, is not very probable. That the principles of systems purely natural should have occur'd in the same order, or nearly so, to different nations absolutely unknown to each other, and very remote in time and place, is not only probable, but I believe matter of real fact in several instances. Nature is always and every where the same, **(46)** appears in the same forms and colours in all ages, in all countries, and on all occasions. Not so the arbitrary complexities of fantastic art. Fanciful art may form images of men cloathed with feathers, with wings to fly, fins to swim &c. But originals or prototypes of such things are nowhere to be found. Gryphons, and wyverns are only creations of heraldic art, and are nowhere to be found in nature. A creature of precisely such a character is the Scandinavian poetry, and that of the Northwalian Bards is a very perfect copy of it.

The Welsh of north Wales had in the 10th and thence to the 13th centuries a very intimate intercourse with the Danish and Norwegian scalds of those ages attendant on the Danish Kings of Ireland. Gruffydd ap Cynan was himself born and educated at the Hiberno-Danish Court, his mother a daughter of the Danish King of that Country, and that King himself a celebrated scald. This king was Auliffe King of Dublin, as he was termed. He was also king of a great part of Ireland, spoke the scaldic language, was skilled in all the scaldic learning of poetry &c. Gruffydd ap Cynan, on recovering the sovereignty of north Wales, introduced the scaldic system of poetry, which firmly established itself there, and absolutely and entirely superseded the **(47)** ancient Bardic system of the Cymry which however continued in south Wales where it has been preserved to the present day, but never revived in north Wales.

It was at, and about, the period mentioned that this intercourse subsisted between the court of Aberffraw and the Danish court of Ireland, never before or after; never with the scalds of any other time.

Mr William Owen, in his communication to Sir R. C. Hoare, gives it as his opinion that Gruffudd ap Cynan introduced only the Irish musical system. That this was introduced by him into north Wales is true, and it is equally true that he introduced the scaldic system of poetry. The works of all the Northwalian Bards of that and the subsequent century clearly prove this in their manner, style and other strong characteristics. Let any one compare those with the poems of Regner Lodbrog &c &c &c, and try then whether he will find himself able to withhold his assent. What of the ancient British mythology, or of poetic learning, appears in the Bards of Gruffudd ap Cynan (as we may call them), must be considered as the dying remains of Ancient British Bardism. Such vestiges or traits occur also, but very rarely, in the poems of those scaldic Bards of north Wales, **(48)** and were only such as had traditionally stuck to the popular memory and thence taken, and from any regular system of genuine British Bardism, either written or traditional.

The genuine manner and character of the partical or prose writings of any particular age wherein any work of the kind I suppose to have been written affords the most cogent evidence of its authenticity. This scaldic style of character of Northwalian poetry continued from the time of Gruffudd ap Cynan until the death of Llewelyn ap Gruffudd in 1282; about 200 years, and soon afterwards died away. It seems to have emigrated about the end of the specified period into Glamorgan, escaping as it were from the interdict under which it had certainly been laid in north Wales by Edward the first. That it had been so interdicted is very clear from numerous passages that might be collected from the works of the Bards from the death of Llewelyn down to the year 1400, tho' I believe that no massacre, as Sir John Wynne has asserted, of the Bards ever took place. An execution of a stubborn Bard, of two or three possibly, might have **(49)** taken place, and magnified into a massacre. I believe that it would be difficult to find sufficient evidence in our old writings for more than this.

About the close of the 13th and beginning of the 14th century, something of the scaldic violence of metaphor and figure appears in the works of those Glamorgan Bards, Casnodyn, Trahaearn Brydydd Mawr, Addaf ap Dafydd, called Addaf Eurych, y Prol, and others of that period; with very great abatement of the scaldic ferocity. Indeed the object of this had been, in some measure removed by the subjugation of most parts of Wales to the Crown of England and the cessation of those wars between the two countries that had kept it alive. The system of its versification became greatly changed, and for the better. It continued indeed alliterative still but much better, more analogical, and more elegant, as well as more practicable and easy principles, and widely different from the scaldic alliteration. It was, properly speaking, a resumption, and at the same time, an improvement of an alliterative manner that had appeared in the poetry of the Bards of the 8th, 9th and 10th centuries, before, it should seem, any intercourse between the **(50)** British Bards and scaldic Bards had taken place. And which had been making slow advances towards its present perfection in S. Wales, and about the later end of the 14th century it attained to a degree of perfection from which it has been falling off by overstrained refinements rather than rationally improving. **(51)**

Bards of the 15th century in S. Wales

About the commencement of the 15th century or rather before, indeed so early as the middle of the 12th century, the Silurian or Glamorgan poetry became tainted with, unless we rather say improved by, the Norman or Provençal style of poetry. About 1150, appeared Rhys Goch ap Rhys ap Rhiccart o Dir Iarll, ab Einion ab Collwyn. We have several pieces by him preserved, mostly on amatory subjects, and in a style of some singularity, he seems to have been acquainted with the poetry of the Norman trouvèrs or with that of the Provençal troubadours. At least he wrote in a manner greatly resembling theirs, their gallantry and many other prominent characteristics of their manner appear in his pieces, what cannot be found in the poetry of any former age in Wales. In these things he boldly copied from the troubadour, or whence besides from whom and where else could he have derived such a manner. Indeed it may be answered that he might easily have found it in Nature **(52)** for the troubadourian poetry has much of Nature in it, and the suggestions of Nature will take place in all countries and ages. But it may be asked how could a Welsh Bard of that age have copied from the Troubadours? The answer may be thus and highly plausible, about from 40 to 60 years before the time of Rhys Goch the Normans under Robert Fitz-Hamon had settled in Glamorgan, many great families of them, with the wealth and in the style, even the power of princes living in great splendour; it [is] well known from history that the troubadours and the Norman trouvères or minstrels frequented the courts or castles of the Anglo-Norman kings and barons, as those barons who had established themselves in Glamorgan were amongst the most wealthy of them there, each of them exercising the powers of sovereign princes, *juria regalia*, and more so, it may be safely averred, than in England. It becomes thence highly probable that the troubadours &c visited their courts or castles, thence their manner and style in poetry would of course become known **(53)** and imitated. But how, it may be asked, could the Welsh Bards have any knowledge of, or intercourse with, those foreign poets? We may thus answer when Sir Robert Fitzhamon had become possessed of the sovereignty of Glamorgan, he bestowed many wealthy lordships therein on twelve of his attendant knights with rights of *juria regalia*. He also bestowed large and wealthy lordships also in this country on several of the native chiefs who had sided with him. Little if anything less than half the county was given to Einion ap Collwyn, a native chief or prince, with the same rights and privileges, but all those chiefs or barons held of him as their sovereign or paramount, and by their tenure (of a foederal nature) they were obliged to attend and assist at his court once every month, and had each of them allotted apartments in the castle of Cardiff, where the chief lord or prince of Glamorgan, as he was termed, held his courts of legislation, judicature &c. Now the Welsh Bards under our present notice, **(54)** Rhys Goch was a grandson of Einion ap Collwyn, of course frequently and honourably at Cardiff Castle equal in rank and privilege with the Norman barons that regularly attended there, himself a regular and systematic or constitutional attendant, and thence unavoidably conversant with those Normans of high rank and dignity that always attended there. He must have become intimately acquainted with the Norman and or Provençal poets who visited either the paramount court of Cardiff or the courts of the other barons, and thence with their language and poetry, and it is well known that the Norman soon became the language of all the higher ranks in this island, and continued so for ages. Again the Welsh Bards were also patronized by those Norman barons as we find by many testimonies to be found in their poems as well as in our historical manuscripts of that period and especially that curious anecdote of Robert Duke of Normandy, who is said, and our authorities are respectable, acquired a knowledge of the Welsh language and its poetry. And we have still extant a Welsh poem said to have been written by him, on the subjects of his own melancholy **(55)** situation. It is of so singular a cast as to preclude the supposition of its being spurious, on reading it we find it so well adapted to Robert's circumstances and unavoidable state of mind, that nothing can be more natural and at the same time expressed in such a singularly allusive manner as could never have occurred to any one who might have attempted any fiction of such a thing. It is enigmatic in many of its sentiments and cannot be understood without taking into consideration the singular events and circumstances of Robert's life. This being done, all is nature and light.

From what has been stated we find that their might, or rather that there must, have been an intimate intercourse between some of the Welsh Bards and the foreign minstrel visitants. Hence an avenue by which the peculiar characteristics of the troubadourian poetry might have found their way into the poetry. That some of the Welsh Bards had a knowledge of the French, Italian and Provençal poetry may also be inferred from several passages to be found in works of the Welsh Bards **(56)** still extant, that allude to the literature of those foreign nations.

Hopkin ap Thomas was a person of distinguished rank, learning and genius about the year 1310. He was also a poet and the greatest patron of the Welsh Bards of that age. He lived in the Vale of Tawy in Glamorgan. A Bard of his time says of him,

'He is the Son of Thomas who had no enemies, a lion who never secluded himself, son of Einiawn the patron of Bards.

His learning is refined, he courts fame, he accumulates Wisdom, a man of perfect physiognomy, a magistrate of perfect and just memory, his accomplishments are those of Solomon, in him are beautifully seen the fundamentals of genius. Complete and just are all his actions, he is the strength of south Wales, the object of their wisely judged affections, the regulator of this sapient region; equal to Italy in sublimities of poetry are the practices of the southern country.'

Meurig ap Iorwerth, another Bard, says of him as follows:

'He is like Bede and Cadocus in his wise answers, he is the author of metres in the French manner, elaborately good **(57)** equal to those of Italy or of Cedig – he is the register of wisdom, of music, of Bardic science, the crown of the affable and humane.'

And Dafydd ap Gwilym soon after speaking of a song he had written says,

ni wnaeth prydydd ffraeth o Ffrainc
Na phencerdd y ryw Saffancainc

Neither eloquent poet of France, nor chief ever made a song like this.

Surely such expressions could never have occur'd to any but such as had some knowledge of French and Italian poetry?

Dafydd ap Gwilym flourished from 1330 to 1360, or something later. He adopted the manner of Rhys Goch ap Rhiccart with more of the troubadourian licentiousness which had not appeared before his time in the Welsh poetry. The particulars wherein the Southwalian poets of this School of Rhys Goch or of D. Gwilym imitated the troubadours are the following. The troubadours attached themselves to married ladies. So did Rhys Goch, D.G., Bedo Brwynllys, and many others. The troubadours sent doves, nightingales &c on embassies of love or friendship. So did the Welsh Bards above mentioned and others. The troubadours delighted in beautiful descriptions of nature, spring, landscapes, arbours &c. So did the Welsh Bards of the School of Rhys Goch &c. **(58)**

This troubadourian style was in S. Wales mostly confined to amatory poetry. The more dignified panegyric or ode continued still to be written in the ancient, and certainly more sublime, Welsh style or manner. In amatory songs the manner of the troubadours was more lively and elegant because [it was] more easy and natural than any thing that had on similar subjects appeared previously in Wales. This manner continued in south Wales down to the days of Elizabeth; down even to the present day, for it prevails in all our amatory songs &c. It was attempted in N. Wales in the 15th [century] but with very little success by any except Thomas Prys o Blas Iolyn, Sion Tudur, and possibly one or two more, both living about the year 1580. But of this manner we find little besides of this description of poetry down to that period, and thence to the present not a single vestige of it. It firmly and lastingly established itself in S. Wales, but was not able to do so in N. Wales.

It must however be confessed that in the troubadourian poetry we find many traits strikingly similar to our most ancient Welsh poetry which was written beyond a doubt before the Provençal language was formed, before ever a troubadour existed. **(59)** Perhaps this may be accounted for from both the one and the other having sprung in a considerable degree from the same origin, from the old Gallic or Celtic Bards? And tho' the Provençals lost their ancient language, yet many of their ancient ideas survived it in the popular memory or traditions, and were taken into the poetry of the troubadours. I do not insist on its having been so in fact, it however appears to me probable that it might have been so. This however will not invalidate my opinion that the Southwalian Bards by their intercourse with the Normans derived many peculiarities from the troubadours, who though they had many ideas pretty obviously derived from their Celtic ancestors had also many others that could not have been the offspring of any other age but that wherein they wrote. And of these last many appear to have passed one way or another into the Welsh poetry of south Wales, and by what channel they could have been conveyed besides that above mentioned, I cannot conceive. Many of those are not such as are commonly suggested by nature in all countries and ages whence curiosity is, of course, engaged in the enquiry whence could they have been introduced and how, or by what means? **(60)**

Modern Poetry of North Wales

For little less than two centuries the lyric poetry of north Wales has been the most stupid that was ever known in any country. About 40 years ago (1760) a very thick volume closely printed and on a small type of Northwalian poetry was published. It chiefly consists of Christmas carols, devotional summer carols and other divine songs, blasphemously so termed. Amongst all those it will be found very difficult to find one of any tolerable merit. If any such can be found it will be amongst the pieces of Hugh Moris a poet of real but ill-directed genius, who lived about the year 1660 and thence to, I believe, 1700. His best pieces however are not devotional. Some are humorous and have considerable merit, but he was in his more serious pieces not able to surmount the execrably bad taste of his country and age. He is however superior to all his cotemporaries. A few pieces of Edward Morris have some merit, I say some. I wish I could say more than that, or half as much of nine tenths of the other poets whose works appear in this pitiful farrago. Alliteration not well understood constitutes the whole excellence of their poetry, so that be obtained no matter what becomes of sense or any thing that amongst other people constitutes poetry. **(61)** A number of other volumes of poetry published in N.W. are of the same character. It remains for to mention a few exceptions (I said a few, I ought to have said very few): the late Revd Gronwy Owain, whose works were printed about 45 years ago, some pieces by the late Revd William Wynne and now living are the Revd Walter Davies of Meifod, David Thomas, commonly called the Snowdon Drunkard, David Richards of Dolgellau not inferior to any but in the unlucky choice of a subject, the Trinity – truly Northwalian. One or two more may perhaps be found of the present day of some revival in N.W. The late Lewys Morris wrote two or three pieces that may be considered as tolerable, and none as excellent [as] 'Caniad y Gog i Feirionydd'. The late Mr Rice Jones of Blaenau near Dolgellau, had a truly poetic genius and wrote a few good things in the ancient Welsh manner, or rather in the manner of the 15th century. He would have been a very superior poet had he cultivated his genius, which may be said to have been truly original and fertile, I will venture to say Shakespearian, but in many instances rather Horatian. He was unable to extricate himself from the ridiculous N. Walian manner. He had a happy genius **(62)** for light lyrics. Had he cultivated on proper principles that species of poetry, he failed in it not for want of genius, but because his fancy had clog'd with the absurd manner of N.W. He attempted a convivial song for the Gwyneddigion Society of London, but profanely stuffed it full of Northwalian devotion, such as may frequently be found in any alehouse in north Wales, where it is a very common thing to hear a gang of drunkards singing Christmas carols and other awkward songs on religious subjects over their cups, with the accompaniments of cursing, swearing, wrangling, &c. Of modern Northwalian songs, I have not found any one besides 'Caniad y Gog i Feirionydd' by Lewis Morris whose only one existing copy would be worth snatching out of the fire.

It may be observed that the most ancient of our poetry is employed on religious and moral topics. It derives this character from our old Druids who made verse the vehicle of religious and moral instruction, that thence derived the devotional character of the modern Northwalian poetry. And such a plan continued and acted upon with that nice propriety that the sacredness of the subjects requires might be of the most important service to the cause of morality **(63)** and religion. But things of this nature in a state of gross abuse and profanation are horribly bad and disgusting.

It is, and has long been, an established custom in north Wales to write Christmas carols and to sing them to the music of the harp in the morning service on every Christmas day, and as frequently as possible new carols are procured every year, when Christholidays, during which they are sung daily, they become the common songs of the country, and are to be heard as the recreations of alehouses as above related.

I once heard a gentleman of considerable learning and of some good sense endeavour to vindicate this practice of singing religious songs in public houses and companies of tours. It kept present to their minds such moral and religious ideas and principles as operated as a considerable check on immoralities of conduct and conversation which otherwise would have occur'd. I was not able to afford my assent to his opinion. Mine was, and is, that such a profanation of religious truths brought them under the meaning of the old proverb 'too much familiarity breeds (ends in) contempt.' They become as it were blunted and cease to make their proper impressions, or rather we become callous to their effects. **(64)** To avoid falling into vicious habits, let us rather practice our religious songs and melodies in private or in little select associations far removed from the scenes and schools of vice and temptation. To be used thus, religious and moral songs may be of most important benefit to society, when such compositions are not debased by vulgarity and eternal sameness of thought and sentiment, which is the raucous cast of the Northwalian carols. They consist of nothing but the most unskilful changes in the same vulgar sentiment, or rather repetitions of it, for changes can hardly be a proper expression.

The amatory songs of north Wales are not a better character. They consist of [a] string of bombastic and awkward epithets, unnatural descriptions of female beauty, with abundance of queer conceits and nothing of nature, or of passion, in elaborately alliterative lines of mere nonsense.

There are in north Wales as there are also in south Wales a great number of little stanzas too natural and simple to be called epigrams in the modern acceptation of the term, but infinitely better. They are generally in simple rhyme and mostly, to their high credit, without alliteration those to be found chiefly in the mouths of the common people, a great number of them on amatory subjects, and excellent of their kind, many of them turn on moral sentiments in the genuine **(65)** manner of the old Druids, and are admirable. Simple as they are, these are some of the best things in modern

Northwalian poetry. It is in this particular line, and in this only, that it seems inclined to follow nature. A collection of these beautiful morsels from every part of Wales, is a desideratum. All parts of the Principality abound with them.

In the year 1451 was held a famous session of Bards at Carmarthen under the patronage of Gruffudd ap Nicolas, David ap Edmund, a Northwalian Bard, won the Bardic chair there by dint of mere alliteration and jingle. On his return he was by his countrymen hailed as conqueror. They were bitten by him and became all of them alliteratively mad, of which mania they have never yet been cured. But the scientific principles of alliteration, as taught them by that wonderful tho' greatly aberrant genius, is now but very imperfectly understood amongst them.

The most popular metres now in use by the Northwalian lyric poets are not the ancient and genial metres of the language, but such as have been borrowed from old English lyrists with English appellations: Leave land, Amarylis, Spanish Raven, Crimson Velvet, Greece and Troy, About the banks of Helicon, Hunt is up (Antesup), Bonny Kate – Queen Dido – Susanna – Sweet Cap. Gramundus, Whitelocks Gyranto (Curranto), **(66)** Moll Symis – Green sleeves, New Taffi – Loath to depart, Armida or Almida, Queens dream – Banks of Ireland – Charms of Love – Lady Byron – King's Farewel – Nightingale – William Taylor, Charity Mistress – Kings Round, Guinea Windsor – Hunting the hare, Hope to have – Black Friars. – Love's a sweet Passion, Sweet Richard – Synselia (Since Celia), Draw Cupid draw, Spanish Gypsies – Cowheel – Passing Bell – Prince Rupert's Conceit – Cast away Care – Parson of the Parish, Heavy heart – Monk's March, and many more of the kind.

All the above metres are imitated from old English songs and ballads, as will appear beyond a doubt to all that are acquainted with the old English poetry of the 16th and 17th centuries, or capriciously constructed Welsh verses or stanzas, awkwardly adapted to English tunes, such as songs, dances, marches, &c of the 17th century and of subsequent periods. The much more natural (to the Welsh language) forms of stanzas and kinds of verse that sprung up spontaneously in, and out of the nature of the Welsh language have been so much neglected in N.W. as to become almost unknown. But in S. Wales they are much more current, not but that here also may be found numerous awkward attempts to force the trochaic and amphibrachic Welsh into the English iambic metres and rhythm, to which **(67)** it will not conform without difficulty and great inconveniency. Rhymes of one syllable, or of the final syllable, long and accented are very numerous in the English. Words of two, three, and more syllables in English end iambically or with accent and length on the last syllable and thus supply monosyllabic rhymes to words of one syllable – *less*, *bless*, &c, may find legitimate rhymes to suit them in *redress*, *repossess*, &c; so *lent*, *bent*, *sent*, &c have their correspondent rhymes in *content, represent* &c. But in Welsh we have no polysyllabic words accented on the last syllable but verbs derived from adjectives in some (not all) of their inflections. All words besides end trochaically, or with the accent on the last syllable but one. Hence it is that in attempts to write Welsh verse with monosyllabic or iambic rhymes we experience a distressing paucity of such monosyllables and other words as are necessary. Hence it is that in such metres not having the great variety of such words adapted to the purpose as the English language has, we are under the necessity of too frequently introducing the few that we possess and very frequently cannot bring them in but on the back (as may be said) of a sentiment that has been too much used before. Hence the very monotonous nature of Welsh poetry written in such verse. But when we write in the indigenous verse of the language with trochaic endings we find ourselves at great liberty and ease and in the midst of the most profuse abundance. The Welsh language accommodates itself to the Italian versification with the greatest ease, **(68)** but not to English iambic metres. But many are tempted to force our language into such verse for the sake of having Welsh songs, Psalms, hymns &c adapted to favourite English tunes. We have indeed many things in iambic verse that are truly excellent, written with ease and elegance. But numerous repetitions of such pieces are not desirable from the necessity of using the same rhymes too frequently, the poet thence falling unavoidably into plagiarisms, and what is perhaps that of the worst kind, sui plagiarism.

In the amatory as well as in the devotional poetry of N.W. the same sentiments and images eternally recur. Their popular poets seem to have not the least idea of the merits and beauties of originality. They never attempted it. This is the general character that runs thro' all their poetry of every kind. All hackneyed and commonplace stuff. They servilely copy from each other and from themselves, never able to exhibit the same sentiment or object in any new light. They seem never to attend to what nature, passion, or fancy might dictate, but to what has been said before by a poet of esteemed celebrity; pilfer every sentiment and idea from him, and have nothing of their own in the composition but a slight variation of language or mode of expression. Lewis Morris had some originality in his pieces, but was too much of a buffoon ever to become a respectable poet. **(69)** Gronwy Owen was a poet, truly a poet on all occasion and great in almost every thing. Where and when has the poet existed that was absolutely great in all things? Hugh Morris was truly original in many of his pieces, and too servile a copyist in others, but he was purely a poet of nature and not of education. He read and wrote his own language, it may be questioned, which he could make a shift to speak a little of any other. Of course great allowances should be made, but he wants not all that are due to him. So much has he been able to rise above what would have fairly entitled him to such allowances.

Edward Morys of Perthi Llwydion, Owen Gruffudd of Llanystumdwy and a few others would have been great poets, had they either from reading or conversation ever acquired just ideas of poetry. They wanted neither genius nor abilities, they were plain uneducated country people. But that the Revd Messrs Samuel of Llangar, Robert Wynne of Gwyddelwern and some other clergymen of learning should not have escaped from the very bad manner and taste of their country, but there not, or but in a very insignificant degree, as appears very clearly by the commonplace Christmas and summer carols &c &c. But it must be allowed that their country and age afforded no proper stimulus to any exertion beyond the common course of things, thus unfavourable are some periods to genius. **(70)** Thus depressive of all its powers, or not possessing the powers of rousing it up into action.

The London Gwyneddigion Society, consisting chiefly of petty clerks, porters, journeymen mechanics, &c – such good sort of men, who certainly mean well but possess not the learning necessary to qualify them to be judges of poetry or of the language – have far more than 25 years ago stuck themselves up for patrons of Welsh poetry. They annually propose a subject, unpoetical enough, God knows, very often publish it in the newspapers, handbills, fly leaves of books and pamphlets, &c, with offers of a silver medal in reward of the best poetical production on the subject. Those who write on the subject must send up their productions in unknown hands and under fictitious names to said Gwyneddigion who being no poets or sons of poets themselves take upon them to judge which of the several pieces sent up is best entitled to the medal and, without being qualified either by nature or education to judge of anything in literature, pronounce *ex cathedra* the sentence, the dread sentence that – that – that too often awards the medal **(71)** to the stupid man of laboured art, of quaint expressions, of nonsensical alliteration, and of what – no body well perceives but themselves – leaving the work of superior taste and brighter genius to be ranked amongst the productions of unsuccessful stupidity, when it would be worthy of a better fate. What stirs and sets in motion the waters of a stagnant pool tends to purify them. In a similar manner the poetic genius of north Wales has been wakened into action and has under the indelicate stimulus of the Gwyneddigion's medal bestir'd itself, and has produced better things than have appeared for a long time, better than could have been expected. But purity of idioms in the language of these productions is woefully neglected, but unluckily this purity of idiom is absolutely unknown to the Northwalian dialect. The modern literary dialect is however common to them as it is to every part of Wales and well understood every where even by the illiterate vulgar: then why not write in it, discarding those barbarous modes of expression that so much abound in the Northwalian dialect? The pieces thus brought into existence are copied too glaringly from such English poems as may be found on the same, or similar subject. This is a misfortune. It is even a great fault, **(72)** but the idea that originality is one of the first requisites of good [?poetry] has never yet been made known to those bards of the Gwyneddigion's institution. The Northwalian poets have doubtless as good understandings and as clear ideas as any other people whatever. They only want instruction, and to be cured of their blind prepossessions in favour of usages which lay poetic genius deep in the mud of ignorance.

There have been a few Northwalian poets in most periods since the days of Elizabeth who have in some degree cultivated the ancient versification, and if they have not attained to the overstrained refinements of the 15th century, or of D. ap Edmund's system, it is so much the better. So far they have receded back a little nearer to Nature. They are not to be blamed for this, tho' it is certainly more the effect of ignorance of that unnatural system than of judgement or good taste. They are however fair objects of ridicule for pretending to a skill in that system which they do not possess, let them however thoroughly acquaint themselves with it not for the purpose of reviving it, but for that of knowing correctly what of it may be proper for preservation and practice, and what to reject. For want of knowing its principles, a laborious lexicographer has fallen into the most glaring mistakes, and the errors he has thereby committed will operate as so many mortal stabs to the reputation which otherwise he would have **(73)** acquired. The system under notice notwithstanding its objectionable parts, its false and overstrained refinements in versification, has faithfully preserved the ancient and legitimate principles of Welsh prosody, principles of which too many at this day are shamefully ignorant. And yet they have been in print and subsequently reprinted ever since the time of Queen Elizabeth, and were in the hands of the author above pointed at. It had also been repeatedly suggested to him that he was ignorant of them, but without effect. The misfortune was he had previously committed himself, had proceeded so far in the road of error that he could not with a good grace recede. That is he appears to have thought so. Others will think differently.

Twm o'r Nant a modern Welsh dramatist, has been called the Welsh Shakespeare, too profanely I am afraid. He more properly ranks with those authors of English interludes and miracles who wrote about the beginning of the 15th century or earlier. Welsh dramatic poetry has been stationary, or rather stagnant, in such a state for more than 300 years. This is a little strange. It has been more written, I cannot say cultivated, in north Wales than in south Wales. Its sole merit consists in low buffoonery and glaring indecency, with a good stuffing of Northwalian religion. **(74)**

Modern Southwalian Poetry

The Southwalian poetry of the ancient schools or systems is not here under consideration.

Songwriting, which constitutes nearly the whole of the popular poetry, is of more ancient date or rather of preservation than in north Wales. This is for the most part written in easy, simple, and thence natural verse without, or with but little alliteration, chiefly trochaic and amphobrachic. Some of it however is in iambic verse. It is more diversified in sentiment and imagery than the popular poetry of north Wales, of course much nearer to nature. Devotional poetry has from early ages been cultivated in south Wales, and on a more natural and rational plan than in N.W.

The S. Walian amatory songs have less of art in their versification than those of N.W.: smoother, more flowing and better adapted to music; have more of nature, passion and sentiment. Some of them are as beautiful and pathetic as those of any other language whatever.

Convivial songs of great merit are also pretty numerous in S.W. Some of them perfect patterns of excellence. A May song by Will Tabwr about 1660, may be instanced as one of these. Others of the same period have great merit, several also of this description by Will Hopkin, a finely natural poet, **(75)** of the earlier part of the last century are worthy of notice. Many of these songs have a good deal of delicate humour. Summer songs, or May songs, harvest songs &c are to be found in S.W., but not as in N.W. profanely devotional; they are of a cheerful and innocently convivial cast.

The brown colt (good ale) and its jockeys has been in Glamorgan a favourite topic for a convivial song, and tho' the subject has long been a hackneyed one, many of its songs have much originality of fancy and humour, with several of a less commendable character. Songs in celebration of rural amusements, bandy play, dancing, maypoles &c are common, or rather have been so till lately; also hunting songs, of which we find some possessed of merit.

Ballads of the same cast as the old English ballads are common, and in much smoother and regular verse, of course better adapted to music. Some of these are simply beautiful. A young man who received his death wound at the battle of St Fagans is the subject of a love ballad superlatively beautiful, and powerfully (I may say excruciatingly) pathetic and at the same time historically true. Indeed all the S. Walian ballads are founded on historical truths, and are often useful as well as good authorities to the historian and antiquary. That fiction was a requisite of **(76)** poetry was not an idea of the Welsh poets, but the contrary, viz. that a sacred adherence to truth should be the primary and indispensable rule. Hence the historical truth of all the Welsh poetry.

Some of the Southwalian popular songs have all the beautiful simplicity of the Scotch popular poetry, are equal to them in sentiment, passion, liveliness of description, and greatly superior in versification. Amongst them may be found some of the finest patterns of British pastoral or rural poetry; truly characteristic of British sceneries, climature, manners &c, having in them nothing of those absurdities of mythology, sentiment, description &c pilfer'd from ages countries climates &c widely different from those of Britain by those who never possessed eyes that could see nature, or hearts that could feel nature; stuff so much delighted in by the stupidity of unnatural learning.

Amongst the classes or orders of the Southwalian Bards there was one denominated *Teuluwr* & *Bardd Teulu*, Domestic Bard; his Poetry was called *Cerdd Deulu*, Domestic Song. It was requisite that it should be written in smooth, easy and **(77)** natural verse, without the metrical refinements of the *cerdd gadair*, chair song, without alliteration &c. but in easy and simple rhyme with just accentuation and quantity. It was required to be thus easy and natural in versification that it might be a proper vehicle of instruction or amusement to those who were not learned in and acquainted with the intricacies and difficulties of chair song. It was adapted to understanding and general mental acquirements of families, of youth, females, servants, and those in general of the lower classes, who equally with the higher and more learned, were entitled to and equally wanted instruction and mental information as well as amusement. It is singular enough that some manuscript tracts in S.W. of considerable antiquity say that the *Teuluwr* (Domestic Bard) is the same as what of old times was called *Derwydd* (Druid), and it may be sufficiently proved that this idea is correct. He certainly was the Bard of useful and of moral instruction in a peculiar sense, as well as of innocent amusement. I say innocent, for the maxims, rules and regulations of his profession strictly forbid immorality and indecency, on severe penalties, amongst others, that of never being, after the commission of such offences, admitted into any family or district **(78)**, never [to] be entitled to the usual or legal fees for any production of his. Hence it is that indecent and immoral poetry is a thing almost impossible to be found in Wales at any period whatever.

This species of poetry was much cultivated in S.W. from remote periods. We may venture to say from the earliest, for it is the poetry of nature and of good sense. We find volumes of it in S. Wales of very considerable antiquity, but nothing of the kind in N.W.; at least it was not there professedly cultivated, or no memorials of any such thing remain in writing or in popular tradition. Notwithstanding this we may fairly suppose that it was at least practiced, if not of regular institution, for it is that kind of poetry that is dictated by nature and passion. The *penillion* or popular stanzas elsewhere mentioned are of its nature, the remains, or rather continuation of it. Besides, tho' not recognized as Northwalian, we now and then find in manuscript a song of this nature purely (rather impurely) in the N. Walian dialect. In the reign of Elizabeth a poet (and not a bad one) named Richard Hughes, Equerry to Queen Elizabeth, wrote songs of this description. Several of them remain and possess considerable merits. Of the same period we find now and then a piece by other authors: **(79)** Edmwnd Prys, a Northwalian *temp.* Jacques I, translated the Psalms into this kind of metre or verse, and mentions it in his short preface as a thing familiarly known under the term carol, (literally love-song) a proof that it existed then in N.W. tho' neglected and even condemned, by their more ridiculously erudite bards of alliteration and silly refinements. Owing however to this neglect and contempt we do not find it cultivated in that country. It is never mentioned in their manuscripts, treatises on the art of poetry which are numerous from about the year 1480 (not earlier unless we include D[afydd] Ddu Hiraddug who was a Southwalian tho' beneficed in manuscripts) down to 1650. And this species of poetry existed in N.W. only in a rude and uncultivated state, written or rather composed by the illiterate class of poets who were termed *clêr y dom* (dunghill poets), and not otherwise or farther noticed, or mentioned by those highly beclouded bards of nonsensical cleverness who by dint of mere jingle monopolized all the poetical fame and emolument, treating the simple pupils of Nature with sovereign contempt. For this reason, an ancient piece of poetry, that may properly be called a song, of any merit cannot be found in N.W. prior to the time of Elizabeth or of Richard Hughes. Of the N.W. songwriting thence downwards **(80)** to the present day a character has been given above. What it was before that period is but little known from reasons already given, but from the few vestiges that remain it should seem that the power classes had their poets called by the other Bards *clerwyr* and *cler y dom* who, by little and little, acquired some imperfect knowledge of alliteration and other jingling and silly arts, and as the more skilful Bards of Dafydd ap Edmund's institution became neglected, and at last extinct, these dunghill minstrels, for to this day they deserve the appellation, rose up into public notice and have stuffed N.W. as tight as a hopsack with such songs and poetry as has been above described, with exceptions that are but few, but few indeed.

The late Lewis Morris had largely swallowed the Northwalian infatuation, and in some of his letters to Mr Edward Richards, insists upon it that N. Wales for ages had nothing in poetry inferior to the alliterative poetry of the 24 metres, (See *Cambrian Register* Vol. II. pp. 542, 544, &c) and that songwriting was a modern thing not much, if anything, earlier than the time of Charles II. Such ignorance is astonishing. Such a boast is just such another as for a nation to plume themselves on never having **(81)** produced any thing in poetry inferior to acrostic, anagram, charade, rebus, enigma &c &c, for many of the 24 metres are still more ridiculous than any of the above kinds of poetry, very often greatly admired by greatly vulgar minds who neither see or feel anything of Nature. This N. Walian boast is nothing less than a boast that they never (at least since the days of Gruffudd ap Cynan) had any natural and rational poetry. National and local prejudices and infatuation blind the human mind as much, if not more than anything else.

It is indeed true that natural poetry (never poetry), songwriting &c was not, or seems not to have been, cultivated or held in any estimation in N.W. ever since the unnatural scaldic taste had been introduced by Gruffudd ap Cynan, which was greatly improved in all its absurdities by D. ap Edmwnd and his disciplines. North Wales was without songs for a long time, or without any that were worth preserving, because it was without good sense, natural taste &c &c. And to this very day the blind infatuation continues. A living N. Walian poet of strong natural parts, had he been poetically educated in the school of nature, has of late been requested to publish a new poetical version of the [?]. He has begun the work, has attempted **(82)** it in rhyme with alliteration, but finding himself sorely trammelled has discarded rhyme and adopted alliteration which, on the Welsh system, will still fetter him too much. He will never be able to preserve the sense of the original, or to give his verse that ease and flow that its adoption to music requires. He has written a long poem in alliterative rhyme of 7 syllable lines and has convinced every one that, had he written in more natural and rational verse, he would have attained to the fame of a great poet. Lewis Morris says that the taste introduced and established by Gruffudd ap Cynan was religiously observed till the time of Queen Elizabeth. I believe that to the disgrace of that long period of nearly 500 years that this is pretty near the truth, for before Richard Hughes, who wrote from about 1590 to 1610, I find not a single piece written in the verse or language of [a] nature that can be clearly ascertained to be Northwalian. I once fancied that I had discovered something worth notice of this nature in a manuscript now in the possession of the Revd Mr Davies at Bangor, wherein are a number of early and very tolerable **(83)** songs. I indeed suspected that the language of many of them was not Northwalian, but recollecting that this dialect was hardly ever used in writing till a very late period, I still presumed that most of them were Northwalian productions, but finding them subsequently in Southwalian manuscripts, the copies more correct with the names and often abodes of their authors, I became convinced that they were not all Northwalian, but that the oldest and greater number of them came from S. Wales. There are however in Mr Davies's manuscript some pieces of this kind by Northwalian poets, especially many by Richard Hughes, two or three very good ones by Rees Cain in amphibrachic verse of 11 syllables, one or two by Edmund Prys the poetical translator of the Psalms, with a few more of inferior merit, (see *Hen Ganiadau Gwynedd*). Songwriting however began from about the year 1600 to be more attended to than heretofore in north Wales, and in the reign of Charles II, it, in the songs of Hugh Morys, attained to some degree of respectability, but not to any tolerable degree of correctness. It has stagnated in the same state ever **(84)** since. All attempt the manner of Hugh Morys without possessing this genius, and N.W. does not appear to have produced a man of sufficient critical knowledge and acumen to write such criticisms as might reform and improve on this, or on any other kind of poetry; not being attempted but by poets of very slender literature, seldom more than that of reading and writing their own native dialect, not being patronized, or even criticized by persons of learning and taste, it will hardly make any advances towards a greater degree of perfection.

To return to the Southwalian poetry of this character, domestic poetry (*cerdd deuluaidd*) as it was termed, was regularly cultivated, it was subjected to rules. It had its principles and characteristics well defined. In short had been digested and reduced to a regular and judicious system of cultivation. We have tracts in manuscript of considerable antiquity scientifically written on it. We have also *Trioedd Cerdd Deulu*, or triads of Domestic Poetry, wherein its principles are well exhibited and expressed. Writings of this nature, or on this subject never appeared in N.W. Of course no regular cultivation ever bestowed on this natural and interesting species of poetry. **(85)** It is true there are many manuscript tracts in N.W. written by various authors from the middle of the 15th to that of the 17th century on the arts of alliteration and the manner of forming the 24 stanzas, established, with infinite absurdity to the exclusion or proscription of all others. Many of those stanzas formed on the most ridiculous principles that can be well conceived. Besides these things those manuscripts treat of very little besides on poetical criticism, or if a very little be sometimes found, it is superficial in the highest degree always, often highly absurd, always quaint and unnatural.

Songs properly so called are found in S. Wales of so early a date as the beginning of the 12th century. The earliest of ascertained date are several by Rhys Goch o Dir Iarll, some anonymous pieces may be of an earlier date, but this cannot be ascertained.

Rhys Goch wrote in a manner singularly original, he finds [a] love messenger in the birds of the air, the wild animals of the wood, the fishes of the sea and rivers, even the rivers and waves themselves, the winds, clouds, day, night, June moon, stars, summer, spring, snow, sunshine (*tês*), angel, devils, dreams, *awen*, **(86)** *ochenaid*, *cân* &c. His manner of describing (*dyfalu*) is original and beautiful, natural, and at the same time a master sketch of art; art that shall be at the same time pure Nature, is the consummation of its excellence. I have applied the term master sketches to the poems of Rhys Goch ap Rhiccart, for they appear to be only sketches, but highly original, capable of improvement, worthy of it, and fortunate in having received a very considerable degree of it, especially in the poems of Dafydd ap Gwilym, who adopted his manner, adhered closely to it, but at the same time greatly improved it, writing in a more dignified and full-sounding, and at the same time more melodious verse, more harmonious rhythm. In short, we may venture to say, brought this very original and beautiful manner to its full perfection. D. ap

Gwilym flourished about the middle of the 14th century, i.e. about 1350, and about 200 years after Rhys Goch. I have already observed that in his works we first perceive lively trails of the troubadourian manner, for several passages in him are strikingly similar to what characterizes the troubadourian poetry: lively description, tenderness & passion, gallantry &c. **(87)**

I have already pointed out the means whereby Rhys Goch might have become acquainted with the troubadours, and their poetry, but if what I have said, or rather conjectured cannot be fairly admitted, the remaining opinions are that both nations, i.e. Welsh and Provençals, being equally descendants of the ancient Celtae, both living in those countries where the ancient Celtic Druids and Bards flourished, but have retained in the public memory, in impressions powerfully made on the public taste and feelings and fancy, and those indelible, the images, sentiments, names &c of those ancient Bards. Or if this will not appear sufficiently probable, it must follow that both derived this manner from Nature. The bards or poets of each nation being equally the pupils of nature, this manner however has prevailed in a very considerable degree to this very day in S. Wales but has been very little, and never with success practiced in north Wales.

We have in manuscripts of the 15th & 16th centuries collections of poetry and moral adages &c by Ceraint Fardd Glas, otherwise called Bardd Glas o'r Gadair; one of the poetical pieces is entitled 'Dewis Bethau y Bardd Glas o'r Gadair'. It is a kind of catalogue in rhyme of all the external beauties of nature, and indicates an eye that could see nature in all its beautiful forms and colours, and as well as [a] mental eye that could **(88)** see, a heart also that could feel what is most truly delightful in intellectual nature; as far as we can depend upon this piece to be of that antiquity to which it refer'd, so far are we able to assert that the beautiful imagery and sentiment of the poetry of the troubadours existed amongst the Bards of Wales from very early periods, long before the Provençal poetry, or even language, became known in the world. But we have from fair analogies very powerful reasons for believing that the piece above mentioned is genuine. (Here introduce it.) A few pretended prophecies were written and fathered on Taliesin, Merlin, &c about the times of Owen Glendower, in favour of Henry VII, against the Church of Rome, by the Welsh followers of Walter Brute in the 14th or 15th centuries, and these are all the poetical forgeries that are known in our language. An anonymous piece has also been now and then, I believe, ascribed to a Bard to whose manner it was very similar. His was rather [a] mistake than deception, so that upon the whole we have very good reason to believe that all the pieces that bear the name of Bardd Glas are genuine, as we cannot perceive that there ever existed a motive for forging a love song, or one descriptive of natural beauty. A beautiful piece of this kind, or on **(89)** any similar subject, would never, we may fairly infer, have been given by any poet to another. He would not have had the useless self-denial to deprive himself of the just fame to which his genius would be entitled. We can not perceive an adequate motive for such a conduct, but I leave to every man his opinion. Mine is that the poem under consideration of Bardd Glas is authentic, for of such poetry it does not appear that we have any spurious pieces in our language.

About the year 1770, the late Mr Morgan Llewelyn of Neath shewed me a manuscript of at least 200 years old which contained a great number of pieces by D.G. Amongst others were properly songs in the metre called in S.W. *cyhydedd gyrcharg, Gyhydedd lefn*; in N.W. *owdl gywydd o'r hen ganiad.* I did not copy them. I had then fallen into the N. Walian mania: I thought no Welsh poetry worth copying or preserving but what was alliterative, according [to] the most fastidiously refined rules of D. ap Edmund. I have since sorely repented, the manuscript has been lost to all the surviving friends of Mr Llewelyn and with it, I fear, those pieces of D.G., full beyond a doubt, of poetical beauty. I am not the first that has been led astray by prejudices and erroneous preconception. I fear tho', I wish I may, that I shall not be the last. I have searched other manuscripts in vain **(90)** for those pieces of D.G. and it is in vain that I have endeavoured to find out where Mr Llewelyn's manuscript went. I have too publicly declared that the manuscript has either been stolen or is unfairly withheld from those to whom it ought to have been resorted, for which reason it will be withheld from me. Had I been prudently silent I should probably have found it out long ago.

It has been asserted by those who are fond of, and wish to explode every thing in verse but what is alliterative, that the language has been preserved in its purity by alliteration, and by that only. The reasons given are a little plausible but facts are stubborn things. The songs of the 15th and 16th centuries are in general written in very pure language. Not so the alliterative, wherein we find very frequently an English word introduced or a Welsh word barbarised for no better reason than because such words were wanted as would alliterate with others that could not be dispensed with. A candid research into these things will prove the truth of what I say. It may however be true in a few instances that alliteration, and more so the severe rules of rhyme, has preserved the orthography of some words, but it has most certainly introduced into the language a greater number of foreign **(91)** words than otherwise would have been ever admitted, and this so early as the middle of the 14th century as we see them in the poetry of Iolo Goch.

The oldest songs, in the proper, or modern, sense of the term, that we have now extant, are a few by Rhys Goch ap Rhiccart, above mentioned. Those by D.G. are about 200 years later, and about 1450 we have one very fine one y Gwilym Tew. About that time and thence to 1480 flourished Llywelyn ap Hywel ap Ieuan ap Gronwy of Llantrisaint in Glamorgan by who we have several most beautiful songs: 'the dream', and another to 'the dawn' are superlatively beautiful. Morgan Powel, Gronwy William, Hopcin Twm Philip, and several others wrote good songs in the time of Elizabeth. Hywel Llwyd and Hywel Llwyd of Llancarvan wrote fine songs about 1650. (Qu? whether they are not one and the same) 'Cân y Porfelwr' [Song of the Pastoralist] by Hywel Llwyd is one of the finest patterns of British pastoral that was ever written in either of our languages. Will Tabwr, about the same period, wrote songs of real wit and humour. The song 'Canmlynedd i nawr' by Hopcin y Gwäydd o Fargam is a piece of exquisite humour.

This natural and easy kind of poetry was much used, and seemingly with success, in the times of Henry 8th, Edward 6th and Elizabeth, in favour of the Reformation by Twm ab Ifan ap Rhys William Cap Du and others. **(92)** Of these pieces or songs, we have a great number preserved. We have also several in favour of the opposite papistical side of the question, and when the dissention from the Church of England took place about the middle of the 17th century, we have many such songs on each side of the question. These songs afford us some historical knowledge not elsewhere to be found. It has in all ages been the uninterrupted practice of the Welsh poets to record in verse the events and occurrences of their own times, and possibly there is no country in Europe whose history can be collected so completely from its poetry as that of Wales. A judicious person beginning early enough in life, might make a very interesting compilation of this nature, but such an attempt will not with ease and speed sufficient find patrons, at least I greatly fear it.

(93) The romance or apologue of Einiawn ap Gwalchmai seems to have some historical truth in it. Einiawn is said to have lived in the time of Llewelyn ap Gruffudd, and that as he mourned in solitude for his death he met the Rhiain y Glasgoed [the maiden of the greenwood]. He stays from home with his mistress till the years of such enjoyment were over, then returns home with a lying account of his having been infatuated by a fiend, having been persuaded thereunto by Dafydd Ddu, whom he brings with him to Gwynedd and prevails on his brother-in-law who was Bishop of St Asaph to benefice him at Dinmeirchion, where he dies. Dr Davies & Edward Llwyd date Einiawn too early and D. Ddu too late in 1340, tho' he might have lived till then being very old 80 at least or upwards. The versification of D. Ddu is precisely that of the middle or later end of the 13th century. In 1340 it had nearly attained its present perfection (i.e. the *cynghanedd*). This will be admitted as very decisive evidence by all who understand these matters, hence we may fully venture to consider them as cotemporaries, **(94)** at least so far, as said to be so in this tale, that is D. Ddu a young man of 20 when Einiawn was grown grey, and so 60 years of age at least. The *cynghanedd* of D. Ddu in Off. B. Mariae [Officium Pavum Beatae Mariae Virginis, Gwassanaeth Meir] is that of 1300 at the latest or rather that of 1280. Anachronisms are seldom to be found in the old Welsh tales. Their authors appear to have kept them as near true history as possible. After all this can hardly be said to have been written professedly as a tale, for Einiawn's apology for his delinquency that he was, as it were, bewitched by a demon or fiend would easily gain credit in that age of superstition, and this tale having been rolled a little about like a snowball would soon increase in magnitude, so that we may fairly enough believe that the writer, Hopcin ap Thomas, believed the whole to be true history. Hywel son of Ednyfed Vychan by his second Wife was Bishop of St Asaph. about 1300.

I therefore conceive that Hopcin ap Thomas recorded this supposed wonderful event as an historical truth and that there is no fraud any where but in the old worn out debauchee, Einion ap Gwalchmai, who invented all that is supernatural in the story to clear himself as far as possible **(95)** from the imputation of profligacy, and it was possible enough in that age for him to do it in such a manner. Indeed, I question where it would not be tolerably possible to succeed in such a tale at this very day in Anglesey, and other parts of north Wales where superstitions, equally unaccountable, still prevail, as the offering of silver groats to St Iestin &c for cursing any person who has incurred the envenomed anger of the devotee. David Thomas, the Bard, declared to me that he himself had been once the messenger to carry such an offering to a saint but whether it was to engage him to curse or to bless with the cure of a particular disorder, I cannot now remember perfectly, for offerings are made for both purposes. See also Bingley's Tour, where many accounts of such superstitions are given, which I know to be true. However some of the Northwalians, being properly ashamed of them, may deny the existence of such things.

The language of this tale is a beautiful specimen of fine Welsh. It was written at a period when the language appears to have been in its golden age, about the same period or not long before it the Mabinogion were written. **(96)** Those tales also exhibit the Welsh language in all its richness of beauty and, I will venture to add, magnificence. The same periods afford other specimens of fine prose writing, and those ought to be studied as the standards of the language. Attempts were in subsequent periods made to write in the same style and, mistaking verbosity for richness, produced nothing but sound without sense. Edward Dafydd of Margam fell considerably into this error in the later part of the 17th century, and others before him, but fortunately I have not seen subsequently any attempt of the kind. The style of the Bible, tolerably good, is what is now generally attempted but seldom with success. Verbosity, empty floridness and bombast are within the reach of a shallow genius but simple and, at the same time, rich and energetic beauty and energy, require a very superior genius such as never appears frequently.

The writings that may justly claim the rank of classics in prose, and to be considered as the standards of the language are, in the first class, the triads: several sets of them, Caradoc of Llancarvan, Ieuan Brechfa, the Mabinogion, Cyfarwyddyd Einiawn ap Gwalchmai a Rhiain y Glasgoed & some others, perhaps Cattwg Ddoeth and Bardd Glas. The Gogynfeirdd are too much in the scaldic style but D. Gwilym must rank with the first, so must a few others.

XIII: On the Welsh literature. Miscellaneous (NLW 13121B, pp. 471–6)

This essay is a celebration of Welsh literature as an unrivalled medium for the transmission of the ancient bardic traditions and, unlike its English counterpart, as a means of making the Welsh 'wiser and better'.

The term civilization seems to be generally understood in a very catachrestical sense. It is taken to signify the ostentations and luxuries of wealth, the follies of fashion, the arts – most of them very iniquitous – of amassing wealth. The tyrannies of unjustly privileged orders. The modes of brow-beating and trampling upon inferiors, whether individuals or communities, of monopolizing rather than generally diffusing knowledge. And to this may be added a rage for false and delusive knowledge, if knowledge it must be called, arts and sciences that are utterly useless, with many that are pernicious and strongly tend to annihilate genuine civilizations. If by civilization we understand such things, it must be confessed that we have attained to it in a very high degree, it may be truly said of it that it has grown so high amongst us as to have its head in the clouds. Let us however take another view of these things from a different and opposite point.

True civilization then signifies such a system of things, of really usefully learning, arts, sciences &c, that are of real utility and comfort to mankind, and supply his real wants; above all such a system of morals, and whatever the advocates of the above system may think of me, I will say religion, as may be effectual to subdue the malignant and foolish passions and propensities of human nature. Instead of fierceness, substitute suavity and kindness of temper. Instead of pride, humility without servility, and, that of which pride is only the counterfeit, as hypocrisy of religion, true dignity of manners. Instead of haughty ostentation, genuine elegance of life and conduct; a benevolent and peaceable, instead of a selfish contentious disposition; a general readiness to serve our fellow creature of whatever name or nation as far as our power extend. Temperance and moderation in all our habits of living; justice uniting with benevolence in all our actions; a general rectitude of conduct such as leaves all at ease about us, such as interfered with the just welfare of no individual within the sphere of our influence. External appearances enter but very little into the question, no further than those real requisites of life: cleanliness and decency. There is indeed a natural elegance that should run through **(472)** all our actions, conduct, and external appearances, thro' all that relate to mental and corporeal, the eye of genuine civilization will always discern it and act upon its principles.

Mere literature is not civilization, it is only the instrument in the hands of other principles that may be used to retard and even destroy civilization, as well as to promote it. When it is made the tool of avarice, of culpable ambition, the ladder to tyrannical authority and power or of vain glory, the pretence for trampling upon those who have not been so fortunate as to attain to its accomplishments, the advocate of oppression, injustice, war, bloodshed and the most audacious rapine; what is it better than the scalping knife of the savage, the dagger of the assassin? What better than these when it becomes the herald of immorality, the champion of infidelity? The diffuser of doctrines and principles that overturn those laws of rectitude that secure good order in society? That deprive man of the best hopes that he has in this world of troubles, that deprive the miserable of the only comforts that remain to them? Pleading its charter of false honour and factitious philosophy in opposition to the well-known and admitted laws of pure virtue and religious morality? Arrogating to itself when monopolizing what the world of tyranny may be pleased to admit as wisdom.

The literature of the Welsh language, whatever defects it may have, is not chargeable with anything of this. It opens no roads to wealth and power, it has no places and pensions to attain to, advances not a single step on the high road to fortune, is not a thing of fashion, held in no respectability by the knaves of fortune or the fools of fashion. And it is for this very reason that it is so effectual in improving the minds and morals [of] those to whom it dictates, softening their manners, and superinducing a suavity and rectitude of disposition and conduct that must be obvious to every eye but that of prejudice. [It] has nothing in view but pure mental improvement, has it not in its power to be ostentatious and arrogant, has no means of so exalting itself over the head of humble poverty, has nothing to trample upon. It is acquired from no other motive than that of becoming better acquainted with the most important truths; for no purposes but those of morality, **(473)** unsophisticated virtue, and that of all others, the most fundamental principle of true civilization, religion. In addition to those most important objects, it has attained to the means [of] acquiring the knowledge of many of the most truly important arts of life, and thus of being useful to man in enabling him to supply his natural wants without creating artificial wants.

English literature has hardly anything in view but improvement of fortune, the sordid acquisition of wealth, not the attainment of virtue and pure morality. Its objects are those of avarice, ambition, power; the means not of instructing those who are destitute of knowledge, but of trampling upon them, and of more effectually holding them in that state of degradation, slavery and mental blindness that best suits its own superciliousness, arrogance, and self-conceit; that best answers the purposes and gratifies the wishes of avarice and pride; calling to his aid the numerous artifices of pedantry, self-interest and vain glory, things of all others the most abhorrent of Genuine civilization; and stifle it in every thing but outward and fallacious appearances, render it a whitened sepulchre, fair without, but all filthy corruption within. It wishes to hold all in the thraldom of ignorance, and consequently, in every other species of slavery but those of a class that has been created by itself, never by nature or the God of nature. There are no views of this nature open to the Welsh literature. The only view to which it can possibly turn its eye is that of doing real good, of instructing the ignorant, of improving the heart and enlightening the mind. Wales will never become truly civilized but by the literature of its own language. English learning may make us coxcombs, knaves, and fools, but so many temptations in its hands held out to seduce us, will never in any valuable degree truly civilize us. It may make us richer, prouder and, what is the acme of its attainments, atheistically philosophical, and thus uncivilize us. But our own native literature has no other tendency than to make us wiser and better. An English writer speaking of the Welsh language (*Monthly Review* for May 1805, p. 45) says, 'if knowledge and civilization be beneficial, there can be no doubt that its disuse is to be desired.' It appears from **(474)** this, and many similar things in other English writers, that the Welsh are considered as an uncivilized people similar probably to an American Indian Nation, that their language is not a literary one. But the fact is that it is by far the oldest literary and, at the same time, living language in Europe. Whatever it may be believed to have been before, it certainly became a literary language in the time of the Roman Empire. Writings in the language of that period are still extant. It never since ceased to be so, in all subsequent ages down to the present the Welsh have written in their own language, and that when other modern tongues were still in their cradles, incapable of any thing in literature worth preserving. Our present literature is far from being so contemptible as many suppose. We have more than a thousand printed books in the language, probably near two thousand. We have ten presses at least in Wales employed in printing Welsh books, besides many that are printed in London. It has three or four periodical publications, or magazines, and is now equal, if not superior, to what English literature was in the reign of Elizabeth and James, everything considered, with much less than those ages had of a strong tendency to retard instead of advancing true civilization, and incalculably less than what the present English literature has. It has no loose immoral books of any kind. None that fuel the unruly passions, none that inculcate the pernicious doctrines of infidelity, none that lead the understanding into those labyrinths of scepticism that lead, never to return, the public mind into the depths of immorality. It has no places, pensions, profitable trades, no offices, employment and high trusts to attain to that might lead it into temptation, that would render it perfectly dead to all the true purposes of civilization, a thing absolutely inconsistent with that avarice, worldly ambition, fake honour &c that leads learning astray, and that afforded Rousseau **(475)** too many powerful arguments on the side that he took of the prize question proposed by the Academy of Dijon. There can be no doubt but that the preservation and retention of the Welsh language will be [the] greatest blessing of all others to Wales. In this language and in no other can civilization and truly useful, free from baleful knowledge, be advanced and sustained amongst the Welsh. Compare the lower classes in England with those of the same order in Wales, and let impartiality decide. I will venture to say that the first are mere savages compared to the last. The modern refined English language has been so replenished with words and technical terms from ancient and modern learned languages, that it is no longer the language of the vulgar, in whose dialect there are in effect no books. And those of this lower order, if they attain to a tolerable knowledge of the learned dialect of their country, find in it such a number of profane, licentious, and in every sense immoral publications, that by such knowledge they become additionally brutalized instead of being civilized. There is certainly more literary knowledge amongst the peasantry of Wales than amongst those of England, and, what is infinitely better, more true morality, more humanity of sentiment, more gentleness of character; and all this derived from the benign impressions made upon them by the literature of their own language, that has nothing in it to counteract such impressions. One circumstance is greatly favourable to Welsh literature, we have only to acquaint ourselves with the power of the alphabet, pronounce every letter, and accent on the penultimate syllable. We have no quiescent letters, none that are used like the English C. G. J. Th Ch &c to express very different sounds. The general radicals of the language are so well known that all derivatives from them are readily understood. Hence it is that the Welsh generally find it **(476)** a very easy task to learn to read their native language. A month is generally supposed to be sufficient to acquire this knowledge in perfection. An old poetical adage says:

Ni bu Cymro'n dysgu darllain
Pob Cymraeg yn ddigon cywrain,
Ond un misgwaith, beth yw hynny,
Os bydd gwyllys gantho i ddysgu,

[There isn't a Welshman who's learned to read,/All Welsh perfectly skilfully,/In less than one month, what is that,/If he has the will to learn]

Many learn it in less, and we need no regular schools, for one neighbour gives another a few lessons two or three times a week for half an hour at a time, and the pupil is soon able to read his native language.

It is an usual thing in Wales for a few young, and sometimes older persons, of both sexes to attend for an hour twice or thrice a week at a place where a good-natured neighbour, and such may always be found, will give them some instructions in reading Welsh, and often in writing. A month of such instructions generally enables the pupil to proceed in his own strength. Reading parties are formed to exercise themselves, one correcting the other, and amongst other things, Welsh songs in manuscripts are read by them, and immoral, or in anything indecent, songs are never written in Wales. And tho' pieces of harmless levity are common enough, such as have a tendency to corrupt the mind and to violate morality are seen but so rarely that they are hardly known. Religious and moral songs are very common, read and sung by most, even the common love songs have generally a moral cast. We very seldom find any wherein some moral sentiment is not introduced. The authors of these are generally common mechanics, labourers in husbandry, sometimes women, and their songs in general have more of pure nature in them than can be generally found in the productions of more learned persons. There is a national passion for poetry amongst the Welsh which has a very good effect upon their minds and general disposition, it would be an easy matter to impress on them thro' the medium of song the best principles of morality and civilization.

Select Bibliography

Ariès, Philippe, *At the Hour of our Death*, trans. Helen Weaver (London, 1981).

—— *Western Attitudes Toward Death: From the Middle Ages to the Present*, trans. Patricia M. Ranum (London, 1976).

Barrell, John, *Imagining the King's Death: Figurative Treason, Fantasies of Regicide 1793–1796* (Oxford, 2000).

Berman, David, *A History of Atheism in Britain: From Hobbes to Russell* (London, 1988).

Bowen, Geraint, *Golwg ar Orsedd y Beirdd* (Caerdydd, 1992).

—— and Zonia Bowen, *Hanes Gorsedd y Beirdd* (Abertawe, 1991).

Boyce, Benjamin, 'News from Hell: Satiric Communications with the Nether World in English Writing of the Seventeenth and Eighteenth Centuries', *Publications of the Modern Language Association of America*, LVIII (1943), 402–37.

Bromwich, Rachel, *'Trioedd Ynys Prydain' in Welsh Literature and Scholarship* (Cardiff, 1969).

—— (ed.), 'Trioedd Ynys Prydain: The *Myvyrian* "Third Series"', *THSC*, (1968), 299–338, (1969), 127–55.

—— (ed.), *Trioedd Ynys Prydein: The Triads of the Island of Britain* (3rd edn., Cardiff, 2006).

Brooke, Charlotte, *Reliques of Irish Poetry* (Dublin, 1816).

Butler, Marilyn, *Romantics, Rebels and Reactionaries: English Literature and its Background 1760–1830* (Oxford, 1981).

Cannon, Jon, and Mary-Ann Constantine, 'A Welsh Bard in Wiltshire: Iolo Morganwg, Silbury and the Sarsens', *Wiltshire Archaeological and Natural History Magazine*, 97 (2004), 78–88.

Carr, Glenda, *William Owen Pughe* (Caerdydd, 1983).

—— *William Owen Pughe* (Caernarfon, 1993).

—— 'Bwrlwm Bywyd y Cymry yn Llundain yn y Ddeunawfed Ganrif' in Geraint H. Jenkins (ed.), *Cof Cenedl XI: Ysgrifau ar Hanes Cymru* (Llandysul, 1996), pp. 59–87.

—— 'An Uneasy Partnership: Iolo Morganwg and William Owen Pughe' in Jenkins (ed.), *Rattleskull Genius*, pp. 443–60.

Charnell-White, Cathryn, *Barbarism and Bardism: North Wales versus South Wales in the Bardic Vision of Iolo Morganwg* (Aberystwyth, 2004).

—— 'Women and Gender in the Private and Social Relationships of Iolo Morganwg' in Jenkins (ed.), *Rattleskull Genius*, pp. 359–81.

Christmas, William J., *Lab'ring Muses: Work, Writing, and the Social Order in English Plebeian Poetry, 1730–1830* (London, 2001).

Colley, Linda, *Britons: Forging the Nation 1707–1837* (London, 1994).

Constantine, Mary-Ann, *'Combustible Matter': Iolo Morganwg and the Bristol Volcano* (Aberystwyth, 2003).

—— *The Truth against the World: Iolo Morganwg and Romantic Forgery* (Cardiff, 2007).

—— 'Ossian in Wales and Brittany' in Gaskill (ed.), *The Reception of Ossian in Europe*, pp. 67–90.

—— 'Pious Frauds and Perjurers: Iolo Morganwg's Truth against the World' in Peter Knight and Jonathan Long (eds.), *Fakes and Forgeries* (Amersham, 2005), pp. 119–34.

—— '"This Wildernessed Business of Publication": The Making of *Poems, Lyric and Pastoral* (1794)' in Jenkins (ed.), *Rattleskull Genius*, pp. 123–45.

Crawford, Thomas, 'The View from the North: Region and Nation in *The Silver Darlings* and *A Scots Quair*' in R. P. Draper (ed.), *The Literature of Region and Nation* (Basingstoke, 1989), pp. 108–24.

Crowe, Richard M., 'Diddordebau Ieithyddol Iolo Morganwg' (unpublished University of Wales Ph.D. thesis, 1988).

—— 'Iolo Morganwg – An Eighteenth-Century Welsh Linguist' in Cyril J. Byrne, Margaret Harry and Pádraig Ó Siadhail (eds.), *Celtic Languages and Celtic Peoples: Proceedings of the Second North American Congress of Celtic Studies* (Nova Scotia, 1992), pp. 305–14.

—— 'Iolo Morganwg and the Dialects of Welsh' in Jenkins (ed.), *Rattleskull Genius*, pp. 315–31.

—— 'Thomas Richards a John Walters: Athrawon Geiriadurol Iolo Morganwg' in Hywel Teifi Edwards (ed.), *Llynfi, Afan, Garw ac Ogwr* (Llandysul, 1998), pp. 227–51.

Curtis, L. Perry, Jr., *Apes and Angels: The Irishman in Victorian Caricature* (London, 1997).

Davies, Andrew, '"The Reputed Nation of Inspiration": Representations of Wales in Fiction from the Romantic Period, 1780–1830' (unpublished University of Wales Ph.D. thesis, 2001).

—— '"Uncontaminated with Human Gore"? Iolo Morganwg, Slavery and the Jamaican Inheritance' in Jenkins (ed.), *Rattleskull Genius*, pp. 293–313.

Davies, Ann Elsbeth, 'Cerddi Serch a Natur Iolo Morganwg' (unpublished University of Wales M.Phil. thesis, 1999).

Davies, Caryl, *Adfeilion Babel: Agweddau ar Syniadaeth Ieithyddol y Ddeunawfed Ganrif* (Caerdydd, 2000).

Davies, D. Elwyn J., 'Astudiaeth o Feddwl a Chyfraniad Iolo Morganwg fel Rhesymolwr ac Undodwr' (unpublished University of Wales Ph.D. thesis, 1975).

Davies, Damian Walford, *Presences that Disturb: Models of Romantic Identity in the Literature and Culture of the 1790s* (Cardiff, 2002).

—— '"At Defiance": Iolo, Godwin, Coleridge, Wordsworth' in Jenkins (ed.), *Rattleskull Genius*, pp. 147–72.

Davies, Hywel M., 'Loyalism in Wales, 1792–3', *WHR*, 20, no. 4 (2001), 687–716.

Davies, J. H. (ed.), *The Letters of Goronwy Owen (1723–1769)* (Cardiff, 1924).

—— (ed.) *The Letters of Lewis, Richard, William and John Morris, of Anglesey, (Morrisiaid Môn), 1728–1765* (2 vols., Aberystwyth, 1909).

Davies, John, *The History of Wales* (new edn., London, 1994).

Davies, R. R., 'Buchedd a Moes y Cymry', *WHR*, 12, no. 2 (1984), 155–79.

—— '"Sweet civility" and "barbarous rudeness"' in idem, *The First English Empire: Power and Identities in the British Isles 1093–1343* (Oxford, 2000), pp. 113–41.

Davis, Michael T. (ed.), *Radicalism and Revolution in Britain, 1775–1848* (London, 2000).

Davison, Carol Margaret, *Anti-Semitism and British Gothic Literature* (Basingstoke, 2004).

Dearnley, Moira, '"Mad Ned" and the "Smatter-Dasher": Iolo Morganwg and Edward "Celtic" Davies' in Jenkins (ed.), *Rattleskull Genius*, pp. 425–42.

Edwards, Huw Meirion, 'A Multitude of Voices: The Free-Metre Poetry of Iolo Morganwg' in Jenkins (ed.), *Rattleskull Genius*, pp. 95–121.

Edwards, Hywel Teifi, *The Eisteddfod* (Cardiff, 1990).

Elliott, Robert C., *The Literary Persona* (London, 1992).

Ellis, Tecwyn, *Edward Jones, Bardd y Brenin (1752–1824)* (Caerdydd, 1957).

—— 'Bardd y Brenin, Iolo Morganwg a Derwyddiaeth', *NLWJ*, XIII, no. 2 (1963), 147–56, no. 3 (1964), 224–34; XIV, no. 2 (1965), 183–93, no. 3 (1966), 321–9, no. 4 (1966), 424–36; XV, no. 2 (1967), 177–96.

—— 'Ymweliadau Iolo Morganwg â Meirionnydd', *Journal of the Merioneth Historical and Record Society*, V, part III (1967), 239–50.

Emsley, Clive, 'An Aspect of Pitt's "Terror": Prosecutions for Sedition during the 1790s', *Social History*, 6 (1981), 155–84.

—— 'Repression, "Terror" and the Rule of Law in England during the Decade of the French Revolution', *EHR*, C, no. 397 (1985), 801–25.

Epstein, James E., *Radical Expression: Political Language, Ritual, and Symbol in England, 1790–1850* (Oxford, 1994).

Evans, J. J., *Dylanwad y Chwyldro Ffrengig ar Lenyddiaeth Cymru* (Lerpwl, 1928).

Evans-Jones, Albert, 'Tad Beirdd Eryri: Dafydd Tomos ("Dafydd Ddu Eryri") 1759–1822', *THSC* (1969), 7–23.

Fairer, David, *English Poetry of the Eighteenth Century 1700–1789* (London, 2003).

Finlay, Richard J., 'Caledonia or North Britain? Scottish Identity in the Eighteenth Century' in Dauvit Broun, R. J. Finlay and Michael Lynch (eds.), *Image and Identity: The Making and Re-making of Scotland through the Ages* (Edinburgh, 1998), pp. 143–56.

Fitzpatrick, Martin, 'The "Cultivated Understanding" and Chaotic Genius of David Samwell' in Jenkins (ed.), *Rattleskull Genius*, pp. 383–402.

Foster, R. F., 'Paddy and Mr Punch' in idem, *Paddy and Mr Punch: Connections in Irish and English History* (London, 1995), pp. 171–94.

Gaskill, Howard (ed.), *The Reception of Ossian in Europe* (London, 2004).

Goffman, Erving, *The Presentation of Self in Everyday Life* (Harmondsworth, 1990).

Goodridge, John, *Rural Life in Eighteenth-Century English Poetry* (Cambridge, 1995).

Gruffydd, R. Geraint, 'The Renaissance and Welsh Literature' in Glanmor Williams and Robert Owen Jones (eds.), *The Celts and the Renaissance: Tradition and Innovation* (Cardiff, 1990), pp. 17–39.

Haber, Judith, *Pastoral and the Poetics of Self-Contradiction: Theocritus to Marvell* (Cambridge, 1994).

Haycock, Marged, 'Metrical models for the poems in the Book of Taliesin' in Brynley F. Roberts (ed.), *Early Welsh Poetry: Studies in the Book of Aneirin* (Aberystwyth, 1988), pp. 155–77.

Heslinga, M. A., *The Irish Border as a Cultural Divide: A Contribution to the Study of Regionalism in the British Isles* (Assen, 1962).

Hill, Christopher, 'The Norman Yoke' in idem, *Puritanism and Revolution: Studies in Interpretation of the English Revolution of the Seventeenth Century* (new edn., London, 2001), pp. 46–111.

Hone, J. Anne, *For the Cause of Truth: Radicalism in London, 1796–1821* (Oxford, 1982).

Hopkin-James, Lemuel J. (ed.), *Hen Gwndidau, Carolau a Chywyddau* (Bangor, 1910).

Houlbrooke, Ralph, *Death, Ritual and the Family in England, 1480–1750* (Oxford, 2000).

Hughes, W. J., *Wales and the Welsh in English Literature from Shakespeare to Scott* (Wrexham, 1924).

Hutchinson, John, and Anthony D. Smith (eds.), *Nationalism* (Oxford, 1994).

Huws, Daniel, *Caneuon Llafar Gwlad ac Iolo a'i Fath* (Cymdeithas Alawon Gwerin Cymru, 1993).

—— *Cynnull y Farddoniaeth* (Aberystwyth, 2004).

—— *Medieval Welsh Manuscripts* (Aberystwyth, 2000).

—— 'Iolo Morganwg and Traditional Music' in Jenkins (ed.), *Rattleskull Genius*, pp. 333–56.

James, Brian Ll., *Thomas Richards of Coychurch* (Coychurch, 1990).

—— 'The Welsh Language in the Vale of Glamorgan', *Morgannwg*, XVI (1972), 16–36.

James, E. Wyn, '"The New Birth of a People": Welsh Language and Identity and the Welsh Methodists, *c.*1740–1820' in Robert Pope (ed.), *Religion and National Identity: Wales and Scotland c.1700–2000* (Cardiff, 2001), pp. 14–42.

Jarvis, Branwen, *Goronwy Owen* (Cardiff, 1986).

—— 'Iolo Morganwg and the Welsh Cultural Background' in Jenkins (ed.), *Rattleskull Genius*, pp. 29–49.

—— (ed.), *A Guide to Welsh Literature c.1700–1800* (Cardiff, 2000).

Jenkins, Geraint H., *Facts, Fantasy and Fiction: The Historical Vision of Iolo Morganwg* (Aberystwyth, 1997).

—— *Literature, Religion and Society in Wales, 1660–1730* (Cardiff, 1978).

—— *'Perish Kings and Emperors, but Let the Bard of Liberty Live'* (Aberystwyth, 2006).

—— 'The Bard of Liberty during William Pitt's Reign of Terror' in Joseph Falaky Nagy and Leslie Ellen Jones (eds.), *Heroic Poets and Poetic Heroes in Celtic Tradition: A Festschrift for Patrick K. Ford*, CSANA Yearbook 3–4 (Dublin, 2005), pp. 183–206.

—— 'Cyffesion bwytawr opiwm: Iolo Morganwg a Gorsedd Beirdd Ynys Prydain', *Taliesin*, 81 (1993), 45–57.

—— '"Dyro Dduw dy Nawdd": Iolo Morganwg a'r Mudiad Undodaidd' in idem (ed.), *Cof Cenedl XX: Ysgrifau ar Hanes Cymru* (Llandysul, 2005), pp. 65–100.

—— 'Glaniad y Ffrancod yn Abergwaun ym 1797' in idem, *Cadw Tŷ Mewn Cwmwl Tystion* (Llandysul, 1990), pp. 256–72.

—— 'Iolo Morganwg and the Gorsedd of the Bards of the Isle of Britain', *Studia Celtica Japonica*, 7 (1995), 365–86.

—— 'The Unitarian Firebrand, the Cambrian Society and the Eisteddfod' in idem (ed.), *Rattleskull Genius*, pp. 269–92.

—— 'The Urban Experiences of Iolo Morganwg', *WHR*, 22, no. 3 (2005), 463–98.

—— (ed.), *A Rattleskull Genius: The Many Faces of Iolo Morganwg* (Cardiff, 2005).

—— (ed.), *The Welsh Language before the Industrial Revolution* (Cardiff, 1997).

Jenkins, Philip, *The Making of a Ruling Class: The Glamorgan Gentry 1640–1790* (Cambridge, 1983).

Jones, Alun R., *Lewis Morris* (Caerdydd, 2004).

Jones, Bedwyr Lewis, *Yr Hen Bersoniaid Llengar* (Dinbych, [1963]).

Jones, David Ceri, 'The Board of Agriculture, Walter Davies ("Gwallter Mechain") and Cardiganshire, *c.*1794–1815', *Ceredigion*, XIV, no. 1 (2001), 79–100.

—— 'Iolo Morganwg and the Welsh Rural Landscape' in Jenkins (ed.), *Rattleskull Genius*, pp. 227–50.

—— '"Mere Humbug": Iolo Morganwg and the Board of Agriculture, 1796–1815', *THSC*, 10 (2004), 76–97.

Jones, Emrys, 'The Age of Societies' in idem (ed.), *The Welsh in London 1500–2000* (Cardiff, 2001), pp. 54–87.

Jones, Ffion M., '"Gydwladwr godi[d]og . . .": Gohebiaeth Gymraeg Gynnar Iolo Morganwg', *LlC*, 27 (2004), 140–71.

Jones, Owen, and William Owen (eds.), *Barddoniaeth Dafydd ab Gwilym* (London, 1789).

——, Iolo Morganwg and William Owen Pughe, *The Myvyrian Archaiology of Wales* (3 vols., London, 1801–7).

Jones, Tegwyn (ed.), *Tribannau Morgannwg* (Llandysul, 1976).

Lake, A. Cynfael (ed.), *Blodeugerdd Barddas o Ganu Caeth y Ddeunawfed Ganrif* (Llandybïe, 1993).

Leerssen, Joep, *Mere Irish and Fior-Ghael: Studies in the Idea of Irish Nationality, its Development and Literary Expression prior to the Nineteenth Century* (Cork, 1996).

—— *Remembrance and Imagination: Patterns in the Historical and Literary Representation of Ireland in the Nineteenth Century* (Cork, 1996).

—— 'Ossian and the Rise of Literary Historicism' in Gaskill (ed.), *The Reception of Ossian*, pp. 109–25.

Lewis, Ceri W., *Iolo Morganwg* (Caernarfon, 1995).

—— 'Iolo Morganwg' in Jarvis (ed.), *A Guide to Welsh Literature c.1700–1800*, pp. 126–67.

—— 'Iolo Morganwg and Strict-Metre Welsh Poetry' in Jenkins (ed.), *Rattleskull Genius*, pp. 71–93.

—— 'The Literary Tradition of Morgannwg down to the Middle of the Sixteenth Century' in T. B. Pugh (ed.), *Glamorgan County History, Volume III: The Middle Ages* (Cardiff, 1971), pp. 449–554.

—— 'The Literary History of Glamorgan from 1550 to 1770' in Glanmor Williams (ed.), *Glamorgan County History. Volume IV: Early Modern Glamorgan from the Act of Union to the Industrial Revolution* (Cardiff, 1974), pp. 535–639, 687–97.

Lewis, Gwyneth, 'Eighteenth-Century Literary Forgeries with Special Reference to the Work of Iolo Morganwg' (unpublished University of Oxford D.Phil. thesis, 1991).

Lewis, Saunders, *A School of Welsh Augustans* (Wrexham, 1924).

Linnard, William, 'Iolo Morganwg and Llantrithyd', *NLWJ*, XXV, no. 3 (1988), 296–312.

Llwyd, Alan, *Gronwy Ddiafael, Gronwy Ddu: Cofiant Goronwy Owen* (Llandybïe, 1997).

Lord, Peter, *Words With Pictures: Welsh Images and Images of Wales in the Popular Press, 1640–1860* (Aberystwyth, 1995).

Lynch, Peredur, 'Yr Awdl a'i Mesurau' in Brynley F. Roberts and Morfydd E. Owen (eds.), *Beirdd a Thywysogion: Barddoniaeth Llys yng Nghymru, Iwerddon a'r Alban* (Caerdydd, 1996), pp. 258–87.

Mee, Jon, *Dangerous Enthusiasm: William Blake and the Culture of Radicalism in the 1790s* (Oxford, 1992).

—— '"Images of Truth New Born": Iolo, William Blake and the Literary Radicalism of the 1790s' in Jenkins (ed.), *Rattleskull Genius*, pp. 173–93.

Miles, Dillwyn, *The Royal National Eisteddfod of Wales* (Swansea, 1977).

Millward, E. G., *Yr Arwrgerdd Gymraeg: Ei Thwf a'i Thranc* (Caerdydd, 1998).

—— 'Eifionydd y Beirdd', *TCHS*, 25 (1974), 42–65.

Morgan, Owen, *The History of Pontypridd and the Rhondda Valleys* (Pontypridd, 1903).

Morgan, Prys, *The Eighteenth Century Renaissance* (Llandybïe, 1981).

—— *Iolo Morganwg* (Cardiff, 1975).

—— 'From a Death to a View: The Hunt for the Welsh Past in the Romantic Period' in Eric Hobsbawm and Terence Ranger (eds.), *The Invention of Tradition* (Cambridge, 1983), pp. 43–100.

—— 'The Historical Significance of Iolo Morganwg', *Transactions of the Port Talbot Historical Society*, II, no. 2 (1981), 59–68.

—— 'Iolo Morganwg and Welsh Historical Traditions' in Jenkins (ed.), *Rattleskull Genius*, pp. 251–68.

—— 'Wild Wales: Civilizing the Welsh from the Sixteenth to the Nineteenth Centuries' in Peter Burke, Brian Harrison and Paul Slack (eds.), *Civil Histories: Essays Presented to Sir Keith Thomas* (Oxford, 2001), pp. 265–84.

Morris-Jones, John, *Cerdd Dafod: sef Celfyddyd Barddoniaeth Gymraeg* (facsimile edn., Caerdydd, 1980).

—— 'Derwyddiaeth Gorsedd y Beirdd', *Y Beirniad*, I (1911), 66–72.

O'Halloran, Clare, 'Irish Re-creations of the Gaelic Past: the Challenge of Macpherson's Ossian', *Past and Present*, 124 (1989), 69–95.

Owen, Hugh (ed.), *Additional Letters of the Morrises of Anglesey (1735–1786)* (2 vols., London, 1947–9).

Owen, Morfydd E., 'Royal Propaganda: Stories from the Law-texts' in T. M. Charles-Edwards, Morfydd E. Owen and Paul Russell (eds.), *The Welsh King and his Court* (Cardiff, 2000), pp. 224–54.

Owen, William, *The Heroic Elegies and Other Pieces of Llywarç Hen* (London, 1792).

Parry, Thomas, 'Dafydd Ddu Eryri', *TCHS*, 41 (1980), 59–81.

Phillips, Geraint, 'Forgery and Patronage: Iolo Morganwg and Owain Myfyr' in Jenkins (ed.), *Rattleskull Genius*, pp. 403–23.

—— 'Math o Wallgofrwydd: Iolo Morganwg, Opiwm a Thomas Chatterton', *NLWJ*, XXIX, no. 4 (1996), 391–410.

Phillips, W. J., 'Iolo Morganwg and the Rees Family of Gelligron', *NLWJ*, XIV, no. 2 (1965), 227–36.

Piggott, Stuart, *The Druids* (London, 1999).

Pittock, Murray, *Celtic Identity and the British Image* (Manchester, 1999).

—— *Inventing and Resisting Britain: Cultural Identities in Britain and Ireland, 1685–1789* (London, 1997).

Ragussis, Michael, *Figures of Conversion: 'The Jewish Question' and British National Identity* (London, 1995).

Ramage, Helen, 'Eisteddfodau'r Ddeunawfed Ganrif' in Idris Foster (ed.), *Twf yr Eisteddfod* (Abertawe, 1968), pp. 9–27.

Rejhon, A. C., 'Hu Gadarn: Folklore and Fabrication' in Patrick K. Ford (ed.), *Celtic Folklore and Christianity: Studies in Memory of William V. Heist* (Santa Barbara, Calif., 1983), pp. 201–12.

Roberts, Brynley F., '"The Age of Restitution": Taliesin ab Iolo and the Reception of Iolo Morganwg' in Jenkins (ed.), *Rattleskull Genius*, pp. 461–79.

—— 'Mab ei Dad: Taliesin ab Iolo Morganwg' in Hywel Teifi Edwards (ed.), *Merthyr a Thaf* (Llandysul, 2001), pp. 57–93.

—— '"Yn Wladgarol, Iaithgarol a Chenedlgarol": Cymdeithas Cymrodorion Aberdâr' in Hywel Teifi Edwards (ed.), *Cwm Cynon* (Llandysul, 1997), pp. 261–84.

Roberts, Michael, '"A Witty Book, but mostly feigned": William Richards' *Wallography* and Perceptions of Wales in Later Seventeenth-century England' in Philip Schwyzer and Simon Mealor (eds.), *Archipelagic Identities: Literature and Identity in the Atlantic Archipelago, 1550–1800* (Aldershot, 2004), pp. 153–65.

Rogers, Pat, *Grub Street: Studies in a Subculture* (London, 1972).

Rubel, M. M., *Savage and Barbarian: Historical Attitudes in the Criticism of Homer and Ossian in Britain, 1760–1800* (Oxford, 1978).

Smiles, Sam, *The Image of Antiquity: Ancient Britain and the Romantic Imagination* (London, 1994).

Smith, Anthony D., *Myths and Memories of the Nation* (Oxford, 1999).

Snyder, E. D., 'The Wild Irish: A Study of Some English Satires against the Irish, Scots, and Welsh', *Modern Philology*, XVII (1920), 687–725.

Stafford, Fiona, *The Sublime Savage: A Study of James Macpherson and the Poems of Ossian* (Edinburgh, 1988).

Stott, Anne, *Hannah More: The First Victorian* (Oxford, 2003).

Suggett, Richard, 'Iolo Morganwg: Stonecutter, Builder, and Antiquary' in Jenkins (ed.), *Rattleskull Genius*, pp. 197–226.

Sweet, Rosemary, *Antiquaries: The Discovery of the Past in Eighteenth-Century Britain* (London, 2004).

Taylor, Clare, 'Edward Williams ("Iolo Morganwg") and his Brothers – A Jamaican Inheritance', *THSC* (1980), 35–43.

Thomas, Keith, *Man and the Natural World: Changing Attitudes in England 1500–1800* (London, 1983).

Thrower, James, *A Short History of Western Atheism* (London, 1971).

Troyer, H. W., *Ned Ward of Grub Street* (London, 1968).

Walker, D. P., 'Ways of Dealing with Atheists: A Background to Pamela's Refutation of Cecropia', *Bibliothèque d'Humanisme et Renaissance*, XVII (1955), 252–77.

Walters, Huw, *Cynnwrf Canrif: Agweddau ar Ddiwylliant Gwerin* (Llandybïe, 2004).

—— 'Myfyr Morganwg and the Rocking-Stone Gorsedd' in Jenkins (ed.), *Rattle-skull Genius*, pp. 481–500.

Waring, Elijah, *Recollections and Anecdotes of Edward Williams* (London, 1850).

Waugh, Margaret, 'The Bard Ate Grass', *Country Quest*, 27/11 (1987), 24–5.

Wharam, Alan, *The Treason Trials, 1794* (London, 1992).

Whitney, Lois, *Primitivism and the Idea of Progress in English Popular Literature of the Eighteenth Century* (New York, 1973).

Whittaker, Paul, 'The Tablature of the Iolo Morganwg Manuscripts (British Library, MS Add. 14970)', *Welsh Music History*, 3 (1999), 252–70.

Williams, Edward, *Poems, Lyric and Pastoral* (2 vols., London, 1794).

Williams, Elizabeth, 'Iolo Morganwg in Denbighshire: Extracts from his Itinerary in 1799', *Denbighshire Historical Society Transactions*, 16 (1967), 82–99.

Williams, G. J., *Agweddau ar Hanes Dysg Gymraeg*, ed. Aneirin Lewis (Caerdydd, 1969).

—— *Edward Lhuyd ac Iolo Morganwg: Agweddau ar Hanes Astudiaethau Gwerin yng Nghymru* (Caerdydd, 1964).

—— *Iolo Morganwg*, BBC Annual Lecture (Cardiff, 1963).

—— *Iolo Morganwg – Y Gyfrol Gyntaf* (Caerdydd, 1956).

—— *Iolo Morganwg a Chywyddau'r Ychwanegiad* (Llundain, 1926).

—— *Traddodiad Llenyddol Morgannwg* (Caerdydd, 1948).

—— 'Brut Aberpergwm: A Version of the Chronicle of the Princes' in Stewart Williams (ed.), *The Glamorgan Historian*, IV (Cowbridge, 1967), pp. 205–20.

—— 'Bywyd Cymreig Llundain yng Nghyfnod Owain Myfyr', *Y Llenor*, XVIII, no. 2 (1939), 73–82, no. 4 (1939), 218–32.

—— 'Eisteddfod Caerfyrddin', *Y Llenor*, V, no. 1 (1926), 94–102.

—— 'Yr Eisteddfod a'r Orsedd', *Y Llenor*, I, no. 2 (1922), 131–8.

—— 'Gorsedd Beirdd Ynys Prydain', *Y Llenor*, III, no. 3 (1924), 162–71.

—— 'Gorsedd y Beirdd a'r Seiri Rhyddion', *LlC*, VII, nos. 3 and 4 (1962), 213–16.

—— 'Rhys Goch ap Rhiccert', *Y Beirniad*, VIII (1919), 211–26, 260.

—— 'Tri Chof Ynys Brydain', *LlC*, III, no. 4 (1955), 234–9.

—— 'Wil Hopcyn and the Maid of Cefn Ydfa', trans. Mrs E. E. Williams, in Stewart Williams (ed.), *The Glamorgan Historian*, VI (Cowbridge, 1969), pp. 228–51.

—— 'William Robert o'r Ydwal', *LlC*, III, no. 1 (1954–5), 47–52.

—— and E. J. Jones, *Gramadegau'r Penceirddiaid* (Caerdydd, 1934).

Williams, Glanmor, *Religion, Language and Nationality in Wales* (Cardiff, 1979).

Williams, Gwyn A., *Artisans and Sans-Culottes: Popular Movements in France and Britain during the French Revolution* (2nd edn., London, 1989).

—— *Madoc: The Making of a Myth* (London, 1979).

—— *The Search for Beulah Land* (London, 1980).

—— *The Welsh in their History* (London, 1982).

—— *When Was Wales? A History of the Welsh* (Harmondsworth, 1985).

—— 'Druids and Democrats: Organic Intellectuals and the First Welsh Nation' in idem, *The Welsh in their History* (London, 1982), pp. 31–64.

—— 'Iolo Morganwg: Bardd Rhamantaidd ar gyfer Cenedl nad oedd yn cyfrif' in Geraint H. Jenkins (ed.), *Cof Cenedl V: Ysgrifau ar Hanes Cymru* (Llandysul, 1990), pp. 57–84.

—— 'People's Remembrancers to a Welsh Republic', *Radical Wales*, 12 (Autumn 1986), 18–19.

—— 'Romanticism in Wales' in Roy Porter and Mikuláš Teich (eds.), *Romanticism in National Context* (Cambridge, 1988), pp. 9–36.

Williams, Ifor, 'Rhys Goch ap Rhiccert', *Y Beirniad*, III (1913), 230–44.

Williams, John (ab Ithel) (ed.), *Barddas* (2 vols., Llandovery, 1862, 1874).

Williams, Taliesin, *Traethawd ar hynafiaeth ac awdurdodaeth Coelbren y Beirdd: yr hwnn a Ennillodd Ariandlws a Gwobr Eisteddfod y Fenni, 1838* (Llanymddyfri, 1840).

—— (ed.), *Cyfrinach Beirdd Ynys Prydain: ys ef Llwybreiddiaeth ag Athrawiaeth ar y Farddoniaeth Gymraeg a'i Pherthynasau, yn ol Trefn a Dosparth y Prif Feirdd gynt ar y Gelfyddyd wrth Gerdd Dafod* (Abertawy, 1829).

—— (ed.), *Iolo Manuscripts: A Selection of Ancient Welsh Manuscripts, in Prose and Verse, from the collection made by the late Edward Williams, Iolo Morganwg; for the Purpose of forming a continuation of the Myfyrian Archaiology; and Subsequently Proposed as Materials for a New History of Wales* (Llandovery, 1848).

Womack, Peter, *Improvement and Romance: Constructing the Myth of the Highlands* (London, 1989).

Wood, Marcus, *Radical Satire and Print Culture 1790–1822* (Oxford, 1994).

Worrall, David, *Radical Culture: Discourse, Resistance and Surveillance, 1790–1820* (London, 1992).

Wright, Herbert G., 'The Relations of the Welsh Bard Iolo Morganwg with Dr Johnson, Cowper and Southey', *Review of English Studies*, VIII, no. 30 (1932), 129–38.

Index